JAMES HILLMAN UNIFORM EDITION

5

Uniform Edition of the Writings of James Hillman
Volume 5

Published by Spring Publications, Inc.
www.springpublications.com

Second, revised printing.

Cover illustration:
James Lee Byars, *Untitled,* ca. 1960. Black ink on Japanese paper.
Estate of James Lee Byars, courtesy Michael Werner Gallery,
New York, London, and Berlin

ISBN: 978-0-88214-583-9

Library of Congress Control Number: 2010013670

♾The paper used in this publication meets the minimum requirements of the American National Standard for Information Sciences—Permanence of Paper for Printed Library Materials, ANSI Z39.48–1992.

JAMES HILLMAN

ALCHEMICAL PSYCHOLOGY

SPRING PUBLICATIONS
PUTNAM, CONN.

The Uniform Edition of the Writings of James Hillman
is published in conjunction with

Dallas Institute Publications, Joanne H. Stroud, Director

The Dallas Institute of Humanities and Culture
Dallas, Texas

as an integral part of its publications program concerned with
the imaginative, mythic, and symbolic sources of culture.

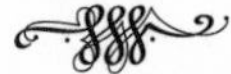

Additional support for this publication has been provided by

Elisabeth and Willem Peppler

The Fertel Foundation, New Orleans, Louisiana

Pacifica Graduate Institute, and
Joseph Campbell Archives and Library,
Carpinteria, California

Contents

Abbreviations used throughout this book are:

Bonus = Bonus of Ferrara, *The New Pearl of Great Price,* trans. A. E. Waite (London: J. Elliot & Co., 1894).

Collectanea = Eirenæus Philalethes [George Starkey], *Collectanea Chemica,* trans. A.E. Waite (London: J. Elliot & Co., 1893).

CP = Sigmund Freud, *Collected Papers*. Authorized translation under the supervision of Joan Riviere, 5 vols. (London: The Hogarth Press and the Institute of Psycho-Analysis, 1924–50).

CW = *Collected Works of C.G. Jung,* trans. R.F.C. Hull, 20 vols. (Princeton, N.J.: Princeton University Press, 1953–79), cited by paragraph number unless indicated otherwise.

Figulus = Benedictus Figulus, *A Golden and Blessed Casket of Nature's Marvels* (London: J. Elliot & Co., 1893).

HM = *The Hermetic Museum, Restored and Enlarged,* trans. A.E. Waite, 2 vols. (London: J. Elliot & Co., 1893).

Jung Letters = *C.G. Jung Letters: Volume 2, 1951–1961,* ed. G. Adler, trans. J. Hulen (Princeton, N.J.: Princeton University Press, 1976).

KY = C.G. Jung, *The Psychology of Kundalini Yoga: Notes of the Seminar Given in 1932 by C.G. Jung,* ed. S. Shamdasani (Princeton: N.J.: Princeton University Press, 1996).

Lexicon = Martin Ruland the Elder, *A Lexicon of Alchemy,* trans. A.E. Waite (London: J. Elliot & Co., 1893).

MDR = C.G. Jung, *Memories, Dreams, Reflections,* recorded and edited by Aniela Jaffé, trans. R. and C. Winston (New York: Vintage Books, 1989).

Minerals = Albertus Magnus, *Book of Minerals,* trans. D. Wyckoff (Oxford: Clarendon Press, 1967).

Paracelsus = *The Hermetic and Alchemic Writings of Paracelsus the Great,* trans. A.E. Waite, 2 vols. (London: J. Elliot & Co., 1894).

SE = *The Standard Edition of the Complete Psychological Works of Sigmund Freud,* ed. J. Strachey, 24 vols. (London: The Hogarth Press and the Institute of Psycho-Analysis, 1953–74).

UE = *The Uniform Edition of the Writings of James Hillman,* 11 vols. (Putnam, Conn.: Spring Publications, 2004–).

Author's Preface

...upon this simple system of many colors is based the manifold and infinitely varied investigation of all things.
–Zosimos of Panopolis (ca. 250 CE)

The following pages were written for different occasions and, except for Chapters 2, 5, and 6, were delivered as lectures. I called the early attempt to present my way of grasping this material, in the 1960s at the C.G. Jung Institute in Zurich, "Alchemical Opus/Analytical Work." My intention then as now is to give psychoanalysis another method for imagining its ideas and procedures by showing how alchemy bears directly on psychological life, more clinically immediate and less spiritually progressivist.

Lectures in New York City and notes for semester courses to university students in 1968 (Chicago), 1973 (Yale), 1975 (Syracuse), and 1979 (Dallas) expanded the sources and the insights they prompted, which are compacted where relevant into these chapters.

All along my work has derived from the extraordinary scholarly achievements of C. G. Jung who opened the field to psychological understanding. Tho' following his footsteps, I have worn my own shoes, that is I try to abjure a grand narrative that encompasses alchemy within an explanatory theory, such as Jung's conjunction of opposites and the realization of the Self, eschewing the temptation to give meaning by translation into universal symbols and noble metaphysics. Instead, I have tried to obey one of Jung's own principles, "stick to the image"–to the colors, the chemicals, the vessels, the fire–images of the sensate imagination as it presents states of soul. "Stick to the image" recovers the ancient Greek maxim, "save the phenomena" (*sozein ta phainomena*), and the phenomena of alchemy present a chaos. "Every other science and art is closely reasoned," says a basic text attributed to Bonus of Ferrara,[1] "the different

1 *Bonus*, 113–14. Who "Bonus" was, where and when he lived remain uncertain.

propositions follow each other in their logical order; and each assertion is explained and demonstrated by what has gone before. But in the books of our Sages the only method that prevails is that of chaos; there is everywhere studied obscurity of expression; and all the writers seem to begin, not with the first principles, but with that which is quite strange and unknown to the students. The consequence is that one seems to flounder along through these works, with only here and there a glimmering of light..."

Obscurity of expression is natural to the psyche. Prime example, our dreams; mere glimmerings. Saving the psyche's phenomena calls for an alchemical method of chaos, a method which indulges the soul's surprising beauty and inventive freedom, and speaks both of the psyche with psychology and to the psyche with imagination.

In preparing this book I received help from and am grateful to Mary Helen Sullivan, the late Gerald Burns, Stanton Marlan for valuable suggestions and keeping me at the task, and Klaus Ottmann for his intelligence, taste, and labor.

James Hillman
Thompson, Conn., March 2010

Cf. J. Ferguson, *Bibliotheca Chemica*, 2 vols. (Glasgow: James Maclehose and Sons, 1906), 1:115.

1

The Therapeutic Value of Alchemical Language: A Heated Introduction

Jung's alchemical work has been relevant for analytical psychology in two main ways. I shall be suggesting a third way.

The first way has been excellently presented by David Holt in his lecture on "Jung and Marx."[1] There Holt shows that Jung imagined his work to be theoretically and historically substantiated by alchemy, and that Jung spent a great part of his mature years working out, in his own words, "an alchemical basis for depth psychology,"[2] particularly the opus of psychological transformation. As Holt indicates, it is to alchemy we must turn to gain the proper placing of Jung's entire endeavor. We need alchemy to understand our theory.

The second way has been profoundly elucidated by Robert Grinnell in his book *Alchemy in a Modern Woman*.[3] There Grinnell demonstrates the incontrovertible parallels between the psychic processes in a modern Italian patient and those that go on in the alchemical opus. Where Holt stresses alchemical *theory* as background, Grinnell stresses alchemical phenomenology in *practice*. We see from Grinnell the continuity or archetypality of alchemical thematics in case-work. Thus, to work with the psyche at its most fundamental levels, we must imagine it as did the

---

1 D. Holt, "Jung and Marx: Alchemy, Christianity, and the Work Against Nature" (lecture given at the Royal Society of Medicine, London, 21 November 1974, under the auspices of the Analytical Psychology Club, London), http://davidholtonline.com/articles/1151738827_Holt_Marx_Alchemy.pdf(accessed February 2, 2009).

2 "My encounter with alchemy was decisive for me, as it provided me with the historical basis which I had hitherto lacked," *MDR*, 200.

3 *Alchemy in a Modern Woman: A Study in the Contrasexual Archetype* (Zurich: Spring Publications, 1973). See also his "Alchemy and Analytical Psychology," in *Methods of Treatment in Analytical Psychology*, ed. I.F. Baker (Fellbach-Oeffingen: Adolf Bonz Verlag, 1980).

alchemists, for they and we are both engaged with similar processes showing themselves in similar imagery. We need alchemy to understand our patients.

The third angle, which I shall now essay, has to do with alchemical language. In brief I want to make this one point: Besides the general theory of alchemical transformation and besides the particular parallels of alchemical imagery with the individuation process, it is *alchemical language* that may be most valuable for Jungian therapy. Alchemical language is a mode of therapy; it is itself therapeutic.

To talk about therapy, we must first talk about neurosis, and here I follow Jung's general theory that neurosis is a "one-sided development of personality" (*CW* 16: 257), which I take to mean the unavoidable one-sided development of consciousness *per se*. I read Jung to mean that neurosis resides in the patterns of our conscious personality organization, in the habitual way we go about our days. Whatever we do here requires repression somewhere else: I do because I repress or I repress because I do. As Jung's own formulation states: "One-sidedness is an unavoidable and necessary characteristic of the directed process, for direction implies one-sidedness" (*CW* 8: 138). Neurosis can be cognitive, conative, or affective, introverted or extraverted, for we can be one-sided in any direction of personality.

Jung's is a beautifully limiting idea of neurosis, keeping it to what some might call "ego-psychology." I wouldn't, couldn't, call it such for reasons we shall come to; but at least Jung's idea of one-sidedness keeps neurosis from complicated explanations in terms of socio-adaptive processes, developmental historicisms, intropsychic dynamisms, biofeedback mechanisms, and other jabberwockies. Neurosis is located right in one's conscious framework (*CW* 16: 12). I am neurotic because of what goes on here and now, as I stand and look and talk, rather than what went on once, or goes in society, or in my dreams, fantasies, emotions, memories, symptoms. My neurosis resides in my mental set and the way it constructs the world and behaves in it.

Now, the essential or at least an essential component of every mental set, of every personality, is language. Thus language must be an essential component of my neurosis. If I am neurotic, I am neurotic in language. Consequently, the one-sidedness that characterizes all neuroses in general is also to be found specifically as a one-sidedness in language.

An important implication of this I will merely brush in passing. This implication is: to discover the specifics of any neurosis, I must examine the specifics of the language essential to it, the styles of speech in which the neurosis is couched. Jung began on this path with his studies in word association; Charles Osgood's semantic differential and George Kelly's psychology of personal constructs could take us into further detail and practicality.

There is much to learn in regard to the rhetorics of the neuroses. For we psychologists listen to the style of speech and not only to the contents of that speech, and to the tone and body of its voice. Archetypal psychology has already begun to examine the language, especially the rhetorical styles of manifest speech, whether in the hour, in dream reports, or written works, and within words themselves. But all this we leave aside today.

The main implication of the proposition that the one-sidedness of neurosis occurs essentially in the one-sidedness of language will lead us directly to the goal of this introduction. To get there quickly let me clear the ground in a hop, skip, and jump. The hop: since language is largely social, the one-sidedness of *my* language reflects society's collective language. Then, the skip: Jung has already defined collective language as "directed" ("directed process," "directed thinking" [*CW*5, chap. 2]), and I have attacked it in various places under its guises of "nominalism," "rationalism," "psychological language," "Apollonic consciousness," and "day-world concepts." Last, the jump: conceptual language, which is nominalistic and thus denies substance and faith in its words, is the usual rhetorical style of "ego," especially the psychologist's "ego," and is the chronic locus of our collective neurosis as it appears in language.

You see that I am claiming, as have Freud and Jung in other ways, a general Western cultural neurosis of one-sidedness. However, I am locating this in our directed-process language, which is *directed from within* (for, after all, who or what directs our directed thinking?) by its inherent syntactical, grammatical, and conceptual structures resulting in conceptual rationalism. *Horrible dictu*, this neurosis is reinforced by the academic training we must each have to become members of the psychotherapeutic profession. By conceptual rationalism I mean writings such as this that account for events in concept-terms rather than thing-words, image-words, craft-words, and also I mean our habitual use of identity verbs (such as "is"), which unconsciously substantiate the very terms we consciously assert to be only nomina. Hence we hypostasize our hypotheses. A rift develops between theory and practice, even a theoretical delusion about practice. Like Jung, we assert our conceptual statements are only heuristic; but because of language we cannot avoid, in practice, substantiating what our theory asserts is only heuristic, only hypothetical. We simply are caught in the literalism of our own language.

We speak in concepts: the ego and the unconscious; libido, energy, and drive; opposites, regression, feeling-function, compensation, transference... When working with these terms we curiously forget that they are concepts only, barely useful for grasping psychic events which they inadequately describe. Moreover, we tend to neglect that these concepts burden our work because they come freighted with their own unconscious history.

Not only, then, as Jung says, are psychological concepts "irrelevant in theory," but, as he also says, the psychologist "must rid himself of the common notion that the name *explains* the psychic fact it denotes" (*CW*8:223–25). Yet we psychologists imagine these concept terms to be thing words, for as Jung continues: "Psychology... is still afflicted with a... mentality in which no distinction is made between words and things." What is this mentality, this affliction?

Is Jung speaking of literalism, that one-sidedness of mind that experiences only singleness of language? In such a consciousness, there is no "as if" between the word and whatever it is conceiving. Then the subjects in our sentences become existing subjects and the objects become objectively real facts. Then such concepts as the ego, the unconscious, the feeling-function, the transference become literally real things. Substantives become substances. So much so that we consider these concepts able to account for personality and its neuroses, whereas I am arguing that these very same substantialized concept terms—ego, unconscious, transference—*are* the neurosis.

As Freud began by deliteralizing the memory of sexual trauma into its fantasy, and as Jung began by deliteralizing incest and libido, we need to deliteralize a host of other substantialized concepts, beginning with "the ego" and "the unconscious." I have personally never met either of them, except in a psychology book.

Enter alchemy – thing-words, image-words, craft-words. The five supposed sources of alchemy are each a technology. Each is a handwork physically grappling with sensate materials. (1) Metallurgy and Jewelry: mining, heating, smelting, forging, annealing; (2) Cloth and Fiber Dyeing: dipping, coloring, drying; (3) Embalming the Dead: dismembering, evacuating, infusing, preserving; (4) Perfumery and Cosmetics: grinding, mixing, distilling, diluting, evaporating; (5) Pharmacy: distinguishing, tincturing, measuring, dissolving, desiccating, pulverizing. To these traditional sources must be added food preparation and conservation, the daily acts of transforming raw materials into tasty and nourishing edibles.

To a mind that has not severed conceptual denotations from metaphorical inference, all these activities with the hands and senses carried meanings about nature, life, death, and the soul. A smith had to know how to manage fire and regulate heat; a pharmacist must make mixtures in the right proportion, else a remedy could kill rather than cure. (The very word *pharmakon* means both poison and remedy.)

The basic stuffs of personality–salt, sulfur, mercury, and lead–are concrete materials; the description of soul, *aqua pinguis* or *aqua ardens*, as well as words for states of soul, such as *albedo* and *nigredo*, incorporate events that one can touch and see. The work of soulmaking requires corrosive acids, heavy earths, ascending birds; there are sweating kings, dogs and bitches, stenches, urine, and blood. How like the language of our dreams and unlike the language into which we interpret the dreams. When alchemy speaks of degrees of heat, it does not use numbers. Rather, it refers to the heat of horse dung, the heat of sand, the heat of metal touching fire. These heats differ, moreover, not only in degree but also in quality: heat can be slow and gentle, or moist and heavy, or sudden and sharp. As well, the heat of horse dung imparts to the heated material properties of horse dung itself. Heat is not abstracted from the body that gives it.

The words for alchemical vessels – the shapes of soul in which our personality is being worked–contrast with the concepts we use, concepts such as inner space or internal object, or fantasy, or patience, containment, suppression or relationship. Alchemy presents an array of different qualities of vessel, different fragilities, visibilities, and forms: condensing coils, multiheaded alembics, pelicans, cucurbits, flat open pans. One uses copper or glass or clay to hold one's stuff and cook it.

Finally, the words for the operations—that which one does in crafting the psyche—are again concrete. We learn to evaporate away the vaporousness, to calcine so as to burn passions down to dry essences. We learn about condensing and congealing cloudy conditions so as to get hard clear drops from them. We learn about coagulating and fixing, about dissolving and putrefying, about mortifying and blackening.

Compare these craft words of alchemy with the words used for the operations of psychotherapy: analyzing the transference, regressing in the service of the ego, developing the inferior function, managing anger, syntonic identifying, showing hostility; improving, denying, resisting, identifying... Not only is this language abstract, it is imprecise. Because of this imprecision in our equipment, our concepts for grasping the movements of the soul, we have come to believe the soul itself is an ungraspable flux, whereas actually the psyche presents itself always in very specific behaviors, experiences and sensuous images.

Before Jung's thought had been touched by alchemy, he raised doubts about the sensuous language that alchemy so relishes. In 1921 he writes in his *Psychological Types*:

> The rational functions are, by their nature, incapable of creating symbols, since they produce only a rational product necessarily restricted to a single meaning, which forbids it from also embracing its opposite. The sensuous functions are equally unfitted to create symbols, because, from the very nature of the object, they are also confined to single meanings which comprehend only themselves and neglect the other.[4]

I read him to be claiming that sensuous perception is as one-sided as conceptual understanding, therewith implying that sensate language clings to its referents (alchemy's concrete stuffs and operations) so that no further connotations emerge. Here, I believe, Jung is confusing the concrete with the literal.

Alchemy took Jung away from the systematic rationalism of the *Types*. We can see now, as Holt quoted, how necessary alchemy was for providing a basis for his depth psychology because alchemy leaves unilateral literalism completely. No term means only one thing. Every

4 C.G. Jung, *Psychological Types or The Psychology of Individuation,* trans. H.G. Baynes (New York: Pantheon, 1923), 141–42.

alchemical phenomenon is both material and psychological at the same time, else alchemy could not claim to be salvific of both the human soul and material nature. It is all metaphor ("symbolic" in Jung's 1921 sense of that word). All analogy. All a *poiesis* of the hand.

Our minds still retain this alchemical propensity for transferring technology into psychology. Psychotherapeutic slang betrays how we truly imagine long before the profession arrives at sophisticated concepts. The language of handwork, of technical grappling, now emerges from the car repair shop. There, in that garage, metaphors abound for our psychic life: realignments, tune-ups, tightening the brakes, refilling the tank so as not to run out of gas, never stalling, never misfiring, and never going flat.

Ever since Jung opened the door to alchemy for psychologists, we have tended to go through it in only one direction: We apply our directed thinking to its fantasy thinking, translating its images into our concepts. White Queen and Red King have become feminine and masculine principles; their incestuous sexual intercourse has become the union of opposites; the freakish hermaphrodite and uniped, the golden head with silver hair, red within the black without—these have all become paradoxical representations of the goal, examples of androgyny symbols of the Self. You see what happens: sensate image disappears into concept, precision into generality. Even the peculiar images of the *Rosarium Philosophorum* (*CW* 16), which call for perplexed contemplation, are asked instead to serve as a handbook for a general psychology of transference.

We could go through the door differently. We might try translating the other way—the actualities of psychotherapy and the language we use to conceive those actualities put into imaginatively precise alchemical words: thing words, image words, craft words. Grinnell's book does just this—and so, conceptually addicted minds find it hard to read, heavy. It *is* hard and heavy precisely because it speaks in the concrete words of the *opus*.

We could also not go through the door at all. For if we see through the concepts to begin with, we do not need translations. Then we would speak to the dreams and of the dreams as the dreams themselves speak. (By "dream" here I mean as well the dream, or fantasy, within behavior.) This seems to me to follow Jung's dictum of dreaming the myth along. To do this we must speak dreamingly, imagistically—and materially.

I have introduced "materially" at this juncture because we are close to the crunch, and the crunch of alchemy is matter. It is the crunch of our practice too—to make soul *matter* to the patient, to transform his/her sense of what matters.

Holt, following Jung, has shown that alchemy is essentially a theory of the redemption of the physical, of matter. If so, then this redemptive process must also take place in our speech, where the absence of matter is most severe, and especially because this deprivation is so close that it is unconscious to us even as we speak. We can hardly expect therapy—so dependent upon speech—to work on this massive curse of Western consciousness, our tortures over matter, if the tool with which we work, our speech, has not itself resolved the curse. Our speech itself can redeem matter if, on the one hand, it de-literalizes (de-substantiates) our concepts, distinguishing between words and things, and if, on the other hand, it re-materializes our concepts, giving them body, sense, and weight. We already do this inadvertently when we speak of what the patient brings as "material," look for the "grounds" of his/her complaint, and also by trying to make "sense" of it all.

Re-enter alchemy. Its beauty lies just in its materialized language which we can never take literally. I know I am not composed of sulfur and salt, buried in horse dung, putrefying or congealing, turning white or green or yellow, encircled by a tail-biting serpent, rising on wings. And yet I am! I cannot take any of this literally, even if it is all accurate, descriptively true. Even while the words are concrete, material, physical, it is a patent mistake to take them literally. Alchemy gives us a language of substance which cannot be taken substantively, concrete expressions which are not literal.

This is its therapeutic effect: it forces metaphor upon us. We are carried by the language into an as-if, into both the materialization of the psyche and the psychization of matter as we utter our words.

Alchemical texts are monstrously arcane. They are compacted with entangled layers of references and analogies. It seems deliberately cultish, supposedly to hide its secrets from the common mind and dogmatic authorities. But there is a more profound, *psychological,* intention behind alchemy's obscurantism.

> The sages did not give a name to any of their things nor compare them with anything unless there is an aspect which requires

> the contemplation of the observer about it and his thinking it over... They did not coin examples or descriptions except in order to point by them to their hidden stone. They did not coin them for fun or for amusement.[5]

The language itself has a psychological effect:

> Man's language consequently must strain to capture the density of meaning ["the hidden stone"] conveyed by the signs. It is this very fact which makes Paracelsian texts themselves difficult to interpret. Their fantastic vocabulary is not designed to define unique, singular characteristics of phenomena; rather, it is constructed to reveal as many depths of meaning as possible–their words are intended to reverberate in the imagination with meanings.[6]

Conceptual language, however, is not self-evidently metaphor.[7] It is too contemporary to be transparent; we are living right in its midst. Its myth is going on all about us, so it does not have a metaphorical sense built in it. I do now know, cannot see, that I am really not composed of an ego and self, a feeling function and a power drive, castration anxiety and depressive positions. These seem literally real to me, despite the experience that even as I use these terms, there is a haunting worthlessness about them. Nominalism[8] has made us disbelieve in all words–what's in a name?–they are mere "words," tools, any others would do as well; they have no substance.

But our psychological language has become literally real to us, despite nominalism, because the psyche needs to demonize and personify, which in language becomes the need to substantiate. The psyche animates the material world it inhabits. Language is part of this animating activity (e.g., onomatopoeic speech with which language is supposed to

5 Muḥammad Ibn Umail, *Book of the Explanations of the Symbols (Kitāb Ḥall ar-Rumūz)*, Corpus Alchemicum Arabicum, vol. 1, ed. T. Abt, W. Madelung, T. Hofmeier, trans. S. Fuad (Zurich: Living Human Heritage Publications, 2003), 73.

6 O. Hannaway, *The Chemists and the Word: The Didactic Origins of Chemistry* (Baltimore: The Johns Hopkins University Press, 1975), 61.

7 "Every modern language, with its thousands of abstract terms and its nuances of meaning and association, is apparently, from beginning to end, but an unconscionable tissue of dead, or petrified, metaphors." O. Barfield, *Poetic Diction: A Study in Meaning* (Middletown, Conn.: Wesleyan University Press, 1984), 63.

8 Cf. the discussion of Nominalism in my *Re-Visioning Psychology* (New York: Harper and Row, 1975), 5–8.

have "begun"). Unless my language meets the need to substantiate, then the psyche substantiates anyway, unawares, hardening my concepts into physical or metaphysical things.

May I insist that I am not proposing to cancel our concepts and restore the archaic neologisms of alchemy as a new *esperanto* for our practice and our dealings with one another. That would be to take alchemical language only literally. I do *not* mean: let us start off now talking alchemy; I mean first let us talk *as alchemists, as if we were talking alchemically*. Then we can talk alchemy, even the old mad terms, because then we will not be using them as literal substitutions for our concepts, employing them as a new set of categories. It is not the literal return to alchemy that is necessary but a restoration of the alchemical mode of imagining. For in that mode we restore matter to our speech—and that, after all, is our aim: the restoration of imaginative matter, not of literal alchemy.

I said that the one-sidedness of neurosis perpetuates in our psychological language, its conceptual rationalism. One-sidedness—that general definition of neurosis—now becomes more precise. It can now be seen to refer to the grasping nature of our grasping tools, our concepts, which organize the psyche according to their shape. Our concepts extend their grasp over the concretely vivid images by abstracting (literally, "drawing away") their matter. We no longer see the clay funeral urn or the iron pot-bellied stove, but "the Great Mother"; no longer the sea just beyond the harbor, the sewer blocked with muck, or a dark pathless forest, but "the Unconscious."

How can we have faith in what we do if our words in which we do it are disembodied of substance? Here again I join Grinnell and Holt who take faith to be the key to the entire psychological and alchemical opus. But I would locate this faith in the words that express, operate, *are* this endeavor. Again: abstract concepts, psychological nomina, that do not matter and bear weight, willy-nilly accrete ever more hardening, leaden immobility and fixation, becoming objects or idols of faith rather than living carriers of it. When we talk psychology, we cannot help but become adamantly metaphysical because the physical imagination has been emptied out of our words.

According to Jung, neurosis is splitting, and therapy is joining. If our conceptual language splits by abstracting matter from image and speaking only from one side, then the as-if of metaphor is itself psychotherapy because it keeps two or more levels distinct—whether words and things, events and meanings, connotations and denotations—joining them together in the word itself. As the *coniunctio* is an imaged metaphor, so metaphors are the spoken *coniunctio*.

Especially, our one-sided language splits immaterial psyche from soulless matter. Our concepts have so defined these words that we forget that matter is a concept "in the mind," a psychic fantasy, and that soul is our living experience amid things and bodies "in the world."

As Jung grew older, he became ever more occupied with this particular split—matter and soul, attempting to join them with ever fresh formulations: psychoid, synchronicity, *unus mundus*. Even if defined as embracing both sides and even if presented ambiguously and symbolically, these words (unlike, for instance, the alchemists' own "soft stone," "hermaphrodite," or "Royal Wedding in the Sea of the Indians") only reinforce the splitting effect inherent in such one-sided language itself. For they too are concepts, without body or image. Thus psychology remains neurotic: we describe a nominalistic psyche without matter (and therefore fantasy and image do not "really" matter, are "only" in the mind or must magically connect to matter in synchronicity), and a de-souled matter that seeks redemption through body therapies, consumer hedonism, and Marxism.

We end with a cultural statement about neurosis and its therapy, similar to ones made by Freud and by Jung. Our neurosis and our culture are inseparable. After political doublespeak, spin, jargonism, and Pentagonese, after sociological and economic scientism and media management of speech, and all the other abuses—even those of Lacan and Heidegger and communications theory performed in the very name of language—that have drained words of their blood, brought into our day a new syndrome, childhood mutism, and made us in psychology lose faith in the power of words so that therapy must turn to cries and gestures: after all this I am passionately urging a mode of recuperating language by returning to speech that matters. I am also harkening back to Confucius who insisted that the therapy of culture begins with the rectification of language. Alchemy offers this rectification.

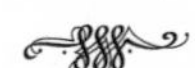

2

Rudiments

I. FIRE

Fire of all things is the judge and ravisher.
–Heraclitus

Would you know the perfect Master? It is he who understands the regulation of the fire, and its degrees. Nothing will prove to you so formidable an impediment as ignorance of the regimen – of heat and fire.
–Thomas Norton

Desire is not enough; in fact, ignorant desire frustrates itself or burns itself away. For desire to be consummated, for the *opus* to come to fruition–in art, in love, in practice of any sort–learn all you can about its fire: its radiance, its flickering instability, its warmth, and its rage. Fire as element below and above the range of human reason requires a "psychoanalysis of fire"–the very title of Bachelard's exemplary study.[1] The art of the fire and the key to alchemy means learning how to warm, excite, enthuse, ignite, inspire the material at hand, which is also the state of one's nature so as to activate it further into a different state.

Of course, the laboratory, the stove, the curcurbits and alembics, the co-workers are imaginary figments as well as materialized phenomena. You are the laboratory; you are the vessel and the stuff going through the cooking.[2] So, too, the fire is an invisible heat, a psychic heat that

1 G. Bachelard, *The Psychoanalysis of Fire,* trans. C.M. Ross (Boston: Beacon Press, 1964).

2 "Both the metallic body and the alchemist suffer and feel joy in the process. Not only do the substances mate in the alembic, the alchemist also at the same

clamors for fuel, breathing room, and regular loving consideration. How to build the heat that can dry up the soggy, soggy dew, melt the leaden oppressions, and distill a few precious drops of intoxicating clarity?

In Greece, in the Asklepian temples where "patients" went to find healing by dreaming, they incubated for a period of time devoting themselves to focused brooding and right procedures in order to be blessed by a beneficent dream. In the Bible, Jonah, abandoned by his shipmates, had to remain for a time in the belly of a great whale sunk in the depths of the sea. In that darkness he generated heat, lost his hair. Solitary confinement; utter internality. This is the *Nekyia,*[3] the night sea journey through the underworld made also by Odysseus, Aeneas, and Hercules, and by Eurydice, Inanna, Persephone, Psyche, by Orpheus, by Christ. Whether this underworld is frigid and ghastly or burning with the hots of hell, it is a realm characterized by temperatures suitable only for demons, ghosts, heroes and heroines, goddesses and shades who are no longer altogether of the upper world. Outsiders. Marginals. Alchemy is a profession of marginals; those at the edge. Those who live from their own fires, sweating it out, self-sustaining their own temperatures which may be at variance with the collective climate. *Tapas*: the ardor of internal heat. In India the sage sits in the Himalayan snow and with his own body heat melts a place to be, contained by his own containment.

Nature's fire is both celestial, descending from sun and stars and lightening, and arising from the earth out of thermal springs, gases, geysers and volcanoes. The alchemist works with both kinds, those coming from beyond into the human sphere, the flashes and fevers, explosive manias and star-struck blindings, as well as the interior culinary fires, the metabolic heats of the body that stew and digest and melt the loins in lust. "The greater the spiritual stature of a person, the greater the sexual passion," says the Talmud (*Tract. Sukkah*). As fire licks and clings to the logs it burns, so passion clings to the bodies of life. "The Clinging" describes the trigram of the second daughter of the *I Ching*. Like the claws of a cat, the paws of a lion, sulfuric fire attaches to the object of its desire or attaches itself to its desire. Intense internal heat as the moment

---

time mates with nature." J. Lindsay, *Origins of Alchemy in Graeco-Roman Egypt* (London: Frederick Muller, 1970), 294.

3 *CW*12:61n; *CW*5:309–19.

of fertility. The bitch is in heat: "*Solo aestu libidinis*," the heat alone of the libido releases Mithras from the stone.

If alchemy is the art of fire, and alchemists, "artists of fire," as many texts repeat, then the alchemist must be able to "know" all the kinds of fire, degrees of fire, sources of fire, fuels of fire. And, the alchemist must be able to fight fire with fire, using his own fire to operate upon the fires with which he is operating. Working the fire by means of fire. Nature works on nature. Alchemy, an art of nature, a natural art that raises the temperatures of nature. "Nature's time is extremely long, and the fashion of her concoction uniform, and her fire very slow. That of Art, on the other hand, is short; the heating is controlled by the wit of the artist, as the fire also is made intenser or milder."[4]

Where science measures heat with degrees of temperature, alchemy observes the different kinds of heat, the qualities of fire. Heat increases as the work proceeds, rising through four classic stages. "Each of these is twice as great as the preceding," says Mylius.[5] Different texts describe the four with different images but the following occur frequently: a brooding hen,[6] slow and mild as of the flesh; the sun in June; great and strong calcining fire; burning and vehement; able to melt lead or fuse iron. Another lists the four as water bath, ash bath, sand bath, and naked flame. Ruland's *Dictionary* fills out the four stages with rich descriptions.[7] "The first grade is very slow, and it is like an inactive lukewarmness; it is called the heat of a tepid bath, of excrement, of digestion, of circulation ... likened to the warmth generated by a fowl when hatching its young." Evidently this fire is generated by brooding, digesting and holding within the lower body, its fermenting bowels and silent womb. Attitudes are lukewarm, diffident. Slowness and the restraint of activity all by themselves are able to develop heat.

---

4 Michael Maier (1617), quoted by J. Read, *From Alchemy to Chemistry* (Mineola, N.Y.: Dover Publications, 1995), 37.

5 J. D. Mylius, *Philosophia Reformata* (1622), quoted by J. Read, *Prelude to Chemistry: An Outline of Alchemy* (Cambridge, Mass.: MIT Press, 1966), 264.

6 "The fire must be light, mild, and moist, like that of a hen brooding over her eggs." *Lexicon*, s.v. "Great Secret of Aristeus."

7 *Lexicon*, s.v. "Ignis Leonis." Norton describes fourteen increasingly hot qualities of heat ("The Chemical Treatise of Thomas Norton," in *HM*2).

"The second grade is fiercer, yet such that it is safe to touch, nor does it injure the hand. They call it the heat of ashes... Cinders on account of their fineness do not produce much air." Chapter 9, below, discusses the role of air; here we can note that this second stage is fed very little fuel. It has little inspiration, no heavy breathing. Instead a stifling dullness, dusty, ashen, dried out. "I kept nothing of myself but the ashes."[8] "Ash on an old man's sleeve/Is all the ash the burnt roses leave."[9] This heat can be touched, handled, coming perhaps from sifting residues, a heat rising from the warmth of reminiscences, "mixing memory and desire."[10] Read Eliot, Proust; read Akhmatova: the fierce heat of fine ashes, unstirred by the breezes of fantasy.

Why fierce? Because ash is the ultimate reduction, the bare soul, the last truth, all else dissolved. "The ash is all," said Zosimos of Panopolis,[11] the "first alchemist," the discipline's patron authority. The *Rosarium Philosophorum* (*CW* 16) says ash "endures," and Muḥammad Ibn Umail, the tenth-century Arab alchemist known to the Latin West as Zadith Senior, writes in his *Tabula Chemica*: "Burnt ash and the soul are the gold of the wise." Fierce? Because we are roasted in our own base nature.

"The third grade will burn the hand, and is compared to boiling sand or iron filings." Desiccation, a condition of soul known in the Middle Ages as *siccitas, acedia*, the dry depression of the soul forced by willful resolve to do its duty. The iron of Mars, angry. The time in the endless desert under a relentless sun. This fire "will burn the hand," so it cannot be handled. It is out of your hands. If the first stage was held in the body and the second in memory, this is the heat of desperate determination, an isolating anger that drives the work ever more hotly.

"The fourth is the highest grade, and is generally the most destructive...a living flame is produced from wood or coals." Bernardus of Treviso says the fourth is "in iron, or in the flame."[12] Besides the obvious association of iron and flame with the smith and the forge, there is a warrior-of-the-spirit implication in the third and fourth degrees. The

8 J. Cocteau, *The Difficulty of Being* (New York: Coward-McCann, Inc, 1967), 32.

9 T.S. Eliot, "Four Quartets: Little Gidding," in *The Complete Poems and Plays, 1909–1950* (New York: Harcourt Brace & Company, 1952), 139.

10 T.S. Eliot, "The Waste Land," in ibid., 37.

11 *Collection des ancien alchimistes grecs*, ed. M. Berthelot, vol. 2: Les Œuvres des Zosime (Paris: Georg Steinheil, 1888), III.lvi.

12 *Lexicon*, s.v. "Ignis."

desert saint, ascetics; "it is death to soul to become moist," said Heraclitus, for whom Fire was the primal principle. All the soul's stickiness is up in flames, vanished into thin air, and the smoky, oily, smelly worldliness of sulfuric desires have been purified. It is a change from "ordinary" sulfur to "clear-burning sulfur (*ignis clare ardens*) or "extinguished fire" (*ignis exstinctus*), "Sulfur deprived of its virtue."[13]

The two hottest fires are intended for the operation called calcination: "The reduction of bodies into Calx by burning."[14] Calx = "any powder reduced by the separation of superfluous moisture."[15] Reduction of confusion to an essence, of moisture or a solid to "a fine powder,"[16] of misty remembrances to a poignant image, of a stubborn blockage to lightweight fantasy. Epitome = Epiphany. The essential realization. Moments in memory or a weave of sensations (odors, tastes) debrided of personal associations, leaving but a calx, an objective correlative of the over-determined issue. No long-winded account of circumstances, only the hot core. No causality. No context or conditions. The truth of what is because of only what is—unalloyed. Utter reduction through heat. "Your material can be cooked only in its own blood," say the texts.

These powders work on other bodies as catalysts and activators, entering into compounds, absorbed and disappearing. Or, like a powdery pigment which, when touched by a living drop of moisture (a pang of grief, a freshet of lust, a flush of hope), can color an entire scene. The alchemist works with these essences, this treated, cooked, conquered nature, not with nature in the raw. The calcined body is the body that has been through the fire, a twice-born body, a subtle body, no longer attached to what it once was and so can become wholly absorbed by the work.

Heat measured in numbers on a thermometer has no palpable qualities, only higher and lower, more or less. Two-dimensional. Heat qualified by a brooding hen, melting lead, by seasons, ashes brings the operator's imagination directly into relation with the fire. Moreover, these heats particularize the fire. Warmth given by a bath feels different from warmth radiating from glowing coals much as the heat from a desert

---

13 Ibid., s.v. "Ignis Extinctus."

14 *Lexicon*, s.v. "Combustio."

15 *Lexicon*, s.v. "Calx."

16 E. J. Holmyard, *Alchemy* (Harmondsworth: Penguin Books, 1957), 45.

wind differs from jungle humidity. The source of the heat qualifies the heat, carries over into the heat its virtues of ash, water, dung, flame. When alchemy uses terms for fire such as "Persian fire" (*ignis persicus*) ("an Ulcer torturing with a fiery heat"[17]), "belly of the horse" (*venter equi*), or "fire of the lion" (*ignis leonis*), it stimulates the careful attention to images, a practice similar to careful scientific observation of the thermometer. Poetic terms take the measure of imagination.

Figulus judges degrees of heat by the hand.[18] "The first degree is that which permits of the hand being held to it... A second degree is that which permits the hand being held to the fire but a short time." Notice that it is the fire that "permits." Fire is the agent, the master of the work. Knowledge of this master must come firsthand; it is not learned from books or lectures on desire. The good cook has burnt a dish or two, and her hand as well. We learn heat from chefs, smiths, potters, embalmers, from curing tobacco, smoking hams and fish, baking pizza, drying tea, fermenting beer, distilling bourbon. Boiling sugar alone requires a subtle language of many shadings, consistencies, degrees.

The hand-knowledge of intensities applies to other disciplines. Like writing: leave the chapter on the desk untouched for three days. Pick it up again only to find it has congealed like cold mutton. The boxer lays off roadwork awhile and his legs lose their dance in the ring. The patient comes to analysis only every two weeks, takes a month off, so the heat never builds and the sessions become sluggish, trivial, diffident.

We can be misled by turning the pages of the old alchemy tracts with woodcuts or the many detailed depictions by the Flemish painter David Teniers the Younger (1610–90) of the alchemist at work, that the fire is external to him. No; the alchemist brings his own caloric participation; he is with the fire, in the fire. That old man in the laboratory concocting solutions with his apparatus, kneeling by the fire, is the old man in the mind, his hands in the furnace of his own body, sweating over the transformation of his own nature—our own acids and sulfurs, our own putrefications, our own bitter salts.

---

17 *Lexicon*, s.v. "Ignis Persicus."

18 *Figulus*, 267–68.

Fire of the Gods

Fire as an infant ever hungry, fire as a child quickly growing, young and blazing, fire as a virgin ever-renewable. Hearth as womb, cradle, embracing the center around which the *opus* circumambulates. We are back with Hestia[19] who sat in the middle of the ancient house, of the King's palace, of the town hall–not as a statue or personified figure, but simply as the fire in the hearth. Just that. Hestian fire asks for care-taking. She is a domesticating fire of culture; a severe restriction of passion; a quiet yet fierce warmth of attentiveness. This fire is the mystery of focused consciousness itself. Hestia came first in the declination of divine hierarchy in prayers, and sometimes in processions, because before all else comes the ability to attend, to be aware. We see the dark and into the dark by grace of her light. Task-mistress, disciplinarian, pure intention, dignity–such are the demands she places on the worker in fire, and alchemy is threaded through with this sort of stern advice.

Other gods, other fires. Or, rather as the master mythographer Karl Kerényi said of polytheism, not many different worlds but the same world styled according with a variety of divinities. Thus alchemists are also children of Hephaestus because their ancestry goes back to smiths and their forges; and children of his wife, Aphrodite, because of their ancestry in the arts of jewelry, perfumery, cosmetics and the coloring of cloth; and of Ares/Mars, her paramour, because of the red fiery heat whose emblems in alchemical shorthand were sword, arrow, knife, lance, instruments that pierce and slay and bring about separations; and of Hermes because of the subtle transformations and secret formulations, the sleight-of-hand manipulations, the mercantile impetus and mountebank pretensions; of old Saturn because the arduous work begins in lead and ends in lead, said Michael Meier, a *via longissima*, a labor of fire-tending fueling, ash-hauling, sleeplessly watching; or of Hades because of its language of cruelties and a heat that putrefies as well as the hell-fire of dried-out death[20] and because of alchemy's origins in embalming and the supposed Egyptian source for the root word *khem* = black, this

19 Cf. J. Hillman, "In: Hestia's Preposition," in *Mythic Figures, UE* 6.

20 R.B. Onians, *The Origins of European Thought: About the Body, the Mind, the Soul, the World, Time, and Fate* (Cambridge: Cambridge University Press, 1951), 288 and 258n5.

"black art," as it was called, which like Hades operates in hiding, away from daily human sight.

Yet among all these it is the fire of Hestia, and of Venus/Aphrodite, that draws us to the work with both duty and love, and a sensual pleasure in colors, smells and textures of the mixtures. Alchemy as a passion, a devotion, a *bhakti* yoga. "The fire is the love fire, the life that flows forth from the Divine Venus... the fire of Mars is too choleric, too sharp, and too fierce..."[21]

Many gods and goddesses, including references to Diana/Artemis and the moon; Zeus's thunderbolts; Eros; the wine and dismemberment of Dionysus. But one figure whom we moderns think of first with fire, Prometheus, is missing! Prometheus does not belong in the alchemical *devotio*, and the work must always be on guard against the "promethean sin," stealing the fire for human use. According to Plato, Prometheus stole fire from Hephaestus, (Aeschylus says from Zeus; Hesiod, from the sun). Plato's version suggests a basic clarification.[22] Hephaestus works with fire for the sake of the work; love, says Plato, prompts him. Prometheus wants the fire for the "good of mankind." The first is aesthetic, even religious; the second ideological. But then Prometheus was a Titan and a dominant of the Industrial Age's titanic capitalism, nationalism and ideological humanism, and the final mutation of alchemy into chemistry (see Chapter 9 below).

Hastening Nature

Since nature has its own heat and works slowly at its own improvement, the alchemist's fire intends mainly to aid nature's own efforts. "Nature's own efforts"—that gives the clue to the misappropriation of fire by Prometheus and by alchemists who sought actual gold and actual cure. Jung recognizes the Promethean sin as it appears in Christianity, although he does not make the link back to the Greek myth. There is a "parting of the ways," writes Jung, between the Christian opus and the alchemical. The alchemist "may play a part in the *perfectio*, which brings him health, riches, illumination and salvation;

21 John Pordage (1607–81), in *CW* 16: 507.

22 Plato, *Symposium*, 197*a*; *Protagoras*, 321*e*.

but ... since he is not the one to be redeemed, he is more concerned to perfect the substance than himself."[23]

The furthest alchemical vision goes beyond the human; it would redeem nature, achieve its perfection, and fire is the means to this end. As one of the four elements that grounds the being of the cosmos, fire belongs not even to the gods. No more may fire be stolen and put to human use than may earth, air and water be appropriated for the benefit of one species alone. The Promethean impulse, and as it became human-centered Christianity, is hardly environmental. Any student of alchemy, any borrower of its tropes for one's own art or practice, doing the work for one's own nature, remains Promethean, a secular humanist, a gold digger.

If alchemy stands behind the natural processes going on in deep psychotherapy, as Jung has shown, and also in the arts, then these activities must also have an aim beyond Prometheus. Soul-making of the individual or even of the collective still remain human. Deep psychotherapy is obliged like alchemy to be focused on "perfecting the substance," not the subject, else it remains morally at fault, like Prometheus for stealing from the gods, and practitioners of therapy will find themselves chained to a rock of dogmatic person-centered humanism.

How do we conceive this service of nature? How does the alchemical paradigm enliven a practice, an art, so that the practice, the art, serves nature? Quite simply: by recognizing the stuffs and tools, the places and constructions having each their enlivening spirits; by recognizing the *anima mundi*—that all things are ensouled, with their own intentions, their own habits and pleasures. Treating things with regard for their properties. Alchemy is animism. Materials entrust themselves to us for their improvement. Nothing may be used without their willing cooperation.

By treating the materials as ensouled, by invoking the spirits of the metals and speaking of their emotional qualities, alchemy found gods in nature, and soul, or animation, in the physical world. The devotion to alchemy was not quite a branch of then-contemporary humanism; less the study of human works of culture and language than a focus upon the non-human mystery of things, their innate potentials, their liveliness. All the pious counsels and moral admonitions, which fill the texts, seem

23 *CW* 12: 451.

laid on to counter the dehumanizing, perhaps demonic, experimentation with that which lies outside human measure. Today's science, investigating similar inhuman powers, omits similar moral counterweights.

Fire produces and permits differing effects on different substances on different occasions. St. Augustine notes that fire blackens wood yet whitens stone, producing contrary effects on materials that are more akin than contrary.[24] Each thing heats in its own style. Know your fire, but know your material as well. For instance: A husband and wife are akin, a couple. They consider entering the vessel of therapy and turning up the heat on their difficulties. The fire may whiten her, yet blacken him or *vice versa*, and they come out as contraries.

When we hasten nature by applying heat, we adapt the heat to the qualities of the substance. Even more, the heat we apply externally by fire must aim at kindling and reinforcing the *calor inclusus* within the substance. Amount and kind of heat are determined by the stuff we are working with. Not too much, not too little. Dosage. Therefore, the hastening of nature has no formula, no clear foreknowledge of hours, days, years. "How long will it take?" asks the patient of the doctor, the singer of his coach, the novelist of his schedule to get this outline into submissable shape.

Bonus of Ferrara replies: "The time required for the whole work is stated by Rasis to be one year. Rosinus fixes it at nine months; others at seven, others at forty, yet others at eighty days. Still, we know that as the hatching of a chicken is always accomplished in the same period, so a certain number of days or months, and no more, must be required for this work. The difficulty connected with the time also involves the secret of the fire, which is the greatest mystery of the Art."[25]

A more subtle passage compares the *opus* with an embryo that requires nine months to mature, each trimester ruled by an element.[26] First the *opus* is nourished by water, then by air, and finally by fire. The transition from water to air, from flooding and dissolving to drying and distance is familiar enough to artisans in any work of concentration.

---

24 Augustine, *The City of God*, XXI.4.

25 *Bonus*, 115–16.

26 *Aurora Consurgens: A Document Attributed to Thomas Aquinas on the Problem of Opposites in Alchemy*, ed. M.-L. von Franz (Toronto: Inner City Book, 2000), 290.

Then, the work is "quickened by fire." It lives on its own. The desire or impetus that has impelled the work exhausts itself, all intentions, expectations, ambitions burnt out in the sheer passion of the doing.

II. FUEL: CHARCOAL AND AIR

In the woodlands and forests of old Europe and still today in parts of Central Asia and Africa, and in Brazil, Japan, India and China the charcoal workers gather their sticks and branches for manufacturing the fuel that was essential to alchemy.[27] The Roman naturalist Pliny the Elder (23–79 CE) laid out carefully the sorts of wood that make the best charcoal and for what particular purposes. Fir, he wrote, takes the bellows better; less smoldering so it suits smiths at their forges. For iron, charcoal of chestnut; for silver, pine.

To an alchemical mind, the purest fire will be fueled with the purest substance. You get from the fire only what the fire is fed. Charcoal is the most desirable fuel because its matter has already been purified. Or died. That is why it is black and so light in weight. All superfluities have been burnt out. It has been through the fire, a twice-born fuel, first as natural wood, then as the essence of that wood. Charcoal: an *opus contra naturam*. Also, charcoal signals in its lifetime the colors of the alchemical opus: black lumps, white ash, yellow flame, red coals. Most mysterious: even the origin of the English word is unknown.

Born in fire and dying in fire, charcoal is fire's devoté. The selfless servant, dried of moisture, with no desires of its own for transformations. Therefore it serves so well as cleanser, absorber, purifier, letting other stuffs pass through its porous body without participation. Neither reagent nor catalyst, charcoal is the fuel that does not interfere, a giver of energy asking nothing for itself in return. This is the quality of energy that fuels the *opus*.

---

27 It is estimated that as much as one hundred million tons of charcoal are still being produced annually. S. Perkins, "Charcoal warms the whole world," *Science Review* 160 (2001), 383.

Even lighter than charcoal is the air on which fire depends. It is the primary fuel, given by the gods as evidenced by the fire of lightning. Pictures of alchemists at their ovens and stoves and smiths at their hearths often show a servant called a "puffer" working a bellows, maintaining the fire by a steady stream of air. There are Egyptian images of these puffers working the bellows as early as 1450 BCE.[28] From indigenous blow-pipe and primitive bellows of animal skin to the blast furnace in ironworks, fire uses air to intensify the heat. To kill a fire, cut off its air.

What is this "air," and how to manage it? Right at the beginning of Western thought about nature and the cosmos, Anaximenes of Miletus (sixth century BCE) proposed an elemental air to be the founding stuff of the cosmos. The idea of an invisible, transparent element that rarefies and condenses and on which fire and light depend, on which, in fact, all life depends, continued to perplex human thinking with theories of ether, phlogiston, aerial angels and winged demons, celestial powers and flying machines, vapors and ghosts, the soul as breath—until the chemical analysis of air during the Enlightenment by Priestley and Lavoisier and the discovery of oxygen (see below, Chapter 9). Fascination with air and imaginative inspiration drawn from it continues in the marvelous treatises by Bachelard on the poetics of air and by David Abram on language, air, and the *ruach* or divine breath.

The character of elemental air also comes from medical and psychological astrology, where air is one of the four foundational elements composing the cosmos. Early texts of psychology presented in the symbolics of astrology teach that air provides fire with coolness, even as air increases its heat; with detachment so that a fire does not burn itself out; with jets of wit, lofty thoughts and mobility of direction, even as it blindly rages. Also, air feeds fire with mental invisibilities, with spirit and a farther, wider vision. A steady stream of narrowed attention quickens the inert charcoal, bringing forth warmth and light.

Fire actually burns air, the flicker of the flame is the same oxygen that we combust. As we live, we are burning, consuming the wind, thereby generating the *calor inclusus* that sustains our days. Our death is expiration, the windbag emptied, the fire out. The act of breathing is our

28 Read, *From Alchemy to Chemistry*, 79.

first participation in the cosmos, circulating in our intimate interiority. Fire lives on mind, and the sustaining heat of our warm-bloodedness depends on inspiration, on fantastic invention, breezy wit and windy rhetoric, on brain-storming, rarefied theories and cool ideas. The mind, a blast-furnace. A breath-soul of inflating words must be continuously fed into the work. The alchemist with his puffer and bellows sucks into his project inspiration from the *nous* of the world, the archetypal mind that moves like the wind around the whole earth. From its four quarters, the life-breath of traditional thought pumps up the work. And so we find the alchemists referring ever and again to other texts, inhaling the thoughts of other doctors of the Art and announcing this dependence as a maxim, "one book opens another," much as painters read philosophers, composers look at architecture, philosophers visit museums, poets translate from distant and dead languages—their fires desperate for fresh currents. For the fire must have words; and the writers whose life is air—Keats, Stevenson, Lawrence—die young of consumption; not burnt out, burned up.

III. METALS

Although alchemy moved from forge to laboratory, working with metals was not left behind. The elemental metals—iron, lead, copper, mercury, tin, or antimony—entered into the compounds, adding their natures to the concocted product. Each of the major metals corresponds with one of the seven planetary bodies that influence the soul by means of their exhalations, the *pneuma*, breath or inspiration, that give specific qualities to the work.

The Doctrine of Correspondence—"as above, so below"—means more than symbolization on earth of the planets in heaven. Correspondence: "congruence; friendly intercourse; mutual adaptation; connection; letter-writing." It means keeping in touch with, receiving messages from. Things on earth, especially the metals in the earth, are in touch with the gods; they bear mythical messages. There is a spirit in the iron, in the lead, a *spiritus rector*, a guiding principle that teaches the artisan.

Lead instructs slowness; copper, quick warmth; mercury, ungraspability and fusibility.

This spirit in the metal, its subtle body, and its shadow, rather than the mineral as such, becomes the focus of alchemy. Thus, the alchemical work with metals is called the "sophistication of the metals." The alchemist tries to release specific qualities from the metal. As a refiner attempts to release the metal from its ore, so the alchemist tries to realize a quality in the metal—the passionate vigor in iron, say, so that the Stone (that goal of the work) be strong, penetrating, purposeful. At the same time, alchemy warns against possession by the very spirit it is seeking, a possession that can have the artisan stuck in the shadow of iron: rigid, martial, burdened, and rusting.

The process is both one of *refining,* by releasing essence from dross, and of *transmutation,* by improving the grade of the metal from lowest to highest, from lead and iron to silver and gold, because the metals themselves are filled with a desire to return to the higher condition from which they have fallen. In each metal is the slumbering wish to transmute to a nobler state.[29] Refining and sophistication aim for purity, a silver that is "sterling," a gold that is 24 carats. Purity: the least possible extraneous admixtures. Purity: entirely self-same. The refined metal is unadulterated; the sophisticated metal has been reduced to its essential qualities. Refinement and sophistication through discipline.

Iron imposes its discipline. Enter the forge of rage, melt, and coagulate, submit to the hammer and harden, be plunged again and again into the fire and the cooling bath. These rigors resonate with the angers of Mars and his choleric temperament, the impatience, the toughness, the imperviousness to malleability, and the need to keep dry from rust.

The Venusian discipline of copper works toward a more sophisticated essence by separating out—drying up, burning away—collective idealizations, traditional constraints, and sentimental overtones, so as to achieve

29 Alchemy ignores the modern distinction between organic and inorganic chemistry. See, for instance, the major and original work of Angelo Sala (1576–1637) on (organic) sugar and (inorganic) salt. Both substances embodied similar Paracelsian principles: the combustible (sulfur), the fluid (mercury), and the heat-resistant (salt). For Paracelsians, and alchemists on the whole, metals and their ores "grew" in Mother Earth like plants. Z.E. Gelman, "Angelo Sala: An Iatrochemist of the Late Renaissance," *Ambix* 41, no.3 (1994), 146–60.

copper's essential beauty shown by the metal's subtle patina of surface. (Venus as goddess of the skin of things—their feel, their shine.)

In Greek, *metalleia* refers to an underground channel or mine; *metalleuontes* is one who searches for metals, a miner; and *metallao* means to search, inquire. A play on words adds a further significance: *metallasso* means to change, alter—perhaps the metals take pleasure in their alterations and enjoy the discipline imposed upon them by extracting their ore-bodies and the smelting. As one book leads to another in alchemical inquiry, so, says Pliny the Elder, one vein leads to another.

The adept provoked by the metal becomes a prospector, exploring deep in the psyche's elemental core for the foundational substances that underlie the surface behavior of things. It is as if the planetary gods in their metallic hideouts push the depths to search further, ever gaining more and more essential knowledge and technical ability from what the metals afford. They become the teachers, the mentors.

The inherent perfectibility of the substances urges all things away from the literal, undifferentiated, and only natural as given or found. The "only natural" may be necessary, but it is insufficient, since the metals themselves ask to be sophisticated. The given soul asks to be worked. In its natural found state the soul is innocent, ignorant, and therefore dangerous. That the material itself asks to be refined, the raw wanting to be cooked, suggests an archetypal basis for the ideas of perfectibility, progress, and as well, evolution.

The primary material condition of a substance conceals its essential nature. It does not even know itself, seeming merely a symptom without worth. The adept works to discover the value in what appears as dull ore or discard slag. His labors move the material from its first or primary presentation to a moment of revelation when it becomes psychologically intelligible. The practitioner seeks not only to free the metal from its dross but to free the meanings of the metal, their linkages with the intelligibility of the cosmos. To the alchemist, the world is signed by the gods and we learn to read their signatures and gain the significance afforded by each thing.

Assumed here is the inherent intelligibility of the world. This innate knowledge does not reside in God's omniscient mind, but is immanent in the world of things, giving to each its specific value and allowing it to be understood. By reading the world as animals do, we adapt to it and can better aid it on its way toward its aims. Alchemy was not merely gold-making for the benefit of the alchemist and his patron. Within the labor was the vision to bring the world itself into a golden age, fulfilling *its* desire for perfection, a soul-making of the world itself.

Nature is constantly at work toward this end. Its own *calor inclusus* or innate heat slowly transmutes the stubbornly resisting primary matter. The alchemist, however, by ingeniously intensifying the heat, could hasten nature's own aims. In his laboratory and at his stove the adept believed he could bring to fruition in a lifetime, or sooner, what nature by itself takes centuries to accomplish.

Although the work is always stated as an *opus contra naturam* (a work against nature), it was of course a following of nature, guided by nature, instructed by the book of nature which the alchemist diligently studied. Thus the best statement for summarizing the alchemical attitude is from Ostanes, whom Jung cites frequently: "Nature rejoices in nature: nature subdues nature: nature rules over nature."[30]

Resistance

Nature subdues nature by means of fire. Heat dissolves the cohesion of a substance; that natural desire to hold to itself as it is. Heat separates the metal from the ore body and can calcine the metal into a more workable condition. In the only-natural state, the substances resist change. They intend to stay as they are and have been for millions of eons, buried and hidden away. Yet the innate urge toward perfectibility welcomes the fire. Hence, they rejoice also in their submission, allowing themselves to be smelted, hammered, and extracted from their home ground.

Resistance of any thing is given with its essential nature. "The power or endeavor, wherewith each thing endeavors to persist in its own being, is nothing else but the given or actual essence of the thing in question," wrote Spinoza.[31] Resistance in the work and to the work is not personal but ontological. Being does not move, said Parmenides, to which Heraclitus replied, all things move. Two differing ontologies.

30 *CW* 9.2: 244 n.

31 *Ethica*, part III, prop. VII. B. de Spinoza, *Opera*, ed. J. Van Vloten and J.P.N. Land (The Hague: Martinus Nijhoff, 1914), vol. 2.

Ontological ambivalence. Ostanes's maxim accounts for the inherent ambivalence in the metals and all through the alchemical art. Ostanes's maxim sophisticates the idea of ambivalence itself. Nature does enjoy its natural state and resists change, yet it also struggles against its predeliction for stasis, subduing itself and making change possible. Nature sophisticates itself, dividing its ambivalence into two aspects—the unchanging and the changing. It is therefore folly to attempt to change the unchanging. Or as the alchemists say: "You cannot make a milk-cow out of a mouse."

What changes and what does not change? What stays the same and what becomes different? In philosophical terms, the existence changes, but the essence remains unalterable. The natural body of the metal may become a liquid, a powder, a vapor; it can combine, shift colors, submit to the effects of other substances. The subtle body, however, persists in its own self-same unalterability.

It takes heat to subdue the innate resistance of a substance, a heat gentle enough to melt the stubborn and fierce enough to prevent regression to the original state. Only when the regression to the original "found" condition—the substance in its symptomatic presentation—is no longer possible, only when it has been thoroughly cooked and has truly separated itself from its historical and habitual mode of being can an alteration be said to have been accomplished. Then the substance, which psychology might call a complex, becomes less autonomous and more malleable and fusible, having lost its independence as an intractable object that objects and resists. Only then can the subtle body of the metal—hardness of iron, the quick warmth of copper, the weight of lead—join the work. "Only separated things can be conjoined," say the alchemists.

IV. VESSELS

The inescapable paradox of fire—of alchemy, of psyche, of intelligent living—consists in this double commandment: *Thou shalt not repress/ Thou shalt not act out.*

On the one hand, fire will act out. Fire spreads; its appetite consumes whatever is combustible. It cannot be concealed. "Three things cannot be hidden," says an Arab proverb, "a camel in the desert, someone in love, and a fire."[32] Fire insists on being visible. It does not want to be repressed, its sparks to be smothered, doused. It will smolder long after the flames have died.

On the other hand, desire may not be released straight into the world. The work is spoiled, say the alchemists, by direct heat. Do not let flames touch the material. Direct fire scorches, blackens the seeds. Fire is quick, and "all haste comes from the devil." *Festine lente*, "make haste slowly," advised a favorite Renaissance maxim.

Do not act out; do not hold in. A paradox. And a double negative that suggests a *via negativa*, a de-literalizing cancellation of both commandments. A mercurial escape from the exhausting oscillation between them. Instead of holding in or acting out, *act in*. Cook in the *rotundum* as one vessel was called, referring both to a container and to the roundness of the skull.[33] Hold the heat inside the head by warming the mind's reveries. Imagine, project, fantasize, think.

Vessels both contain and separate. *Separatio* is one of the main operations in the work. Each substance, each quality, must be distinguished from the *massa confusa* of the primary material, the original supporting confusion. Although the two operations of separation and conjunction are referred to again and again as basic to the work all along (also termed "dissolve and coagulate"), the *separatio* is the more fundamental. This again because "only separated things can be conjoined."

Any substance held in a basket or a jug has been separated from the undifferentiated bulk simply by virtue of a container. The material stuff is no different, and yet it is altogether differentiated by its form. Your beer in a bottle, my beer in a can, are the same and not the same. Water in a jar is jarred water, like bottled water, fountain water, river water. The moment the water running from the tap fills this vase or that bucket, the water has taken on shape.

---

32 *The Secret Heart* (1946), a film directed by Robert Z. Leonhard, starring Claudette Colbert, Walter Pidgeon, and Lionel Barrymore, opens with the following written prologue: "There are three things you cannot hide: Love—smoke—and a man riding on a camel—an old Arabian proverb."

33 *CW* 14:731–32; 13:113–18.

We cannot handle all suffering, all evil, all ignorance, all emotion—only that particular part that has been separated out and given a recognizable form.

Water itself comes in a variety of conditions, from raindrop to ocean, from stagnant marsh to white cascade. The vessels which hold it have edges and bottoms. It is not merely a question whether you are too wet or too dry, too runny and sloppy or too parched and brittle, but how is your moisture *shaped*. Humanity shapes, as birds shape their nests and burrowing animals shape their tunnels. And we shape our graves and burying vessels—abhorrent the bodies of the dead heaved into a pit, shapeless.

Whatever we deal with has to be held in some way. Even oceans have their shores.

> If God had not given us a vessel
> His other gifts would have been of no avail.[34]

Vessels come in every sort of shape and size, made of all kinds of materials, from river reeds and willow twigs to thick clay for pots, wood for barrel staves, metal and glass for beakers. Some vessels are quick to heat but crack easily. Some are opaque, others transparent; some flat and open to allow evaporation, others tightly sealed to intensify the pressure. Vessels: methods of containment. Can you take the heat? Are you opaque and dense, slow to warm so no one can tell what is going on inside? Sometimes it is less an issue what is in the vessel, the nature of the stuff being contained, and more one of shape: leaky, fragile, brittle, solid, full to overflowing, empty, cracked... "I'm doing fine, in great shape."

Vessels are the way we embrace events, store them, style them. Prior to weapon and tool, the vessel. Hunt the mastodon; cook the meat; but the leftover must be kept, and the water brought from the river. "His other gifts would have been of no avail." Along with the sharp flints and stone axe-heads for cutting, the spear points and fish hooks—instruments of killing, there are baskets and slings and gourds and pots—instruments

34 The maxim is attributed to Albertus Magnus and quoted in "The Chemical Treatise of Thomas Norton," *HM* 2:62. Norton adds to Albertus "and that vessel is glass." "Moreover, the size and shape of your vessel should be in proportion to the quantity of your substance, and to all other conditions of the experiment."

of keeping. Since the former lasts through time, while the latter more easily fragments and decays, our picture of early human life puts the male hunter in the foreground and the female gatherer, keeper, and sorter in the background.

Vessels present the style of a culture. One image tells a story: a chipped, dirty toothbrush glass for whiskey in a cheap bed-sitter by Graham Green; pop-up beer cans, Styrofoam cups, jokey ungainly coffee mugs, motel wastebaskets with plastic liners. The bruhaha over wine-glass shapes, stems, thinness... By their vessels ye shall know them.

"Let your glass distilling vessel be round or oval... Let the height of the vessel's neck be about one palm, hand-breadth, and let the glass be clear and thick (the thicker the better, so long as it is clear and clean, and permits you to distinguish what is going on within... The glass should be strong in order to prevent the vapours which arise from our embryo bursting the vessel. Let the mouth of the vessel be *very* carefully and effectually secured by means of a thick layer of sealing-wax."[35]

Three observations to draw from this passage: (1)"To distinguish what is going on within": insights must be clear, not vague and cloudy. (2) "Vapours which arise from our embryo [can burst] the vessel": the living seed of the work is not viable for life, must not leave the vessel; and, while it is germinating, it gives rise to fantasies which seek to escape into the world (in programs and projects). (3) "Let the mouth of the vessel be *very* carefully... secured": Treat the work-in-progress as a secret. Guard your open mouth. Watch carefully what and how and to whom you speak about what is going on within.

Within? Where is that? Within the vessel, whatever the vessel may be: wherever there is a contained and separated focus, a holding zone, something cooking. You are not the vessel, nor is it necessary to believe that "within" is within you—your personal relationships, your psychic processes, your dreams. Interiority is within all things—the garden bed that is in preparation, the poem that is the focus of attentive emotions. Keep a close watch on these interiorities; by watching we are vesseling, for it is the glass vessel that allows the watching, and watching provides the very separation and containment expressed concretely by the glass vessel.

35 Philalethes, "An Open Entrance," in *HM* 2:182.

The watching alchemist is also the observed. Inside the vessel, creatures form, strange images of excited materials, Kings and Queens, little homunculi–miniature figures with faces and eyes. The alchemist becomes the subject of interior observations. The human will's intentions submit to imagistic guidance, a kind of poetic influence of "others" as the vessel brings them to life.

Glass

Glass: like air, like water, made of earth, made in fire. Blown glass melts, liquefies, glows, expands, takes on all sorts of shape, size, thickness, brilliance, and color. It can take the heat. Glass lets us see what is going on within it, behind it. Glass, the vessel of inside revelation, capturing and transmuting the glimpse or glance into studied observation. Inside the glass curcurbits, depicted in the *Splendor solis* and the *Trésor des trésors,* glorious figures go through their alchemical transmutations. Glass holds precious blood in a vial, roses in a bowl, wine in a decanter.

By removing the *opus* from forge to stove, glass makes alchemy possible, and psychological. Glass also makes the science of chemistry possible in the laboratory of controlled *in vitro* observation and experimentation.

Glass also separates observer from observed. It is the material of distancing, separating events from life by means of fragile transparency, enclosing them each in its own "house" as the glass vessels were sometimes called. Because the clear glass preferred by alchemy is itself hardly visible, its invisibility allows the visibility of the *opus*–but only when the glass is shaped into a vessel, that is, affords containment. Glass slide, glass countertop, looking-glass are not enough for the alchemical work.

The parallels with psyche are obvious. The psyche too is invisible; we grasp it only in reflection or we identify it with its contents–this dream, that feeling or memory. Psyche appears to be only what it contains. Glass, like psyche, is the medium by which we see into, see through. Glass: the physical embodiment of insight. The illusion of glass makes content and container seem to be the same, and because we see the content before we recognize that it is held by glass, we do not at first see its shape, its density, its flaws since our focus is fixed on the contents. Glass as subtle body requires a subtlety of noticing. The sophistication of the material needs sophistication of insight.

The alchemical mind was occupied with noticing properties. Which qualities, which attributes, are the "virtues," in Paracelsus's terms, of a substance? Natural things could be grouped, even classified, by their adjectives: hard, cold, bitter, wintry, could bring together phenomena from all three kingdoms—animal, vegetable, mineral. Because the world is inherently intelligible we can discover where each phenomena belongs by means of the study of properties, care with adjectives.

The Bain Marie

The glass vessel is itself vesseled. It can sit in a pot of ash or sand, but more often it is inside a larger container of water: the *bain marie* or Mary's Bath.

Heat penetrates the stuff in the glass vessel by means of water. Both fire and water cooperate to regulate the heat, though neither element touches the substance directly. An ingenious method of indirection, bringing together two notorious enemies, fire and water, to serve the *opus*.[36] Usually when they meet, they hiss and spit and let off clouds of scalding steam, but the *bain marie* protects them from killing each other, and protects the substance from elemental warfare.

The *bain marie* appears in alchemical tradition as an ancient invention, from Egypt perhaps, coming from a practitioner named Mary the Jewess,[37] identical with or confused with Maria Prophetessa. The *bain marie* supposedly developed in the kitchen of a Jewish lady, mystic, experimenter, cook. Today's cooks still use the vessel as a "double-boiler."

As long as water fills the bath, the substance cannot burn, cannot even boil away. The heat of the bath increases ever so gradually in order to loosen and relax the stubborn resistance of the substance by means of gentle warmth. Like your body in a warm tub, which gradually rises in temperature as you draw in more hot water. The warmth permeating the glass vessel from the bath is another way of imaging sympa-

36 CW12, fig. 72.

37 R. Patai, *The Jewish Alchemists* (Princeton, N.J.: Princeton University Press, 1994), chap. 5: "Maria the Jewess."

thetic attention, gentle encouragement, all-embracing tolerance. Knots, boundaries, strictures give way.

"Perform no operation until all becomes water." Before you can do anything at all psychological, you must dissolve the initial mindset with which you approach a problem. Problems themselves are fixed positions. The word "problem" refers in its primary meanings to chess, math, battle strategy—all very tight conditions. We yield and let go, and the mind, set on resolutions, lets go of its own mindset that seeks the resolutions. Will power turns to lassitude in the bath.

Perform no operation until all has become water: rational analysis must wait for emotion to flow, reveries to float, collect in pools, stir, sink, find outlets. Discriminations blur. This and that melt into each other; right and wrong and their guilts grow soft and mushy; they hardly matter, no hard facts, no sturdy sureties to cling to. All yields to the warming water. We become gentler with ourselves. We lose intention for arrival, no hurry. A bath is not a shower. We are the substance, our body and our mind enter the vessel of the soul, Mary's bath. We are the cook and the cooked, unable to feel the difference.

The Pelican

The stoppered vessel serves well for sublimation (raising a substance to a higher level) and for precipitation (a substance at the bottom may produce either drops or liquid at the top or a fine white precipitate). But for more subtle operations a special closed vessel is required: the Pelican.

This glass container has a fat round body stretching upward and out of the body into a long neck that curves downward and rejoins by inserting into the body, thus allowing a circulation of the same matter through various stages from below to above and then back down again.

The Pelican sophisticates the familiar alchemical image of the Ouroboros, the snake that bites its own tail. The Pelican, too, is a tail-eater: the lower end is consumed by the upper end, the head, but the process does not stop there with mental reflection. The head sends its product down again into the body, repeatedly. A continuing circulation ensues. What arises to the head does not escape. As the substance melts, steams, sending vapors upward, cloudy ideas form, pressures increase, lighter, uplifting feelings swirl. But these inspirations and hot ideas are reprocessed down as too unripe, too soft-boiled, too unreal. Rather, they are fed back into the vessel as further nourishment. It is the *opus* that must be fed, continued at all costs.

Repetition. *Iteratio*, they called it. "But I've been here before; "I've done this already." The same again and again.

The Pelican embodies sacrifice; it is a sacrificial vessel. It is the instrument of ritual. An essence of ritual is the complaint: "Yet again." *Iteratio, circulatio*, biting your own tail, eating your own body that feeds your own body. The process is closed into itself, lives on itself, feeds off its own images, including the images of emerging product, of goals, of futures. The sacrifice of non-arrival. Getting nowhere, utopia as goal.

Hence the term "Pelican," since that bird, according to lore, drove its bill into its own breast to draw the blood that fed its young. Christ was this pelican, nurturing his faithful with his own life-blood. The pelican is thus a wounding, a repetitive ritual, a sacrifice, and a humiliation all at once. And, a necessary instrument for feeding the *opus* from within itself. What arises during the work belongs to the work, not to the world. Before the vessel may be opened, its contents must be thoroughly psychologized, refined, sophisticated; its concretizations vaporized. Maintain the heat; stopper the vessel; find pleasure in repetition. The soul is being nourished by its wound.

Yet more subtle: the Double Pelican. The depictions show two pelicans interlinked, side by side or face to face. What emerges from the body of the vessel on the left flows through its neck into the body of the vessel on the right, and vice versa, i.e., the cooking contents in the vessel on the right flows through its long curved neck downward into the body of the vessel on the left. Exchange of reveries, like lovers interlocked, joined by mutual imaginings. A model of co-generation, partnering, intimate kinship. *Yab/Yum*. Native Americans in some locales smoked their tobacco in similar ritual pairings. By means of a tube in my nose, I inhale your exhalations, and in reverse: as I blow my smoke out, you breathe it in. Cross-fertilization of spirits.

The soul requires psychic material. The residues of the daily world, *Tagesreste* as Freud called them, may fill the vessel but do not feed it. Information and influences only nourish after they are mulled and brewed a while. Think of the soul as a cow with several stomachs; reflection as regurgitation. *Pepsis* was one of the terms used for what went on in the vessel: *pepsis,* Greek for digestion; transubstantiation of the raw into the cooked. Turning the events of the day into experiences, which is one definition of soul-making. Alchemists warn against undigested material—extraneous comparisons, borrowed interpretations, theories and explanations. They say "read," and yet they say, "nothing found in books is of any use." All that is needed is already given, providing it be properly cooked.

The Pelican offers an image for the wounding that the work causes. We feel the cost in blood. "Things must be cooked in their own blood," is an oft-repeated admonition. We feel the draining in the body for what might come later but is now entirely unknown, the Pelican's offspring, children of the imagination, for "Imagination bodies forth/The form of things unknown."[38] The Pelican: vessel of psychological faith, a phrase used by a keen student of alchemy, Robert Grinnell,[39] for an attitude or a devotion that calls for nothing less than giving in, giving over to the opus all personal demands one has upon it, for its sake, come what may.

The Void in the Vessel

Each vessel has its particular shape. Inside is emptiness. Each vessel is shaped around this emptiness. Because our Western culture declared "Nature abhors a vacuum," we abhor emptiness. ("Empty" from Old English meaning "at leisure, unoccupied," that is, not working, unfunctional.) For us, the void in the vessel is just that: empty. We regard vessels from the outside, admiring the glaze on the pot, the cut of crystal, the weave of a basket, and handle of a jug. When valuing the inside, then by measure only: how much does it hold? A pint, a quart, a bushel?

In Buddhism, the void is less a vacuum than a positive force.[40] The inside shapes around itself the outer visible form. The "stillness" of the

38 W. Shakespeare, *A Midsummer-Nights' Dream,* Act. 5, Sc. 1.

39 R. Grinnell, "Reflections on the Archetype of Consciousness: Personality and Psychological Faith," *Spring: An Annual of Archetypal Psychology and Jungian Thought* (1970), 15–39.

40 E. C. Eoyang, "'Vacuity,' 'Vapor,' and 'Vanity': Some Perspectives on the Void," *Tamkang Review* 16, no.1 (1985): 51–65.

Chinese jar (T.S. Eliot)[41] begins inside; the exquisite shape we see is the stillness emanating from the void. Always this specific void inhabits this specific shape.

Culture affects the shape of vessels and therefore they reveal mysterious qualities of a culture that its other arts and written texts might not as well express. Strange shapes, perfected forms of different Chinese dynasties, Greek pots, Etruscan, Phoenician, French Roccoco, Picasso's ceramics, Morandi's clusters of quiet bottles. Barrels and casks, pitchers and jugs. The long-neck beer bottle, the old Coke bottle, the milk bottle with the bulge for yellow cream. The Roman *futile* that could only tip over, the goat skin of wine, the metal canteen shaped differently for each nation's army. Vessels expose the invisible *Zeitgeist,* the visible formed by the invisible.

Western phrenology and Romantic medicine expressed a similar idea, attributing the contours and crevices in the human skull to the force of the brain, and within that organ, the power of mind or soul. Phrenologists penetrated to the "inner nature" of a person by studying and measuring the palpable bumps of the skull. They claimed to read a person's gifts and deficiencies, the very inmost character, from the hills and valleys of cranial topography.

These ways—Oriental and Romantic—of considering inner emptiness suggest that each emptiness has its individual shape and is contained in a quite particular manner. Your void is not my void, and hers is different again. The way a person holds his or her lacunae is already a revelation of what is being held. General terms, simplistic diagnostics—abandonment, need, identity crisis, low self-esteem, depressive mood, dependency, masochistic helplessness—cannot adequately describe, let alone understand, the force of the void.

Because our collective Western natures abhor a vacuum, we reach out to fill the emptiness with anything, everything from junk food to junk self-help, from drink and shopping and the novelty of games and gadgets to the commiseration of soul-mates, or simply endless tears. Alchemy, however, suggests these feelings of emptiness are indications of a vessel forming. The void is building a shape, a particular shape. Perhaps several vessels. Modes of containing. Modes of measuring. Modes

41 T.S. Eliot, "Four Quartets: Burnt Norton," in *The Complete Poems and Plays,* 121: " The stillness, as a Chinese jar still/Moves perpetually in its stillness."

of differentiating. The reality of the psyche is forcing its way into life and reshaping one's life by means of the feelings of emptiness.

Sometimes the void can be located physically. Right here, in my belly; just behind my heart I feel light-headed, dizzy. Sometimes it appears in a dream as falling through space, a pothole, a dark cave, a huge vacant lobby, an egg-shaped object.

So long as we do not attribute formative power to the hidden inside of the vessel, we will continue to read its function in one direction only. The pitcher holds water, the vase holds flowers, the basket, fruit. The void inside is merely a receptacle; the water, the flowers, the fruit are what count.

A reverse reading says the jug is moistening, the vase flowering, the basket fruiting. The master painters in Holland and in nineteenth-century France showed the poppies and irises and roses, the pears and apples and grapes emerging from the hollowness of their containers, the void as source of beauty. If you examine the vases holding the flowers, the baskets and plates on which the fruit lies, these vessels are each manifestations of particularized shapes, colors and textures, and they are inherent to what they display. "If God had not given us a vessel/His other gifts would have been of no avail."

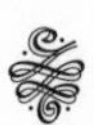

V. OVENS AND STOVES

Vessels contain the substance, but the fire itself must be contained. The heat that charges through the work and makes alchemy possible requires a container equal to its burning force. Desire needs direction.

Clay cracks, glass breaks, wood burns, metal melts. What vessel can hold the *opus maior*? The methods implied by the vessels—clay's earthiness, the reflection and lucidity of glass, the materialistic naturalism of wood, and the disciplined hardness of metal—each fall victim to the great heat. The soul madly burns for "gold," how else account for the insanity of alchemy, the folly, the miserable privations and persecutions and the exalted ambition of those who pursued it to their deaths.

The elixir that would cure all ills, grant longevity and immortality of soul as well as fame, fortune, and the company of kings—these were the visions of alchemical desire. So excessive, so extreme that they could only come from the Gods. Such was the imagination of Zosimos who retells a Jewish tale (Genesis 6:1–4) as if alchemy's origins:

> Angels were taken by passion for women. They descended to earth and taught them all operations of nature ... They were the ones who composed chemical works ... Their book is called *Khema* and it is from them that chemistry [*kumia*] received its name.[42]

Alchemy starts in desire; desire needs direction. Ethical suppression cannot master desire. The essence of fire is out of our control. It comes from the celestial region, from angels, from the gods and the earth's burning bowels. Hence the shamanistic aspect of the smith as fire master, and the crime of Prometheus's humanism.

Furnus, the furnace as response to fire. The *Furnus* takes responsibility for the fire. Equal to the forces of fire must be the rigor and fantasy of the stove. It must be able to govern fire's wild combustibility, and a Chinese text refers to the "sacrifice to the stove (*tsao*) and you will be able to summon 'things' (i.e., spirits)."[43] *Furnus*: a logic of strong, well-built, carefully joined, enduring system. Ground rules, bricks and mortar of the trade, iron-clad discipline of the church or school or society which keeps the living spirit in focus, concentrated, and able to withstand the blaze of inspiration, the flashes and sparks of passion that would ignite grass fires and scatter the intensity.

Direction, aim, purpose, concentration, focus. *Focus*, Latin for hearth. The fire-resistant stove is ruled by its own governing principle: to resist the fire. Rules are made to keep the fire in bounds. A stove is constructed; it is a construct, a conceptual system. Its design has designs on the fire, designating its direction and quality.

Assay furnaces, cupelling furnaces, silver-refining hearths, iron-smelting furnaces, glass-melting furnaces, furnaces for smelting lead or tin and for separating silver from copper, and hearths for the production

42 Patai, *The Jewish Alchemists*, 56.

43 A. Waley, "Notes on Chinese Alchemy," *Bulletin of the School of Oriental Studies*, London Institution, VI, no. 1 [1930], 2.

of mercury and resin.[44] Back-burners and front-burners, multiple vents, multiple heats, hideaway ovens, warmers, hot grills of orange coals. Some alchemical stoves had more than forty different cooking places. Multiple heats for multiple materials and concomitant multiple operations. The stove: the discipline of multiplicity. Knowing where each thing best belongs; a place for every operation and each thing in its place. Placing as the art of cooking.

Again, Maria the Jewess is considered, by Zosimos at least, to be the source for the early description of furnace construction, which would logically necessarily follow from her invention of the *bain marie*.[45]

Kinds of cooking, multiple operations: evaporation in a flat pan lets the steam dissipate; distillation achieves from a messy mass a few drops of clarity; sublimation brings a material upward from the sedimentation at the bottom of the vessel; congelation allows matters to cool down and solidify into a definite shape; fermentation encourages the stuff to enrichen from within its own obscurity.

Multiple operations, multiple stoves.[46] Ascending furnace drives the heat upward; descending furnace drives the heat downward; sand furnace surrounds the vessel in ashes, the warmth coming from yesterday's fires: soft, gray, dry, burnt out, yet still giving off warmth; reverberating furnace in which the heat bounces off the interior walls, cooking by echo, repetitions that build intensity; blasting furnace increases the flame by means of a current of air for liquefying and melting minerals; bladder furnace suspends material in a bladder with its mouth protruding outside the oven. These are but some described in technical works on ovens and condensed in Ruland's *Dictionary*, entry on "Furnus."

"Olde Men imagined for this Art/A special Furnace for every part."[47] Norton invented his own furnace "unknown to the Ancients." "I set it up...at a very considerable outlay...It is so constructed that sixty different chemical operations, for which diverse kinds of heat are required, may be carried on in it at the same time, and a very small fire...supplies

44 B. Meitzner, *Die Gerätschaft der chymischen Kunst: Der Traktat "De Sceuastica Artis" des Andreas Libavius von 1606* (Stuttgart: Franz Steiner Verlag, 1995).

45 Patai, *The Jewish Alchemists*, 90.

46 Cf. C.R. Hill, "The Inconography of the Laboratory," *Ambix* 22 (1975), 101–10, with numerous illustrations.

47 Holmyard, *Alchemy*, 193.

a sufficient degree of heat for all these processes."[48] He goes on to describe other stoves he is perfecting, their ingenuity, their economy of fire (fuel), their multiple service, their capacity for regulating degrees of burning intensity—and which furnace types are best for which particular operations, e.g., purging and drying for exaltation.

If the stove disciplines the fire and directs the heat, it embodies rules and cautions that alchemists love to pronounce. Hardly a text can be found that does not find fault with other texts and the errors in their procedures, or succumb to giving warnings, advice, and moral admonitions. Norton's treatise insists upon five "rules or concords":

> The first rule to be observed is that the student's mind should be in perfect harmony with work. The desire of knowing this Art should hold a dominant place in his mind; else all his labors will come to nothing. The second concord is that he should know the difference between this Art and those who profess it. The third kind of harmony is that which should exist between the work and the instruments. The fourth concord assigns to the work the place which is most suited to its execution. The fifth concord is the sympathy which should exist between your work and the celestial sphere.[49]

Were we to imagine that rules for the alchemical opus are equally valid for psychoanalytic work, then these five rules could be restated in contemporary terms: (1) Knowledge of the psyche in all its vicissitudes, rather than of oneself or of the patient, should hold a dominant place in the practitioner's mind. (2) The value of psychological work is not measured *eo ipso* by the examples of those who practice the profession of psychology. (3) Since concepts are instruments of psychological practice, they must harmoniously further the intentions of the work. (4) Your place of practice shall suit your style of practice and its aim. (5) Practice expresses a cosmology. There should be a harmony between cosmos and clinic, between your broadest view of the world's ultimate order and the intimate work with the suffering of souls.

48 "The Chemical Treatise of Thomas Norton," *HM* 2:62.

49 Ibid., 59–60.

VI. THE SPIRIT OF FIRE

More rudimentary than the tools, stuffs, and procedures used by alchemy is the fire upon which all depends–the element with which this chapter began and now ends. Fire is the first principle, the root metaphor. As the work is governed by fire, dependent on fire, so is alchemical thinking about the work. Consequently, the characteristics of fire archetypally propel alchemical reflection in a specific direction.[50]

Thinking requires language. The idea that fire transforms matter is not only an empirical idea witnessed when a flame burns a wood chip to a black cinder. That transformation was already implied by the Greek term for matter, *hyle* (wood, timber), which later accreted more abstract meanings of Aristotelian potentiality (able to be transformed) and Christian fallenness (able to be redeemed). As wood submits to fire, so material nature submits to spirit by which it is purged, transformed and raised.

Any worker in fire can easily perceive fire's primary characteristics. It rises. Its heat overpowers and changes materials. It gives off light. It cannot be touched directly. It cannot be satiated. *Ascension, transmutation, enlightenment, intangibility, insatiability:* these five ideas empirically witnessed in the laboratory affect the formulations of alchemical texts and later commentators on these texts. In brief, fire gives alchemy its spiritual readings.

Ascension: In the fire of the work, or on fire with their work, alchemists are subject to fire's defiance of gravity, and they imagine their work pointing upward in accord with the flames and the heat they are attempting to control. From lower to higher; from inert to active; heavy to light; small, aimless and smoldering to intense and leaping. A ladder of values and stages of progress: imperfection to perfection; disease to health;

50 The paradigmatic figure for this direction is the Belgian chemist and physician Jan Baptista van Helmont who regarded himself as a *philosophus per ignem*, a philosopher by fire. This mystical, yet empirical, thinker held that God communicates "by means of fire–the penultimate chemical means of inquiry. Fire is a concentration of light, and in its destructive power... it is a divine creation." B. Heinecke, "The Mysticism and Science of Johannes Baptista van Helmont (1579–1644)," *Ambix* 42, no. 2 (1995), 72.

particular to universal; mortal to immortal—*medicina cattolica*, panacea, resurrection, diamond body, gold, saved from hell-fire by divine fire, the salamander who survives fire, the phoenix rising from the ashes.

Transmutation: An inner fire is at work all through nature lifting it in stages from impure to pure. Witness the accomplished transmutations in particular pockets of rock: crystals, precious jewels, nuggets of gold. Evolution is built into the mineral body of the earth. Though fire may calcinate a substance to powdery ash, blacken it to "death," nonetheless, downward and disintegrative effects are appropriated by the overall model of improvement. Light at the end of the tunnel; darkest before dawn; Gethsemane and Golgotha before the Resurrection. Whatever fire touches it alters: All things are subject to its transformative omnipotence. Even water evaporates, rock melts to lava, and the strongest iron bends to its will. The flame of the spirit overcomes all material resistance.

Enlightenment: Fire lights up the dark. By means of it we can see in the dark, advance into the dark, hold back the night. Yet, this same fire sharpens and deepens the dark. Standing close by its light, near into the fire (lamplight, candle flame, camp-fire), the corners and shadows of the farther perimeter become pitch, impenetrable. The more light, the more darkness, requiring ever brighter enlightening. Light and dark, contraries defining each other; eventually, opposites warring each other. Enlightenment, a *via longissima* because unconsciousness increases in proportion to illumination. Resolution of the paradox? An epiphanic illumination, only an apocalyptic fire of spiritual awakening evacuates darkness itself: "Death and Hades cast into a lake of fire" (Revelations 20:14]; "O Death where is thy victory?" (1 Corinthians 15:55).

Intangibility: Because fire cannot be touched directly, it must be grasped indirectly, by hints, paradoxes, analogies, allegories, cryptic ciphers and arcane symbols. Gnostics, Rosicrucians, Kabbalists. The "black art" of hidden knowledge. Anything usually perceptible to the common eye is not the alchemical gold; all things, the mind itself, must be initiated, sophisticated. Only an elite, initiates of the occult, a priestly caste, reclusive and disciplined, having suffered long in the mystery, done their mortifications and their praying, can work the fire.

Insatiability: When Thomas Norton describes the qualities required by an alchemist's servants, his job description could as well cover a nursemaid. Caring for the fire in many indigenous cultures belongs among the tasks of women and the old. Like a baby, fire wants only to grow and its appetite is insatiable. It must have regular feedings, enough air, and nothing indigestible–wet straw, rotted wood, dirt-covered roots, clumped dung. As it grows it seeks to leap out of the cradle, go off on its own, and spread its sparks. Alchemy's insatiability is sometimes disguised, sometimes blatant. Insatiable, the expansion of terms, differentiation of stuffs, kinds of vessels. Insatiable, the appetite for learning: "One book opens another." Insatiable, the desire for the golden goal. Even the last stages of the *opus major* are limitless: *exaltatio, multiplicatio, rotatio*. And alchemy does not let itself be reduced to simple formulae and normative rules, as if, because of the fire, alchemy cannot come to a cohesive system required by its own operations of coagulation and conjunction. Like the spirit, it goes where it wants, follows its impulse. Like the spirit, fire is on a mission, to ignite fires ever further afield, converting the day into combustibles to fatten its own flames.

These five leading ideas so apparent to any "worker in fire" together support an alchemical metaphysics. The archetypal ascending impulse within fire gives alchemy its spiritual vision, translating its images and insights into messages for the upward path. The Christianism of alchemy's main authors derives not only from their historical context: that they were writing in a strongly Christian era. Their redemptive metaphysics is determined even more by their archetypal context: the spiritual ascensionism of elemental fire.

A passage from Aristotle can save alchemical psychology from this archetypal determinism and the spiritual reading of alchemy. Aristotle writes:

> For the growth of fire is unlimited while there is something to be burnt, but in all things which are naturally constituted there is a limit and a proportion both for size and for growth; and these belong to soul, but not to fire, and to principle rather than matter.[51]

Since soul recognizes itself in its images and since the making of images (*poeisis*) is soul's primary natural activity,[52] "the definite principle" that

51 Aristotle, *De Anima: Books II and III (with passages from Book I)*, trans. D.W. Hamlyn (Oxford: Oxford University Press, 2002), 19 (416*a*).

52 *CW* 13:75; 11:889, 769; 8:618. Cf. J. Hillman, *Re-Visioning Psychology* (New

governs the "increase of fire" are images. They are the essential rudiments of the entire work. They are what the alchemist sees and smells and touches with his hands—and what he imagines. Focus on them limits the infinite metaphysical speculation ("the increase of fire") to just what is just now. Alchemical descriptions in language and pictures are coagulations serving to condense the volatility of the engaged psyche into actual presentations. Alchemy: a study of presentations as these appearances portray, define, and affect the soul. Consequently, alchemy's insatiable spiritual drive, its "fire," requires psychological limitations, an alchemy of soul such as this rudimentary chapter and the book as a whole intend.

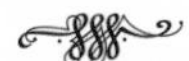

York: Harper & Row, 1975), xvii: "[Jung] considered the fantasy images that run through our daydreams and night dreams, and which are present unconsciously in all our consciousness to be the primary data of the psyche. Everything we know and feel and every statement we make ... derive from psychic images."

3

The Suffering of Salt

Some seek not gold, but there lives not a man who does not need salt.
–Cassiodorus

Toward a Substantial Psychology

Alchemical salt, like any other alchemical substance, is a metaphoric or "philosophic" salt. We are warned in various alchemical texts not to assume that this mineral is "common" salt, our table salt or sodium chloride. Yet, as we shall see, this alchemical salt is indeed common to us all–and not only as the physiological content necessary to our blood and fluids.[1] It may well be that the epithet "common," which is curiously attached only to salt of all our everyday comestibles, reveals that salt

1 Animal life depends on common salt. Horses (according to breed, size and location) require up to 40 pounds a year, cows up to 80. Humans consume about ten pounds (not including the amounts in already prepared edibles). "You and I each contain about eight ounces of salt–enough to fill several shakers. [Salt] is involved in muscle contractions including heartbeats... nerve impulses... digestion. Without salt the body goes into convulsions, paralysis, death. Put blood cells in a salt-free fluid and they burst." (G. Young, "Salt: The Essence of Life," *National Geographic* [September 1977], 381.) Since the need for salt is so basic, governments relied on salt monopolies and salt taxes for a sure source of funds. Salt-tax rebellions ensued, for salt represented the common people's common need so that its control was an injustice affecting life itself. The defeat of the secessionist South in 1865 has been attributed to a salt famine and a Chinese law states that a man deprived of salt for a fortnight would be too weak to tie up a chicken. (R.P. Multhauf, *Neptune's Gift: A History of Common Salt* [Baltimore: The Johns Hopkins University Press, 1978], 3–19.) So valuable was salt that it was imported great distances (for instance, from Sicily via Venice to the peasants in the upper Rhone valleys in Switzerland). In Africa blocks of Sahara salt were sold to sub-Saharan economies in exchange for gold dust, ivory, and slaves. Salted food is synonymous with "holy" food in ancient Hebrew. (F. Braudel, *Civilization and Capitalism, 15th-18th Century*, vol. 1: *The Structure of Everyday Life*, trans. S. Reynolds [Berkeley: University of California Press, 1992], 209.)

is the substrate of what is meant by "commonly human," so that salt is the archetypal principle of both the sense of the common and common sense. Already you can see how we shall be working in this chapter: we shall be activating the image of salt (1) as a psychological substance, which appears in alchemy as the word *sal*; (2) as an operation, which yields a residue; (3) as any of many physical substances generically called "salts"; and (4) as a property of other substances.

The word *sal* in alchemical texts, especially since Paracelsus, often indicates the stable basis of life, its earth, ground, body. However, the term also more particularly refers to alums, alkalis, crystallizations, bases, ashes, sal ammoniac, potash, as well as to the sense qualities equivalent to these materials: bitterness, astringency, pungency, mordancy, desiccation, and crustiness, dry stings and smarts, sharpness and pointedness.

These qualities of human life belong to the very substance of character. Indeed, bitter and mordant qualities are not only as common and basic as salt, but they are as essential to the embodiment of our psychic nature as is salt in our physical bodies. Our stinging, astringent, dried-out moments are not contingent and accidental; they are of our substance and essence.

This *psychological* approach to salt has two major predecessors: Ernest Jones's "The Symbolic Significance of Salt in Folklore and Superstition" (*Imago* 1 [1912])[2] and C.G. Jung's richly condensed chapter in *Mysterium Coniunctionis* (*CW* 14: 234–348).[3] The main differences between their approaches and mine lie in our different aims. Where they examine salt in a scholarly manner in order to gain an objective meaning of this alchemical substance, I am attempting to bring over to the reader its substantiality as a commonly recognizable experience. Where Jung does a metapsychology of alchemy, I am trying to do an alchemical psychologizing. Hence his chapter on salt, and Jones's mainly anthropological amplification, are indispensable backgrounds, even though they offer less experiential closeness to the material. I intend that my speaking about salt will bear traces of salt with it.

2 Reprinted in E. Jones, *Essays in Applied Psychoanalysis*, vol. 2: *Essays in Folklore, Anthropology and Religion* (London: Hogarth Press, 1951).

3 Both essays were re-issued and excellently introduced by Stanton Marlan in *Salt and the Alchemical Soul* (Woodstock, Conn.: Spring Publications, 1995).

Our model is the microcosm/macrocosm and the doctrine of correspondences between them. A man or a woman is a smaller arrangement (*kosmos*) which all things in nature are proportionately represented. Not only is the macrocosmic world personified and alive with subjective qualities that we nowadays allow only to human beings, but the microcosm of the human being, because it is a microcosm of nature, is also a mineral, physical object, consisting of substances such as salt. The difference between this psychological substantiality and that of chemistry, which too holds that mineral and physical elements enter into the composition of a human being, is that the chemical model does not require consciousness or soul. There is a radical split between conscious subject and the physical substances. Whereas the alchemical model suggests: as within, so without. The physical world has its interiority and subjectivity because it is a larger arrangement of the soul's nature. For alchemy, both human and world are ensouled. Intelligence, meaning, display—these are potentially present and afforded throughout.

The microcosm/macrocosm model requires a micro/macro-awareness. It asks that we feel into the world of matter with sensitivity for qualitative differences. It asks that we find in our objective experiences analogies with and metaphors of physical processes and substances. The micro/macro model works in two directions. While endowing the world with soul, it also indicates that human nature goes through natural processes of an objectively mineral and metallic sort. Our inner life is part of the natural world order, and this perspective saves us from taking ourselves so personally and identifying what goes on in the soul with the subjective ego. Thus, salts belong to the very stuff of the psyche. *Sal* describes one of our matters, something that is mattering in us and is the "matter" with us—too much, too little salt, or salt at the wrong times and places, or combined wrongly.

Alchemical psychology describes a myriad of substances. William Johnson's *Lexicon Chymicum* of 1652 and Martin Ruland's *Lexicon Alchemiae* of 1612 list hundreds of words referring to materials. These can be reduced to a system of seven basic stuffs deriving from metallic seeds of the traditional planetary gods: all sorts of words may refer to silver, for instance, and its operations, and each of these words connote as well the planetary principle of the moon in a particular phase or guise or combination. A variety of the sevenfold system is that of three substances plus a fourth, the "tetrasoma," which in itself combines four of the primary planetary metals (lead, copper, iron, and tin or antimony). The threefold system, in which salt finds a major place, derives mainly from Paracelsus,[4] the Swiss radical philosopher of nature, religious physician, and eccentric whose system of sulfur, mercury, and salt was a more subtle and chemical mode of imagining than the more gross and metallurgical model of the seven.

Because of the interrelated complexities of these substances, alchemical models are polytheistic, that is, one cannot speak truly of any element alone. Whatever is said about salt is always contaminated, and must be so contaminated by the materials, vessels, and operations with which it is in interaction. Psychic materials are always in diffuse interpenetration, with other materials and do not remain singly self-consistent, and so require multiple interpretation. In fact, this very contamination is part of their definition: let us say that alchemy is soft-edged. Lines between its elements cannot be drawn hard and fast because these elements are also elementary living natures. The technique of isolation, so essential

4 Although various of salts were alchemically known in antiquity (Theophrastus, Pliny, and later Geber and Rasis), not until Paracelsus was salt elevated to one of the *tria prima*, more fundamental than the seven planets and the four elemental temperaments. Paracelsus re-founded alchemy on a tripartite scheme by introducing salt as a new third term. This "third" position is characteristic of Paracelsus in that he opposed both Aristotle and the Scholastics on one side and Galen on the other. His tradition, as Walter Pagel shows ("Paracelsus: Traditionalism and Medieval Sources," in *Medicine, Science, and Culture: Historical Essays in Honor of Owsei Temkin*, ed. L.G. Stevenson, R.P. Multhauf [Baltimore: The Johns Hopkins University Press, 1968], 57ff.), was Platonic and Neoplatonic, especially in following the tripartite cosmo-anthropology of Marsilio Ficino—body, soul, spirit—whom Paracelsus admired. It is in his advocacy of the third principle that I see the importance of Paracelsus for Jung as a spiritual ancestor (*CW* 15: 1–143; *MDR*, 200 and 220). Both warned against theological spiritualism on one side and empirical materialism on the other in order to hold the middle ground of soul or psychic reality. Part of the so-called "elusiveness" of Paracelsus (O. Temkin, "The Elusiveness of Paracelsus," *Bulletin of the History of Medicine* 26 [1952], 201–17) can be attributed to this mercurial middle ground. Although Paracelsus usually identified sulfur rather than salt with the middle integument, it was his advocacy of salt and his own saltiness (the physical, practical, common, vernacular, purgative, sharp-tongued, bitter, uncombinable nature of his character) that shows this substance to have been as fundamental to his nature as it was to his thought. He died, by the way, in Salzburg. (On the three lines of thinking, see O. Temkin, *Galenism: Rise and Decline of a Medical Philosophy* [Ithaca: Cornell University Press, 1973], esp. 128–70.)

to the method of modern natural science, arbitrarily forces nature to comply with an isolating kind of consciousness and its epistemology, which cuts, separates, and opposes in order to know.[5]

Alchemical salt is usually in a tandem with sulfur and what is said about salt is usually from a sulfuric standpoint. For example in Paracelsian alchemy, salt is frequently imagined as soul (sulfur as body and mercury as the spirit combining them). The illustrative image is the egg, whose yolk (sulfur)–oily, smelly, sticky and vital–is its body, whose shell (salt)–fixed, inflammable, crusty and enclosing–is its soul, and whose white (mercury)–connecting yolk and shell, mutable, slippery, volatile, changing its shape and consistency–is the egg's spirit. Or the shell (salt) may be the body; the yolk (sulfur), the soul.

I have found that it is better to consider each component to have its own sort of body rather than to insist that salt is always soul (or always body)[6] in a one-to-one equation. We must remember that a psychic substance does not and cannot mean one thing. We find that alchemists shifted "body" to equal this or that depending on the task at hand. The same is true in our psychic work today: certain problems take on body or cry for release from body, or lose their embodiment, so that no single aspect of our psychic lives can consistently be named "body." As Robert Sardello has often said, body is most elusive. When body is equated with sulfur what is meant is the excitable, palpable urgency, the body of generative passions and will. When body is called salt what is meant is the fixed, consistent, stable body that encloses any existent as its outer shell. Paradoxically, salt may mean the inner core: for salt was imagined by Khunrath as the center of the earth. Perhaps the best way to understand "body" in this context is by the action of a substance: that which coagulates or brings embodiment about therefore must itself be body. Sometimes sulfur is the coagulatory agent; sometimes coagulation is attributed to the power of salt.

The tandem of salt and sulfur continues in modern lives and modern dreams. A woman in analysis oscillates between burning enthusiasms for

---

5 "Science" from *scire*, to know, is cognate with *scindere*, to cut, divide, and has the same probable root as schism, shed, and shit (as separation). Cf. E. Weekley, *An Etymological Dictionary of Modern English* (London: John Murray, 1921.)

6 Cf. *CW* 14: 322–23. Salt is also Christ, Mercurius, and thus the spirit as well as the soul, and body or earth.

new people, projects, places. She is ready to catch fire at any moment, bringing a richly fat imagination and vital energy to life. She also has times of depression: drinking alone self-enclosed, encrusted, bitter with residues of what has been, stuck for hours in a square chair at a square table, feeling low and base, sunk to the center of the earth. There is no direct connection between her sulfur and her salt. They oscillate in "mood swings." An alchemical therapeutic approach would not temper one with the other, but would touch both with mercury, that is, free them from their alternating concretism by means of psychological insight. The first step is to see how impersonally autonomous the swings are and how they constellate each other, as do sulfur and salt.

In another case, a young man, finding it hard to yield some of his childish innocence and the rich life in the lap of the mother and the gods, dreams first of walking with his girl through a salt desert, then of their sharing salty meat together, and then of a strange man who runs a stand on the street, handing the dreamer a salty sausage-type roll instead of what he had ordered—a roll or bun filled with yellow, sweet-cream custard. The dreamer is offended. He had wanted the savor and joy of sulfur in the sweet soft things that slip down with no effort.[7] But the strange man-in-the-street (Mercurius himself, perhaps) hands him the bitter sting of salt that can bring tears to one's eyes. We shall now have to explore the nature of this salt.

Salt Mines: The Mining and Making of Salt

But first—where is the salt to be found? How do we mine it, make it, prepare it. Eirenaeus Philalethes replies: "Descend into yourself, for you carry it about with you..." It is to be found in "Man's blood out of the body, or man's urine... Mark well that those bodies which flow forth from our bodies are salts and alums."[8] As there is salt in the macrocosm, so can it be mined from within microcosmic human nature. In fact, because salt is "the natural balsam of the living body" (*Paracelsus*, 1:259) we descend into the experiential component of this body—its blood,

7 A classical psychoanalyst would likely find the contrast between sausage roll and creamy bun to symbolize an opposition between male and female genitalia.

8 E. Philalethes, "The Secret of the Immortal Liquor called Alkahest or Ignis-Aqua," *Collectanea*, 12–13.

sweat, tears, and urine–to find our salt. Jung (*CW* 14: 330) considers alchemical salt to refer to feelings and to Eros; I would specify his notion further by saying that salt is the mineral, impersonal, objective ground of personal experience making experience possible. No salt, no experiencing–merely a running on and running through of events without psychic body.[9]

Thus salt makes events sensed and felt, giving us each a sense of the personal—my tears, my sweat and blood, my taste and value. The entire alchemical opus hangs on the ability to experience subjectively. Hence it is said in "The Golden Tract": "He who works without salt will never raise dead bodies."[10] The matters are only macrocosmic and chemical, out there, dead, unless one works with salt. These intensely personal experiences are nonetheless common to all–both intensely mine and yet common as blood, as urine, as salt. In other words, salt acts like the ground of subjectivity ("That which is left at the bottom of our distilling vessel is our salt–that is to say our earth."[11]). It makes possible what psychology calls felt experience. We must turn to this same ground to mine our salt.

"Felt experience" takes on a radically altered meaning in the light of alchemical salt. We may imagine our deep hurts not merely as wounds to be healed but as salt mines from which we gain a precious essence and without which the soul cannot live. The fact that we return to these deep hurts, in remorse and regret, in resentment and revenge, indicates a psychic need beyond a mere mechanical repetition compulsion. Instead, the soul has a drive to remember; it is like an animal that returns to its salt licks; the soul licks at its own wounds to derive sustenance therefrom. We make salt in our suffering and, by keeping faith with our sufferings, we gain salt, healing the soul of its salt-deficiency. D.H. Lawrence said:

> I am not a mechanism, an assembly of various sections.
> And it is not because the mechanism is working wrongly, that I am ill.
> I am ill because of wounds to the soul, to the deep emotional self

9 In common cookery salt is used for "contracting" the fibers of meat. *Mrs. Beeton's Household Management* (Ware, Hertfordshire: Wordsworth Editions, 2006), 269.

10 *HM* 1: 22.

11 Ibid.

> and the wounds to the soul take a long, long time, only time can help and patience, and a certain difficult repentance ...[12]

The alchemical substances offer distinctions in kinds of suffering. Salt, for instance, may be distinguished from lead, in that the first is sharp, stinging, acute: it burns in on itself with wit and bite, corrosive acrimony, making sense through self-accusation and self-purification. It is purgative. Lead, however, is chronic and dense, a heavy, oppressive, gloomy suffering, without specified focus, senseless. It is constipative. Whereas salt says "it hurts," lead says "I can't." Where salt tastes the details of its pain by remembering precisely and with piercing agony, lead cannot see, does not know, remaining paralyzed and sunk in a general, abstract obliteration of empirical memory.

The curing of these conditions also differs: salt requires a pinch, feeling the pinch of the event that stings; lead seems to require time, waiting it through, that patience Lawrence speaks of. What results from the salt cure is a new sense of what happened, a new appreciation of its virtue for soul. The result of the lead cure is depth, weight and gravity, more fullness and the ability to "hold it" and "bear it." The two contrast also in two literary genres of suffering: irony (salt) and tragedy (lead). The first tends toward common human experience while the second tends to give distance from that experience. Of course, there are "leaden salts" in alchemy, that is, conditions in which the leaden and the salty aspects of suffering are so combined that the distinctions are hard to notice: usually that which dulls and blankets the nature of salt is a result of lead. The task becomes one of separating lead from salt, black mood from recollection, poisoned spirit from subjective experience, the fateful inescapable destiny from the personally culpable wrong-doing.

Salt may also be mined from whatever is stable. As the principle of stability whose alchemical sign was a square,[13] salt can be mined from

---

12 "Healing," in *The Complete Poems of D.H. Lawrence* (Ware, Hertfordshire: Wordsworth Editions, 1994), 513.

13 See H. Silberer, *Problems of Mysticism and its Symbolism*, trans. S.E. Jelliffe (New York: Moffat, Yard and Company, 1917), 395–96. Concerning salt as square or cube, Silberer makes a nice differentiation: "Crystallization produces the regular form; fixation, the density." The scanning electron microscope shows the structure of common salt to be rather like hard-edged squares or small flat cubes. Cf. the alchemist Edward Jorden (1569–1632) in A.G. Debus, *English Paracelsians* (London: Oldbourne Press, 1965), 163.

the rocks of concrete experience, those fixities which mark our lives with defined positions. These places are not merely solid facts—my degree, my property, my car accident, my abortion, my war record, my divorce; these are also places where psychic body is salted away and stored. These rocks, when recognized and owned, belong to the history of my soul, where it has been salted down by the fixities of experience, giving a certain crystallization to my nature and keeping me from inflammations and volatilizations.

As salt is not flammable,[14] it seems not subject to heat: we make salt less in ardor than in recrimination, less by desire than by memory of desire. "Ash on an old man's sleeve/Is all the ash the burnt roses leave" (T.S. Eliot, "Little Gidding"). Ash is the memory of the fire; not a burnt-out cinder, but the fixed inflammable essence of a love that once flamed to heaven.

Though we cannot make it by fire, we do make salt by means of dissolutions. Salt is soluble. Weeping, bleeding, sweating, urinating bring salt out of its interior underground mines. It appears in our moistures, which are the flow of salt to the surface. "During the work the salt assumes the appearance of blood" (*CW* 14: 337). Moments of dissolution are not mere collapses; they release a sense of personal human value from the encrustations of habit. "I, too, am a human being worth my salt"—hence my blood, sweat, and tears.

It is curious how we are fixated upon our wounds. Psychology speaks of trauma, invented a traumatic theory of neurosis and post-traumatic stress disorder. Why does psychology go back to the hurt child for grounding psychic development, and why does the psyche itself need to look back? It seems the soul must have its signal remembrance engraved into its psychic body so that it knows it has or is a body. Pain implicates us at once in body, and psychic pain in psychic body. We are always *subjected* to pain, so that events that hurt, like childhood traumas, abuse, and rape, force our subjectivity upon us. These events seem in memory to be more real than any others because they carry the force of subjective reality.

---

14 On fire and salt, see Jung, *CW* 14: 319. The "fire" hidden in salt is its dry power or spirit even if it remains itself inflammable. Common sodium chloride melts only at 800° C. Yet there is a "fire" hidden in salt, for common table salt is composed of "a metal so unstable that it bursts into flame when exposed to water; and a lethal gas (chlorine)" (Young, "Salt," 381).

Viewed from the perspective of salt, early traumas are moments of initiation into the sense of being a "me" with a subjective personal interior. We tend to fixate on *what* was done to us and *who* did it: resentment, revenge. But what psychologically matters is *that* it was done: the blow, the blood, the betrayal. Like the ashes which are rubbed into the wounds at initiation rites to purify and scarify, the soul is marked by its trauma. Salt still is touched to the body in Christian Baptism, and eaten still at Jewish Pessach in ritual remembrance of trauma.[15] A trauma is a salt mine; it is a fixed place for reflection about the nature and value of my personal being, where memory originates and looking back into personal history begins. These traumatic events initiate in the soul a sense of its embodiment as a vulnerable experiencing subject.

The paradigmatic story of "looking back" is that of Lot's wife (Genesis 19:26). (Lot and Lot's wife were even used as alchemical terms for salt—cf. Johnson's *Dictionary*.) Because Lot's wife could not refrain from looking back at the destruction of Sodom from which they had been saved, she was turned to a pillar of salt. Jewish commentators[16] say that her mother-love made her look behind to see whether her married daughters were following; and Christian comments on Luke 17:32 (Clement of Alexandria, *Exhortation to the Greeks*, 94) also see the source of her move in remembrances of family and relatives, personal subjectivities of feeling. Evidently, family fixations are also salt-mines. The disappointments, worries, smarts of mother-complex love—the evening with the photograph album, the keepsakes—are ways the psyche produces salt, returning to events in order to turn them into experiences.

---

15 The touch of salt and bitter herbs at Jewish Passover brings back the memorial image of the Red Sea and the desert. The image must not be forgotten because it is part of what makes this day different from any other day, i.e., remembrances help differentiate and fix significance. Salt initiates the youngest child (naive soul) into the bitter images of the soul. When, however, remembrance becomes more than a touch, over-salted, then "not forgetting" becomes literalized into history as facts. Then we become stuck in the past rather than sticking to the image, and the salt acts no longer as an imagistic remembrance, but becomes a literalized historical experience.

16 L. Ginzberg, *The Legends of the Jews*, 7 vols. (Baltimore: The Johns Hopkins University Press, 1998), 1:255 and 5:241–42. The same commentaries note that the destructive rain that fell on Sodom while Lot's wife was looking back on that place of lustful desire was a rain of brimstone (sulfur), i.e., salt longing for sulfur.

The danger here is always fixation, whether in recollection, earlier trauma, or in a literalized and personalized notion of experience itself: "I am what I have experienced." Paracelsus defined salt as the principle of fixation (2: 366).[17] This term, like projection, condensation, sublimation, reappears centuries later in psychoanalysis where it is defined by Freud:

> Fixation can be described in this way. One instinct or instinctual component fails to accompany the rest along the anticipated normal path of development, and, in consequence ... it is left behind at a more infantile stage.[18]

Here we have Genesis 19: 26 recapitulated in modern psychoanalytic language. The image of Lot's family on its journey is now presented as a "path of development." Parable becomes theory; the story salted down as science.

Among these sources of salt, urine holds a special place.[19] According to the model of the macrocosm/microcosm, urine is the human brine. It is the microscopic sea within, or the "waters below." Jewish legends[20] explain that salt is included in all sacrifices as a remembrance of the act of Creation by the separation of the waters above from those below, their having been torn asunder, and the salt remembers these lower waters and their weeping at having been cast down from nearness with God.

Urinary salts are residual traces afloat in the lower person. They are essential remembrances that betray our inner nature, its color, smell, opacity. Bladder disorders and urinary symptoms and dreams may refer to an awakening to the lower waters, to the fact that there is psychic life in the lower person independent of what goes on above, and this life is all intense, burning, personal necessity, which no one else can tend for you and for which time and place and privacy must be found.

---

17 Cf. J. Read, *Prelude to Chemistry: An Outline of Alchemy, Its Literature and Relationships* (London: G. Bell and Sons, 1936), 27.

18 S. Freud, "Psycho-Analytic Notes Upon an Autobiographical Account of a Case of Paranoia," in *Collected Papers*, 4 vols. (London: Hogarth Press, 1924–25), 3: 453.

19 Cf. Philalethes, "The Liquor Alkahest," for a short treatise on urine. For a recipe of "piss and vinegar" see *HM* 2: 74 ("The Testament of Cremer"). The urine is to be collected from an "unpolluted [virginal] youth."

20 Ginzberg, *Legends of the Jews*, 5: 18.

A patient dreams: "My urine is to be examined with various chemicals. I have in front of me several glass bottles with different chemicals, but I don't know how much to take of each of the chemicals for each of the little bottles and how I am to get my urine into these little bottles." Psychoanalysis as urinalysis suggests very careful discriminations of private, internal residues, and making clear (glass) distinctions among them. It is as if the urinary salts must be separated from generalized memory and generalized suffering and examined for their quite specific particulars. For the dreamer the task is double: *dosage* (how much to take) and *focus* (capturing the flow in narrowly accurate perceptions). It is an exercise in "eachness"—a term fondly used by William James to counter the global thinking and feeling of wholeness.

Urine of the virgin boy (between eight and twelve years) was often mentioned as a starting substance for the work. This "urine of the boy" is one of the many names for the *materia prima.* It refers to the salts in the microcosmic sea before the Fall, that is, the archetypal essence of each particular character before it has accumulated personal residues: salt not as the result of events, but as prior to events. The virginal condition is not empty or blank, even if unsullied by experience. These salts have their own specific gravity and qualities—that is, there is an *a priori* salt in our "boy of the soul," who is defined by the fixed intensities that are the demanding urgencies of ones own particular essence. The salts in the urine of the boy are these archetypal traces of character essence. Platonic remembrances that are virginal because they are given intact with one's nature and that can be opened by the alchemical opus.

Johnson's *Dictionary* states simply: *"Urina puerorum est mercurius."* Of course, Mercurius's names are legion; when, however, a substance is overtly named such, there is immediate significance for soul-making. This implies that the ambitions of puer fantasy, which Freudian psychology has attributed to the urinary phase of the little boy's development, take on revelatory significance. It is not merely "urinary erotism"[21]—that I can sexually fertilize the world or extinguish its fires or start rivulets. The urinary ambition of the "boy of the soul" is also an expression of my salt, the essence of myself, my base. "Look," it says,

21 H.A. Murray, "American Icarus," in *Puer Papers,* ed. J. Hillman (Irving, Texas: Spring Publications, 1979), 91ff.

"see my piss—this is me." There is a potent spirit to be found in the silly piss of one's little boy (even perhaps in his bed-wetting).

We can feel the primordial salt of the puer in the bitter pains of ambition that burn before any accomplishment, and also in the sense of remorse that stings before there have been external events to rue. Burning intensities can plague a childhood before worldly experience has begun, and these same salty pains reappear when the boy of the soul is constellated. In the *urina puerorum* is a remembrance of things *a priori* that load an act in the world with more salt than puer consciousness can sometimes bare: huge guilts, high-pitched hopes, even suicide. For the puer comes not only on wings of flights and in games of love; he comes, too, smarting with a memory of beauty and what one is on earth for.

The *urina puerorum* suggests that with the right operation we can recover the salty aspect of the puer. The salt to put on the tail of puer flights is already there to begin with, if we but know the right operation for recovering it. One operation which alchemy suggests for making salt is evaporation.

The watery boy who floats in and out with the tides of emotion and follows the streams of least resistance can be fixed by the salts buried in his own tissues. These give regularities, densities, squareness, and body. When the tides of the sea are exposed to sunlight and their flow stopped, salt crystallizes; so can salt be gained by the evaporation of the microcosmic flood. For this operation, alchemists used a wide-open, flat pan; all things exposed in broad daylight and all the upward pressure allowed to escape. The steam, the smoke, and the cloudy vapors ascend to dissipate in hot air. We lose the lushness of feelings, the flush of high hopes, the dumb bogs of inertia; and, as the moistures recede, something essential crystallizes in the dry air. Here, the sealed hermetic vessel would be wrong. Evaporation means not taking events deeply and intensively but rather flattening the affects and letting a pressure steam away by itself until it comes down to itself. Evaporation to a salt: this is the common salt of the everyday table of the world which is at the same time one's own crystallized experience of it.[22]

22 Since there are many salts, there are many operations to produce it, evaporation being but one. Others are calcination, putrefaction, distillation (salt as a by-product), coagulation.

The alchemical idea that urine contained a potent spirit, a mercurial *lumen naturalis* (light of nature) became evident in 1669 when the German Hennig Brand—called the "last of the alchemists"—cooked urine mixed with sand and produced a soapy residue that glowed.[23] Phosphorous had been discovered. The word etymologically means "light-bringing." It is an epithet for the morning star, for Lucifer, and for Hermes. Indeed, *urina puerorum est mercurius.*

The When and How of Salting

Albertus Magnus declares: "Salt is necessary for every solution."[24] This seems a strange statement, inasmuch as we have been imagining salt as the principle of fixity, of bitter crustiness. Solutions, in contrast, seem to connote fluid, passive, receptive conditions, allowing bitterness to dissolve and crustiness to melt. The *solutio,* however, in alchemical psychology is one of the very few basic operations and because of its ubiquity throughout the entire opus, it cannot be defined in only one way. Evidently, a genuine solution must have the capacity to stabilize. It must sustain a condition, not merely dissolve it.

The alchemical *solutio* does not suggest simplified problem-solving. Rather, it requires salt in order to affect the material in a lasting way. The salt mines of which we spoke in the previous section are both deposits of salt and attempts at solution. When we sit still and sweat it out, we are stabilizing and adding salt to the solution so that it becomes a genuine one. Problems seem not to go away until they have first been thoroughly received.

The issue at stake here is the capacity to internalize, to admit and receive a problem into one's inner nature as one's inner nature. This would be to salt it. A problem reaches its solution only when it is adequately salted, for then it touches us personally, penetrating to that point where we can say: "*Fiat mihi*; all right; I admit, I give in; it's really my problem; it has to be." The taste of this experience is bitter, and it humiliates, and it lasts—a lasting solution.

---

23 I. Asimov, *The Search for the Elements* (New York: Basic Books, 1962), 35–36; cf. R.P. Multhauf, *The Origins of Chemistry* (London: Oldbourne, 1966), 22f.

24 Albertus Magnus, *Libellus de alchimia,* trans. V. Heines (Berkeley: University of California Press, 1958), 61.

A second use for salt is in order to "slay sulfur."[25] Remember: salt is square and blue,[26] and it coagulates. When sulfur flares up it can be slain by a pinch of salt, the pinch that kills, whether a tearful eye, a sharp-tongued remark, a grain of common sense. Salt wounds and slays the impulsive reactions, because it recalls the pain incurred in similar events. Salt gives us the awareness of repetition; sulfur, only the compulsion. Perhaps the exalted *sal sapientia* (salt of wisdom, wisdom of salt) is nothing more grandiose than salt's ability to inhibit sulfur.

As there are psychologies of sulfur that preach action and base themselves on desire, drive, and will, examining psychological events in terms of behavior and its reinforcement or control, so there are psychologies of salt. These tend to literalize the idea that personal suffering is necessary for every solution. They insist upon the self-improvement of interior life. They advocate guilt and penance and working through, examining subjective history, personal feelings, traumata. Alchemical psychology corrects this sort of literalizing by presenting the personal factor that so dominates in psychologies of salt to be impersonal and commonly general. Then, when we work at our self-correction, betterment, purification, we realize that it is not the self that is the focus of our good work; it is the salt. We are simply working on the salt. In this way, the salt in alchemical psychology helps keep the work from flaming up in the egoistic inflation of personal guilt. I am alone responsible; it's all my fault.

Salt is especially missing in young people. A young and careless man dreams of visiting Jung in his house, which turns out to be a laboratory in a huge salt dome where a wizened Jung explains how he works on making salt. Another young man full of promise and void of accomplishment dreams of a beautiful, running deer that springs into a river, its antlers high above the water, crosses, and then collapses on the other bank in desperate need of salt. A transition of the spirit had been made, but only through exhaustion does it come home to the dreamer how badly he needs to conserve, not only his leaping, bounding, rutting spirit but also the experiences of his dream life where his spirit shows itself.

---

25 *HM* 1:154–55 ("The New Chemical Light").

26 Debus, *The English Paracelsians*, 163: "Salts are proper to blew colors" (citing Edward Jorden's *A Discourse of Naturall Bathes, and Minerall Waters* [London, 1631]). Jorden also wrote probably the first treatise in English on hysteria.

Unless the animals of his imagination are salted they may simply vanish in spiritual heroics and aesthetic highs. Yes, we catch the bird by putting salt on its tail.

Why is young love so bitter and study for exams so bloody? Are these not rituals of the salt, ways of intensifying that thicken matters and cement them in place? Bitter love is a salt cure, curing the tender soul, with tears, recriminations and, finally, some sort of stabilized pattern. The backwards and forwards of lovers' fights between tearing passion and passionate tears enact stages of the salt/sulfur conjunction. The salt component "that just won't let go" helps preserve the relationship, when sulfur would burn it out or turn it black.

As macrocosmic salt keeps meat and fish, and pickles vegetables, so we need salt in microcosmic ecology for fixing, toughening, preserving. We can't swallow and digest all that happens in a day, or in a night–so we need long hours of pickling events in glass jars for later staring at, sharing and consuming. If we would keep something, we salt it down, salt it away. The decaying impulse of young nature–the fresher and purer the substance, the surer and sooner it rots–is held in abeyance. Salt gives us time, endurance, survival. It seasons youth by removing excess moisture, thereby preserving the soul through dryness. Dry souls are best, said Heraclitus, which Philo turned to mean, "Where the earth is dry, the soul is wisest"–*sal sapientia*. Analysis shrinks.

"Salt causes matters to thicken." It acts as "knot and cement."[27] What modern psychology speaks of as "integration of personality" and "integrity of character," alchemical psychology refers to as salt, for it is this sophic substance that effects internal adhesion, knitting and knotting events into experience, shrinking generalities into specifics. Salt gives the sense of significant detail, crystallizations that pack with importance what might otherwise have been a bland evening of "waste sad time stretching before and after" (T.S. Eliot, "Burnt Norton"). We want to meet someone at the party who can put sting into a conversation. At a family affair it is usually a crusty old Aunt or Grandfather who adds the salt. The flow of unexperienced events suddenly condenses and remains fixed as we are shriveled by a penetratingly salty observation.

---

27 D.R. Oldroyd, "Some Neoplatonic and Stoic Influences on Mineralogy in the Sixteenth and Seventeenth Centuries," *Ambix* 21 (1974), 148 (citing the French alchemist Nicolas Le Fèvre [1615–1669]).

There is another time and place for salt: when the soul needs earthing. When dreams and events do not feel real enough, when the uses of the world taste stale, flat and unprofitable, when we feel uncomfortable in community and have lost our personal "me-ness"—weak, alienated, drifting—then the soul needs salt. We mistake our medicine at times and reach for sulfur: action, false extraversion, trying harder. However, the move toward the macrocosm may first have to go back toward the microcosm, so that the world can be *experienced* and not merely joined with and acted upon as an abstract field. World must become earth; and this move from world as idea to tangible presence requires salt.

Ruland says: "Nothing can be tangible without the presence of salt." Salty language, salty wit, salty sailors, soldier's pay (*salarium*=salary), worth one's salt, a salted bill, a salted bitch (lustful), a dose of salts—these express the tangible values of the base, workaday, and common earth that our feet walk upon and our hands touch. This language of salt connotes each human being as "salt of the earth": only those well-born and high-placed can afford to sit "above the salt."

The mines of common experience offer this salt: the saws and skilled physical know-how of the old-timer, the age-old crystallizations of common law and common speech. Each of these is like a salt mine, and we can bring down our high-falutin' notions and half-cocked ideas by earthing them in commonality. Salt gives what one has in one's head a worth among people, a tangible value on earth. Commonality, however, needs to be distinguished, from being practical and finding application. To earth an image is not simply to sell an invention. Rather, to salt or earth one's winged speculations is to express them with a common touch; tangibility of style.

Earth is also a local sense. There is salt in local speech: accent, patois, dialect, idioms. Whether one-liners that are grainy epitomes (New York) or drawn out tales that meander across the land (Texas), local speech makes words tangible. The difference between dialect and dialectics, between patois and jargon, between earthy humor and dirty joke, between local idiomatic and national idiotic ("televisionese") is all a matter of salt.

"Salt is not added in equal portions to every kind of food; and this circumstance should be diligently considered by the physician" (*Paracelsus* 1:264). Now we are talking about dosage. Salt requires particularizing;

it forces one to take note of the specific taste of each event. Tangibility means recognition and discrimination of specific natures. This sheds a new light upon the idea of the common: it is evidently not merely collective and general. What is common, however, is a sense for the particular—the water in this village is softer and sweeter than the water on the other side of the valley; these game birds need to hang another day; you can't use that kind of nail in this kind of wood; when the fever turns into sweating, you have to give even more liquids. Paracelsian medicine turned to the patient and tried to make acute differential perceptions; yet it also tried to be a medicine of and for the common people in earthy dialect. We have perverted the meaning of "common" to denote *all* or *usual* or *equal*: whereas "common salt," alchemically speaking, refers to the sharp perception of inherent natures that brings out their individual properties so that we can understand the right dosage.

As we become salty, the caution of salting tends to reverse. Where once it was necessary to catch the bird and conserve experiences, we begin to find ourselves slowly pickling in brine. Events don't let us go: they return to our heart's blood, leap with tears to the eye, bring us to break out in cold sweat over a past deed, burn in the bladder. (Paracelsus speaks of the "evil there is in salt" [1:259].) No longer the conscious application of salt, salting now becomes autonomously psychic. The soul forces its tangibility upon us and brings home our common and base susceptibility to human pain. Perhaps this is the eros of salt Jung writes about, or the wisdom of it, or the black earth and shadow associated at times with salt in alchemy; or perhaps it is the ashes and dry earth to which we are returning, the soul's essence becoming fixed, intimations of immortality that first feel like personal pain.

Paracelsus writes (1:43): "Salt corrects and fixes leprous Luna, cleansing it from its blackness." Thus salt is also a "corrective"—and particularly a corrective of lunatic nigredo conditions by fixing them. A bitter despair, a drawn-out moody meanness, a corrosive worry, a stubborn self-ignorance are leprous. These conditions eat through their own skin, spread contagiously. One picks at oneself. These conditions make the reflective power, which belongs with Luna, splotchy, coming out only in spots, here and there, tatters of whiteness that leprously perpetuate the condition rather than clearing it. Although "leprous" in alchemy generally meant "impure," Paracelsus seems to be speaking of a sickness of reflection itself, when the powers of the moon become sicklied over, Hamlet-style. Rather than having the body of a clear insight, such reflections attack one's own embodiment—my actions, my nature, my self.

Salt corrects this illness of reflection by means of fixing precisely what it is that is wrong. The blackness refers to the generalized stain obscuring reflection, those introspective attempts to see into the dark that only further darken the mind. The acute attack of salt particularizes the mental state by means of a precision of feeling. Exactly what, when, where, and how must be felt, so that the "general mess of imprecision of feeling" (T.S. Eliot, *East Coker)* can be spotted, and each spot cleared one by one. The larger disaster is corrected by the smaller sense of it. Accuracy means acuteness; painful to the self-eating wasting disease while cleansing it of too much lunar reflection.

A woman dreams of a small, bottomless lake of salt and there are warnings to stay out of the water. She falls in and the water is so thick that it doesn't feel liquid. A long piece of salt catches her right arm and begins to pull her under. With effort she disengages from it and manages to climb out by finding toeholds in crevices of solidified salt along the bank. Public, collective opinion warns against what it sees as a bottomless salt pit of depression. But she falls in, despite prudent opinion and her intention. When she is in this lake, it is so dense and coagulated that the water no longer flows. Stuck. (Salt causes matter to thicken, says one of our texts.) Here this thickening is like the process of identification: she has become immersed in the thickness of her suffering, which at the same time is the place of her becoming more cohesive, stable and solid. One piece of this generalized lake of salt, one crystallized moment of it—a remembrance, a guilt, a bitter point of pain—catches her arm of action and pulls her further inward and downward. Disengagement happens by effort, particularly by finding toeholds in already memorial, crystallized experience from which the moisture has dried out. She can actually make her way out by standing upon what she has already been through. She is afforded a way out of the bottomless lake by standing on a solid "bank," by "banking" on something solid that is there whenever the bottomless lake is there. The way out is at the edge, her marginalization. Like cures like: the disengagement from identification with salt takes place *not* through the efforts of the right arm which only drag her further under, but through small basic understandings that can be found in the little depressions and faults (crevices) of her solidified subjective experience.

The Fervor of Salt

Our account has attempted to bring home the experience of salt in alchemical psychology. We have come to see salt to be the ground of subjectivity. Salt fixates, corrects, crystallizes and purifies, all of which it can do to subjectivity itself. This purification of subjectivity shall more particularly occupy us in this final section where the connection more clearly emerges between salt and virginity.

We have already met its hard and square, densive-protective nature. For example: the egg analogy of Paracelsus, where salt was the shell; and in the writings of Joseph Duchesne (Quercetanus, c. 1544–1609), where salt appears in the hard matter of things, their roots, bark and bones, those parts that are clotted, cemented, coagulated or congealed.[28]

We may go so far as attributing to this substance that tendency in writings about salt to conclude with a clotted thought, a reduction to a basic idea. The multiple nature of salts, their multiple origins and effects, that the term refers to so many different qualities of experience and chemical materials (alums, alkalis, ashes, etc.)[29]–all tend to congeal into a single basic principle. For Jones this idea was "semen"; for Jung, it was "Eros." The stuff of which we write becomes the stuff with which we write and we are affected by the material we work with. As we would take in the reader, captivating and convincing, so does the material because it, too, is ensouled, captures our imagination: we lose mercurial volatility and sulfuric richness and become reduced ourselves to repetitions, moral constraints and fixities of expression as we attempt to go ever inward, accurately defining the pure roots and bones, crystallizing that experience called "*sal.*" The importance of salt as value (expressed

---

28 Debus, *The English Paracelsians,* 94 (citing Duchesne's *Le Grand miroir du monde* [Paris, 1595]).

29 For a treatise showing many salts and the different operation for each, see R. Steele, "Practical Chemistry in the Twelfth Century," *Isis* 12 (1929), 10–21. (Rasis's practices are reported in Bonus of Ferrara, *The New Pearl of Great Price: A Treatise Concerning the Treasure and Most Precious Stone of the Philosophers or the Method and Procedure of this Divine Art,* trans. A.E. Waite [London: Vincent Stuart, 1963], 366–71.)

above in terms of soldier's pay) instead becomes an overvaluation of either the place of this substance within the alchemical opus or of one's interpretation: an overvalued idea due to an overdose of salt.

This effect of salt proceeds from its own fervor, *a fervor of fixity* which can be distinguished from the fervor of sulfuric enthusiasm and its manic boil of action, as well as from the fervor of mercury and its effervescent volatility. Salt's fervor is rather holy, cleansing and bitter; immovably fixed; fanatic.

You will recall that Paracelsus (1:258) held that we eat salt to cherish our nature of salt and that we desire salt for its own sake. Salt desires itself. Its appetite works in us and through us for itself. It is fixed upon itself. Where sulfur and mercury are found in and by means of other events, salt is the experience of feeding on experience. By closing out the other principles, it can intensify its own interiority. A salt mine right there in whatever we call 'mine.' Thus *in extremis,* salt eats into its own nature, corrosive as lye in its own self-reflective purifications: recriminations, repentance, ashes, lustrations toward an ever-purer essence. Its suffering is self-caused. This is the salt that turns all reds to blue–blue in the senses of cold, puritan, celestial, exclusive, loyal, doleful, deadly (cyanide, cobalt, prussic).[30]

Here we may review those images of pure salt that we have already seen: of the virgin boy's urine, white crystal, final ash. Here, too, belong the images of the salt desert as if it were heaven: the Elysian fields become a Dead Sea, celestial, immaculate and barren, a crystalline ground of self-laceration, that sense of being grounded in long-suffering nobility, which negates even the *fiat mihi.* For nothing comes from the Great Salt Lake when one has oneself become purely salt, like Lot's wife. As salt fixates and purifies itself, suffering becomes fanaticism.

The intensity of this fanaticism appears in alchemical language both as ammonia, caustic soda, alkali, white lime, and as natron, the white salt of niter, which is a destructive, explosive powder. (Even table salt is delicately flammable, an unstable metal–sodium.)

Some alchemists recognized as salts whatever appeared in crystalline form. May we imagine that a salt crystallizes to bind its inherent fervor? These fanatical salts manifest themselves more in political and doctrinal

30 Cf. below, chap. 5, "Alchemical Blue and the *Unio Mentalis.*"

affairs, although similar attitudes appear as well in the concretistic *askesis* of paranoid schizophrenia. The very virtue of salt—its down-to-earth, concrete commonality—seems a virtue only in combination with other elements. Alone, salt fixates on itself, attempting to become the pure elixir which alchemy insists is always the result of many combinations.

The inherent capability of salt to crystallize its own essence is what I would call the inherent virginity of salt. By virginity here I mean the self-same, self-enclosed devotion to purity. I believe it is this aspect of salt that is alchemically associated with the cold, hard aspect of Luna, the queen as "bitch."[31] The Luna-sal connection is discussed at length by Jung, who considers salt another term for the moon, another manifestation of the more general principle of "the feminine."[32]

In ancient Rome, salt was indeed the province of the virginal feminine, the Vestals.[33] They prepared the sacrificial animals and sprinkled each with salt to make it holy. The Vestal (i.e., an initiated and ritualized) Virgin was the mistress of the salt; she understood how to handle it. Here is the virgin, not in the fervor of fanaticism, but the virgin as *mediatrix*; she knows the right dosage, a pinch, a touch, a grain, not a state. Jung quotes Picinellus: "Let the word be sprinkled with salt, not deluged with it."[34] The dosage of salt is an art: it must be taken *cum grano salis*, not corrosive, bitter irony and biting sarcasm or fixed immortal dogma, but the deft touch that brings out the flavor. Even the salt of wisdom (*sal sapientia*) and the salt of common sense become crystallized and destructive when taken alone, squarely, or imagined straight, for it is in the very nature of salt to literalize itself and conserve itself into a crystal body. Any insight or experience preserved as truth or faith becomes virginal: it closes into itself, becomes unyielding, dense and defended. Too much salt. We are each virginal when we are preserved from experience by preserved experience.

---

31 *CW*14:174ff. Robert Grinnell (*Alchemy in a Modern Woman* [Dallas: Spring Publications, 1973]), expands upon the "bitch" in depth.

32 *CW*14:234, 240, and 320–55.

33 S. Demetrakopoulos, "Hestia, Goddess of the Hearth," *Spring: An Annual of Archetypal Psychology and Jungian Thought* (1979), 65–68, with notes. Cf. for details of the preparation of the *mola*, G. Dumézil, *Archaic Roman Religion*, trans. P. Krapp, 2 vols. (Baltimore: The Johns Hopkins University Press, 1996),1:318.

34 *CW*14:326.

Hence the importance of the Vestal Virgins. Like cures like. Their conscious virginity enabled them to handle the purifying power of the salt. As initiates in the cult of salt, they must have understood the dangers of its "corruptive ferment."[35] Society is always in danger of the fervor of salt–puritanism, fanaticism, terrorism–and the preservation of Roman culture depended upon the Vestal Virgins.[36] This suggests that a psychological understanding of the power of salt and its dosage is necessary for the human body, the soul's body, and the body politic. Too little and principles go by the board; too much and a reign of terror ensues.

We can recognize when the principle of fixation has become a fixation of principle. Then salt is unable to be combusted and released by sulfur or is unable to be touched or stained by mercury: neither life nor insight possible, only dedication, fervid and pure. Alchemical psychology protects itself from salt by its composite thinking, in mixtures, a bit of this and a bit of that. Alchemical salt is always yielding its body to sulfur and mercury, to the love for it of spirit and soul, *fiat mihi*, let it be done to me, receptive to other powers, touching them and in touch with what it is not, the alien and unredeemed. For the function of salt is not its own conservation, but the preservation of whatever it touches. Images of the Virgin Mary, welcoming the alien, letting all things come to her and affording protection by giving her body to whatever their condition, by giving that touch which brings out their flavor and blesses their earth–this presents the soluble salt, Stella Maris. For as Arnold of Villanova said, "The salt that can be melted" is the desirable salt.[37] "Prepare this salt till it is rendered sweet."[38]

As a final example of the fervor of salt, or what the alchemist Khunrath[39] imagines as a hell fire in the midst of salt, perhaps a too-bright light in which purity burns with a consuming passion, we close with an "alchemical text" by D.H. Lawrence from his 1915 novel *The Rainbow*, the chapter called "First Love."[40]

---

35 Philalethes, "The Liquor Alkahest," 22.

36 Cf. Demetrakopoulos, "Hestia, Goddess of the Hearth," 68.

37 *CW* 14: 240.

38 *HM* 1: 177 ("The Glory of the World").

39 *CW* 14: 337; *HM* 1: 176–77.

40 D.H. Lawrence, *The Rainbow* (London: Penguin Books, 1995), chap. 11. Other passages exhibiting saline, lunar, metallic metaphors, and even a chemical view

The scene is set among haystacks under the moon, at a wedding feast. Images of fire and darkness pervade, and those familiar alchemical opposites appear when "red fire glinted on a white or silken skirt." The principal figure, Ursula, "wanted to let go."

> She wanted to reach and be amongst the flashing stars, she wanted to race with her feet and be beyond the confines of this earth. She was mad to be gone. It was as if a hound were straining on the leash, ready to hurl itself after a nameless quarry into the dark.

She invites Skrebensky to dance. "It was his will and her will ... locked in one motion, yet never fusing, never yielding one to the other."

> As the dance surged heavily on, Ursula was aware of some influence looking in upon her ... Some powerful, glowing sight was looking right into her ... She turned, and saw a great white moon ... And her breast opened to it ... She stood filled with the full moon, offering herself ... She wanted the moon to fill in to her, she wanted more, more communion with the moon, consummation.

Skrebensky takes her hand and wraps a big dark cloak around her, and they sit. She desires desperately to fling off her clothing and flee away to the moon, "the clean free moonlight." Skrebensky, too, takes on a metallic quality, "a dark, impure magnetism. He was the dross, people were the dross."

> Skrebensky, like a load-stone weighed on her ... He was inert, and he weighed on her ... Oh, for the coolness and entire liberty and brightness of the moon. Oh, for the cold liberty to be herself ... She felt like bright meta ...

And her hands clench "in the dewy brilliance of the moon, as if she were mad." Then a strange rage fills her and her hands feel like metal blades of destruction. "Let me alone," she said. She throws off his dark cloak and walks towards the moon "silver-white herself."

They begin again to dance, and a struggle starts between them. She feels "a fierce, white, cold passion in her heart." And though he presses his body on her, as if to make her feel inert along with him, there remains in her body a "cold, indomitable passion." "She was cold and

---

of human character in the relationship of Ursula and Skrebensky, appear in chap. 15, "The Bitterness of Ecstasy."

unmoved as a pillar of salt." To him she feels "cold and hard and compact of brilliance as the moon itself," and he wishes to set a bond around her and compel her to his will.

> They went towards...the great new stacks of corn...silver and present under the night-blue sky...the silvery-bluish air. All was intangible, a burning of cold, glimmering, whitish-steely fires. He was afraid of the great moon-conflagration of the corn-stacks...He knew he would die.

Ursula becomes aware of the power she holds: "A sudden lust seized her, to lay hold of him and tear him and make him into nothing." Her hands feel hard and strong as blades and her face gleams "bright and inspired." Skrebensky again draws her close to him.

> And timorously, his hands went over her, over the salt compact brilliance of her body...If he could but net her brilliant, cold, salt-burning body in the soft iron of his own hands...He strove...with all his energy to enclose her, to have her. And always she was burning and brilliant and hard as salt, and deadly.

He puts his mouth to her mouth, "though it was like putting his face into some awful death," and her kiss was "hard and fierce and burning corrosive as the moonlight..."

> Cold as the moon and burning as a fierce salt. Till gradually his soft iron yielded, yielded, and she was there fierce, corrosive, seething with his destruction, seething like some cruel, corrosive salt around the last substance of his being, destroying him, destroying him in the kiss. And her soul crystallized with triumph, and his soul was dissolved with agony and annihilation.

I have let D.H. Lawrence present the figures and scene of my conclusion for several reasons. First, to exhibit again the connection between psychology and literature, to suggest their interchangeability. Second, to bring witness to the ever-presence of alchemical imagination—in this case the *sol et luna* conjunction as sulfuric iron and salt. (I do not believe we can reduce these images and this rhetoric to the influence upon Lawrence of his father, a miner, or of the mining milieu of his native place.) Third, to show personalities as composed of and carried by imaginal substances—metallic seeds, chemicals, impersonal minerals, the hard and enduring natures of the gods working through our wills. And, fourth, to raise a veil and sound a warning concerning undifferentiated lunar consciousness.

As the twentieth century was setting, a full moon was rising. Much as solar enlightenment and its obsession with clarity, optics, measurement, royalty and categories of hierarchical order possessed the Western mind from the sixteenth century until the Romantic revolution, so moonbeams infiltrated into the late twentieth century: Right-sided brains and left-handed cults; herbals and vegetables, fragrant candles and healing rites; fears of seas rising and the aquifers going saline; wiccans, pop-visions of Our Lady, Artemis freedoms, Diana power, lesbian politics, the ordination of women priests; women governors, senators, generals, CEOs, history as "herstory"; marching mothers and the salt tears of grieving, the moon-balm of compassion to all creatures large and small. All the goddesses crowded within. "The Feminine" as a fervor of salt; new sanity and old lunacy indistinguishable in the moonlight.

Too close to the moon can be madness. "Love burns in changes of the moon." Says Robert Duncan, "She comes so near to earth/And makes men mad./O misery!" ("The Venice Poem"). We watch this moon too close to earth in Ursula, whose lunacy is a death-dealing fanaticism, bitter, assertive, caustic, sterile, corrosive salt. We witness Ursula's body turning to salt as she becomes infused with her subjectivity. Like Lot's wife, she is self-occupied. Because salt is the soul of the body, it can reach us through body-subjectivity. We become pure body-experience, and transmute the event of the other into a mere instrument of the experience. Thus the body turns to salt; it remains untouched, its virginity preserved even while it is being embraced because no conjunction is happening, only the intense experience of subjectivity.

There is a confusion here between the urge for purity and the desire for liberty. The Vestal Virgin submitted utterly; there was no possibility of imagining liberty together with purity. The result of this confusion is a fervid and lonely purism, a vestigial virgin without her ritual and isolated from her cult, burning with divine eros, yet seeking the white light for herself, her devotion to the moon poisoned by the salt of subjectivity. "People were the dross." Purism is the salt in the soul that allows no recovery; it is also the passion for revenge. "Carthage must be exterminated," said obsessed, fanatical Cato; its soil sown with salt. Purism as utter destruction.

Each planet, each worship, each archetypal perspective has its kind of terror. There is a terror in the moon, in the purity of a single-minded devotion that its salt can claim. The terror arises not simply from its so-called dark side, from Lamia and Hecate's bitch or Lilith, but from the moon's sway over the salt in the seas and our microcosmic flood. From the analysis in this chapter we may understand purism as the fixation of salt into a literalization of the preservative principle.

Owing to the inherent relation between Luna and Sal, purism is the main danger in any devotion to the moon. To invoke the moon is to invite the salt,[41] and unless we are trained in the nature and power of salt as were the alchemists and the Vestal Virgins, we become unwitting terrorists of the night, no matter how noble our dedication. Fanatical singleness frees one from the power of the other but at the expense of destroying the other's core existence. We may stand tall, but we stand alone, cold and barren as the moon.

Ursula had not been trained in alchemical psychology where we learn that the moon is not a stopping place. Both alchemy and astrology consider the moon a way station to the other planets,[42] just as the microcosmic moon, the human psyche, indicates various gods. The moon implies others; it is no sovereign solar king producing its all-important, self-sufficient light out of itself. It reflects light from beyond itself. For an alchemical psychology, devotion to the moon extends to what the moon reflects—a variety of other powers.

In everyday use salt is an emetic and a purgative. It can rid us of poisons. In the right dilution it is medicinal and hastens healing. Because it purifies, it was sprinkled on the sacred flour and sacrificial animals by the Roman vestals. That purity was apportioned precisely, ritually, uncontaminated by any other element. Especially, no water. The virgins were issued only the amount of water they would use each day and the water was held in an unsteady jar (the *futile*) so that none could be kept. Purity cannot allow dilution.

---

41 One name for salt was "common moon" (*HM* 1:177). The affinity of *sal* and *luna* was metallurgically witnessed in the process of gold-making: When salt is added to a gold/silver *compositum* and it is exposed to red-hot heat for a period, the salt "attacks" the silver, driving it into the walls of the crucible where it forms sliver chloride, letting the purified gold run free. This process compares with the "attack" of salt on leprotic lunar reflection, freeing the light of intelligence from hyper-subjectivity. (R.J. Forbes, *Metallurgy in Antiquity*, second edition [Leiden: Brill, 1971], 180.)

42 *CW* 14:217–18. "Luna represents the six planet... She is multi-natured."

We each need a Vestal Virgin to guide our hand in apportioning our fervid dedication and the grains of inherent bitterness which accompany dedication and give it its zest. The very same salt that is honest wisdom, sincere truth, common sense, ironic wit and subjective feeling is also salt the destroyer. Dosage[43] is the art of the salt; a touch of the virgin, not too much. This dosage only our individual taste and common sense can prescribe. Only our salt can taste its own requirements.

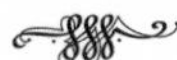

43 It was Paracelsus and his school (Debus, *The English Paracelsians*, 32–35) that "went to great pains to determine the correct dosage with their medicines." The concern with dosage derived most probably from the iatro-chemistry of mineral and metallic salts as specific medicines. If the Paracelsians taught the art of dosing salts, salt was the principle that taught the Paracelsians.

4

The Seduction of Black

The principal of the art is the raven.
–C.G. Jung

The Color of Non-Color

Black and White–these two non-colors to the Newtonian eye of science are, to the eye of culture, the first of all colors–the truly primary colors.

Two University of California ethnologists published a survey of the words for colors in some ninety-eight languages.[1] From this base, they made a wider, universal claim, reporting that all languages have terms for black and white, dark and light, obscure and bright. Furthermore, if a language has a third color term, it will be red; and if a fourth and fifth, yellow or green.

For us, their principal finding, and the one least contested by others, is the primacy of the black-white pair. All cultures, it seems, make this distinction, this fact suggesting the importance of the diurnal rhythm,[2] and, particularly for psychology, that contrast[3] is essential to consciousness.

---

1 B. Berlin and P. Kay, *Basic Color Terms: Their Universality and Evolution* (Berkeley: University of California Press, 1969). See below for a fuller presentation of the Berlin-Kay scale.

2 G. Durand, *Les Structures anthropologiques de l'imaginaire: Introduction à l'archétypologie générale* (Paris: Presses Universitaires de France, 1963).

3 Contrast favors an aesthetic mode of distinction, unlike the logical severity of opposition and contradiction, which are often insensitively applied to contrasting colors, as if black and white or green and red were warring opponents rather than radically differing co-relatives.

Among sub-Saharan African peoples, the three primary colors–black, white, and red (and I am translating more metaphorically concrete expressions into our abstract color terms)–form the very ruling principles of the cosmos. They are not merely color words, names of hues.

We find a similar idea in the three *gunas* in Indian cosmology: black *tamas,* red *rajas,* and white *sattva* enter into the composition of all things. The anthropologist Victor Turner states that these three colors "provide a primordial classification of reality."[4] They are "experiences common to all mankind," like archetypal "forces," "biologically, psychologically, and logically prior to social classifications, moieties, clans, sex totems, and all the rest." For culture, black and white, as well as red, precede and determine the way human life is lived.

Turner's claim separates the "culture" of color from the "science" of color. From the cultural viewpoint, colors are not secondary qualities, reducible to physical sensations in neurological systems in the subjective perceiver. On the one hand, colors have to do with light, reflection, optics, and nerves; on the other, they have something to do with the world itself. They are the world itself, and this world is not merely a colored world, as if by accidents of light and chemistry, or as if decorated by a painterly god. Colors present the world's phenomenal actuality the way the world shows itself, and, as operational agents in the world, colors are primary formative principles.

Even the rainbow derives its colors from the phenomenal world (rather than from the refraction of light) according to the mediaeval imagination: "From the heavens it derives the fiery color; from water, the purple; from air, the blue; and from the earth the grassy color."[5] Whether the earth takes its colors from an invisible, colorless light above or composes that light by means of its own elemental hues (green grass, blue water), the rainbow joins visible and invisible. The Torah says God set forth the rainbow as a visible sign that the cosmos is sustained by invisible principles. The rainbow also declares the double principle that the display of beauty goes hand in hand with discrimination, the spectrum of finely differentiated hues.

---

4 V. Turner, *The Forest of Symbols: Aspects of Ndembu Ritual* (Ithaca, N.Y.: Cornell University Press, 1967), 90.

5 C.B. Boyer, *The Rainbow: From Myth to Mathematics* (New York: Thomas Yoseloff, 1959), 85.

Only in a physically reduced worldview, a worldview reduced to and by physics, can black be called a non-color, an absence of color, a deprivation of light. This privative definition of black ignores the fact that black appears in broad daylight in naturally given pigments and in other phenomena from charcoal and obsidian to blackberries and animal eyes. Moreover, the negative and primitive definition of black promotes the moralization of the black-white pair. Black, then, is defined as *not* white and is deprived of all the virtues attributed to white. The contrast becomes opposition, even contradiction, as if day would be defined as non-night, and a blackberry be defined as a non-whiteberry.

The law of contradiction, when moralized, gives rise to our current Western mindset, beginning in the sixteenth and seventeenth centuries, the Age of Light, where God is joined with whiteness and purity, while black, with the *privatio boni*, becomes ever more strongly the color of evil. Northern European and American racism may have begun in the moralization of color terms. Long before any English-speaking adventurer touched the shores of West Africa, fifteenth-century meanings of "black" included: "deeply stained with dirt; soiled; foul; malignant, atrocious, horrible, wicked; disastrous, baneful, sinister..." When the first English-speaking sailors spied natives on West African shores, they called these people "black." That was the first generally descriptive term they used—not naked, not savage, not pagan—but black. Once named, these native peoples were cursed with all the meanings implied in that term. The English term "white" to characterize an ethnic group first occurs in 1604, after the perception of Africans as "black." The moralization and opposition between white and black continues to this day in general English language usage, as white equals good, and black equals bad, dirty, foul, sinister, and evil. "White" as a term for Christians had become firmly established by 1670 in the American lexicon.[6]

Disdain for black is not only contemporary, Western, and English. The color black in the Greek world, and in African languages also, carried meanings contrasting with white and red, and included not only the fertility of the earth and the mystery of the underworld, but also disease, suffering, labor, sorcery, and bad luck.

---

6 W.D. Jordan, *White Over Black: American Attitudes Toward the Negro, 1550–1812* (Chapel Hill: University of North Carolina Press, 1968), 94.

Black, however, is no more cursed than any other color. In fact, color terms bear extremely contrary meanings. Each is weighted down with a composite of opposites—yellow with sunshine and decay; green with hope and envy; blue with puritanism and prurience. The curse of black comes only when color terms are laid onto human beings, a curse of our Anglo-American culture that has burdened the majority culture by labeling it white, thereby loading it with the archetypal curse of white supremacy.

Could there be an archetypal aspect to darkness that might account for our disdain, as well as the fear, the physiological shudder, it can release? Does the human eye prefer light to darkness? Is the human being heliotropic, fundamentally adapted to light? Is visual perception its preferred sense, as we witness in the embryo where, from its earliest weeks, the rudimentary optical system begins to form before many others?

If the human animal has an innate predilection to light, then the exclusion of black as a color term substituting for "darkness" might find justification. The exclusion of darkness favors adaptation to the phenomenal world and optimal functioning within it by means of our primary organs of sense, the eyes. Then, we might conclude that the definition of black as a non-color belongs to the ocular identity of human consciousness. The eye becomes the *pars pro toto* for habitual human consciousness, and black threatens the very core of this identity. This threat, however, is precisely its virtue!

The Alchemical Nigredo

The cosmic significance of these three primary colors appears as well in early Western science, that is, in the tradition of alchemy. Of the three, black plays an especially important role as the base of the work and even enters into the formation of the word "alchemy." The root *khem* refers to Egypt as the black land, or land of black soil, and the art of alchemy was called a "black" art or science. The Western alchemical tradition traces its source to the *techne* of Egyptian embalming, dyeing of cloth, jewelry, and cosmetics.

The first four color terms—black, white, red, and yellow—are also the primary color terms embracing the entire alchemical *opus: nigredo, albedo, xanthosis* or *citrinitas,* and *iosis* or *rubedo.* These color terms describe:

(1) stages of the work; (2) conditions of the material worked on; and (3) states in the psyche of the artifex or worker-alchemist. Each color term combines three distinct categories which our modern consciousness keeps separate: the method of working, the stuff worked on, and the condition of the worker. For our epistemology, there is no inherent or necessary relation among method, problem, and subjectivity.

For example, for any alchemical substance to enter the *nigredo* phase and blacken, the operations must be dark and are called, in alchemical language, *mortificatio, putrefactio, calcinatio,* and *iteratio.* That is, the modus operandi is slow, repetitive, difficult, desiccating, severe, astringent, effortful, coagulating, and/or pulverizing. All the while, the worker enters a *nigredo* state: depressed, confused, constricted, anguished, and subject to pessimistic, even paranoid, thoughts of sickness, failure, and death.

The alchemical mode of science maintained the law of similitudes among all participants in any activity: the work, the way of working and the worker. All must conform; whereas in science the subjectivity of the experimenter may be radically separated from the experimental design and from the materials of the experiment.

Alchemical method, by contrast, treats each problem according both to its and the alchemist's nature. That is why no comprehensive system can be drawn from alchemical texts; why measurement plays an indifferent role; why the inventions of each alchemist are stridently opposed by other alchemists; and why even the materials worked on are so radically differentiated—so many kinds of salt, so many names for mercury, so many styles and shapes of instruments.

The radical idiosyncrasy of, and yet deep concordance among, method, problem, and subjectivity also account for why depth psychology finds alchemy so useful a background for the work in its laboratories: the consulting rooms where *nigredo* conditions are all too familiar.

We may read this conformity among worker, the worked on, and way of working, backwards; such a reading may offer psychological insights that cannot be gained from a Cartesian-Newtonian science that separates worker from the work. From alchemy, we learn that if you as a worker in any field on any project—from research to marriage, from business to painting—become exhausted, dried out, stuck, depressed, and confused, then you have indications of a *nigredo* phase, and the material you are encountering is itself dark and obstinate. This "depression" signifies neither a failure of your personality nor of your method. In fact, the very difficulties in your method and the darkness of your fantasies indicate that you are in the right place and doing the right thing just because of the darkness.

The optimistic and more Christianized readings of alchemical texts give the *nigredo* mainly an early place in the work, emphasizing progress away from it to better conditions, when blackness will be overcome and a new day of the *albedo* will resurrect from obfuscation and despair. Christianized readings seem unable to avoid salvationalism.[7]

This, however, is only one possible reading. The texts make very clear that the *nigredo* is not identical with the *materia prima,* a much larger basket of conditions. The *nigredo* is not the beginning, but an accomplished stage. Black is, in fact, an achievement! It is a condition of something having been worked upon, as charcoal is the result of fire acting on a naive and natural condition of wood, as black feces are the result of digested blood, as blackened fungus is the result of decay. Because depression, fixations, obsessions, and a general blackening of mood and vision may first bring a person to therapy, these conditions indicate that the soul is already engaged in its opus. The psychological initiation began before therapy's first hour. Jung says of the *nigredo:* "It is right that the magnum opus should begin at this point."[8]

Black Intentions

What does black intend to achieve? Why is it an accomplishment? Let me briefly list what blackening performs, without using the mystical language of John of the Cross, Simone Weil, and other proponents of religious darkness. First, as non-color, black extinguishes the perceptual colored world.

Second, the blackening negates the "light," whether that be the light of knowledge, the attachment to solar consciousness as far-seeing prediction, or the feeling that phenomena can be understood. Black dissolves meaning and the hope for meaning. We are thus benighted.[9]

---

7 E.F. Edinger, *Anatomy of the Psyche: Alchemical Symbolism in Psychotherapy* (Chicago and LaSalle, Ill.: Open Court, 1985).

8 *CW* 14:708.

9 See below on the *sol niger,* which radically shifts the meaning of "benightedness"

Third, the two processes most relevant for producing blackness—putrefaction and mortification—break down the inner cohesion of any fixed state. Putrefaction, by decomposition or falling apart; mortification, by grinding down, as seeds in a mortar are refined into ever thinner and smaller particles. Newton himself wrote: "[F]or the production of *black*, the Corpuscles must be less than any of those which exhibit Colours."[10] The thickness and solidity of the materials he worked with, Newton said, became more attenuated by fire and by putrefaction, "the more subtle dissolver." Black matter was the least formed and the most susceptible to dissolution—or in our language, chaos.

This "subtle dissolver," when mixed into other hues, brings about their darkening and deepening or, in alchemical psychology's language, their suffering. Black steers all varieties of brightness into the shade. Is corruption, then, black's intention?

An answer depends on what is meant by "shade." Surely, this intention is not merely the sullying of innocence, the staining of the only natural, that necessary preliminary to all alchemical thinking. Hence, we are not dealing merely with the corruption of natural innocence. The "shade" that black afflicts pertains to the deeper and invisible realm of shades, the Kingdom of Hades, which is the ultimate "subtle dissolver" of the luminous world.

We can begin to see—through a glass darkly—why the color black is condemned to be a "non-color." It carries the meanings of the random and the formless. Like a black hole, it sucks into it and makes vanish the fundamental security structures of Western consciousness. By absenting color, black prevents phenomena from presenting their virtues. Black's deconstruction of any positivity—experienced as doubt, negative thinking, suspicion, undoing, valuelessness—explains why the *nigredo* is necessary to every paradigm shift.

Black breaks the paradigm; it dissolves whatever we rely upon as real and dear. Its negative force deprives consciousness of its dependable and comforting notions of goodness. If knowledge be the good, then black confuses it with clouds of unknowing; if life be the good, then black stands for death; if moral virtues be the good, then black means

into a kind of illumination.

10 B.J.T. Dobbs, *The Foundation of Newton's Alchemy, or 'The Hunting of the Greene Lyon'* (Cambridge: Cambridge University Press, 1975), 224.

evil. If nature is conceived as a many-colored splendor, then black signifies the entire *opus contra naturam*, translating the great phenomenal world into the inked abstractions of letters, numbers, and lines, replacing the palpable and visual given with the data of marks and traces. By deconstructing presence into absence, the *nigredo* makes possible psychological change. The change derives from black's dissolving effect on all positivities. "Negation brings fluidity";[11] psychic energy or libido (whose root means downflowing, like liquid) moves from its coagulations, seeks new goals.

Therefore, each moment of blackening is a harbinger of alteration, of invisible discovery, and of dissolution of attachments to whatever has been taken as truth and reality, solid fact, or dogmatic virtue. It darkens and sophisticates the eye so that it can see through. Thus, black often becomes the color of dress[12] for the underworld, urban sophisticates, and the old who have seen a lot.

Because black breaks the comforting paradigms, it is the color preferred by the spiritually driven and politically pressuring reformers and "outsiders"—adolescents, rebels, pirates, ladies of the night, cultists, bikers, Satanists, puritans, anarchists, hitmen, priests—all the "non-conformists" who then become trapped by their own identification with black.

Though alchemical maxims say that the work must resemble a "raven's head" in its blackness and that this raven is "the principle of the art," these sayings identify the depth of black's radicality. They do not intend radical identity or identification with black. Black is itself not a paradigm, but a paradigm breaker. That is why it is placed as a phase within a process of colors, and why it appears again and again, in life and in work, in order to deconstruct (*solve et coagula*) what has become an identity. Those who wear the black shirt and the black robe, the black hood, and black undergarments as signs of radical identity become thereby neither anarchists, outsiders, nor reformers, but fundamentalists. Hence the rigid severity and monotheistic literalism of revolutionaries.

Alchemical psychology teaches us to read as accomplishments the fruitlessly bitter and dry periods, the melancholies that seem never to

11 T. Kawai, "The Function of Negation in Japanese Society, Art and Psychotherapy," privately circulated paper, with permission of the author.

12 J. Harvey, *Men in Black* (Chicago: University of Chicago Press, 1996).

end, the wounds that do not heal, the grinding sadistic mortifications of shame and the putrefactions of love and friendships. These are beginnings because they are endings, dissolutions, deconstructions. But they are not the beginning, as a one-time-only occurrence. Such would be a literal reading of the alchemical process, which is not a unidirectional model, progressing in time. It is an *iteratio*; black repeats in order for the deconstruction to continue, as shown, for instance, by Figure Nine of Jung's commentary on the alchemical *Rosarium*.[13] The soul returns, the King and Queen are joined—yet out of the ground emerge the dark birds. Are these birds "the seduction of black," drawing the psyche back to the protective comfort of all-too-familiar complaints, the nest of the *status quo ante*? "What you must be particularly careful about... is to prevent the young ones of the crow from going back to the nest when they have left it."[14] I want neither to condemn you to permanent blackness nor to relieve you from it by promising the return of the colored world, which alchemical psychology presents in gorgeous images. My aim has been neither.

Blacker Than Black

I am moved by another intention: to warn. And warning, too, belongs to the *nigredo*, for it speaks with the voice of the raven, foretelling dire happenings that may result from the seduction of black. Remember how nineteenth-century colonials feared going black; how Joseph Conrad perceived a madness and a horror in the heart of darkness; how the black plague, the black knight, the black shirt, and the black inquisitor haunt historical Europe; and how the scariest images of childhood, from chimney sweep, magician, black widow, the Rottweiler and the Doberman, to skeletons in the *danse macabre* and the Grim Reaper himself stalk the halls of fantasy—all in black. To socialize these fears into race relations does not get at the archetypal imagination of these fears.

Let us be clear: Negro is not *nigredo*, although a figure in a dream called "black," as any dream phenomenon so named, may usher in, and represent, the blackening. But especially in a racist society, we must keep very distinct the epithets that arbitrarily color human beings on the one

13 *CW* 16: 285.

14 E. Philalethes, "An Open Entrance," *HM* 2: 192.

hand, and, on the other, cosmic forces that shape the soul apart from human beings. What civilized society fears is black magic: the magical pull of black attraction, the soul's desire to descend into darkness, like Persephone unto Hades.[15] We fear what we most desire and desire what we most fear .

The essence of this fear lies in the black radix itself: that it is implacable, indelible, permanent, a crucial component of the *aqua permanens*—that sense of psychic reality underlining and underlying all other realities, like an awareness of death. Thus, the tragic paradox of black. It sticks like tar[16] to its own self-same negativity. As it curses other colors by darkening their brightness, it curses itself as well, by making itself "blacker than black," beyond the touch of Mercurius duplex.

In other words, the color required for change deprives itself of change, tending to become ever more literal, reductive, and severe. Of all alchemical colors, black is the most densely inflexible and, therefore, the most oppressive and dangerously literal state of soul. Hence clinicians fear that *nigredo* conditions of depression will lead to literal suicide, revenge to violence, and hatred to domestic cruelty. Hence, too, reductive moves and "shadow" work in therapy feel so concrete and confining.[17]

Of course, as painters know, there are many saturations of black. Part of the painter's opus is the differentiation of blacks: blacks that recede and absorb, those that dampen and soften, those that etch and sharpen, and others that shine almost with effulgence—a *sol niger.*[18] Nonetheless, the alchemical maxim "blacker than black" states an ultimate radicality

---

15 Cf. J. Hillman, *The Dream and the Underworld* (New York: HarperCollins, 1979), for a fuller psychological treatment of the Hades realm.

16 Philalethes, "An Open Entrance," 192: "The whole is dry as dust, with the exception of some pitch-like substance, which now and then bubbles up; all presents an image of eternal death. Nevertheless, it is a sight which gladdens the heart..."

17 Bachelard writes, "Any color meditated upon by a poet of substances finds black a substantial solidity, a substantial negation... Black feeds in the depth of all color; it is their intimate abode." G. Bachelard, *La Terre et les rêveries du repos* (Paris: Corti, 1948), 27 (my translation).

18 "There is a black which is old and a black which is fresh. Lustrous black and dull black, black in sunlight and black in shadow. For the old black one must use an admixture of blue, for the dull black an admixture of white, for lustrous black, gum must be added. Black as sunlight must have grey reflections." The Japanese artist Hokusai, as quoted by the American painter Ad Reinhardt. *The Pursuit of Comparative Aesthetics: An Interface Between East and West,* ed. M. Hussein, R. Wilkinson (London: Ashgate Publishing Limited, 2006), 239.

beyond all different shades and varieties. What is blacker than black is the archetypal essence of darkness[19] itself, at times named by alchemy as night, Satan, sin, raven, chaos, *tenebrositas*, black dog, and death...

Since Mercurius is hidden and the *albedo*, an unpredictable grace, what can "cure" the *nigredo*? What can release the soul from its somber identification? This is the question posed in every analysis, and posed during the *nigredo* moments of every life. The alchemist answer: decapitation. According to Jung, the black spirit is to be beheaded, an act that separates understanding from its identification with suffering. Because, "in the *nigredo* the brain turns black,"[20] decapitation "emancipates the *cogitatio*." Blackness remains, but the distinction between head and body creates a two, while suffering imprisons in singleness. The mind may begin to recognize what the body only senses. Decapitation allows the mind to be freer from the body's identity.

Of course, decapitation makes sense as an operation only as a treatment for the *nigredo*. It is, of course, contraindicated–even redundantly senseless–for those conditions of the soul where the head is barely attached and rarely recognizes anything the body feels. And, of course, the alchemical "body" refers not merely to the physical flesh and its symptoms, but to all imaginal perspectives that are trapped in habitual concretisms.

Decapitation is therefore a *separatio*–to use an alchemical term for the basic therapeutic move of making distinctions, or analyzing. Despite the fixity of *nigredo* moods and their repetitious thoughts, analysis separates the material–dreams, moods, projections, symptoms–from the mind's literal identification with this material. The dense and oppressive material becomes images that can be entertained by the mind. Mental images emancipate us from the slavery to the *nigredo*; though the material remains dark, decapitation allows the mind to cogitate the darkness.

Alchemy advises "beware of the physical in the material." It is not the "material" of suffering that poisons the work with despair, but the "physical," that is, the substantive naturalistic mind that prevents an imaginative appreciation of the material. Just this imaginative appreciation is what alchemical psychology offers. Patients, and any of us at many

---

19 S. Marlan, *The Black Sun: The Alchemy and Art of Darkness* (College Station: Texas A&M University Press, 2005).

20 *CW* 14:733.

times who are "unable to imagine" are often trapped in the *nigredo* by past traumata, and caught by the "physical in the material." These same patients, however, may be trapped as well in the nigredo of their therapists who have not been decapitated and whose cogitations have not been emancipated from reductive, naturalistic,[21] and historicist understanding of what's going on.

Literalism is surely the most obdurate of all our habitual concretisms. By this "literalism" I mean singleness of meaning, identification of any concrete embodiment with its "word," that identity between word and thing so that words become things. Decapitation also frees the word "black" from only *nigredo* meanings, therewith freeing phenomena (including persons) called "black" from the indelible fixities of *nigredo* projections.

Remember here that the "word" in our culture is inked in black, and this selection of color for ink may be more than merely convenient and efficient. The very blackness of the inked letter supports its indelible fixity and abets the cursing power of literalism.

Perhaps, then, the contemporary attempts at multiple meanings (poly-semy), of separating the signifier and the signified, of playing with the ambiguity of "trace," troping, displacing, and insisting upon difference and, as well, the absenting of all certitudes from positive propositions, these deconstructive moves may be French modes of decapitating the *cogito*—freeing the mind from the singleness that I condemn as literalism. The entire French effort may be alchemy-like attempts (the arcane obscurantism of deconstructive talk sounds indeed like the language of the alchemists) to invite Mercurius duplex back into the discourse from which French logical clarity had excused him.

Although I can grasp an alchemical intention in contemporary French thought, I do not profess its method: it stops short and remains an exercise of the *cogito*. The guillotine blade never quite cuts through. The brain remains blackened, and so the cogitations of its mind are read by critics as nihilism, Euro-pessimism, cynicism, negative theology, and the latest fashion in existential despair, and therefore deconstructionism becomes one more habitual concretism of Western thought.

---

21 On the "naturalistic fallacy," see J. Hillman, *Revisioning Psychology* (New York: Harper & Row, 1975), 84–86.

It stops short before the *nigredo* turns blue. After the black comes the blue–not cynical, but sad; not hard and smart, but slow. The blues bring the body back with a revisioned feeling, head and body rejoined. The alchemists spoke of this as the *unio mentalis,* which I elaborate in Chapter 5 below. Blue gives voice to the *nigredo,* and voice unites head and body. Darkness imagined as an invisible light, like a blue shadow behind and within all things.

The principal concretism against which this present chapter has been contending is the Newtonian convention, upheld by the dictionary,[22] that excludes black from the realm of color because it is not concretely visible in the spectrum. Perhaps, however, the fault is not Newton's at all but results from black's cursed literalism, its desire to be outside this world, in the underworld of invisibilities, or in the dark kingdom of death. Perhaps black cannot lift the curse from off its own head, so that it becomes our job, each of ours, to decapitate the *nigredo,* to emancipate our minds in a post-Newtonian manner.

Sol niger dispels the *nigredo* curse because it is "blacker than black." As Stanton Marlan shows,[23] we may be blackened and yet enlightened. *Sol niger*–one name for the ultimate aim of the whole alchemical endeavor–blackens with "unassimilable" darkness. It feels to be an "intolerable image."[24] Yet it is an image of *sol,* an illuminating sun that may darken all day-world positivism, but not all insight. As negation of negation, the black sun ontologically eradicates the primordial dread of non-being, that unfullfillable abyss–or, the abyss becomes the unbounded ground of possibility.

Negation conceived as theological evil, a stage in a dialectical process, or a Manichaean power gives a positive function to darkness, enhancing the seduction of black. We succumb to the reverse of solar optimism, and descend into a positivist negation revealed as "the horror, the horror," into pessimism, cynicism, despair, and suicide as a rationally valid answer to a *nigredo* view. But *sol niger* shines invisibly through every such negative coagulation. Darkness and translucence both, a true de-

22 *Oxford English Dictionary,* s.v. "black": "Opposite to white, colourless from the absence or complete absorption of light... no distinguishable colour."

23 S. Marlan, *The Black Sun,* chap. 4.

24 N. Micklem, "The Intolerable Image: The Mythic Background of Psychosis," *Spring: An Annual of Archetypal Psychology and Jungian Thought* (1979), 1–19.

capitation of the ordinary mind. Hence Philalethes can speak of "eternal death that gladdens the heart."

This emancipation of the mind means more than thinking dark thoughts with a blackened brain or suffering the body's obstinate depressions. It means the incorporation of invisibility within all perceptions, never losing the dark eye or ignoring the soul's desire for shades and sorrows. Hades never far from brother Zeus. To be benighted is only the beginning; to be black, to see black–that's how the *nigredo* inescapably affects us. But, to see by means of black, to see the habitual as mystery, the apparent as ambiguous, shifts the concretistic fixities into metaphorical images. This is the emancipation of the *nigredo* from literalism. Like cures like; we cure the *nigredo* by becoming, as the texts say, blacker than black–archetypally black, and thereby no longer colored by all-too-human prejudices of color.

Becoming blacker than black would also bear upon the chaos and tragedy of what are misnamed "race" relations and are more truly color relations because they are reflections in the human sphere of alchemical processes whose intentions only peripherally concern people. For the desire of alchemy was not merely toward the human soul; it sought the soul of the world. Alchemy is a cosmological work; to follow an alchemical psychology at once leads to working with the world. Alchemy would re-animate the dense and neglected, sometimes called "matter," and alchemy demands an ever-returning descent into that darkness, that invisibility sometimes called Hades.

By continuing to regard black as a non-color and segregating it from the bright beauty of the Newtonian prism, our faulty cosmology remains unable to find a place for the *nigredo,* except as "shadow" phenomena such as crime, cruelty, racism, imprisonment, toxicity, and the mental disorder of depression. Also, our science-infected psychology, by locating *nigredo* phenomena only in subjectivity as human moods and human failures, continues its delusional method that disconnects the work from the worker and from the ecological world worked on.

Worse is the danger that our Western epistemology loses its ability to correct its own bright blindnesses by making radical paradigm shifts. The conversion of black from non-color to color, from negative to negation of negation, is therefore not merely an issue of societal reform regarding the inclusion of darker peoples and darker shades of existence.

The inclusion of black among the colors becomes a way for Western consciousness to decapitate the naive fundamentalism of its hopefully-colored illusions.

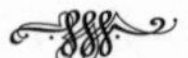

5

Alchemical Blue and the Unio Mentalis

the soul
vanishes
the soul. vanishes. into the shape of things
–Robert Kelly

I. THE BLUES

Transitions from black to white sometimes go through a series of other colors,[1] notably darker blues, the blues of bruises, sobriety, puritan self-examination; the blues of slow jazz. Silver's color was not only white but blue. We may consider blue a transitional color, either resulting from the suffering of silver (salt and vinegar) or resulting in silver.[2] Either way, blue has an affinity with both black and white,

---

1 Cf. Norton's *The Ordinal of Alchemy* (*HM* 2: 38–39): "Physicians have discovered nineteen colours intermediate between white and black in urine ... Magnesia [a term for white] throws out a mild, pure splendor in the subtle state of our Art; and here we behold all colours that ever were seen by the mortal eye–a hundred colours, and certainly a good many more than have been observed in urine; and in all those colours our Stone must be found in all its successive stages. In the ordering of your practical experiments, and in conceiving the different parts of the work in your own mind, you must have as many phases, or stages, as there are colours."

2 Ruland lists twenty-seven kinds of blue-colored silver. Norton writes (*HM* 2: 45): "Silver may easily be converted into the colour of the lazulite, because ... silver, produced by air, has a tendency to become assimilated to the colour of the sky." So strong is the association of blue with silver and whitening that even when modern chemistry disputes alchemical testimony (deriving a blue pigment from silver treated with salt, vinegar, etc.), it assumes the alchemists had some to-us-unknown physical justification for their claim. (Dorothy Wyckoff points out that silver "so treated would not give a blue pigment. Nevertheless, this recipe, with variations, is found in many old

both *nigredo* and *albedo*. Even more, however, blue is a condition of soul not in transition, not in movement, but all its own, multiple, complex, many-shaded.[3] Soul vanishes as a weighted, leaden substance, burdening my personal interior and appears as a shadowy resonance, an undertone, a further dimension in things as they are. Wallace Stevens says in his extraordinary poem on this theme, "The Man with the Blue Guitar": "Things as they are/Are changed upon the blue guitar."[4] "Soul" moves from noun to adjective and adverb, becoming the universal qualifier, less something here or there and more a mood or shade anywhere. The mind begins to become psychological, discovering soul as a second layer (if not the very first), which gives metaphorical depth and psychic value to things as they are.

Hence blue becomes necessary to our explorations of white, silver, and the *albedo*. To do them justice we must first have gained a blue eye.

The blue transit between black and white is like that sadness that emerges from despair as it proceeds towards reflection. Reflection here comes from or takes one into a blue distance, less a concentrated act that we do than something insinuating itself upon us as a quiet removal. This vertical withdrawal is also like an emptying out, the creation of a negative capability, a profound listening–already an intimation of silver.

These very experiences Goethe associates with blue:[5]

> [B]lue still brings a principle of darkness with it. (778)

---

collections, so it must have some value." Albertus Magnus, *Book of Minerals*, ed. D. Wyckof (Oxford: At the Clarendon Press, 1967), 192–93n. Is not the claim based rather on fantasy, a sophic silver of a whitened imagination that knows that blue belongs to silvering, and therefore sees it?

3 For the rich complexity of blue, see M. Pastoureau, *Blue: The History of a Color* (Princeton, N.J.: Princeton University Press, 2001); W. Gass, *On Being Blue: A Philosophical Inquiry* (Boston: David R. Godine, 1976); and A. Theroux, *The Primary Colors* (New York: Henry Holt, 1994). These authors do not draw upon alchemy.

4 W. Stevens, "The Man with the Blue Guitar," in *The Collected Poems of Wallace Stevens* (New York: Vintage Books, 1990), 165.

5 J.W. von Goethe, *Theory of Colours*, trans. C.L. Eastlake (Cambridge, Mass.: MIT Press, 1970). Also, W. Kandinsky, *Concerning the Spiritual in Art*, trans. M.T.H. Sadler (New York: Dover, 1977), 38: "Blue ... retreat[s] from the spectator ... turning in upon its own centre ... When it sinks almost to black, it echoes a grief that is hardly human."

> As a hue it is powerful, but it is on the negative side, and in its highest purity is, as it were, a stimulating negation. Its appearance, then, is a kind of contradiction between excitement and repose. (779)
>
> As the upper sky and distant mountains appear blue, so a blue surface seems to retire from us. (780)
>
> [I]t draws us after it. (781)
>
> Blue gives us an impression of cold, and thus, again, reminds us of shade. We have before spoken of its affinity with black. (782)
>
> Rooms which are hung with pure blue, appear in some degree larger, but at the same time empty and cold. (783)
>
> The appearance of objects seen through a blue glass is gloomy and melancholy. (784)

Sadness is not the whole of it. A turbulent dissolution of the *nigredo* can also show as blue language (cursing a blue streak), *l'amour bleu, la bleu* of absinthe and the "blue ruin" of gin, Bluebeard, blue murder, the black-and-blue contusions of Lynch's *Blue Velvet*, and the cyanotic bodies of Dietrich's *Blue Angel*, early Picasso, Schiele, and Van Gogh's hungry poor.[6] And—in blue movies, as pornography was once called.

Pornographic films are blue because they are saturated with depression and cynicism. Not merely the concrete graphics of an anatomy lesson, the Saturnian labored repetitions, the grindings, the grunts and the grunge, but also where they are watched: mongrel bars, truck-stop back rooms; the fixed stare in blue-smoky air.

This is the realm of the alchemical blue dog[7] (*kyanos*, blue; *kynos*, dog); blue takes on a dog-like quality: hang-dog and dirty dog, both. Why does depression seek porn? For arousal? For Eros and Priapos and Venus to come to life? Rather, I think, to maintain the depression, to re-direct the verticality of desire downward and backward (doggy fashion), clipping the wings of eros. Pornography—an *opus contra naturam*,

6 See Gass for the weird and sexual blues, especially. On the cyanotic aspects of blue, see Jung's remarks on Picasso's blue period (*CW* 15: 210), which Jung compares with a *Nekyia* to the realm of Hades: "We enter the underworld. The world of objects is death-struck, as the horrifying masterpiece of the syphilitic, tubercular, adolescent prostitute makes plain."

7 For a thorough examination of the erotic alchemical dog in a particular case, see R. Grinnell, *Alchemy in a Modern Woman* (Dallas: Spring Publications, 1989), 101ff.

a counter-instinct of the psyche, perverting the conventionally natural, enslaving, torturing; an erotics of despair.

Like the "black dog," as Winston Churchill named his desperate depressions, the blue dog, too, points its nose down, in touch with sadness and the bones buried in the underworld and its goddesses of decay and destruction with whom a dog often keeps company. Yet, the texts say that the dog is "of celestial hue," and the "ithyphallic old man" representing this dog is "winged" (*CW* 14: 177). The dog of blue may be material in its attachment, but not physical in its purpose. Its nose points beyond its fondness for filth, beyond to the lunar land where the fascinating power of images possesses the mind.

The mind engulfed in its obsession, shame and disgust, and faced with the impotence of its will to suppress the hounding fantasies, is forced to admit psychic reality—even though the admission comes through a back alley. Thus, the alchemical dog, as an instinctual energy of the blue phase, is called "the begetter," who brings a "divine logos" (*CW* 14: 176–77) or archetypal intelligence (like "The Hound of Heaven" in Francis Thompson's famous spiritual poem that doggedly pursues for a purpose), in this case hidden in the dirt.

According to Kalid (*CW* 14: 174), this dog "preserves bodies from burning and from the heat of the fire." The lower we go into the slow, blue, dank underworlds of eros, the less likely we are subject to the puer's erotic flame. Therefore, too, the dog is carrier of diseases (*CW* 14: n280). The pathologized mind is better able to withstand the lunar ablutions of the *albedo* that would wash away all stains. The dog is guardian and keeper of faith with the human condition, its base in a baseness which cannot be transcended.

When pornographic, perverse, ghastly or vicious fantasies start up, we can place them alchemically within the blue no-man's land between *nigredo* and *albedo*. We will look for bits of silver in the vice. A mirror of self-recognition is forming by means of horror and obscenity. The soul's *putrefactio* is generating a new anima consciousness, a new psychic grounding that must include underworld experiences of the anima itself: her deathly and perverse affinities expressed alchemically by the "moon bitch" (*CW* 14: 181), "rabid dog" (*CW* 14: 182)[8] and lunacy that comes

8 On lunar lunacy, see below, chap. 6; also J. Hillman, "You Dirty Dog," in *Animal Presences*, *UE* 9: 150–60.

with the moon goddess, Diana.[9] The dark blue of the Madonna's robe bears many shadows, and these give her depths of understanding, just as the mind made on the moon has lived with Lilith so that its thought can never be naive, never cease to strike deep toward shadows.[10] Blue protects white from innocence.

The vertical direction, as Jung reaffirms (*CW* 12: 320), is traditionally associated with blue.[11] Ancient Greek words for blue signified the sea.[12] In Tertullian and Isadore of Seville, blue referred to both the sea and the sky,[13] much as the Greek word (*bathun*) and the Latin (*altus*) connoted high and deep by one word. The vertical dimension as hierarchy continues in our speech as blue blood for nobility, blue ribbons, and the many mythological images of "blue gods": Kneph in Egypt and Odin's blue wrappings,[14] Jupiter and Juno,[15] Krishna and Vishnu, Christ in his earthly ministry like that blue Christ-man seen by Hildegard von Bingen.[16]

---

9 The blue dog offers another reading of the Diana/Actaeon tale. The dogged hunter, drawn by fantasies of the nude female body, is ravaged by the concretism of his desire rather than its obscure object–the lunar *albedo*. Concretism belongs with the dog who, it is jokingly said, has only three concerns: eating, defecating, and copulating, equivalent with Freud's oral, anal, and phallic phases of the libido. For rich discussions of the Actaeon tale, see T. Moore, "Artemis and the Puer," in *Puer Papers*, ed. J. Hillman (Dallas: Spring Publications, 1979), and W. Giegerich, *The Soul's Logical Life* (Frankfurt am Main: Peter Lang, 1998), chap. 6.

10 Cf. *CW* 12: 322: "And how can man reach fulfillment if the Queen does not intercede for his black soul? She understands the darknes..." This passage follows Jung's discussion of "blue."

11 Cf. J.E. Cirlot, *A Dictionary of Symbols* (London: Routledge, 1962), 52.

12 T. Thass-Thienemann, *The Interpretation of Language*, vol. 1 (New York: J. Aronson, 1973), 307; E. Irwin, *Color Terms in Greek Poetry* (Toronto: Hakkert, 1974), 79–110, "*Kyaneos*."

13 P. Dronke, "Tradition and Innovation in Medieval Western Color-Imagery," *Eranos Yearbook* 41 (1972), 67. On the (light) blue sky, see Gaston Bachelard's chapter on "The Blue Sky" in his *Air and Dreams: An Essay on the Imagination of Movement* (trans. E.R. Farrell and C.F. Farrell [Dallas: The Dallas Institute Publications, 2002]). The underworld as an airy place, and blue, appears in the Navaho cosmology. The next to the deepest (red) world is blue, inhabited by blue birds, see G.A. Reichard, *Navaho Religion: A Study of Symbolism*, 2 vols. (New York: Pantheon Books, 1950).

14 H. Bayley, *The Lost Language of Symbolism* (London: Williams & Norgate, 1912), 78–79. Bayley derives "blue" from words for "truth"–a curious example of archetypal fantasy displayed as etymology.

15 Cirlot, *A Dictionary of Symbols*, 51.

16 Dronke, "Tradition and Innovation," 98 (*Scivias*, II:2). A blue Christ is deviant

The transit from black to white via blue[17] implies that blue always brings black with it. (Among African peoples, for instance, black includes blue;[18] whereas in the Jewish-Christian tradition blue belongs rather with white).[19]

Blue bears traces of the *mortificatio* into the whitening. What before was the stickiness of the black, like pitch or tar, unable to be rid of, turns into the traditionally blue virtues of constancy and fidelity. Country-and-Westerns sing the blues of desertion and fidelity. "Gone and left me," "done me wrong," "but I can't help lovin'." I may be ruined and bruised, yet still my heart's still loyal. No way to put something behind me and get on. Blue remembers, and the black in it doesn't let things go. The tortured and symptomatic aspect of mortification—flaying oneself, pulverizing old structures, decapitation of the head-strong will, the rat and rot in one's personal cellar—give way to mourning.

---

if not heretical. The image does, however, add support for Howard Teich's argument that blue represents a lunar masculinity, neither solar red (male) nor lunar white (female) but a conjunction prior to the familiar red & white pairing. Teich contends that blue was repressed in Christian symbolism. It was not a canonical color as are violet, white, green, and black. Does blue carry an indelible etymological taint? *Kyanos* cognate with Skr. *cunya* "empty, vacant, vain," *cuna-m* "absence, want;" Latin, *cavus* "hollow." *Caerulus* (Lat. dark-blue sky) is cognate (via Skr. *Cyama*) with dark, vanish, leave, be left. *Livid* (Lat. blue) belongs to a group of words meaning slipping away, shrinking, vanishing, flowing. *Blue* (Germanic) itself belongs to "a large class of color names... meaning... marked, rubbed, smeared," stained and colored in the sense of "discolored." (F. A. Wood, *Color-Names and their Congeners* [Halle: Niemeyer, 1902], passim.) Compare to these etymologies of blue this digest of Goethe's evaluation: "[Blue] stands on the negative side or polarity of colors where deprivation, shadow, darkness, weakness, cold, distance, an attraction to and affinity with alkalis are to be found." (K. Badt, *The Art of Cézanne*, trans. S. A. Ogilvie [Berkeley: University of California Press, 1965], 59.)

17 The black-white mixture in blue appears in an old British expression, "blue skin": a "person begotten on a black woman by a white man." One of the "blue squadron" meant "a lick of the tar brush." (*Lexicon Balatronicum: Dictionary of Buckish Slang, University Wit, and Pickpocket Eloquence* (London: C. Chappel, 1811).

18 D. Zahan, "White, Red, and Black: Color Symbolism in Black Africa," in *Color Symbolism: The Eranos Lectures*, ed. K. Ottmann (Putnam, Conn.: Spring Publications, 2005), 217–18.

19 The blue/white association is not only in Marian symbolism, since blue plays an especially spiritual role in Jewish mystical and cult symbolism, cf. G. Scholem, "Colors and their Symbolism in Jewish Tradition and Mysticism," in *Color Symbolism*, 1–44.

As even the darkest blue is not black, so even the deepest despair is not the *mortificatio,* which means death of soul. The *mortificatio* is more driven, images locked compulsively in behavior, visibility zero, psyche trapped in the inertia and extension of matter. A *mortificatio* is a time of symptoms. These inexplicable, utterly materialized tortures of psyche in *physis* are relieved, according to the procession of colors, by a movement toward melancholy, which can commence as a mournful regret even over the lost symptom: "It was better when it hurt physically—now I only cry." Blue misery.

With the appearance of blue, self-reflective feeling becomes paramount and the paramount feeling is the mournful plaint. Rimbaud[20] equates blue with the vowel "O"; Kandinsky[21] with the sounds of the flute, cello, double bass, and organ. These laments hint of soul, of reflecting and distancing by imaginational expression. Here we can see more why archetypal psychology has stressed depression as the *via regia* in soul-making. The ascetic exercises that we call "symptoms" (and their "treatments"), the guilty despairs and remorse as the *nigredo* decays, reduce the old ego-personality, but this necessary reduction is only preparatory[22] to the sense of soul that appears first in the dark imagination of depression as it blues into melancholy.

Let us say, blue is produced by a collaboration between Saturn and Venus. According to Giacento Gimma,[23] an eighteenth-century gemmologist, blue represents Venus, while the goat, the Saturnian emblem of Capricorn, is blue's animal. The Zodiacal symbol of Capricorn

---

20 Rimbaud's sonnet "Voyelles" where blue equals O, Omega. "Vowels," in *Rimbaud Complete,* trans. Wyatt Mason (New York: Modern Library, 2002), 104.

21 W. Grohmann, *Wassily Kandinsky: Life and Work* (trans. Norbert Guterman (New York: Harry N. Abrams, 1958), 89.

22 "The blue-clothed" is a current Persian way of naming Sufis for which "various explanations have been given." H. Corbin, *The Man of Light in Iranian Sufism,* trans. N. Pearson (Boulder, Colo.: Shambhala Publications, 1978), 157n121. Supposedly, blue dress is "appropriate to those who are still in the first stages of the mystic life." Dark blue clothing is worn when "the lower psyche [*nigredo*] has been overcome, as though one were in mourning for it."

23 G.F. Kunz, *The Curious Lore of Precious Stones,* (Philadelphia and London: J.B. Lippincott Company, 1913), 31. A century before Gimma, Cesare Ripa lists in his painter's dictionary (*Iconologia*) these figures who should be robed in blue: Astrology, Goodness, Poetry, Steadfastness, and also Inconstancy. (Picasso's blue prostitute? Or at least the shadow side of the fidelity-truth-constancy construct.)

extends slowly from the depths to the heights; immense range and immense patience, devotion and obsession indistinguishable. Where blue brings to Venus a deeper melancholy, and to Saturn a magnanimity (another virtue of blue according to Gimma), it also slows the expansion of whiteness, for it is the color of repose (Kandinsky).

Thus blue is the retarding factor in the whitening. It is the thoughtful anxiety of depression that raises deep doubts and high principles, wanting to understand things fundamentally and get them right. This effect of blue on white can appear as feelings of service, labor, duty, and disciplined observance of the rules, civil conformities like the blue cross, blue collar, blue helmet, and blue uniforms, which personified figures of these feelings might carry in public. The effect can also appear in the blue moods of a guilty conscience. There is indeed a "moral aspect of the whitening"[24]—and I think this is precisely the effect of blue. The whitening implies neither a lessening of shadow nor awareness about it.

The alchemical *albedo* is hardly a shadowless innocence. Tho' the sigh of despair may turn to a sigh of relief, the blue stain remains. There is now more psychic space to carry the shadow's full, mysterious stature, a higher sky and deeper sea. The soul whitens as the shadow comes out of the repressed and is aired in life. One drop of bluing makes the laundry whiter. "Soul vanishes into the shape of things," because the soul's private interiority spreads out, tinging the world with serious weight, much as blues give shadow-depth and more palpable form in oil-painting. In fact as the world's blue shadows emerge, sadness is felt in the world itself, as if held together and wrapped round by sorrow.

If the alchemical white depends on blue, then that blue depends on black. The influential *Emerald Tablet* (in Latin ca. 1150 CE) states: "When the black exceeds the white by one degree, it exhibits a sky-blue color."[25] Evidently, the blue streaks and blue flames of celestial aspirations require a modicum of depression, a drop of putrefaction.

---

24 M.-L. von Franz, *Aurora Consurgens* (Princeton, N.J.: Princeton University Press, 1966), 243.

25 Dronke, "Tradition and Innovation," 76. Cf. this paradox from Wittgenstein: "In a picture in which a piece of white paper gets its lightness from the blue sky, the sky is lighter than the white paper. And yet in another sense blue is the darker and white the lighter colour." L. Wittgenstein, *Remarks on Color,* ed. G.E.M. Anscombe, trans. L.L. McAlister and M. Schättle (Berkeley and Los Angeles: University of California Press, 1978), 1:2.

A degree of darkness is the saving grace of inspiration. In fact, the saving grace of Mary's light blue may lie in an imperceptible black madonna cloaked within her robe.

II. ANIMUS AND ANIMA

I have understood the Jungian notion of blue as "the thinking function" to refer to blue's ancient association with the impersonal depths of sky and sea, the wisdom of Sophia, moral philosophy and truth. Images painted blue, says the Christian Neoplatonist Pseudo-Dionysius, show "the hiddenness" of their nature.[26] Blue is "darkness made visible."[27] This depth is a quality of mind, an invisible power that permeates all things, like air—and blue, said Alberti, in his great Renaissance work *On Painting,*[28] is the color of the element of air.

When the darker blues appear in analysis, I gird myself, expecting that we are now in for the highs and deeps of animus and anima, or what Jungians sometimes call "the animus of the anima." (Did you know that a "blue-stocking" meant a learned lady, that "blueism" meant "the possession or affectation of learning in a woman," and that just plain "blue" once meant "fond of literature"?)[29] These deep blues are inflations with the impersonal, the hidden. They do not feel high but come across rather as ponderous philosophical thought, judgments about right and wrong and the place of truth in analysis. What seems, and even is, so deep, however, is actually far off and away from matters at hand.

---

26 *Pseudo-Dionysius: The Complete Works,* trans. C. Luibheid (Mahwah, N.J.: Paulist Press, 1987), 189 (337*b*).

27 Cirlot, *A Dictionary of Symbols,* 51.

28 Leon Battista Alberti, *On Painting,* trans. J.R. Spencer (New Haven: Yale Univ. Press, 1966), 50. To an earlier mind, the "airiness" of blue could be physically demonstrated by the fact that blue paint is a most fugitive color, fading fast because it had no native pigment, only unwieldy crushed lapis lazuli brought from the Oxus region of Central Asia. On the history and technology of blue paint, see Badt, *The Art of Cézanne,* 62, 79.

29 These references can be found in T.L.O. Davies, *A Supplementary English Glossary* (London: George Bell & Sons, 1881), 68–69.

What we are talking about "seems to recede from us" and "draws us after it" (Goethe) in the seductive manner of the anima.[30]

Jung (*CW* 14: 223) describes this lunar state as a "bluish haze," "a deceptive shimmer... magically transforming little things into big things, high into low, ... into an unsuspected unity." The animus of the anima can fog analytical precision with hazy ideas and pseudo-wise, unifying generalities.

Howard Teich attributes to Jung himself a haze of imprecise generality regarding the place of blue in the alchemical work. Blue, says Teich, signifies a *male* lunar quality.[31] Jung's opposites are too formulaic (Luna = feminine = anima = white), leading Jung to miss a crucial phase: the union of sames within the "male" component–male solar with male lunar represented by blue. To bypass blue neglects the man in the moon or the moon in the male who brings sensitivity, receptivity and compassion to the hyperactive sulfur of the red King. The King must be complete, regally purpled with blue, before joining the Queen. Prior to the *opus maior* or grand conjunction, the male or animus must be tempered, learn the somber chords of a minor key.

The joining of likes precedes the union of opposites. According to Teich,[32] these likes are twins, and stand as one in the blue uniped (*CW* 14: 721f.) and as the blue brother in Navaho mythology. The joined twins share one soul and one spirit. They are imagined as complements (both together) rather than as opposites (either/or). They may be paired in the guises we find all through this chapter (depression and libido, celestial and underworld, passion and compassion, fantasy and reason, and especially as anima and animus or psyche and logos. Psychology itself depends on this complementarity, this *unio mentalis*, if it would do

---

30 For a full phenomenology of anima in Jung's writings, see J. Hillman, *Anima: An Anatomy of a Personified Notion* (Putnam, Conn.: Spring Publications, 2007).

31 H. Teich, "Commentary on Where Two Came to their Father," unpubl. ms., 10: "Although curiously absent in classic accounts of alchemy, the color blue does indeed appear... representing a critical stage of the transformation process that fails to receive much notice... the color blue signifies a union of solar and lunar aspects in the masculine psyche, prerequisite to the final "union of the opposites," masculine and feminine." Cf. Jung's answer to "Why is blue missing?" (*CW* 12: 320).

32 H. Teich, "Changing Man: Archetype of the Twin Heroes," *Proceedings of the 7th International Conference on the Study of Shamanism* (San Rafael, Cal., September 1990), 313–16; and further, under the same title, in *Chrysalis: Journal of the Swedenborg Foundation* 6 (1991), 157–64.

justice to the anima in the animus and the animus in the anima. Then soul nurtures an active intelligent spirit and spirit instigates a receptive understanding soul.

By remembering that "the animus of the anima" is a psychic spirit attempting to enlighten the soul by deepening or raising it into impersonal truths, I am better able to get through these thought-heavy analytical sessions. I realize, thanks to Goethe, that these deep blue conversations of "stimulating negation" (negative animus thoughts, negative anima judgments) have soul-searching intentions. A work of distancing and detaching (Goethe) is going on, an attempt at reflection that is still stained with the *nigredo* because it burrows too far, pushes too hard, neglecting the immediate surfaces from which silver catches its light.

Nonetheless, the "negatives" that so obsess reflection with dark intuitions and sterile ruminations are enlarging psychic space by emptying out the room (Goethe) of its former fixtures. As the soul tries to work its way out of darkness by means of philosophical effort, the whitening is taking place. The animus is in service of the anima. Even the negative mood and critique, and my own withdrawal that I feel during these exercises, belong also to this blue way toward whitening. The *nigredo* ends neither with a bang nor a whimper, but passes imperceptibly into breath-soul (anima) with a sigh. It helps to remember an image from Rabbi Shim'on ben Yoḥai told by Gershom Scholem.[33] The ascending flame is white, but right below as its very throne is a blue-black light whose nature is destructive. The blue-black flame draws stuff to it and consumes it as the whiteness flames steadily on. The destructive blue and the white belong in the same fire. As Scholem comments, by virtue of its very inhesion in the *nigredo*, the blue flame is able to consume the darkness it feeds upon.

The blue transition is delicate; things can go wrong. Both anima and animus (from Greek *anemos*, stream of air, wind) can blow us away.[34] When the element of air and the far imagination of blue conjoin, an archetypal possession can ensue.

---

33 Scholem, "Colors and their Symbolism in Jewish Tradition and Mysticism," 41–43.

34 R.B. Onians, *The Origins of European Thought: About the Body, the Mind, the Soul, the World, Time, and Fate* (Cambridge: Cambridge University Press, 1951), 168–73 on etymology and early usage of *anemos*; also J. Hillman, *Anima*, 91.

Texts caution about red coming too soon, the work turning black, about too high a heat, burning the flowers, and glassy vitrification. Many risks, many ruinous steps. What can go wrong with blue? Watch out for literalizing the image, or, as the alchemists say: "Beware of the physical in the material." Physical, of course, means also metaphysical—the literalization of airy ideas into dense and dogmatic truths. Any blue that becomes pure blue is not true blue.

The connotations that we have uncovered in this amplification indicate the importance of blue in the alchemical process. Were the white to come merely as a clearing off, something essential would be missed. Something must incorporate into the *albedo* a resonance of, a fidelity to, what has happened and transmit the suffering with another shading: not as grinding pain, decay, and the memory of depression, but as *value*. Value belongs to the phenomenology of silver (as discussed in Chapter 6). Recognition of the value of psychic realities is not born merely from relief of black distress. The blue qualifies the white with worth in the ways we have mentioned, and especially by its introduction of moral, intellectual and divine concerns. Thereby blue brings to the whitened mind a capacity for *evaluating* images, devotion to them, and a sense of their truth, rather than only reflection upon their play as fantasies. It is the blue which deepens the idea of reflection beyond the single notion of mirroring, to the further notions of pondering, considering, meditating. The mind conjoined with imagination is drawn away from itself. This inward distancing is upward and downward, both; darkened and enlightened, moral, immoral, and amoral.

III. IMAGINATION IS REALITY[35]

The colors that herald white are spoken of as Iris and the rainbow, as many flowers, and mainly as the brilliance of the peacock's tail with its multiple eyes.[36] According to Paracelsus,[37] the colors result from dryness acting on moisture. We naturally believe that moisture brings color as to bushes and fields after rain. But alchemical thinking does not follow the easy and usual; the alchemical process is an *opus contra naturam*. For Paracelsus, then, color enters more significantly when the profligate profusion of the mind dries up and the essentials of things can stand bare. Hence the importance of black as the suppression of color and the absence of light. The *nigredo* scorches and blights the simplistic fallacies of naturalism.

Drying releases the soul from personal subjectivism, and, as the moisture recedes, that vivacity once usurped by feeling can now pass over into imagination. Blue is singularly important here because it is the color of imagination *tout court*. I base this declaration not only on all we have been exploring: the blue mood which sponsors reverie, the blue sky which calls the mythic imagination to its farthest reaches, the blue of Mary who is the Western epitome of anima and her instigation of image-making, the blue rose of romance, a *pothos*[38] that pines for the impossible *contra naturam* (and *pothos*, the flower, was a blue larkspur or delphinium placed on graves); I call also on Wallace Stevens's blue and Cézanne's blue.

---

35 R. Avens, *Imagination Is Reality* (Dallas: Spring Publications, 1979).

36 "Then take silver, well purged from all metals... then seal up the oil of *Luna*... and set it in a *Balneo* to putrefy until it show all colors, and at last come to be crystalline white." ("The Bosom Book of Sir George Ripley" in *Collectanea Chemica* [London: Stuart & Watkins, 1963], 137.) *Paracelsus*, 1: 83: "When the regimen of the fire is moderated, the matter is by degrees moved to blackness. Afterwards, when the dryness begins to act upon the humidity, various flowers of different colors simultaneously rise in the glass, just as they appear in the tail of the peacock, and such as no one has ever seen before... Afterwards, those colors disappear, and the matter at length begins to grow white..." Cf. *CW* 14: 388, 391–92, and passim in *CW* 20: "peacock," *cauda pavonis*, etc.

37 Ibid.

38 See J. Hillman, "Pothos: The Nostalgia of the Puer Eternus," *Senex & Puer*, *UE* 3: 179–92.

Blue "represents in (Stevens's) work the imagination ... such as the romantic or the imaginative in contradistinction to the realistic."[39] And it was as well for Stevens the color of intellectual stability and "reason." "Both the intellect and imagination are blue,"[40] just as Stevens's poetry presents that combination of thought and image so successfully.[41] The appearance of blue in the coloration process indicates that span of the spectrum where thought and image begin to coalesce, images provide the medium for thoughts while reflections take an imaginative turn away from the dark and confined frustration of the *nigredo* and toward the wider horizon of mind. The blue instrument moves soul from sounding its small lament to the great breath of Kandinsky's organ, its largo, the spacious march of philosophizing that can incorporate the hurts of one's history into a tragic sense of life.

As with Stevens, so with Cézanne,[42] "When he was composing ... only a visionary's or a poet's imaginative conception ... could be of help to him. It was impossible for him to start out from an isolated real thing seen."[43] He based his painting on "shadow paths and contours"[44] out of which "real things" emerged as local high points. The imaginative conception, the visionary shadow, originates and supports the real thing seen in nature. "The deepest shadow color in Cézanne's paintings, the one which supports the composition and is most appropriate for shadows,

---

39 E. Kessler, *Images of Wallace Stevens* (New Brunswick, N.J.: Rutgers University Press, 1972), 198.

40 Ibid., 196: "'The Man with the Blue Guitar,' Stevens's most overt use of blue as symbol, is in the poet's own words a work of 'pure imagination.' The color is perhaps best characterized as a symbol for speculative thought, or simply for the mind."

41 "The poet, in order to fulfill himself, must accomplish a poetry that satisfies both the reason and the imagination." Wallace Stevens, *The Necessary Angel: Essays on Reality and the Imagination* (New York: Vintage Books, 1951), 42.

42 "Cézanne is mentioned far more frequently in the critical prose of Stevens than is any other modern painter." (James Baird, *The Dome and the Rock: Structure in the Poetry of Wallace Stevens* [Baltimore: The Johns Hopkins University Press, 1968], 84.) See 82–93 on their likeness; although Baird emphasizes their common concern with structure, I am stressing their common regard for blue and its implications for their imaginal view of their work.

43 Kurt Badt, *The Art of Cézanne*, 56.

44 Ibid., chap. on "Shadow-Paths and Contours." Cf. Keats's sonnet on blue, where he writes: "What strange powers/Hast thou, as a mere shadow!" *The Complete Poems of John Keats* (New York: Random House, 1994), 240.

is *blue*."[45] The blue "shadow" contrasts markedly with the Jungian notion of shadow blackened by repression, guilt, and moralism. "When [Cézanne] used blue in this way, he transcended any special connotation which had attached to its former uses. Blue was now recognized as belonging to a deeper level of existence. It expressed the essence of things and . . . placed them in a position of unattainable remoteness."[46] The blue shadow is the imaginal ground that allows the eye to see imaginatively, the event as image, creating at the same time a remoteness from real things (Cézanne) of the green world (Stevens), a remoteness felt in the nostalgia that blue brings.

This nostalgia, however, is neither sentimental nor wishful—not vapid blue, baby-boy blue, or lavender blue. For Stevens, the ultimate blue is utterly real, a burning blue, approximating gold, red and fire, an aurora, the dawning of things as vividly alive. "When the sky is so blue, things sing themselves,"[47] writes Stevens, and in a letter explains: ". . . the amorist Adjective means blue as a world metamorphised into blue as a reality."[48]

Blue thus brings a double nostalgia, both for what cannot ever be, the lost and gone, remoteness as removal of the soul from its home, and a nostalgia for the blue intensity, the azure vision, the *lapis lazuli* of the goddesses' hair and the moments when "things sing themselves," and the soul is finally at home.

Once the black turns blue, darkness can be penetrated (unlike the *nigredo* which absorbs all insights back into itself, compounding the darkness with literal, impenetrable introspections).[49] The shift to blue allows air so that the *nigredo* can meditate itself, imagine itself, recognize that this very shadow state expresses "the essence of things." Here is imaginal consciousness affirming its own ground, and able to

---

45 Ibid., 56. The blue of Cézanne drew particular comment from both Zola and Rilke—no mean imaginers themselves. Badt, *The Art of Cézanne*, 56–58.

46 Ibid., 82.

47 "Debris of Life and Mind," in *The Collected Poems of Wallace Stevens*, 338. This azure blue is amplified below, chap. 10.

48 *Letters of Wallace Stevens*, ed. Holly Stevens (Berkeley and Los Angeles: University of California Press, 1996), 783.

49 See below, chap. 10, for a detailed exposition of the difference between a *nigredo* and a blue reading of the symptom presented in the famous early psychoanalytic case of Anna O.

transform the ground of massive concretism, as in Monet's painting of Notre Dame Cathedral.

> One day Claude Monet wanted the cathedral to be a truly airy thing–airy in its substance, airy to the very core of its masonry. So the cathedral took from the blue-colored mist all the blue matter that the mist itself had taken from the sky. Monet's whole picture takes its life from this transference of blue, this alchemy of blue.[50]

Cézanne writes, "Blue gives other colors their vibration, so one must bring a certain amount of blue into a painting."[51] From his perspective, blue would be the crucial color in the palette of the peacock because it transforms the other colors into possibilities of imagination, into psychological events, that come to life because of blue. Jakob Böhme writes, "Imagination of the great Mystery, where a wondrous essential Life is born," results from the colors.[52] The full flowering of imagination shows itself as the qualitative spread colors so that imagining is a coloring process, and if not in literal colors, then as the qualitative differentiation of intensities and hues which is essential to the *unio mentalis*.

---

50 G. Bachelard, *The Right to Dream,* trans. J.A. Underwood (Dallas: Dallas Institute Publications, 1988), 26.

51 Ibid., 57. Compare Kessler's remark on Stevens's blue as "that human faculty which attempts to unify the disparate colors in external nature." The Blue Rider group in Germany is another instance of a union of thinking and imagination. "... blue was both Kandinsky's and Marc's favorite color." "We thought up the name (*Der Blaue Reiter*) while sitting at a cafe table ... Both of us were fond of blue things, Marc of blue horses, and I of blue riders." (Kandinsky's own account, 1930) in Grohmann, *Wassily Kandinsky,* 78. The mystical inwardness in the depiction of "nature,"' the dislike for "'green," and the metaphysical reflection they brought to imagining all accord with the "blue" tradition. Duke Ellington is reported to have "hated green." Kandinsky places green in the "Bourgoisie–self-satisfied, immovable, narrow ... In music, the absolute green is represented by the placid, middle notes of a violin." Kandinsky, *Concerning the Spiritual in Art*, 38–39. For a wholly different perspective, lifting green to high spiritual value, see H. Corbin, "The Green Light," in his *The Man of Light in Iranian Sufism,* trans. N. Pearson (Boulder, Colo.: Shambala, 1978).

52 In the same passage of Boehme (*Mysterium pansophicum,* quoted by Jung, *CW* 9.1: 580), we find that first there comes a "bright-blue," then various other color analogies to it and then "it is like blue in green, yet each still has its blueness, and shines." The blue/green tension (discussed below) is also noted by Boehme, who can see them as joined yet retaining their difference.

Jung's bias towards unity and synthesis shields him from an essential implication of this moment in the *opus* and the texts he is explaining. Jung writes (*CW* 14: 397): "The *cauda pavonis* announces the end of the work, just as Iris, its synonym, is the messenger of God. The exquisite display of colors in the peacock's fan heralds the imminent synthesis of all qualities and elements which are united in the "rotundity" of the philosopher's stone."

Rather than a messenger of God (a statement Jung takes unreflectingly from Khunrath (*CW* 14: 392), Iris is a messenger of many gods, and therefore indicates neither the integration of all the colors, as Jung writes, nor "the coming of God" (ibid.). In fact, the following paragraphs (*CW* 14: 395f.) refer to an author (Penotus) who "correlates the *coniugium* with the 'dii mortui' (dead gods), presumably because they need resurrecting." These passages also refer to the phases ruled by Mars and by Venus and to Juno whose bird is the peacock.

Rather than insistence upon unity and an amplification with Christian meanings of resurrection (*CW* 14: 397) the text implies resurrection of the dead gods buried in the culturally repressed and which appear in differentiated display of multiple colors in both rainbow and the peacock's many-eyed fan. Iris's message is simple: her vaporous substance proclaims it, a substance that is all and only appearance. Look with the eyes of the heart[53] at my shining body and you will see the gods in the power and beauty of color. Their infinity actualizes in the infinite variety of shades and hues that compose the world.

When the colors shine in the peacock's tail so, too, do the eyes whereby they can be seen. Imaginative vision precedes the whiteness itself, otherwise the white earth cannot be perceived as the transfiguration of nature by imagination. For this new perception, the perception of colors, too, goes through a transubstantiation into a mystical or painterly sense of them as substances. They are complexions on the faces of light, revealing the basic quality of nature: its endlessly subtle and multiple intensities. Colors shift from being phenomena of light to essential phenomena in themselves.[54] Light, as a generalized Newtonian

---

53 Cf. J. Hillman, *The Thought of the Heart and the Soul of the World* (Putnam, Conn.: Spring Publications, 2014).

54 Again, the motto of this book from Zosimos: "... upon this simple system of many colors is based the manifold and infinitely varied investigation of all things."

abstraction, shifts to being the presentation of color and secondary to it, so that the *terra alba* is not sheer white in the literal sense but a field of flowers (*multi flores*),[55] a peacock's tail, a coat of many colors.

The transubstantiation announced by the alchemical peacock reverses the history of philosophy. (The color optics of Newton and Locke, of Berkeley and Hume belong to the concentrated subjectivism of the *nigredo* with its neglect and negation of phenomenal nature.) Color now becomes a primary quality again, the thing itself as *phainoumenon* on display, the heart in the matter, prior to such abstractions as bulk, number, figure, and motion. Where color is, the world is as we see it–not merely green as naturalistic sense-perception believes, but green because of its blue shadows.[56] Even in the simplistics of the

---

55 The many flowers appear in Corbin's white earth. He speaks of this "sacred botany," which gives whitened consciousness a sensuous reality and particular content (rather than a mere snow field or white light). The flowers are an appearance in our Western context of the anima as Flora, the flowering of the imagination as rooted living forms. Corbin says, "The flowers play the part of the materia prima for alchemical meditation. This means mentally reconstituting Paradise, keeping company with heavenly beings." (Henry Corbin, *Spiritual Body and Celestial Earth: From Mazdean Iran to Shi'ite Iran,* trans. N. Pearson [Princeton, N.J.: Princeton University Press, 1977], 31–32.) Von Franz gives a variety of splendid passages on the many flowers (*Aurora Consurgens,* 391–95, referring to Jung), which she interprets as "components of our psychic totality, the self" and "indicate a blossoming of psychic relationship" as "human relationships" (395). The reduction of the flowers to the personalistic "our" passes by the very material she has assembled, where she states, "In Greek alchemy flowers and blossoms are an image for spirits or souls" (392). It is "the heavenly beings"–the imaginal figures–with whom the psychic relationship now occurs. We are witness to *their* blossoming and we are their gardeners.

56 The persistent opposition between green and blue, raised to a principle by the Blue Rider group of painters and overemphasized as an opposition between nature and imagination in Stevens (Kessler, *Images of Wallace Stevens,* 185–who counts 163 mentions of each of the two hues in Stevens's work), needs fresh reflection. Blue and Green were the names of rival factions in the Roman circus, and the rivalry of the colors continued for at least a thousand years in actual clashes between parties during the theological and political disputes in the Byzantine Empire (A. Cameron, *Circus Factions: Blues and Greens at Rome and Byzantium* [Oxford: Clarendon Press, 1976]). Scholars themselves are divided; some (e.g., Gregoire, Mango) attribute blue to upper classes who upheld more orthodox and imperial positions, and others (e.g., Villari) exactly the reverse. The difference of scholarly opinions confirms the factioning power of the colors under scrutiny. As well, another persisting fantasy attests to the problematics of blue and green. It is said that many earlier and "primitive" cultures and their language did not know blue as we do, could not even "see" blue as we do because of cultural evolution and the increasing importance of cortical

kindergarten color-wheel, green is secondary to blue, the primary. The natural world depends on the primacy of the imaginal, which affords deep, many-leveled implications to sensory data. Because of blue, the green world yields metaphors, analogies, intelligible instruction, providing reservoirs of beauty and insight. The world is as we see it in our dreams and poems, visions and paintings, a world that is truly a cosmos, cosmetically adorned, an aesthetic event for the senses because they have become instruments of imagining.

The *multi flores* and the myriad eyes in the peacock's tail suggest that the colored vision is multiple vision. One must be able to see polychromatically, polymorphously, polytemporally, polytheistically before the *terra alba* appears. The movement from a monocentric universe to a cosmos of complex perspectives begins with blue since it "gives the other colours," as Cézanne says, "their vibration." Then the alchemical colors vanish and are replaced by a brilliant white lustre. Here one might be so dazzled by the new brilliance of mind as to take white literally, as if white meant only and literally one thing–whiteness–thereby forgetting the multiplicity which made the whiteness possible.[57] The multiplicity must already have been built into the mind as the Cézanne vibrations, shadings and subtleties that are both there in things and

---

discrimination. An only green world, separated form blue, suggests an archetypal (Western?) fantasy of paradise and the happy savage. A cosmos without nostalgia, depression, or perversion, no luring withdrawal and mysterious remoteness, everything given, nothing implied. The linguistic confusion of green and blue states a fusion of nature and imagination, as in Japanese where the term *aoi* can mean both blue and green, and in another imagistic language, Irish, where *gorm* and *glas* could mean both blue and green (C. Tóibín, "Forward," in *In Lovely Blueness* [Dublin: The Chester Beatty Library, 2001]). Cf. further Theroux, *The Primary Colors*, 56–60.

57 Cf. *CW* 14: 388 for an example of forgetting the multiplicity. Jung writes: "The 'omnes colores' are frequently mentioned in the texts as indicating something like totality. They all unite in the *albedo*, which for many alchemists was the climax of the work. The first part was completed when the various components separated out from the *chaos* of the *massa confusa* were brought back again to unite in the *albedo* and 'all become one.' Morally this means that the original state of psychic disunity, the inner *chaos* of conflicting part-souls which Origen likens to herds of animals, becomes the *vir unus*, the unified man." This interpretation identifies totality with unity, whereas totality can also mean both each and every. Moreover, Jung's moral interpretation sees the many as "disunity," *chaos* and *confusa*, and places man above animal. Jung does give, however, other passages contrary to his own view, for instance, Khunrath (*CW* 14: 392): "At the hour of conjunction the blackness and the raven's head and *all the colors in the world* will appear…" (my emphasis).

there in the eyes of the mind by which things are seen as images. It is as if we enter the world without preconceptions, startled by the phenomena where everything is given and nothing taken for granted.

To experience in this manner is to recover innocence—hence the brilliant white luster. Ruskin called it "the innocence of the eye ... a sort of childish perception of these flat stains of color, merely as such, without consciousness of what they signify."[58] Attention shifts from the signification of perception to sense perception itself. We notice and are affected by sense qualities—What is there? In what way is it there? What is it doing there, and doing to me?—rather than: How did it get there? Why? What use is it?

We are arriving at the essence of the *unio mentalis*: the transformation of imagination, and a radical shift in the very idea of imagination. After the despair of blue and the desire of blue, the inventive virtuosity of this force has so saturated our hearts and sight with a heaven- or hell-sent sense of life, imagination having become so pervasive a power, it can no longer be confined to a mental function or conceived as one psychological capacity among others. In fact, imagination can no longer belong to human psychology, but must like grace be accorded archetypal attribution, something descended into our lives from an imaginal realm. The gift of imagination in any human person is first of all a gift from the blue yonder, where the colors themselves begin, much as the rainbow reaches down from an imagined somewhere, and where it touches the earth no fact can find.

Colors are a primary presentation of archetypal differentiation, each color a celebration of the sensuality of the cosmos, each shade and hue tincturing the psyche with a set of moods and attaching it to the world with particular affinities. These become our taste, our aversions and delights.

In recognition of the power of color, those dedicated to transcendence and favoring colorless abstractions, mathematical purity, a spiritual *via negativa* and a metaphysics of void, attack the colors as only appearances, only derivative of the effect of light on the optical system.

58 Quoted from E.H. Gombrich, *Art and Illusion* (Princeton, N.J.: Princeton University Press, 1961), 296.

They march to the mountain tops with eyes averted.[59] The spiritual path parts company with alchemy which indulges in the palpable, the oleagenous and the vivid. Alchemy plunges into the colored matters of this world; its devotees are disciples of color.

As an archetypal grace given with the cosmos, the colors donate their imaginative force to our creativity. How else account for the blue masterpieces in the arts? Gershwin, for instance, or Miles Davis? Is it merely a convention that names their music blue? Or does blue's archetypal power affirm its imaginal reality by means of these masterpieces? Blue made the music blue as it makes our souls sorrow. Blue's specific gift is to the mind so that its sight can be insight, its vision visionary, and metaphor its terra firma. Blue's appearance in the world brings a primordial shading to all existence, beginning the world anew from and for imagination, as at the very beginning of the world when the face of the deep creates the sky and seas in its image.

IV. *UNIO MENTALIS*

This inquiry, these images, and the figures whom we have summoned—Cézanne, Stevens, Monet, Kandinsky, Rimbaud, Kelly, Wakoski, Bachelard, Jung, Picasso, Marc—reveal something of the nature of the *unio mentalis*. Jung, expanding on Gerhard Dorn, considers the *unio mentalis* to be a union of reasoned judgment and aesthetic fantasy (*logos* and *psyche*) (*CW* 14: 755), freeing soul from body (*CW* 14: 739), prior to further union with body (physis, physics, world, *unus mundus*) (*CW* 14: 759f.). The *unio mentalis*—the first goal of the *opus*—as union of *logos* and *psyche* is nothing other than psychology itself, the psychology that has faith (*CW* 14: 756) in itself and indicates and activates the *albedo* following the blue. This psychology, which gives an "inner foundation" (*CW* 14: 758) and "inner certainty" (*CW* 14: 756), Jung elsewhere describes as *esse in anima* (*CW* 6: 77–78)—being in soul.

---

59 Cf. "Peaks and Vales," in *A Blue Fire: Selected Writings by James Hillman*, ed. T. Moore (New York: HarperCollins, 1989), 114–21.

Yes, blue can activate. Despite Goethe's reflective remoteness and cool distancing of blue, the *unio mentalis* is spirited, animated; animus in the anima. A wind blows through it. *An Open Entrance* (*HM* 2: 194) reports that as the material begins to swell up and blossom with many colors, the green of Venus becomes like a hyacinth, "i.e., blue" (*CW* 14: 393). This is a phase of Mars (*CW* 14, p. 289 n 22). A blue Mars? This paradoxical image suggests both a more thoughtful Mars and a martial quality to blue, a florid activity of the mind itself. For under the aegis of Mars the rainbow and the peacock's tail shine forth.

Dorn's statement, "the blue colour *after the yellow* [my italics]," would seem to reverse the standard progression of colors in which blue precedes yellow as yellow precedes red. The *unio mentalis*, however, must be reaffirmed prior to the reddening, else the passage to red could omit obscurity, mystery and the values that blue brought to the *albedo*. The yellow must be psychically contaminated by the blue which is hidden within it and which, as Dorn goes on to explain, "will lead to the complete blackness or putrefaction after a very long time" (*CW* 14: 723). In short, *simple progression through defined stages is not alchemical psychology*; a psychological mind has suffered the *unio mentalis* where black shadows hound every phase and every hue, mainly by means of blue.

A mind casually joined comes easily apart, so that putting the blues behind us as too nostalgic, too sad, too complicated and subtle lets the mind divide against itself. Without the blue bridge of metaphor we fall into black-and-white thinking: either/or, fact/fancy, good/bad... Crucified by opposites. Strung out by the logic of contradiction. Thus the *unio mentalis* is neither a progression from black to white nor a synthesis of black and white. Rather, it is a descent of the mind from that cross, an ever-present possibility of *poiesis* by a mind remaking itself out of whole blue cloth that underlies and can undermine oppositions.

The nature of the achieved *unio mentalis* can be garnered from the accounts of those we have summoned. They suggest that the *unio mentalis* is the interpenetration of idea and mood, of perceived world and imaginal world,[60] a state of mind no longer concerned with sharp distinctions

60 Perceived world and imaginal world appears together in the phenomenon of blue bird feathers. A vivid blue hue is not a pigment, not a dye, but a reflection of light that bounces off the thin opaque covering of the black physical feather. The blue we see is not materially there, purely a reflection, much as the blue of the sky.

between things and thought, time and timelessness, nostalgia and prophesy, appearance and reality, or between intellect that builds theory and soul that invents fantasy. We have colored this *unio mentalis* "blue" because the blue we have been encountering transfigures appearances into imaginal realities and imagines thought itself in a new way. Blue is preparatory to and incorporated in the white, indicating that the white becomes earth, that is, fixed and real. When the eye becomes blue, that is, able to see into thoughts and envision them as imaginative forms, then images become the ground of reality.

The effulgent blue "tincture" (witnessed severally below, in Chapter 10) does not altogether transcend the blue of mood and derangement because that azure occurrence is concocted, according to Dorn (*CW* 14: 703) from an underworld experience, also called "wine" (*CW* 14: 681–83).

Wine has a vernacular relationship with blue drunkenness, blue noses, and blue laws of prohibition, and at the other end of the spectrum wine is the carrier of divine drunkenness in the mystical states of Rumi and Kabīr. Here, we should immediately recall Heraclitus's saying that Dionysus and Hades are one, so that the *unio mentalis* brings obscurity (Hades) with it, deranges the usual mind and suggests a Dionysian mystery.

A blue lens may allow us to see into that most perplexing of the ancient cults and the Dionysian experience. Wine offers truth and theatricality, both regret and joy, or in dreadful diagnostic terms, both "depression and libido" which Stephen Diggs finds to be the secret of jazz, declaring Dionysus the god of "The Blues Revolution."[61]

While red and yellow feathers (and green feathers partly as well) derive their hues from pigmentation, a blue feather is a phenomenon of structure and light. See A. Portmann, "Das blaue Wunder," in *Aus meinem Tierbuch: Zoologische Skizzen* (Basel: F. Reinhardt, 1942), 102–10.

61 S. Diggs, "Alchemy of the Blues," in *Spring: A Journal of Archetype and Culture* 61 (1997), 40f. Two longer erotic poems are characterized by both depression and libido: "Blue Nude" by Robert Kelly (*Kill the Messenger* [Boston: David R. Godine, 1979], 181) and "Blue Monday" by Diane Wakoski (*Inside the Blood Factory* [New York: Doubleday, 1968], 9. "You paint my body blue," says Wakoski, "I cannot shake you out of the sheets." Loss, rejection, bruised soul—and desirous longing. Kelly finds a solution in the last line of his poem packed with sexual recollections by saying: "Deep inside the image there is time for everything." Imagination is able to contain both depression and libido by virtue of blue distancing.

Albert Murray explains: "The fundamental function of the blues musician (also known as the jazz musician)... is not only to drive the blues away... but also to evoke an ambiance of Dionysian revelry in the process."[62] The god in the disease cures the disease; like cures like; drive away the blues by means of the blues.

These authors keep Hades and the underworld in close and tight. Because the blues are based on the most dissonant of all intervals (the tritone), it was once known as the "Diabolus in musica" and for a time actually illegal. Moreover, "most idiosyncratic to the blues is flattening... failing to reach the pitch," "as if to say come back to earth."[63]

Of the consciousness brought by this mystery, as Dodds, Otto, and Kerényi have told us—nature comes alive. The god's presence permeates communal existence as a somber shadow that gives a joyous vibration to all things, or as Goethe described blue, "a kind of contradiction between excitement and repose."[64] The *unio mentalis* implies a divine drunkenness[65] including that which the normal *nigredo* mind considers pathological.

I cannot call Dionysus directly "blue" despite the fact that his hair and eyes, in the Homeric hymn to him, are *kyaneos*. He sees with the blue eye, and to see him our eye must be colored in the same way. I can, however, connect this Lord of souls and wine with Kessler's summary above of Cézanne's blue: that "depth of meaning," that "deeper level of existence" which both holds the world communally as "existing together" and yet "in a position of unattainable remoteness."

"Tibetans say that goddesses have lapus lazuli hair."[66] When myths say gods have blue hair or blue bodies, they have! The gods live in a blue place of metaphor, and they are described less with naturalistic language than with theatrical "distortion." "Divinity escorts us kindly,

---

62 A. Murray, *Stomping the Blues* (New York: Da Capo Press, 2000), 17.

63 Diggs, "Alchemy of the Blues," 36.

64 Compare the two contrasting characters of elemental Earth in Bachelard: energetic activity and repose (*Earth and Reveries of Will*, trans. K. Haltman [Dallas: The Dallas Institute Publications, 2002] and *Earth and Reveries of Repose* [Dallas: The Dallas Institute Publications, forthcoming]).

65 On divine drunkenness, see D.L. Miller, *Christs* (New York: The Seabury Press, 1981).

66 G. Snyder, "The Blue Sky," *No Nature: New and Selected Poems* (New York: Pantheon Books, 1992), 78.

at first with blue," writes Hölderlin.[67] Mythical talk must be full of hyperbole; the gods live in the highs and deeps. To depict them rightly we need the expressionist's palette, not the impressionist's. Precisely this shift into mythical perception occurs with the *unio mentalis*. We now "imagine" the nature of reality, and dark-blue becomes the right color to express Dionysus's hair, because it is the natural, reasonable hue for the hair of this god in this hymn, a most realistic depiction, a poetic truth (as Vico would claim).

One of these peculiar depictions that nourish the alchemical imagination is the uniped, explained by Jung (*CW* 14:720–25, with plates). This one-legged figure has a blue foot; in another depiction, blue undergarments; a third shows the blue foot tipped with black. This singular figure neatly shows the power of the freakish imagination to overcome the naturalistic fallacy of a two-footed pedestrian standpoint. As well, the uniped insists that its blue still retain it black stain.

That stain? A remnant of the *nigredo* of which Jung says in this context (*CW* 14:722), "psychic contents free themselves from their attachment to the body." Not from the body but from *attachment* to it; a freedom from the literalization of body, of bodily events as only body. Not bodilessness but a different sense of body as joined with the mind, as filled with mind (and mind with embodied thought). The single blue foot on which the body stands allows it to be flesh and mystery both.

This flesh clothed in blue returns us to the earlier theme of the blue dog. Long ago it was imagined by a heretical "Gnostic," Justinus, that the creator god was none other than Priapos,[68] an idea scathingly vilified by a Father of the early Church, Hippolytus of Rome, finding it against the Holy Writ, therefore heretical, therefore pagan.[69] But Scholem's discussion of the rainbow as Jahweh's sign of the covenant between heaven and earth says: "The Hebrew word for bow, *keshet*, denotes in Hebrew literature not only rainbow but, in the rabbinic literature,

---

67 "Die Gottheit freundlich geleitet / Uns erstlich mit Blau." "Der Spaziergang," in F. Hölderlin, *Sämtliche Werke, Briefe und Dokumente*, ed. D.E. Sattler, vol. 12 (Munich: Luchterhand Literaturverlag, 2004), 44.

68 R.M. Grant, *Gnosticism and Early Christianity* (New York: Harper and Row, 1966), 19.

69 Hippolytus, "Refutation of All Heresies," in *The Ante-Nicene Fathers*, vol. 5, ed. A. Roberts, J. Donaldson, and A. Cleveland Coxe (Buffalo, N.Y.: Christian Literature Publishing Co., 1886).

also penis."[70] Further, the term, *brith*, or covenant, that the rainbow signifies also applies to circumcision. The colors of the rainbow find their concentrated location in the *sefirah Yesod*, the mystical phallus, called the basis or foundation in those images of the human body representing the Kabbalah's cosmic tree that stretches from heaven down to earth. The genitals transmit the force of the above to the below, and this below—the last *sefirah, Shekhina*, the world soul—is pure blue.[71]

To translate these esoteric references into the blue dog's perverse obsessions we discover this: Invisible Hades appears in the world as Dionysus.[72] There is a divine (i.e., invisible, unfathomable) impulse that seeks to enter ordinary life. It wants to know the soul in the Biblical sense. Carnal knowledge, intimate knowledge, knowledge of intimates. (Hence the innumerable images of copulation throughout alchemy.) The soul longs for this copulation, and sings its longing in the blues, blueing its own flesh, drawing the divine down into the ordinary body. (Hence the blues' libidinous mood.)

That truck-stop backroom, the dense fascination[73] with flickering images is also a soul world, a receptacle of divine penetration. There are divine seeds in all things, bits and pieces of Dionysus's torn apart body vibrating through all creation.[74] So, of course, porn is tawdry, jazz low-down and dirty, earth-bound like a dog, no matter how high the bird flies on trumpet notes or coke. The blue-clothed flesh does not translate to mean wrapping impulses in protective puritan constrictions of single-willed self-control. More liberally, that uniped implies standing like an unwobbling pivot on the pediment of imaginal realism, an understanding given with the blue dog where fantasy is utterly concretistic and the mundane utterly fantastic. This, too, is a unio mentalis.

---

70 Scholem, "Colors and their Symbolism in Jewish Tradition and Mysticism," 37.

71 Ibid., 40.

72 On the Hades/Dionysus identity, see J. Hillman, *The Dream and the Underworld* (New York: Harper & Row, 1979), 44, 171, 177, and passim. The source is Heraclitus, D.15: "... Hades and Dionysus are the same, him for whom they rave and celebrate Lenaia."

73 P. G.W. Glare, *Oxfod Latin Dictionary* (Oxford: Clarendon Press, 1982): *fascinum*, the penis; *fascinosus*, lecherous; *fascinatio*, casting a spell, bewitching.

74 The mythological notion that the dismembered Dionysus as life-force is promiscuously present in all things is discussed in J. Hillman, "Dionysus in Jung's Writings," in *Mythic Figures, UE* 6: 15–30.

The alchemist works under a ruling maxim, "*solve et coagula*" (dissolve and coagulate). Blue literalizations must be dissolved lest the archetypal power coagulate into a monocular metaphysical vision.[75] Not the body and the rocks must become blue, but the mind. Unless the mind continues its laborious artful practice of *solve*–dissolving the literal into its fantasy–the mind can become possessed by a single feature of archetypal blue's imagination: e.g., Yves Klein's manifesto and demonstrative acts; William Gass's persistent tracking of blue's erotic language as if led by the blue dog; Howard Teich's narrow psychologizing of blue into a component of male personality.

Of all those who have allowed blue to inundate their work perhaps only Stevens and Cézanne maintained the complexity of the color. They continued to the end dissolving and coagulating and dissolving again blue's multiple shadings, never letting the *unio mentalis* fixate into a singleness of mind or mood.

A *unio mentalis* is a mind that can hold quietly all that blue evokes, realizing that the mind has moved into a poetic sensibility, dissolved its conceptual obsession into language. "In short, the color blue is in part a pure linguistic artifact."[76]

The beginnings of color terms for "blue" in Greek and Latin were likely "borrowed by prose from poetry,"[77] from oral recitation, from the throat's singing, as the blues today carry the poetic tradition and express the thought of the heart's imagination. If poetry is the source for the deepest blue, so we have had to go to figures like Stevens and Cézanne for more understanding of the soul's coloring process and the psychology of the *unio mentalis*. This turn to poet and painter tells us also who are the alchemists of the modern day.

The poets and painters, and the figures in us who are poets and painters, are those struggling with the continuing problem: the transubstantiation of the material perspective into soul through *ars*. Artifex now artisan.

---

75 The exasperating complexity of blue–that it recedes, depresses, and exalts–often forces on its devotees a monochromatic reduction that idealizes one specific component, most famously, the Blue Revolution of Yves Klein.

76 Theroux, *The Primary Colors*, 59.

77 C. Rowe, "Concepts of Colour and Colour Symbolism in the Ancient World," in *Color Symbolism: Six Excerpts from Eranos 41-1972* (Dallas: Spring Publications, 1977), 351.

The alchemical laboratory is in their work with words[78] and paints,[79] and psychology continues its tradition of learning from alchemy by learning from them. They tell us one further thing about the white earth: if the imaginal ground is first perceived by artistic method, then the very nature of this earth must be aesthetic–the way is the goal. We come to the white earth when our way of doing psychology is aesthetic. An aesthetic psychology, a psychology whose muse is anima, is already hesitantly moving, surely moving, in that white place.

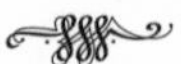

78 Cf. the essay revisioning Freud as alchemist by Randolph Severson," The Alchemy of Dreamwork," in *Dragonflies* 1, no. 2 (1979), 91–121; also P. Kugler, *The Alchemy of Discourse: An Archetypal Approach to Learning* (Diss., C.G. Jung Institute, Zurich, 1979), which concludes with the sentence: "Matter is transformed into imagination."

79 John Constable, the British landscapist, quoted this sentence as if his motto (or an alchemical motto): "The whole object and difficulty of the art (indeed of all the fine arts) is to *unite imagination with nature.*" Gombrich, *Art and Illusion*, 386.

6

Silver and the White Earth

Preface

Allow me to set forth as clearly and rationally as I can what I shall be about in this strange chapter. It starts from two large ideas. The first comes from Hegel who said that in insanity the soul strives to restore itself to perfect inner harmony. For Hegel, insanity is an essential stage in the development of the soul, and a stage upon which the soul purposefully performs.[1] Insanity belongs to soul-making.

The second large idea comes from alchemy. In alchemical soul-making, gold is necessarily preceded by silver. This means that gold comes out of silver, red comes from white, sun from moon, brighter awareness from lunacy. Alchemical soul-making proposes that the final idea of sun conjuncted with moon means nothing less and no other than a condition of being in which solar brilliance and awakeness and moon-madness are marvelously conjoined. The *mysterium conjunctionis* is illumined lunacy.

Let us proceed now to put the Hegelian and the alchemical propositions together—but not too quickly, especially not before we have examined some of what is implied by these alchemical words: silver, Luna, whitening. This, the *albedo* aspect of alchemy, has been remarkably neglected in our solar fever and gold rush. Any usual description of alchemy will tell you that it is an art of gold-making (whether physical or "sophic"), and that the alchemists aimed, by means of devotion, wizardry, and technics, to transpose base metals into noble gold. And though these same accounts all agree that silver is the penultimate major phase and gold's very partner, there is extraordinarily little written about

1 *Hegel's Philosophy of Mind: Part Three of The Encyclopaedia of the Philosophical Sciences*, trans. W. Wallace (Oxford: Oxford University Press, 1971), 125ff.

silver. (The terms "silver," *albedo,* "whiteness," and "Luna" (moon) tend to signify each other.)

This lacuna may be attributed to a masculine bias throughout alchemy and the repression of what is so neatly and undifferentiatedly (hence monotheistically) called "the feminine," since silver in general symbolism carries a female sign (though not always).[2] I do not accept this feminist explanation for the lacuna regarding silver; I think it has more to do with the archetypal nature of silver, Luna, and whiteness. I further believe that our investigation will tell not only more about the general neglect of silver, but also something more fundamental about the neglect of "the feminine" derived therefrom.

Certainly I need make no disclaimers concerning the value of alchemy for psychology, the case having been so well accomplished by Jung earlier in this century, and by Jung[3] and then by von Franz and Edinger. But perhaps I do need to emphasize the particular relevance of alchemy for psychopathology.[4] After all, is alchemy not a prolonged witness to mad men at work upon themselves?

Alchemical Silver: Its Nature and Psychological Properties

Silver is the metal of the moon, the seed of the moon in the earth.[5] Others are copper as seed of Venus and lead as seed of Saturn. The

---

2 *Figulus,* 285: "Silver is masculine."

3 Jung considered alchemy the fundamental paradigm and background for his psychology (cf. *MDR,* 205 and 221). A good third of Jung's writing is directly or tangentially concerned with alchemy, proportionally far more than he wrote about typology, psychiatry, association experiments, eastern wisdom, or parapsychology.

4 Cf. R. Grinnell, *Alchemy in Modern Woman* (Dallas: Spring Publications, 1973).

5 On "how the metals are produced in the Bowels of the Earth," see Sendivogius, "The New Chemical Light," *HM* 2: 90f. Also: Albertus Magnus's *Book of Minerals,* especially Book Three, "Metals in General"; B. Dibner, *Agricola on Metals* (Norwalk, Conn.: Burndy Library, 1958). Agricola's *De re metallica* was translated into English in 1912 by a mining engineer (together with his wife), Herbert Hoover, born the son of a village blacksmith and later President of the United States. An alchemist in the White House! On the relation of planetary gods with metals (going back to Babylonian and perhaps Sumerian times), see J. R. Partington, "The Origins of the Planetary Symbols of the metals," *Ambix* 1 (1937), 61–64. On the history of metals in general, see L. Aitchison, *A History of Metals,* 2 vols. (New York: Interscience, 1960); on silver, R.J. Forbes, *Metallurgy in Antiquity: A Notebook for Archaeologists and Technologists* (Leiden: Brill, 1950).

metals were imagined to be made of coagulated moist vapors, like a condensed gas whose spirit could be released by the proper operations. Because the metals were inherently moist, that is, embodying phlegm, they had a phlegmatic tendency to be passive or inert, requiring fire. Resistance to change is given with the seeds of our nature and only intense heat can move human nature from its innate inertia.

By considering metals as seeds, alchemy kept less to the distinctions between vegetable and mineral (organic and inorganic) kingdoms. Seeds are living forces; a metal such as silver is a *vis naturalis* with encoded intentionality, a capacity to move, form bodies, enter into combinations, take on a history, branch into ramifications; but through all such activities and transmutations it remains true to its own "blood." These ore-bodies were not dead matter to be pushed around but vital seeds, embodiments of soul; not objective facts but subjective factors. The alchemical view incorporated into its theoretical premises what modern natural science is now stating as new: the observer and observed are not independent of each other.

That the planetary spirits are in the earth as metals reminds us that the gods are within the world, buried in the depths of earthly affairs, under our feet as we walk. We walk on their heads and shoulders, they hold us up, though we may suppose them placed into heavenly orbit by our human fantasies. Though they are right there in our ground, they only become manifest when we search them out.

Precisely this is what the word "metal" means: "search." Homer uses the verb *metallao*, translated as "to search." *Metalleia* means search for metals, while *metallon* as a mine or quarry means a place for careful inquiry, scrutiny, researching.[6] The idea of a planet as a metal—and not only a heavenly body or a personified god—induces the activity of searching deeply into nature for the *deus absconditus*. Metallurgy stands not only at the beginning of empirical physical science, it is also the beginning of theoretical research. Metals act as seeds forcing the mind to bestir itself with inquiry. As Pliny the Elder (*Naturalis Historia*, 33:96) says: "Wherever one vein is found, another is not far to seek." And it is the prospector who embodies the prospective view of psychological quarrying: looking ahead, going on further, searching out further veins.

6 H.G. Liddell and R. Scott, *Greek-English Dictionary* (Oxford: Clarendon Press, 1996), s.v. *μεταλλάω, μεταλλεία, μέταλλον.*

The words for silver in several quite differing languages converge upon an idea of whiteness: Egyptian *hd* means white; Hebrew *keseph* means shining white metal; the root *radj* of both Greek *argyros* and Latin *argentum* means white, bright, shining, gleaming. The Greek *argos*, besides bearing the root meanings of white and glistening, also denotes swift, as hunting dogs. In the very word for silver are the hounds of Artemis/Diana, Goddess of the Moon, her elusiveness and danger, and it is an alchemical convention to interchange white, silver, and moon—and Diana too. The flash, gleam, and swiftness of silver appear in the Argo, the ship of Jason's argonauts, that vessel necessary for journeying to the Golden Fleece in the realm of the Sun. Here, too, an alchemical conjunction presented as mythic configuration, confirming our thesis: the way to the gold is via the silver.

Silvering, in short, is whitening, the *albedo* stage of the work, and the lunification of the material refers to any process—lustration, calcination, coagulation—that can bring forth a white and gleaming condition of the soul in the material. Transmutation to silver means cleansing and purifying which at the same time means becoming more essential and durable. These qualitative changes refer especially to the shining forth, or bringing to light, the moon character of the soul, including even its "blues."

Silver's color was not only white, but blue. Ruland lists twenty-seven kinds of blue-colored silver. Norton writes: "Silver may easily be converted into the color of the lazulite because ... silver produced by air has a tendency to become assimilated to the color of the sky."[7]

---

7 *The Ordinal of Alchemy* (*HM* 2: 45). The assimilation of silver (white) to the color of the sky compares with this paradox from Wittgenstein: "In a picture in which a piece of white paper gets its lightness from the blue sky, the sky is lighter than the white paper. And yet in another sense blue is the darker and white the lighter colour," *Remarks on Colour*, trans. L. L. McAlister and M. Schättle (Berkeley: University of California Press, 1978), I.2. So strong is the association of blue with silver and whitening that even when modern chemistry disputes alchemical testimony (deriving a blue pigment from silver treated with salt, vinegar, etc.), the modern mind assumes that the alchemists had some, to-us-unknown, physical justification for their claim. Is not the claim based rather on fantasy—a sophic silver of whitened imagination that *knows* that blue belongs to silvering, and therefore *sees* it? Cf. Dorothy Wyckoff's note to her translation of Albertus Magnus's *De mineralibus* (*Minerals*, 192–93).

Here we need to distinguish briefly between white as a name for the *materia prima* (*ethesia alba*, *magnesia alba*, virgin's milk, etc.), when white refers to unworked innocence, an Endymion sleep[8] of marshmallow dreamings, sweet, shy virginity, and the like, on the one hand and on the other, that white of the *albedo*, a cooling that results from violent tortures, long-suffering patience, and intense heat. All whites are not the same white,[9] and only the *albedo* white refers to alchemical silver as a state of consciousness that proceeds not from the soul as simply given but from the work done upon it.

The moon's body consists of air. Its earth is not our earth, for "it hath been permeated through and through by ether," says Plutarch.[10] To bring the metal of the moon within our mental grasp means to be able to catch and hold onto the subtle invisibilities of air. "Minerals have their roots in the air..."[11] Whereas contemporary psychology imagines the fertile element to be earth, alchemical psychology considers air the nourishing principle. When fire is the secret of the art and sacred principle of the work, then air is the nourisher and earth the smotherer. For Paracelsus, "by the air alone are all things nourished" and earth "supplies a terminus for the element of fire (growth)."[12] Earth limits, fixes, and stops. But modern materialism has elevated earth and emptied the air to insubstantiality.[13] Contemporary earthbound psychology warns of the dangers of air: inflation, puer, airy-fairy; never does it notice the clods of its own standpoint or the dry dust settling on its pages.

---

8 Cf. R. López-Pedraza, "Moon Madness–Titanic Love: A Meeting of Pathology and Poetry," in *Images of the Untouched*, ed. J. Stroud and G. Thomas (Dallas: Spring Publications, 1982).

9 This crucial distinction between naive and sophisticated white is further elaborated below. Muḥammad Ibn Umail gives a varety of names for the "intense whiteness," which is called "The second whiteness" (*Book of the Explanations of the Symbols [Kitāb Ḥall ar-Rumūz]*, Corpus Alchemicum Arabicum, vol. 1, ed. T. Abt, W. Madelung, T. Hofmeier, trans. S. Fuad [Zurich: Living Human Heritage Publications, 2003], 9).

10 "Concerning the Face Which Appears in the Orb of the Moon," in *Moralia* XII, Loeb Classical Library (Cambridge, Mass.: Harvard University Press, 1951).

11 Quoted by E.A. Hitchcock from an unspecified tract in his *Remarks upon Alchemy and Alchemists* (Los Angeles: Philosophical Research Society, 1976), 41.

12 *Paracelsus*, 2:266.

13 On the importance of air for psychotherapeutic work with anima (soul), see J. Hillman, *Anima: Anatomy of a Personified Notion* (Putnam, Conn.: Spring Publications, 2007), 143–45, and below, chap. 9, "The Imagination of Air and the Collapse of Alchemy."

If the moon's earth is ethereal, we must imagine the metal of the moon as a subtle air body that nourishes the fires of the spirit and the passions of the soul by the continual generation of images, of fantasies. Imagine this metal then as a nontangible whitened air, a silvering white body, ethereal like the orb of the full moon floating, suspended in dark azure receptivity, a hard, cool and bright mind at its full, whose effects are both nourishing as well as desiccating and astringent.[14] For this coolness and dryness is precisely what the fire rejoices in and is fed by.

By contrasting silver with its companion metals we can better discern its native properties. Like copper, silver is conductive, yet it is *not red*. Like gold, it is weighty, noble, precious and beautiful, but *harder* and less malleable. Like tin and lead, it is grayish or white and can be made useful, but unlike them it has *luster*, takes a high polish, and reflects. And, like mercury in its first appearance, silver is coagulated into a more *steady state*, not dispersible, fragmentary, and free-running. These comparisons indicate that silver is a cool white conductor, not a red hot one because it has a "frigid and humid body";[15] that it has a certain innate stiffness; that it ennobles the useful by taking on polish by means of which polish it reflects; that it does not easily flow, but tends toward the steadiness and stateliness of self-consistency.

The equation used so frequently in alchemy, Luna = silver,[16] is not a true identity. Silver corresponds with Luna only in certain respects. It is less the moon of Lilith, of the night and the dead, and certainly less the little crescent, the tiny virgin girl at the beginning. Nor is silver the fluctuating moon of the tides, the blood and vegetation, going through phases, turning with time; nor the moon's salty bitterness and its commonality. In short, silver presents the moon's full brightness, its completion or elevation. It is the metal of a Great Light, to use the traditional way of speaking, an archetypal principle of immense potency equivalent to the *opus major* of the First Great Conjunction, the anima realized as an imagination so solid, a soul so bodied, that the reflections of its images whiten the earth of mundane consciousness.

---

14 *Lexicon*, 41.

15 Philalethes, "The Fount of Chemical Truth," *HM* 2:265; also *Figulus*, 304: "Cold and moist."

16 Cf. *The Works of Geber*, ed. E.J. Holmyard, trans. R. Russell (London: J.M. Dent & Sons, 1928), 16; *Lexicon*, 209; *Paracelsus*, 1:8–9 for three more examples where Luna and silver are synonymous.

Again and again, gold and silver are spoken of in one breath, the two perfect metals, the King and Queen. The subtle difference between them shows, for instance, in these adjectives: "true" gold and "fine" silver.[17] Gold involves us in truth, and all that truth would establish by its power, an everlasting kingdom, physical or metaphysical, moral and spiritual. Silver involves us in aesthetic value, discrimination, appreciation, refinement which is also an end (*finis*) in itself.

To review the properties of silver: It is hard and dry having been cleansed of both the stickiness of sulfur and of its own phlegmatic and viscous moisture (*Minerals*, 4:5)—that is, philosophic silver neither adheres to its reflections, nor is it passively moved by its images. The psyche of silver is "hard and dry"; brilliant. Silver rings and reveals its true nature by resonating when struck. Moreover, its truth is in its ring, the ring of truth, that instantaneous aesthetic response of the senses to stimuli affecting the psychic body, which is "frigid and humid."

The body of silver does not burn, nor does it ignite other things, and because of its "cold" conductivity perhaps, "silver is best for sticking molten metals together (*Minerals*, 3:2.1). The cool, silver psyche, though seemingly "unrelated," can establish relations between the most burning issues and hold them together, yet without fusing them into a false compromise (amalgam). It mediates, attaching molten factions by means of its own detachment. Silver toughens gold because gold cannot be drawn into strands and sheets according to Albertus Magnus unless alloyed with silver. Unalloyed gold cannot "bear the blows of the hammer" (*Minerals*, 3:2.3). A true alloy is neither too moist (malleable) nor too dry (rigid), and, as Albertus says, poor alloys, because of their "stuttering" mixture, break under the hammer.

17 "Verissimum aurum et finissimum argentum," D. Geoghegan, "A License of Henry VI to Practice Alchemy," *Ambix* 6 (1957), 14. The Near Eastern word root for silver (*kaṣpu*) derives from "to refine," as the Arabic (*ṣarîf* = pure silver) has the root meaning of "refined metal." Cf. R. J. Forbes, *Studies in Ancient Technology*, vol. VIII (Leiden: Brill, 1971), 247. Let us recall here that refinement and purity are not identical. Alchemical refinement meant a "sophistication" of the metal, its transmutation into a differentiated and subtle power. Whereas our notions of refinement today tend for it to mean a higher percentage of self-sameness, singleness, and concentration. The alchemical notion is more aesthetic; the modern, more quantitative and simplified.

Silver is required for the opus of gold-making, for evidently it is the hard lunar mind, solid in the realization of its imaginative forms, which allows gold to be hammered into specific shape and take on definition. Alchemical gold is a *red* elixir, we must remember. It is active and incarnated, a universal medicine, a multiplying power in the world, a philosopher-king, just as this universal ambition of the gold appears in the worldly gold-making ambitions of the alchemist. Gold is not a transcendent spiritual state of awareness, a mystical saintliness of light, truth and perfection only, but rather these virtues shaped and defined for which shaping into precise forms, silver is required.

Besides these qualities, silver mirrors. " A mirror," says Albertus,

> is caused by moisture which is solidified and is capable of taking a good polish; and it receives images because it is moist, and holds them because it is solid or limited (*terminatum*): for it would not retain them in this way, if the moisture were not incorporated and limited by a boundary.[18]

If silver mirrors because it is both receptive (moist) and solid, then solid receptivity is the kind of consciousness that serves to mirror. Notice how necessary it is for mirroring to have incorporated or digested one's own moisture and to be limited by one's own boundary. One cannot mirror if one too easily flows; and one cannot mirror everything, but only what one can receive and to which one is solidly present within the limits of one's own borders. Mirroring is not blank receptivity; it requires focusing.

Air, Albertus goes on to say, "does not retain such images, although it receives them... having no boundary, it does not focus them into one place and shape... but acts only as a medium through which the images pass, and not as a limiting boundary that gives them being."[19] The airy mind cannot fix and reproduce even its own images. They only pass through and we ourselves are only media, unless fixed by a sense of limitation. When we are engaged in a limited project within a limited frame (a deadline, say), we are better able to imagine than when we remain in pure possibilities; such imagining is not speculative, a mirroring that

18 *Minerals*, 3:2.3.

19 Cf. Norton, *The Ordinal of Alchemy* (*HM* 2:45): "The cause of a mirror is fixed humidity; and for that reason it is also smooth, because air receives no impressions, and is incapable of confining itself."

actually images anything because it is without terminus, without a fixed end or focus. For the mind to mirror images, it needs a specific case, or a specific event in that case, which brings into being true speculation with more solidity than do generalities drawn from many instances. These are mere air, mirroring nothing specific. Precision and focus belong to the mirroring of silver; they are inherent to the very metal of imagining. We cannot image without being precise, and what is not precise, not limited, not focused, is not an image.

Silver serves one more purpose that we may not neglect. It has the "power of stirring up the inherent sulfur of quicksilver" ("Tract of Great Price," *HM* 1: 255). Benedictus Figulus says: "Mercury can be animated only by the white ferment of silver."[20] Surprisingly, this cold metal of the moon animates and activates both fundamental elements, sulfur and mercury. Does this not mean that the entire opus requires mental ferment, the animation of thought and reflection, the active intervention of imagination, and that perhaps even lunacy as a state of activated silver is the silver at work upon mercury, quickening, animating Mercurius, the God and guide of the whole opus, stirring up a white ferment by which he becomes lunatic?

As Luna is the recipient of all planetary influences[21] and as white contains all colors, so silver incorporates all previous metals and phases into its body. Unlike the moon, however, silver is not a starting place. It is usually not one of the many names for the *materia prima*;[22] it is not given but must be concocted, that is, prepared through the *opus contra naturam*, essential to which preparation is blackness. "Your substance will never

20 *Figulus*, 281.

21 Cf. *Paracelsus*, 1: 8–9. Sendivogius notes in "New Chemical Light" (*HM* 2: 98) that "the virtues of the planets descend, but do not ascend" and since "the last place is occupied by the moon," it is this principle that receives and passes downward the influences of the others. The silvered psyche by nature reflects images from the polytheistic universe; it is by nature polytheistic and infers *a priori* the other planets and their metals. Refined, sophisticated silver cannot mean pure, exclusive, or single; it cannot be defined except in terms of a thoroughly concocted and digested multiplicity of virtues, which have descended into it and whose lights it sheds. Its body has received theirs, as the moon receives their invisible rays. A consciousness reflecting this silver will therefore never be able to stand alone, or to conceive or imagine in an isolating, univocal, or mono-theistic style.

22 The exception that proves the rule is in Ruland's lexicon: the eighty-first epithet for the *materia prima* is "silver" (*Lexicon*, 225).

be white, if it has not first been black. It is by means of putrefaction and decay that it attains the glorified body of its resurrection."[23]

"Sulfur burns silver when it is sprinkled upon it in a molten condition, and the blackening of silver shows that it is burnt by the sulfur" (*Minerals*, 5:5). (Witness the effect of egg yolk on a silver spoon.) Even tough molten silver is relatively unaffected by sulfur; when the surface of solid silver is treated with molten sulfur, it "burns" the silver black, an effect that does not occur when molten sulfur is applied to wood, stone, or gold. These curious empirical events suggest that only cold and hardened silver is subject to sulfuric urges while the silver yielding to its own heated intentions remains untarnished.

Albertus reasons that sulfur affects silver in this manner because of their innate affinity. How might this affinity be characterized? Silver retains in its body a modicum of sulfurous moisture. Avicenna[24] considered "white sulfur" (together with "pure mercury") to constitute silver, and Bonus writes that "Silver suffers from a phlegmatic leprosy because it contains a proportion of combustible sulfur."[25] Let us imagine that the reflective lunar mind, despite its stable and astringent properties, retains an affinity for scorching passion. (After all, as Rasis says, manifest silver is copper [Venusian] as manifest copper is silver [Lunarian] within.)[26] This susceptibility of silver for molten sulfur derives from an innate proportion of combustible sulfur, its own oily humor of desire, like an astringent schoolteacher falling into sin despite her brilliance and "frigid and humid body," like Hephaestus leaping upon cool Athene, like Persephone herself, purely modest and yet subject to being covered by the copulatory passion of black Hades, as if within Persephone there lies the secret moisture of affinity with Hell.

The coolness of the image, whether of the moon or of the underworld, and the cool detachment by which we see through to the image, can become seized, as if from without, by the *calor inclusus* or innate heat of love lurking within it. So there will be within each moment of silver—creative fantasy, mental thought, mirrored reflection— propensity

---

23 Philalethes, "Celestial Ruby," *HM* 2:255.

24 Cf. E.J. Holmyard, *Alchemy* (Harmondsworth, Middlesex: Penguin Book, 1957), 94.

25 *Bonus*, 272.

26 Rasis's *Book of Alums and Salts* cited in *Minerals*, 3: 1.8.

to burn with sulfur. Perhaps, the less activated this innate heat of love within imagining (i.e., the less manifest the copper or the more humid and viscous the sulfur), the more the silver of the psyche is subject to sudden scorching of its outer skin, by which I understand the exteriorizing and literalizing of the innate sulfur into desires that no longer can see themselves as images (the blackening of the silver). Hence the importance of recognizing, as we are trying to do in this chapter, all that silver implies. We would activate it so that it not blacken, that our images not be burnt by their innate vitality.

But such passion is also curiously phlegmatic. The "phlegmatic leprosy" (leprosy being a technical term for imperfection) that may make silver splotchy or black (i.e., a sporadic or spottily intermittent consciousness; reflections that do not illumine but rather poison, eat away, or blacken) seem to be caused by phlegm, a Greek word meaning morbid inflammation, which also came to refer to a dull, passive, and untemperamental temperament.

Thus the affinity between sulfur and silver indicates that the mind can be inflamed by the hot urge to action, its reflective ability instantaneously darkened. This propensity, in even the most solid coagulated silver, to respond to the call of molten sulfur is because silver phlegmatically suppurates within its own nature. It is gummed up by the fetid phlegm of its own mental activity that does not get out of its head, coagulates there, sticks to itself, self-poisons.

There is evidently more going on within silver than meets the eye in its white clear surface: a passive fantasy, a mental viscosity or laziness, accompanies the mind's own brilliance.[27] Hence, the long hours of waste ("can't get going"), the phlegmatic leprosy that accompanies intellectual activity. There is inertia and dullness even in the midst of sovereign thought. Hence, too, the necessity for passive (phlegmatic) fantasy along with active imagination. Active and passive, fancy and imagination are inseparably coterminous in the nature of silver. It seems

27 There is a curious pun in Greek that underscores an inherent contradiction in silver: *argos* as shining, gleaming, swift-footed, and related etymologically to white, silver, etc., and *argos* as idle, lazy, fallow, unwrought, slow, slothful, do-nothing, related etymologically to "not working the ground." The various etymological and associative meanings of *argos* are discussed further in E. Irwin, *Colour Terms in Greek Poetry* (Toronto: Hakkert, 1974), 215–18. Also of interest is the fact that the invisible wind, air itself, was considered "white," i.e., silvery (*argestes*), ibid., 169–73.

that this morbid inflammation within silver necessitates leisure as the legitimate companion of the life of the mind. From the viewpoint of an alchemical psychology, leisure is the phlegm of silver, its necessary leprosy, so that the sociology of leisure grows out of the seeds of the metals in both man and world. The leisure class, considered effete and bloodless as the noble class or as the intellectual and academic elite or as those who live off their silver as money (*rentiers*), represent in the public body the component of silver including its phlegmatic indolence.

Without this silver, both swift and sluggish, without this whitened airy body, there is no gold. "No gold is generated except it first hath been silver."[28] And there is no conjunction: the power of gold remains charlatan, a red without white, blood without mind, *actus* without potency, truth without fineness, "deeds without image" (*ein Tun ohne Bild*), as Rilke warned.[29] Or as Keats insisted, truth and beauty do abide together. The alchemists' ceaseless warning that "our gold is not the common gold" was a warning against neglect of the silver. We must first establish the airy body of imaginal reflection before we can comprehend the gold as image and not grasp it as the natural metal.

If the alchemical process is witness to the way of gold-making, first we must realize the whitened mind of gleaming images, maintaining silver's aesthetic sense so that gold can become "philosophic" gold, truth emerge from beauty, deeds signify images rather than the merely singular realm of solar energies, heroes, and shining forth. It is the lunar mind within the gold that imagines the gold from within and is its prior ground, restraining its *multiplicatio* with coolness, enabling the gold to recognize that it and in its power is held to the enactment of psychic images. Only those deeds that generate from silver, that embody the reflection of images and mirror this reflection, may rightly be called true gold.

---

28 *Figulus*, 277.

29 *Duineser Elegien* IX, in R.M. Rilke, *Sämtliche Werke*, 12 vols. (Frankfurt am Main: Insel Verlag, 1975), 2:718.

Mining the Silver

Alchemy usually tells where we may find the substances we need. Sulfur for instance, says the English Benedictine, Kramer (*HM* 2: 154) is found in "All things of this world–metals, herbs, trees, animals, stones are its ore." Sulfur can be got from whatever catches our attention, blazes up. It comes from the natural world and our worldliness. It may be mined from any compulsion, fascination, or attraction in the macrocosm. Salt, as we saw above, is mined from our internal microcosmic world. "Descend into yourself, for you carry it about with you," says Eirenaeus Philalethes.[30] Tears, sweat, semen, especially blood and urine. We recover salt from our interior subjectivity and it refers us back to its source in the residues and tastes of experience.

Where then does silver come from? Let us first recall that this mining of the metals is a metaphorical operation. Benedictus Figulus says: "My son, understand here the Luna Metaphorica, not the literal."[31] The author of "The Open Entrance" writes: "All these things are to be understood with a grain of salt. You must understand that... I have spoken metaphorically; if you take my words in the literal sense, you will reap no harvest except in your outlay."[32] We must discover psychological modes of silver mining, mining it from conditions of the psyche in which silver is buried or to which it is alloyed. A psychological silver mine often can be located at that place I have called "mine," a place of ego appropriation where it is assumed there is nothing deeper here, no buried reflection, no occulted metaphorical fantasy. The work with silver moves us from being mine owners to mine workers, going into the depths of our minds, freeing the bright metal from its dumb ore.

(1) Antiquity, that is Lucretius, Strabo, Diodorus, considered silver to result from a forest fire, a holocaust.[33] A gigantic fire rages through a forest, charring the greenwood, decimating nature and, after that ruin, a thin stream of silver emerges. Silver, they infer, comes out of gigantic psychic disasters. It results from burnout. We claim it only after the woody bowers of protective naturalism have been totally blackened.

30 *Collectanea*, 12.

31 *Figulus*, 304.

32 *HM* 2:183.

33 Forbes, *Studies in Ancient Technology*, 201.

(2) The second and most usual discussions of silver mining in medieval and Renaissance alchemy refer to it together with lead. As the two planets Moon and Saturn are often linked—as beginning and end, as both cold and to do with death, as associated with dogs and poison, as supporters of *mens*—so, as Forbes says, "the history of silver-mining is inseparably bound with that of lead."[34] Silver is protected by lead, according to Albertus Magnus, from being burnt,[35] yet the method for extracting silver from mixed lead-silver ores was by repeated calcination (drying heat), quenching the hot amalgam in a sharp liquid (sal ammoniac or vinegar), and distillation requiring calcination again.

The protection of lead and the release of silver from lead as a white dove indicates the precious and noble nature attributed to silver.[36] A whiteness with the wings of a dove can emerge from a leaden state that seems completely to enclose it. The dull and heavy heart of lead conceals a dove of silver (sometimes magnesia). To extract it, we need dry heat and vinegar. Silver does not come forth easily, and a "ton of smelted lead usually contains only a few ounces of silver."[37]

The release of the dove does not separate it from its weightiness, that *gravitas* of the spirit. It carries lead into its silver. Imagine the lead becoming winged, mobile, airborne, hovering over the operations with serious attentiveness (as a dove with outspread wings stays suspended over a scene in medieval icons). The spirit no longer caught in immanence only, immersed in laborious struggles with the dull and dense.

Lead, as the metal of Saturn—cold, heavy, dense—was not used widely before Roman times. Like silver, it was not technically as practical as were iron and copper, so that both lead and silver, like Saturn and Moon, were more otherworldly, religious and mystical than the more worldly planets and metals of Mars (iron), Venus (copper), and Jupiter (tin). Typical of the Roman approach were the practical uses found for lead and silver, plumbing and utensils for daily life. Silver decoration, for instance, was the boast of high society. Pliny gives details.[38]

34 Ibid., 197.

35 *Minerals*, 3: 1.8.

36 *CW* 12, p. 437n and fig. 178.

37 Aitchison, *A History of Metals*, 1: 46.

38 Pliny, *Naturalis Historia*, 33:49–54.

Vincent of Beauvais in the Middle Ages considered lead to be debased silver.[39] Silver that had "fallen" or aged or lost its nature and purity became lead. The implication is clear: leaden states are "fallen" or "lost" psychic reflections, the dove solidified, buried in dumbness; leaden states are so hard to carry ("heavy as lead") partly because we feel the oppressed silver within them that cannot find its way free; and when silver was extracted, what remained was a new *materia prima,* a heavier, darker lead—plumbago.

Though we may extract a silver moment from our leaden body, these extractions leave behind an even heavier and denser condition.

Depression is the price of silver. Melancholy has, ever since Aristotle's *Problemata,* been the disease of thinkers. The more white reflection the more burdened lead; as we produce silver, we increase the lead. This is surely familiar: an insight may be shining in itself, but it makes no dent on the gray mood from which it came. We have the feeling of lead poisoning, a state of being swallowed by lead, lost in the lead mine—it's all so long and slow. What use, we feel, these silver mirrorings, this trickle of light, if the caughtness of depression does not lift. The truth, however, is that *the depression is the mine.* This is the lead necessary for the silver, even if the silver is neither useful nor functional in altering the lead. We mine silver from lead, but not to do away with the lead, for that would close down the mine.

It would be too narrow to perceive the dove only as an emblem of Christian ascensionism, i.e., that good is only above and all sublimation upward. Wallace Stevens writes of "the dove in the belly,"[40] invoking a holy spirit fluttering in the bowels of the deeps and signaling tremendous sensitivities. The dove in the belly quickens the life of images, whose birth pangs and death throes are concurrent, analogous, even indistinguishable.

Here we must remember the curious metallurgic fact that silver corrupts in air. It tarnishes. It converts with the chlorides in rainwater, so that it is naturally found mainly together in argentiferous lead ores. Only very rarely can silver be found unalloyed under the earth in mountainous regions. Silver blackens in air and cannot always gleam as gold. Silver requires polishing, attention, a bit of rubbing and fussing;

39 Forbes, *Studies in Ancient Technology,* 204.

40 *The Collected Poems of Wallace Stevens* (New York: Alfred A. Knopf, 1978), 366.

it calls for worry. Since exposure makes it lose its shine, it is best hidden, protected. It is covered with blackness, by silence and dullness, and by hiding itself invisibly in lead. Perhaps this is why we cannot find much about it directly in alchemy. It is nearly always coupled with gold: ("What is occult in gold is manifest in silver, and what is manifest in gold is occult in silver").[41] Manifest silver has the brilliant and precious qualities of gold, and when we try to imagine the nature of silver using solar consciousness, silver becomes at once occulted, which then depresses silver into an amalgam with lead.

(3) The third place from which we may mine our silver, besides from the ruins of our ragings and from leaden despair, is from the brain. Figulus speaks of the *Luna Cerebrum*.[42] Many tracts, including some by Paracelsus, place the moon or the metal silver with the brain. The brain is the silver organ as the heart is gold.

By brain here I mean of course the metaphorical brain, the subtle brain, the brain of the fantasy body as well as the bodies of brain fantasies. Fantasies, in other words, whatever their nature, contain silver. This silvered brain presents itself in descriptions of silvery fantasy forms. For instance: "The reign of the Moon lasts just three weeks: but before its close, the substance exhibits a great variety of forms; it will become liquid, and again coagulate a hundred times a day; sometimes it will present the appearance of fishes' eyes, and then again of tiny silver trees with twigs and leaves. Whenever you look at it you will have cause for astonishment, particularly when you see it all divided into beautiful but very minute grains of silver... This is the White Tincture."[43]

These shapes and patterns, these variegated filigrees are ways to find silver: in the bits and grains and swimming sparkles of reflection, dream fragments and tinselly fantasies, twigs of branching thoughts, a hundred times a day, the interlaced connections, marked by the interior "uhs" and "ahs," our awareness resonating in our throats, as the whitening mind emerges in its night.

Ruland writes in his lexicon: "Silver is found in conglomerated masses looking something like buds distributed in the branches of a tree... At other times it assumes the shape of little sticks, or other similar figures.

41 Rasis, *Book of Alums and Salts*, cited in *Minerals*, 175n.

42 *Figulus*, 24.

43 "An Open Entrance," *HM* 2:193.

Agricola testifies that he has seen perfect specimens of metallic instruments such as shovels and small hammers taken from the ore. I myself have beheld natural figures or images of small fish, lions, wolves, etc."[44] Agricola, the metallurgist, saw silver in nature in the very shape of the shovels and hammers of his interest. Silver comes in the shapes of fantasy; it can be mined from our brain's projected, imagined figurations. (Muhammad, by the way, also considered silver the metal of images: amulets in the Moslem faith were forbidden to be made of any metal but silver.)[45] Silver as the metal of imaging indicates that imaging itself may be the mode of mining silver and whitening the brain.

(4) A fourth mode of mining silver is from the money complex.[46] Ever since Roman times, silver has been the metal of money, so that the word itself "silver," *argent* in French, is generic for money. The curiously constant alchemical pairing of silver and gold repeats in monetary habits, for the value of silver is tied intimately with that of gold. During classical times (Pericles), the relationship was 10:1; still today, though silver is economically more valuable than gold because, as a commodity, it is consumed faster than produced and industrially more necessary. Silver fluctuates more in relation with the price of gold than in accordance with its own worth.

The debasement of the value of silver in relation to gold during the third century has been considered a symptom, if not a contributing cause, of the decline of Rome. At the very end of the Empire (397–422 CE), the ratio between them dropped from 1:1 to 1:18 in just twenty-five years. But the total collapse of the values of silver came during the heyday of Western materialism, between 1870 and 1930, a debasement of silver that cannot be accounted for wholly in terms of new mines and mining methods.

Mining silver from the money complex is exceedingly difficult (as discussed in seminars often by Rafael López-Pedraza). The more the value of silver decreases, the more material seems the culture in which silver is used as money. As values become materialized, the more silver

44 *Lexicon*, 40, s.v. "argentum."

45 J.E. Cirlot, *A Dictionary of Symbols*, trans. J. Sage (New York: Philosophical Library, 1971), 216.

46 For more on the "money complex," see J. Hillman, "Imagination Is Bull," in *Animal Presences*, *UE* 9, 58–75, and "Soul and Money," in *City & Soul*, *UE* 2, 355–66.

it takes to assert a value. The more materialistic a person's values are, the less philosophic silver to be found, that is, the less the person is able to reflect on money as other than "what it can buy." As money becomes only an item of exchange, without value itself or stimulus to reflection, its worth is wholly external: what you can get for it. Money's main value then is materializing it into something else.

The monetary question–what is the *intrinsic* value of coinage, what is it backed by–is not only a monetary question. It is philosophical inasmuch as it raises issues of internal and external relations and referents: do the coins refer to their exchange value only or do they bear internal values in and for themselves, as concretizations, tokens of the ideas of worth and the good.

Psychotherapists generally have not faced the deeper issues of money and have taken over the exchange notion without realizing what they are thereby perpetuating in the soul of the patient and the soul of the community. When an analyst interprets money in a dream as an equivalent for energy–much money means much energy, and money in hand means disposable energy–silver is being further debased. For this view is purely functional and utilitarian. The money in itself has no backing except as a counter for something egocentrically desirable: energy.

This view of money affords no psychic reflection, no silver can be mined from it, and one could just as well have dreamt of a car or a horse or an outboard motor as equivalent energy symbols. Instead of value, money comes to mean power: what you can do with it, get for it, valuable only in being put to use, spending and owning, which further reinforces inflation of the individual and the society. Need I insist that practicing psychologists, despite their devotion to self, soul, and the process of individuation, reinforce the crassest kinds of materialism when they appropriate from the conventional and "only-natural" world the meanings they attribute to images.

The utilitarian and materialistic notion of money contrasts with Greek silver coinage. Coinage was invented in Asia Minor; it was the Greeks who replaced utilitarian money–cakes, bars, and spits of metal–with the marvelously-crafted coins of silver showing the heads and animals of gods and bearing witness to local pride. A silver bar is like a contemporary dime in the U.S. But a Greek coin of silver refers back to a specific place, its culture and its god. Greek coins were at one and the same time «a true mirror of Greek religion, history, and economics, as well as Greek love of beauty,"[47] an aesthetic joy, a standard of value, and a tribute to the gods of the place—all at once. No distinction here between commerce and piety, and silver was the substance of this valorization of commerce by the gods.

Money has long lost this silver backing. It is no longer an instrument of reflection, but has instead become the bottom line of anti-reflection. The ultimate excuse we give when we don't wish to go further into the depth of something is that it "costs too much." That stops talk and thought. What we mean ultimately by the word "realistic" is money. Really real reality has come to be equated with money. The ultimate literalism is the economic fallacy, by which I mean considering money as wholly outside the psyche.

Mining silver from money means simply remembering the psychic value, the value for soul, in money issues. An argument over money is a silver quarry—money anxieties as we age; marriage fights over household spending; inheritance claims, insurance, indemnities; analytical fees—these can become valuable mirrors of where the soul is entrapped in matter. Here we are offered a chance to move through the material and quantitative levels to a mirrored insight, seeing one's own shadow face and the face of the specific god backing the contested coin. Each time we take money on its meanest terms by giving an economic excuse—"I'm doing it for the money"—we are back with Nero and Diocletian, debasing silver, the betrayal of value as exchange only. There can be no betrayal of Christ by silver were not silver first debased. The soul is sold not to the devil for money, but to money itself when it becomes the measure of worth rather than the affirmation of value.

(5) Comparable with the red (gold) and white (silver) of alchemy are the two currents that circulate through the psychic physiology of kundalini yoga, the red *pingala* and the white *ida*. According to Gopi Krishna's biographical account,[48] the experience of *ida* leads to a whitening of the perceptual world and to the internal sensations of silver

47 L. Lanckoronski and M. Lanckoronska, *Mythen und Münzen: Griechisches Geld im Zeichen griechischen Glaubens* (Munich: Ernst Heimeran, 1958), 8–9.

48 G. Krishna, *Kundalini: The Evolutionary Energy in Man,* with an introduction by F. Speigelberg and a psychological commentary by J. Hillman (Berkeley: Shambhala Publications, 1971), 66–67, 72–73, and 136–48.

streaking through the body attended by cooling.[49] There is definite connection between the lunar *ida* channel, silver, whiteness, and coldness: Silver is "cold," says Figulus.[50] Why not mine it from our cold conditions?

Relevant here are the ancient notions of the underworld as a place of refrigeration, and the etymological meanings of "psyche" as cool, cooling, cold.[51] Plutarch's essay "On the Principle of Cold" states that "coldness is what binds together,"[52] and because coldness expresses the astringent element and planet earth (as warmth does the fire and sun) it is the nature of cold to harden. According to Francis Bacon, the inmost earth is cold, passive and static.[53]

Bacon's fantasy is an archetypal one (that is, both widespread and valuable), that the cold depth of things is a place of death, an underworld where the existence of sunlight and warmth thins to psychic essence, beings as solely images. One of the connotations of *ida* is "nonexistence,"[54] and the transition to silver as in Gopi Krishna's case is a chilling death experience.

Dreams of snow might be placed within this context. They may refer less to frozen feelings and chilled relationships, and more to the freshly

---

49 Gopi Krishna describes the *ida* experience with these terms: "the lunar nerve"; "imaginary cold current"; "a sound like a nerve strand snapping and instantaneously a silvery streak passed zigzag through the spinal cord, exactly like the sinuous movement of a white serpent"; "a bright silvery sheen"; "silvery luster"; "milky luster"; and "freshly fallen snow." This passage is particularly relevant: "It appeared as if a thin layer of extremely fine dust hung between me and the objects perceived...The dust was on the conscious mirror which reflected the image of objects. It seemed as if the objects seen were being viewed through a whitish medium, which made them look as if an extremely fine and uniform coat of chalk dust were laid on them ...The coat hung between me and the sky, the branches and leaves of trees, the green grass, the houses, the paved streets, the dress and faces of men, lending to all a chalky appearance, precisely as if the conscious centre in me... were now operating through a white medium, needing further refinement and cleaning" (ibid., 140–41). Cf. my commentary, ibid.,156.

50 *Figulus*, 304.

51 Cf. J. Hillman, *Dream and the Underworld* (New York: Harper & Row, 1979), 168–71.

52 *Moralia* XII, 954*a*.

53 G. Rees, "Francis Bacon on Verticity and the Bowels of the Earth," *Ambix* 26 (1979), 202–11.

54 Krishna, *Kundalini*, 157; A. Bharati, *The Tantric Tradition* (London: Rider and Company, 1965), 173–77.

fallen snow of the *ida* experience, or to the appearance of the white sulfur and whitened mercury, the magnesia-like chalk dust that begins to coat objects with a new luster, creating on the one hand a sense of the remoteness and unreality of ordinary life, while on the other hand congealing and firming psychic reality into the white earth. The hardening of fantasy into obdurate psychic fact requires cooling. Alchemy speaks of congelation as one of the major operations. The coldness here is not bitter, but relieving, as if the psyche comes home to itself, losing some of its airy flightiness, its attraction for the flame, its succulent attachments, becoming more firm and solid, achieving its kind of earth by becoming cold. Coldness then is a mode of descent by astringency, drying, grounding and hardening the mind, solidifying the silver, developing its stability and passivity, so it can better receive its own matter in the cool mirror of reflection. Those introverted, schizoid, intuitive persons (called cold, remote, and withdrawn in clinical descriptions) are the very ones to whom the shapes and reflections of the mind carry the most conviction.

Why not then turn to our coldest conditions for mining silver? I am thinking particularly of hatred, which is a fixture of psychic reality as natural to our individual underworlds as was the frigid river Styx (the name means hateful, hatred) to the mythological underworld and to the gods.[55] The palace of this hatred goddess was propped up by silver pillars (Hesiod, *Theogony*, 777), and no water was ever colder.

Perhaps our hatreds are not personal only, but necessities of silver, firming the mind with supportive principles, giving determinate backing to its mirror. If in love we may not see; in hatred every line of the other stands out in cruel detail. Maybe hating belongs to silver-making, and is a requirement for the conjunction with gold, where the vision of perfection gilds all things with a golden glow. Maybe the conjunction also means a conjunction of the *shadows* of gold and silver—golden love tempered by a hatred that cools the heart's optimism with astringent perceptions like a cold-silvered glass at the back of the mind. The work with silver polishes the hatred. The personal salty nature of hating and its sulfuric compulsion become "translucent," so that the personal object of hatred and the personal feelings resolve their narrowness of focus into

55 Cf. Hillman, *The Dream and the Underworld*, 57–59.

the face of an image, like a frightful Japanese, Tibetan or Greek mask. Not harden the heart, but harden the mind, for the courage and faith that gold brings assumes true value only when it is married with these cold depths of earthed insight that hatred so well provides.

(6) Silver may also be gained from the dark side of the moon, the face of the psyche turned away from life on earth and toward the further reaches of planetary influences. I am now talking about an aspect of Luna that turns its back on the earth and does not participate in daylight concerns. Yet this place is traditionally inhabited by waiting souls and dead souls, *daimones*, shades and ghosts whose presence is felt when our consciousness is like blackened silver, a darkness primordially given and not merely a tarnishing from exposure to events. We sense this blackened silver as premonitions and omens, as poisonous moods and lunatic fantasies that descend into us, as if from the moon, without any relation to the dayworld. There is silver in these absentminded conditions, ghostly, separated, wraith-like, and we regain the reflective metal by mining our superstitious hauntings and forebodings for psychic images and nuggets of thought.

According to Plutarch's essay on the face in the orb of the moon, our composite personality—body, soul, spirit—goes through at least two deaths or separations.[56] The first, which Plutarch calls the death of Demeter, occurs on earth and separates soul and spirit from body, swiftly and violently: natural death. The second death takes place on the moon. This death belongs to Persephone. It separates mind (*nous*) from soul, gently and by slow degrees, resulting in mindless souls and soulless minds. These souls on the moon become, as it were, free-floating fantasies, disembodied and mindless both, wholly images or *eidola* (945*a*). They are driven by "the affective element gone astray in delusion" (945*b*). However, these alienated moony souls can be ordered by the moon, says Plutarch, *if they stay there* in that place and condition, for in time they shall receive new light and can return to earthly affairs and human body in a sane condition.

Plutarch's mythology of afterlife is also a psychology of lunacy for it describes the condition of bodiless, mindless souls under the sway of "counterterrestrial Persephone" (944*c*), waiting for return to the light.

56 Plutarch, "Concerning the Face Which Appears in the Orb of the Moon," 943*a* to the end.

These are the souls who have "lost their minds" or "gone out of their minds"–or whose minds have gone out of them–whom we separate by placing in lunatic asylums, a place apart, like the dark side of the moon, where the dominant gods of the place do seem like Hecate, Lilith, and Persephone. In the asylum, the death of Persephone, separating mind and soul from each other, occurs before the death of Demeter. One might expect suicide in an asylum.

According to Plutarch, the souls in this condition of darkened silver (as I am calling it), images without reflection of themselves as images–wholly in the dark, yet nonetheless psychic–cannot wait patiently in their lunacy. Driven by delusional belief in affects (944*f*), they wish to enter bodies too soon, giving rise to various monstrous conditions like Tityus and Typhon, even confounding the Delphic oracle (945*d*), i.e., the ability of images to cast their inherent intelligence forward as providential insights, setting limits, measure, and pattern to human behavior. Evidently, for Plutarch the embodiment of a fantasy (*eidolon*) in a mindless way leads to precipitate embodiment ("acting-out"), a direct entrance of soul into world without having been ordered by the moon. Prolonged habituation with lunar darkness or blackened silver allows the right embodiment that cannot occur until the soul succumbs fully to Luna. Succumbing to her dark side opens one to the paler lights of the planetary influences, the multiple rays too tenuous to be noticed in monocular sunshine. Then the soul can enter the world aware of itself as image. It is this silver of the imaginal that backs the reflective mirror by which we recognize ourselves as images. We return to the world with the *eidola* of the imaginal that became real only when we were on the moon, deluded, daimonic, without recourse to Demeter.

I speculate (silver is also worked by speculation: speculum = mirror; species = likeness, apparition, image, coin) that it is precisely this silver from the far side of the moon that provides the backing for the mind, so that it can recognize in earthly matters the planetary influences, the presence of the gods who give the world its inherent intelligibility. On the moon, in lunacy, the soul gets "both tension and strength as edged instruments get a temper, for what laxness and diffuseness they still have is strengthened and becomes firm and translucent" (943*d*). Without sufficient silver we mistakenly believe affects to be more real and reliable than images. It takes a sojourn with Persephone to tighten the laxness of the soul's sentimentality, to hone an edge on the mind's knife. Without sufficient silver, we mistakenly believe—because we dare not speculate, because we debase silver, because we would not be cold, because we fear the airy body—that images are given by the object imaged; whereas they appear only in a glass with a silver background, reflecting to us ourselves as image. For photography, silver is the essential metal for fixing light, so it can strike a picture. For psychology, no silver, no image; no image, no reflection.

(7) The last place of silver mining is even more complex and subtle than our decoction from money or the moon. This one has to do with sound. Ruland's 1612 lexicon says that silver especially is resonant: it resonates, resounds, re-sounds. We are now moving from the silvery shapes of fantasy into their silvery sounds—shapes as sounds. For instance, the manner of constructing early musical instruments as well as the shapes of Hebrew and Arabic letters have supposedly been derived from the moon's varying forms.[57] The patterns of our speech and the structures of musical tones are thus legendarily attributed to the moon. Silver connects with eloquence also in Christian symbolism, especially the eloquence of the Evangelists who fulfill what is said in Psalm 12:6: "The words of the Lord are pure words: as silver..." and in Proverbs 10:20: "...tongue of the righteous is as silver." Clichés still refer to silver-voiced sopranos and silver-tongued orators. William Jennings Bryan, the most renowned orator in American history, gave his most renowned speech in defense of silver.

In Shakespeare's play about two moonstruck and lunatic lovers, Romeo says (in the balcony scene of Act 2): "How silver sweet sound lovers' tongues by night/Like softest music to attending ears." In Act 5, when the musicians enter and parade their wit, the First Musician answers the question "Why music with her silver sound?" doubly: "Music hath a sweet sound" and musicians "sound for silver"—our theme again of silver and money.

I here aim at the throat, and turn to William Faulkner for an astounding passage connecting moon, silver, money, blackness, and the throat. The story in *Go Down Moses* called "Pantaloon in Black" gives "moonshine" a new significance, for it is not simply that colorless drink made in secret by the light of the moon; it is a cold liquid silver that the

57 Cirlot, *Dictionary of Symbols,* 206.

goin-crazy black man in the story pours into his throat again and again as he proceeds to a lunatic denouement of murder over a few bits of money. The scene is set in moonlight, the character moves through solid silver air, his throat filled solid with the silvering, glinting, shivering, chill liquid air of the drink.

The curious stress Faulkner lays on the *solidity* of this spirit, the substantiality of the air in the throat which produces lunacy, appears in another, radically different, context: the *viśuddha* chakra of the Kundalini yoga system. That chakra is one of seven centers of the subtle or imaginal body. *Viśuddha* is in the throat; it is depicted by a white elephant. Its element is ether, and it refers to the word, the voice in speech and song.[58] Here air becomes essence (ether). It takes on weight, and words can carry armies on their backs. We meet here the enduring solidity of the mind, where what we say and sing matters with the density and durability of an elephant. Jung says of the *viśuddha* chakra: "The power of the elephant is lent to psychic realities,"[59] and: "Psychical facts are the reality in *viśuddha*."[60] Only in *viśuddha* does one "trust the security of psychical existence."[61] Words, concepts, thoughts, the interior logos that talks to us in our semiconscious grunts and hums, the voices of the spirit, the adumbrations of the mind where they reach downward to the heart and upward to the forehead—all this in the throat center becomes utterly and massively real, yet whitened, without visible hue or tint. Nothing is as heavy or bears more weight than what sounds from us, just as the tone and pitch of our actual voices—the catch, the rasp, the flat nasal monotone—reveal the shape of our souls.

If silver can be mined from the throat, we would also have to learn to hear with silver, whiten our ears so as to tune into resonances. This is the art of hearing musically, letting the word resound, as the Second Musician plays upon the First Musician's silver sound of music, doubling the meaning, catching an additional inflection from the words. Mining silver from our very syllables: *Silben* as *silbern*. After all, what is psychotherapy but the art of listening, and speaking.

---

58 The swift silver ship of the Argonauts "had, in the oldest accounts, the gift of speech." K. Kérenyi, *The Heroes of the Greeks* (London: Thames & Hudson, 1959), 252.

59 *KY*, 56.

60 Ibid.

61 Ibid., 46.

We seem to be opening into a *psychology of viśhuddha,* and not only one originating in *mūlādhāra* (sex, family, and society), *svādhiṣṭhāna* (the heroic battle with the dragon of unconscious waters), *maṇipūra* (furies and energies, the gut gestalts of personal emotion), or *anāhata* (feelings). As part of its polytheistic enterprise, archetypal psychology sits on the back of various animals, tints its abstractions with differing colors, and works the mines of many metals, not only the depressive lead of Saturn and the quicksilver of Hermes. Imagine! Words not only angels with silver's trumpet, but descendents of the mammoth; tusked words, shouldering their way into our minds, shaggy and towering above our frantic actions, so close to the jugular.

The silvering by which we hear the soundness in words implies that they are worlds themselves and do not need to gain authentication through reference. Words sound their own depths of reflection—allusions, alliterations, etymologies, puns, the guises of rhetoric. These resonances in words are the singings of angels hitherto throttled by the golden rules of logic, objective reference and definition. We are in the realm of voices, lunacy: the mind sounding itself, sounding its depths, hearing its essential nature as a choir of voices, discordant, antiphonic, responsive, the dead souls in us speaking, ghosts swaying on the family tree, the unborn clustered on the moon, all sounding; talking with our voices and listening to them, hallucinatory.

These ghosts, their voices are silver's modes of mentation; mind mirroring mind. Silver gives us pause, that particular nobility of mind of which Hamlet speaks in his exemplary reflective soliloquy (Act 3, Sc. 1). "The native hue of resolution" (gold alone?) that leads to "enterprises of great pith and moment" are "sicklied o'er with the pale cast of thought" and "lose the name of action." This anima hesitation immediately brings its personified exemplar, Ophelia on stage. The tragic disjunction between them demonstrates the impossible *coniunctio* ("no more marriages") of two lunacies, each turning away from the other and turning the other way.

Hallucinatory, lunatic: "For *viśhuddha* means just what I said: a full recognition of the psychical essences or substances as the fundamental essences of the world, and not by virtue of speculation but of fact, namely as *experience.*"[62] These "psychical essences," which are the fundaments of

62 *KY,* 47. Jung's use of the plural ("essences or substances") compares with the

the world, become experiences when the mind is silvered and the images vividly engraved. Such experiences from the perspective of other centers and other gods may be called lunatic.

To recover the silver, by which I mean to be established in the value of reflection, in the sense of psychic beauty, in clarity; in short, to be of sound mind or sane, we have to hear all things reverberate as words, and shed all words of their outer darkness (that darkness which comes from their reference outward for body, a move that disembodies the word of its own substantiality, its body of air, its native voice). By listening to words themselves, we allow them to ring ever more clearly, as if the whitened ear can actively debride speech of its literalisms. This ear hears for rhetoric, for rhythm, sound, breath, and silence; for evocation of psychical essences, a call to the elephant, its trumpet, so that everything said or read matters to the soul because it bears psychic matter. If we would refashion with grace our psychological language, its books and talks and therapeutic hours, we must calcine and lustrate our ears.

Listen to the words: they shine in their own silver. Ultimately, the mirror is more firm and real than the world it supposedly mirrors, the image brighter than the object, all things sounding. "The world itself becomes a reflection of the psyche."[63] "[The elephant] is supporting those things which we assume to be most airy, the most unreal, and the most volatile, namely human thoughts. It is as if the elephant were now making realities out of concepts."[64] In crossing to *viśhuddha*, "one should even admit that all one's psychical facts have nothing to do with material facts. For instance, the anger which you feel for somebody or something, no matter how justified it is, is not caused by those external things. It is a phenomenon all by itself."[65]

These lunatic phases are silver mines. When we enter the mine we go lunatic for a spell. Jung speaks of the *viśhuddha* experience as "a very

---

silvered dove "as an image of plurality" analogous with the traditional symbolism of the Church where the dove image presented the "multitude of the righteous" (M.-L. von Franz, *Aurora Consurgens* [Princeton, N.J.: Princeton University Press, 1966], 238–39). Evidently, the *albedo* in alchemy and the anima in Jung's descriptions resist unification, even definition. Cf. Hillman, *Anima: An Anatomy of a Personified Notion*.

63 *KY*, 50.

64 Ibid., 55.

65 Ibid., 49.

critical kind of adventure."[66] These places, or phases, do not require mining in the heat of passion or the heart's feeling. They are forges without heat and hammer where silver separates from the ore-body and runs off clear as a mirror, whitening the whole earth. Neither holocaust nor filigrees of fantasy, nor depression, i.e., silver mined only from lead; now simply the ring of cool metal that sounds an event back with another resonance, strangely paranoid or depersonalized. Suddenly metaphor. "What really matters in a metaphor is the psychic depth at which things of the world, whether actual or fancied, are transmuted by the cool heat of the imagination. The transmutative process that is involved may be described as *semantic motion*."[67] Meanings shift; words move into things; things, into words.

Literary critics speak of voice, overtones, tenor (and the technical term for the elephant in the *viśhuddha* chakra is "vehicle").[68] We are at the throat of metaphor—not merely metaphor as a figure of speech and semantic problem, but as an ontological vision with a psychic base in the subtle body of *viśhuddha* consciousness and an alchemical base in silver. "Metaphor is the dreamwork of language," begins Donald Davidson's essay[69] and Nelson Goodman concludes his: "In metaphor, symbols moonlight."[70] Metaphors are psychological language—and all alchemy is metaphorical, the *luna metaphorica* that Benedictus Figulus spoke of—making subtle everything we ever may have assumed to be only empirical fact, whether events in the world, our own flesh, even the elemental minerals in the earth. Alchemy transmutes the world to the dream, which it does in the laboratory of its language.[71]

Hence silvering is so essential to this work, and so hidden, that complaint we began with. Silver is hidden because it is buried all through

---

66 Ibid., 50.

67 P. Wheelwright, *Metaphor and Reality* (Bloomington: Indiana University Press, 1962), 71.

68 On metaphor as tenor and vehicle, see I. A. Richards, *The Philosophy of Rhetoric* (Oxford: Oxford University Press, 1936), 100.

69 "What Metaphors Mean," in *On Metaphor*, ed. S. Sacks (Chicago: University of Chicago Press, 1979), 29.

70 "Metaphor as Moonlighting," in ibid., 175.

71 Cf. the essay revisioning Freud as alchemist by Randolph Severson, "The Alchemy of Dreamwork: Reflections on Freud and the Alchemical Tradition," *Dragonflies: Studies in Imaginal Psychology* 1, no. 2 (Spring 1979), which concludes with the sentence: "Matter is transformed into imagination."

the alchemical work itself, within every word, as the metaphorical resonance that transfers everything said and done to a psychic level. Silver is necessary from the beginning, else we cannot rightly hear the instructions. "Throw away the books," say the alchemists, meaning "discard the literal," so as to hear the spirit in the letter.

However, if silver is the mineral that grounds metaphorical consciousness, then a psychology that takes its stand, as does alchemy, in a metaphorical ontology—all is in semantic motion—will have to bear the pathology of lunacy. To hear the world speak, to consider emotions not "ours," to remain on the dark side of the moon and transmute matter into dream—and especially that semantic motion toward meaning everywhere coupled with coldness and hardness—invite depersonalization and paranoia.

These pathologies might lead us to imagine that silver is pure reflection, subjectivity supreme. But in an alchemical universe the metals are in things as well as in us, so that things reflect and resonate with subjectivity as much as we who are mineral bodies even as the "objective" world breathes and desires. The word "subjectivity" cannot apply, for what is subjectivity without a subject? In a *viśhuddha* psychology that speaks from the throat, there are only psychical essences, resonances belonging to nobody or to the ore body of silver.

What is reflection then when there is no subject reflected, neither emotion nor external object? No fact at all?

The very idea of reflection transmutes from witness of a phenomenon, a mirroring of something else, to a resonance of the phenomenon itself, a metaphor without a referent, or better said, an image. And these images or subtle bodies do not reflect a borrowed light, later, dimmer, after. Silver does not come after gold, but precedes it. So images have their own hardness, their innate gleam and ring. They are not reflections of the world, but are the light by which we see the world. The psyche comes to each moment of the world from the moon—not just once at birth in a mythology of creation, but at birth each day, right now. This light by which the world reflects in us is the light of silver, hidden like the moon in sunlight, hidden because it is white and swift, yet all the while giving the soul's differentiated worth to each particular thing that the sunlight shows as the same, for the sun beams magnanimously on all things alike; this is the light of silver that the alchemical work strives to reconstitute and refine.

Terra Alba, *the Whitening, and Anima*

Albedo is another alchemical term for Luna and for silver. In alchemical color symbolism white is the principal stage between black and red, a transition of soul between despair and passion, between emptiness and fullness, abandonment and the kingdom. *Albedo* is also the first goal of the work, coming after the *nigredo* has divided the world into mind and matter, yet before the *rubedo* restores the subtle body to its carnal keeper. Because of alchemical warnings about the "reddening coming too fast" and about the black crows creeping back down into the nest, the *albatio* or "whitening" is essential to slow the reddening on the one hand, and on the other to raise the blackness from its inertia. As a state between, the *albedo* is referred to as bride, Mary (as intercessor), moon, dawn, and dove. As a state between, it is both closely attached to what it joins and yet is distinct from them. It thus corresponds with that middle realm and mediating attitude we speak of as "psychic reality,"[72] so that the descriptions of the *albedo* and of the white earth teach about the nature of psychic reality and the operations of the *albatio* teach how reality becomes psychic; and psyche, real.

Beware here! There are at least two sorts of white "conditions which often look alike / yet differ completely" as T.S. Eliot says in "Little Gidding." There is, as mentioned above, an original white, the primary Luna or virgin's milk, pure virgin, smoke, cloud, the lamb, spittle of the moon, urine of the white calf, summer, white moistures, lye, syrup—all names for the primary material,[73] all names for those early and repetitive miseries of the soul: the syrupy nostalgias and overeager kisses, tender calf love, the mouth of salivating desirousness (Freud's oral phase), the days under the cloud, summertime, the agenbite of introspective lye, the smoke that neither clears to fire nor dissipates, and above all, that psychic innocence of self, world and others that psychology has renamed "unconsciousness." This primary white is pre-black. It appears in figures of speech, behavior, and in dreams, whether made up at night or by admen: the toothpaste smile, spot removers, milk shakes and ice cream, white linen trousers and Mr. Clean, ski resorts (the resort to skis), aspirin consciousness, "jes' fine, jes' fine."

---

72 Cf. *CW* 14: 630.

73 *Lexicon*, s.v. "Materia Prima et huius Vocabula."

Primary white is immaculate (without stain or blemish), innocent (without hurt, harmless), ignorant (without knowing, disregarding), unsullied and unsoiled. This condition cannot be the *terra alba* because there is no earth to whiten. The work begins on these original white conditions, blackening them by scorching, hurting, cursing, rotting the innocence of soul and corrupting and depressing it into the *nigredo*, which we recognize by its stench, its blind impulse and the despair of a mind thrashing about in matter, lost in its introspective matters, its materialistic causes for what went wrong.

Our white, the second white or *albedo*, emerges from that black, a white earth from scorched earth as the silver from the forest fire. There is a recovery of innocence, though not in its pristine form. Here innocence is not mere or sheer inexperience, but rather that condition where one is not identified with experience. Virginity returns as impersonality. Or let us say, memory returns as image, the evening with the photograph album and you are not the person there on the film and maybe not the person turning the pages. Experience and experiencer no longer matter as the "images that yet/fresh images beget" release one from the *nigredo* of personal identity into the mirrors of impersonal reflections.

This second whiteness is also not mere ignorance, a disregarding insouciance of the world and its ways. Rather, it is that casualness with the world and its ways, which results from psychic realities taking precedence over more earthbound perception, which attempts to resolve psychic difficulties either away from the world or into the world. *Albedo* prefers neither introversion nor extraversion, since the differences between soul and thing no longer matter, that is, are no longer imagined in the material terms of *nigredo*.

These two whites combine in anima, one reason that anima is such a complex psychological affair. She is the White Goddess[74] and also Candide/*candida*, the little innocent. The two whites shadow each other, so that latent in blank innocence and its seductive stupidities is the yearning of Candida for the whitened mind, while shadowing the sophisticated White Goddess is both the snow blindness of purity and the blinding by lunatic imaginings, being "out of it," which delude one again and again into that same uncaring ignorance that was the primary

74 For a splendid phenomenology, see R. Graves, *The White Goddess: A Historical Grammar of Poetic Myth* (New York: Farrar, Straus and Giroux, 2000).

material. Because of these white shadows, we must take pains in this section to differentiate the sophisticated white from its fall into the primary condition.

Transitions of color in our moods, tastes and dream figures reflect alterations in the material of the soul. Inasmuch as alchemical psychology equated change in color to change in substance, the *albedo* is not only a state between but a condition per se. It is, however, difficult to speak from this condition: either one tends to feel it as betterment, as rising from the dark, greeting whiteness in the Christian symbolism of baptism and resurrection or one tends to feel it as a not-yetness, a silent potential (Kandinsky),[75] an absence, that has still to become the color of fire itself (Corbin).[76] We shall try, nonetheless, to stay in the middle ground speaking of white as if we stood in its earth.

When the word earth appears in most psychological contexts, it weighs us down: earthy rituals and earthen pots, mother earth and earth sciences, gravity and the grave. Psychology assumes earth is material. As Patricia Berry[77] has written on Gaia, Demeter, and the Archetypal Mother, "earth" is that projective device by means of which we unload ourselves of matter, an elemental dump for the modern mother complex. We imagine earth only with a material imagination, that naturalistic fallacy which identifies the element Earth with natural dirt and soil: to be earthy, we must be dirty and soiled. Psychology insists Earth be our red body, brown mother, black madonna. Open the *Whole Earth Catalogue* and there amid the concretisms of bedrolls, ridgepoles, herbs, and

75 "White is a symbol of a world far above us, of silence—not a dead silence, but one full of potentialitie… It is a blank that emphasizes the beginnings, as yet unborn," W. Grohmann, *Wassily Kandinsky: Life and Work* (New York: Harry N. Abrams, 1958), 88.

76 "The Realism and Symbolism of Colors in Shiite Cosmology," trans. P. Sherrard, in *Color Symbolism: The Eranos Lectures,* ed. K. Ottmann (Putnam, Conn.: Spring Publications, 2005), 45–108. I have deliberately denied myself any alchemical discussion of the *rubedo* here, for it would require an entire shift of perspective, rhetoric, and images.

77 "What's the Matter with Mother," in P. Berry, *Echo's Subtle Body: Contributions to an Archetypal Psychology* (Putnam, Conn.: Spring Publications, 2008), 9–22.

canoes you will search in vain for the material ways of the mind and the qualities of *psychological* soil, inscapes of arid plains, muddy swamps, hidden banks where green lovers entwine, where there are also bedrock faults and islands, whole continents of the mind, an imaginal geography whose catalogue covers the whole earth because Gaia is also a region of soul—white earth.

Although the modern naturalistic earth of psychology is a supportive element, it mainly supports heroic spiritual fantasies. Even Bachelard lumps earth together, not only with supportive repose, but with the fantasies of will (forging, cutting, conquest, work, and action).[78] The dumb and supine materialization of earth, as well as the fantasy that it needs attack (mining, plowing, moving) insults Gaia, as Berry says, buries her under our dirt, forces her to bear our misplaced concreteness, depriving her of her own inner sky, Uranos, her own luminous and celestial possibilities. As a goddess, Earth is also invisible. She generates immaterially, unnaturally. She supports perhaps most where she is seen least, in psychic territories of repose, like the void in the vessel that is the vessel, like the rest within all rhythms, the hollowness in the drum,[79] working her will within the intangible forms of things into their visible matter.

The gross notions of earth in contemporary psychology betray its materialism; this psychology is so heroic and spiritualized that mother must carry its grounding. No wonder that modern psychology cannot leave its philosophy of development, its laboratory concretism and reliance upon measurement, its reductive explanations. It has not found another earth that would give support and yet not be materialistic.

This other earth is described in Henry Corbin's book *Spiritual Body and Celestial Earth*. There is a marvelous Earth, an imaginal place (or placing in the imaginal) whose "soil is a pure and very white wheat flour."[80] It has a physics, a geography, climates and fertilities. This, too, is a ground, the earth our heads touch just as our feet touch this earth here.

---

78 G. Bachelard, *Earth and Reveries of Will: An Essay on the Imagination of Matter*, trans. K. Haltman (Dallas: The Dallas Institute Publications, 2002).

79 Cf. D. Miller, "Red Riding Hood and Grand Mother Rhea: Some Images of a Psychology of Inflation," in *Facing the Gods*, ed. J. Hillman (Dallas: Spring Publications, 1980), 92–94, on the drum and the *magna mater* who may be both Rhea and Gaia. On alchemy's rhythms, see Bachelard, *Earth and Reveries of Will*, 195.

80 *Spiritual Body and Celestial Earth: From Mazdean Iran to Shi'ite Iran*, trans. N. Pearson (Princeton, N.J.: Princeton University Press, 1989),156.

Our heads are always reaching up and out to the celestial earth. And the problem of head trips is not that they are trips or that they are heady, but that they are not grounded. To ground these flights of fancy and ideational excursions, psychology sends the head down again to the material earth, insisting it bow down to the dark madonna of tangible concrete existence. Psychology fails to grasp that spacey head-trips are in search of another ground way out, an attempt to reach the atopic, placeless, far-fetched *terra alba* of anima inspiration. It is as if psychology hasn't read the Bible, page one, reminding of two firmaments, above and below.

Corbin's work opens a radically different perspective toward grounding and earthing: the firmament above is an archetypal, angelic ground of the mind. The mind descends from archetypal configurations; it is originally in converse with angels and has this angelic originality forever possible, so that all terrestrial and material events can be led back by the act of *ta'wil* (return) to the original ground in the white earth. If we ground ourselves in the upper firmament everything is turned around; by turning everything around (seeing through, metaphorizing, *ta'wil*) gross matters become subtle. To make the *terra alba*, one must start in the *terra alba*. Anima consciousness, or the *albedo* in alchemy, offers a different mode of perception. Seeing, listening, attending all shift from the gross attachments of the *nigredo* to a new transparency and resonance. Things shine and speak. They are images, bodies of subtlety. They address the soul by showing forth their souls.

What is here presented in the subtle language of Corbin and alchemy, can as well be stated in the gross language of our usual psychology. The phase called whitening in alchemy refers to the emergence of psychological consciousness, the ability to hear psychologically, and to perceive fantasy creating reality (*CW*6: 78).

As long as the psyche is struggling in the *nigredo*, it will be emotionally attached, stuck in materializations, fascinated by facts, grinding away. It will sense psychic "material" mostly as dense and difficult: (she has such long dreams; I get confused listening; he's a hard case; the hours drain me, exhausting, depressing—a long mortification). The gnosis of the *nigredo* is mainly diagnostic and prognostic. Its eye is on the materialization of predictions, fascinated by the various forms of *putrefactio*, which clinical psychology calls "diagnoses." (The DSM diagnostic manual is a catalogue of *materia prima* becoming *nigredo* states, like one of Ruland's lists.) The *nigredo* eye looks for what's wrong, the *caput corvi* (raven's head) of foreboding prophesy. It is caught by *physical* questions, whether in etiology (is it an organic, neurological problem?), in transference (touch or not to touch?), or in treatment (pills, body work, or maybe dance therapy?). Grossness casts a cloak of physicality over the subtle body of the patient.

The grounding of mind in whitened earth is what I have written about at other times as the "poetic basis of mind"; consciousness—not the product of brain matter (left or right, it's still matter), society, syntax, or evolution—but a reflection of images, an ongoing process of poesis, the spontaneous generation of formed fantasies. So, for the deepest comprehension of mind, we are obliged to turn to poetry. We must go to the moon people, the lunatic poets, who say, like the poetic clown in Marcel Carné's film *Les Enfants du Paradis*, "La lune, c'est mon pays." Poetry gives us chunks of whitened earth, moon rocks, which when seized upon with Apollonic mission prove dead and worthless. (Imagine! the greatest deed of our age's heroic quest was to capture and bring home to actual earth a tangible souvenir of the physical moon. The insanity of literalism.) But when the moon rocks are turned over in the imaginative hand, then ideas, songs, dreams, dances—essences of mind—emerge. These ores of the moon, these mythopoeic materials, are the primordial seeds out of which soul life comes. Platonic psychology says that souls originate on the moon, which means nothing less than psychological life begins in the places of our lunacy. Of course, Hegel insisted that lunacy was purposeful to the soul's development.

The lunar ground, and therefore silver, whiteness and anima, assume a favored place in a psychology that begins in a poetic basis of mind, i.e., in an imaginal or archetypal psychology. The tradition of this psychology, such as we find in Medieval and Renaissance accompaniments to alchemy like the *Picatrix* or Marsilio Ficino's *Book of Life*, starts on the moon. The moon, says Ficino, rules the first year of life and every seven-year cycle thereafter; the moon is *primus inter pares*, first among equals. All prayers to the planets and all influences from them pass by way of the moon, according to the *Picatrix*. The moon is intercessor, the landing place between outer space of the spirits and the mundane world of the natural perspective. What passes by way of the moon becomes lunatic, that is, enters imaginal reality. The direct prayer from us to them and the literal planetary message from them to us become fantasy images, metaphorical. It is this sense: that all occurrences must first be imagined, that they begin as images, that the very cycle through which anything turns, including ourselves, is a psychological process, that soul fantasies are the ground and seed in all we think and do, want and fear—this is the *terra alba*.

The *terra alba* is a climate and geography, with palaces and persons, a richly imaginal place, not mere abstract wisdom. In Corbin's accounts the celestial earth is full of spiritual bodies; or let us say that the subtleties of soul are embodied in the *mundus imaginalis* by primordial persons, eternal archons, angelic essences who offer human consciousness a grounding in hierarchical principles, enabling a human being to recognize what is essential, what comes first, and what is of lasting worth. It is a place of truth. Its orientation toward truth, however, is eastward rather than up or down, toward the orient, dawn's early light, glimmer of silver, hard to see by and declare.

This hierarchical sensitivity to values, truth and first things, coming as it does via personified forms who are these firm subtleties themselves, brings us to truth psychologically—in vision, dream, fantasy dialogue—and so we gain a *psychological* apprehension of truth. We are instructed by the silvered mind rather than by spiritual enlightenment. This truth evokes reflection and the illumination of the senses, especially the ear, else we could not hear voices, the messages (angels), the angels who are not only there in that other earth, but here in this earth that can be whitened by a mind that perceives whitely, metaphorically. Although silvered perception of truth may be polished to hard and cool sophistication, it is nonetheless glancing, oblique, a poetic truth that includes poetic license—even truth as fantasy and truth of fantasy—so that it may not seem truth at all in the rational eyes of reason alone. Ray (of the sun), radiant (bright), radius (of the circle or a straight measuring rod), *ratio*, and rational are etymological cousins—archetypal descendants of the Sun.

We cannot hold Corbin's accounts of the lunar earth in our solar minds, in our usual hands, any more than our usual ears can get anything from poems. They are so remote from daily consciousness, so farfetched and arcane. ("The moon is the arcane substance," *CW* 14: 154.) Even if alchemy says that "earth and moon coincide in the albedo" (ibid.), they feel miles apart, like death and life. How can they be co-present and how can we be real and imaginal, sane and lunatic at the same time? The answer is closer than we realize: the "white brain stone" (another term for the white earth and the arcane substance, *CW* 14: 626) is an actual experience any day. Poems, dreams, fantasies are wispy, haunting, elusive, arcane, calling for petrifaction by definite fixation techniques (memorizing, recording, depicting). At the same time these shimmering gossamer psychic materials are dense and impenetrable: "I had this powerful dream, but couldn't keep it." "I can't see through it; it escapes me." "I had it once, but can't get it again." Little tiny things, yet so hard to crack—poems, dreams, fantasies. And, full of impact, shocking us, hurting us, driving us to the far corners of lunacy, unforgettable, possessed by beauty, by anima, a mere whim or poetic phrase. The substantial language about matters that supposedly have no substance at all shows the subtle body in the solar world. These experiences that so annoy our everyday awareness are the apprehension in the mind of the white earth dawning.

What is this dawning? How is it felt? Precisely, as feeling. What dawns is not a "new day" but the day in a new way. Rosy-fingered dawn, as Homer called her, touches all things aesthetically. It is as if the world had a new skin, imagination become flesh. There is an erotic hue, an Aphroditic cast, pleasure. The goddess of Dawn (Eos) is both daughter of the Sun (Helios) and sister of the Moon (Selene). She holds together silver and gold and is engaged in multiple affairs of love. The consciousness that dawns now awakens into the world as into a rosy-armed embrace, the white earth inviting with smiles because it is a lover.[81]

81 Dawn comes in little ways in dreams—rising, early morning, "the alarm," breakfast, pulling up the window shades—and in those significant dreams "just before waking" or which end with "I woke up." Dawn also appears in sexual eroticism, not only at actual dawn but in any amorous flush that pinks the horizon. According to myths, young men (pueri?) are particularly subject to being Dawn's lovers, carried up and away by her. On the erotics of Dawn, see P. Friedrich, *The Meaning of Aphrodite* (Chicago: University of Chicago Press, 1978), 36–48. From this mythological-archetypal perspective, the *Aurora Consurgens* (attributed to Thomas Aquinas by Marie-Louise von Franz whose very title means the rising up of dawn will of course be suffused with erotic mysticism as it depicts the conversion of its author by the anima to love.

The white earth shows in dreams, but not necessarily as snow fields, white sands, or azure-silver celestial scenes. What shows rather is the whitening of tangibles, common familiar objects: painting the house white, a white jacket, silvered things. When a blade, needle, thimble, dish or dress is silver, then silvering is occurring *to* these activities (one's knifing, fingering, stitching, serving) and silvering is occurring *by means of* these activities. That is, by means of knifing, sewing, robing, the psyche is being silvered or whitened. Things themselves are becoming psychic; the psyche's thingness, and its thinking (Heidegger), are beginning to show reflection: things as images, images things; the *Dinglichkeit* of psychic phenomena.

Those silver containers of which the Grail is the classic example refer us back to the etymologies of silver as shining, glistening, glancing. A silvered or white chalice, cup, bowl, spoon, jar, or mug present containment, shape, and reflection in one and the same image. Shaping is a mode of reflection, and reflection is a way of holding things and putting them in definite shape.

A silvered container differs from an earthenware pot, wooden box, leather bag, glass bottle. Each permits and prevents certain kinds of holding; each depicts attitudes to psychic contents. When the cup is silver, then there is swiftness in our holding mode, a keen quick grasping-for silver and white mean flashing, swift, and light. The silver receptacle shows mental intelligence, a rapid understanding. But silver tarnishes, clouds over, so that it tends to lose the insights that once shone clear. At the same time, silver as the precious metal of money *values* what it holds, or rather it holds by giving worth, dearness to events.

Of course, the silvered container is usually thought of as the chalice for the blood. The *rubedo* first requires a receptive soul and a comprehensive understanding, else it streams in the firmament, reddening the world with manic missionary compulsion, the *multiplicatio* and *exaltatio* as conversion, moneymaking, and fame. But the *nigredo,* too, requires a silvered vessel. ("Take the black which is blacker than black, and distill of it 18 parts in a silver vessel."[82]) It seems that the best way to hold the blackest of the black–that irremediable and inert pathology–is again with a silvered soul, that quality of understanding appropriate to the

82 *Bonus,* 355.

holiest of essences, the enlightened and receptive mind that belongs to the white anima. Only she can distill from the utter blackness some trickle of possibility.

Silver may also appear in the sky: airships, white forms, missiles. If the airy element is the ground and place of mental life, then the mind is projecting out new directions, shaping new forms, exploratory speculations. It may be reaching for the moon, not merely escaping the earth. Whether or not the waking personality can follow its night soul in these directions is a therapeutic question, but silvering in the realm of air is a process as regular as natural dawning, dew, starlight and the throat of larks, and silvering appears in dreams as well as in nature.

The white ladies in dreams and sickbed visions (in a silver gown, head in light or white cloaked, a dead beloved, the man with the silver badge or instrument) are figures of the white earth calling one to another inscape by sounding music, shearing away, opening passages, instructing, beckoning. They are "calls" away from life who signal the death of one's embeddedness in the body of the world. We fear them and are wonderfully impressed when they ask us to come across the border. But what border? I think it is less the simple, literal line between life and death and more the one we've drawn around love, holding it from death. The white lady or the silver man makes the passage easier by bringing one's love to death, a loving death, moving Eros to Thanatos, so that we may follow more easily into deep unknowns, ready to go, anytime mount the stair, all aboard for White City.

Although the remarkable phenomenology of visionary white figures has been examined by Aniela Jaffé,[83] there is something further to be said about white animals. They have been called witch, spirit, ghost, or doctor animals, but what really is happening to the soul when a whitened or silver-blue-gray animal appears?

First of all, the animal is now a shade of itself, "dead" or psychized. The figure is now both a psychic presence as well as an animal presence. Its body is now subtle. Second, by virtue of its color, it belongs to the *albedo*. It is an animal of the anima, an anima animality. The animal is no longer a terrestrial natural figure, what psychology calls "instinct," but this animal, this instinct, appearing in white, shows that the *terra alba* is

83 A. Jaffé, *Apparitions: An Archetypal Approach to Death Dreams and Ghosts* (Dallas: Spring Publications, 1979), 79ff.

also a place of vital life. There is animality in whiteness; instinctual body in silvered subtleties.

A whitened animal is one that reflects itself; animal action hearing itself, knowing itself. Reflex and reflection joined in one image, desires that self-respect, the sulfur whitened to sure-footed awareness, an animal faith. No wonder that such animals are "doctor animals"; they are the guides of soul, image guides, who can sense their way among images. Their territory is the white earth, the silver land, where the mind and voice of the soul's intelligence rule. They bear intelligence, bring reflection in their white forms. The best way to keep them near is to treat them with the food they live on: intelligence, speech, words, thoughts. Speak with them: Doctor Dog, Frau Doctor Cat. Talk is their soul food.

Of all these phenomena—silver vessels and instruments, white missiles and animals—perhaps the most singular event of the *albedo* is the puzzlement of consciousness. The mind as it was is baffled by the paradoxes of its whitening, a paradox expressed even in the term "white earth." Wittgenstein's *Remarks on Colour* show an excellent mind struggling, during the last eighteen months of his life, with white and anima. We may read his questions and statements with a metaphorical eye as if they came from an old alchemical text having to do with the whitening of consciousness. Even more—as if white were the color of psyche, and of psychology:

> But what kind of a proposition is that, that blending in white removes the colouredness from the colour?
>
> As I mean it, it can't be a proposition of physics.
>
> Here the temptation to believe in a phenomenology, something midway between science and logic, is very great. (II–3)

> What then is the essential nature of *cloudiness* [*des Trüben*]? For red or yellow transparent things are not cloudy; white is cloudy. (II–4)

> Isn't white that which does away with darkness? (II–6)

> "The blending in of white obliterates the difference between light and dark, light and shadow"; does that define the concepts more closely? Yes, I believe it does. (II–9)

> If everything looked whitish in a particular light, we wouldn't then conclude that the light source must look white. (II–15)

The question is: is constructing a 'transparent white body' like constructing a 'regular biangle'? (III–138)

Nor can we say that white is essentially the property of a–visual–surface. For it is conceivable that white should occur as a high-light or as the colour of a flame. (III–145)

A body that is actually transparent can, of course, seem white to us; but it cannot seem white and transparent. (III–146)

But we should not express this by saying: white is not a transparent colour. (III–147)

'Transparent' could be compared with 'reflecting.' (III–148)

We don't say of something which looks transparent that it looks white. (III–153)

We say "deep black" but not "deep white." (III–156)

Consider that things can be reflected in a smooth white surface in such a way that their reflections seem to lie behind the surface and in a *certain* sense are seen through it. (III–159)

What constitutes the decisive difference between white and the other colours? (III–197)

What should the painter paint if he wants to create the effect of a white, transparent glass? (III–198)

White seen through a coloured glass appears with the colour of the glass. That is a rule of the appearance of transparency. So white appears white through white glass, i.e., as through uncoloured glass. (III–200)

This much I can understand: that a physical theory (such as Newton's) cannot solve the problems that motivated Goethe, even if he himself didn't solve them either. (III–206)

Why do I feel that a white glass must colour black... while I can accept that yellow is swallowed up by black? (III–208)

We often speak of white as not coloured, Why? (III–210)

Is that connected with the fact that white gradually eliminates *all* contrasts, while red doesn't? (III–212)

> I am not saying here what the Gestalt psychologists say: that the *impression of white* comes about in such and such a way. Rather the question is precisely: what is the impression of white, what is the meaning of this expression, what is the logic of this concept 'white'? (III–221)

The logic of the concept white is precisely what we are working on in this essay, in order to show it to be a psycho-logic, "something midway between," and something both transparent and cloudy, a strange third that cannot be made into a "regular biangle." This psycho-logic also attempts to account for feelings such as Wittgenstein's that "white does away with darkness," "that a white glass must colour [stain, lighten, tincture] black," and that "white eliminates all contrasts" [the *albedo* as relief]. Moreover, as consciousness moves from the darkness of the materialistic perspective toward the white earth, we can understand why Wittgenstein finds that Newton's physical approach cannot answer the kinds of questions set by Goethe.

Despite the intellectual puzzlement, whitening frequently comes first as an experience of emotional relief, a lightening after blackness and leaden despair, as if something else is there besides; within the misery, the tremor of a bird. Burnout cools; the *ida* stream of Kundalini showers the exhausted and bitter soul with gentle dew. A mood dulcet, a descending grace. Traditional symbolism speaks of white as the color of pardon appearing after the black of penitence. We say: "It's lifted"—not so heavy, not so frantic. "I feel I'll make it." All the while there is a new sense of trust in what's going on. For Dante, white was the color of faith. This faith, however, is not adamantine as a credo, or an iron anchor, and feels rather like sweet anticipations of another chance, a second coming, and that one can go on because somewhere down the line there is a holding place (that same gray ash, dry sand, sere leaf now white earth).

A whitened holding place must be imagined with a whitened mind. For the *terra alba* is not merely rest after struggle; it is not rest at all in the sense of surety. In fact, "white is motion, black is identical with rest" (according to that same twelfth-century text, which concludes with the famous "emerald tablet").[84] So the *albedo* is experienced also as the *motion* of psychic reality, what we have come to call "psychodynamics" and "processes"—so long as these are not literalized into systems upon which we can rest content. For when motion becomes a *system* of motion, rather than the actual moves the psyche makes, then we are again in a *nigredo*, that is, densely unconscious. Our language (psychic energy, process of individuation, development, psychodynamics) is stifling actual movement in concepts about movement. The *nigredo* must speak in the past tense as part of the *mortificatio* and *putrefactio*, whereas the white abjures reports of "what happened" and how it got this way, in order to move with the actual images. *Albedo* talk speaks rather of "what's going on," this move and that: how the psyche is moving and what moves the patient and the analyst make in response.

Another sense of the turn to whiteness is shelter: less exposed, less raw, less delivered over to the fires and floods. Wounds swathed in white dressings; untoiling lilies; milk, flowing and coagulating[85] into the more solidly putrefied culture of cheese. The soul has now a tabernacle; Mary as refuge. There is some structure and a place where it can tend to its motions; it finds itself placed within itself and not driven "out."

We also find ourselves easing off, no longer purging the bowels of *putrefactio*, no longer guilty. Complaining gives way to recollections in tranquility: the memories are there but no longer hold one to their rack. The sense of sin is washed, *ablutio*. The material has sweat itself into moistening, and we may even find a sense of humor. Ironic chagrin relieves shame. The voice now speaking in the inner ear and the words now coming from the inner figures of imagination tell us "it's all right," "take it easy," "let it be," "give yourself a chance." The white lady brings peace. She sits in the garden with a wide lap.

---

84 P. Dronke, "Tradition and Innovation in Medieval Western Color-Imagery," *Eranos Yearbook* 41 (1972), 74–76.

85 On milk and the coagulation of the white, see *Bonus*, 277–82. The coagulated substance is "female," having received the coagulating impetus from the "male." Another name for it is the (white) earth (von Franz, *Aurora Consurgens*, 10). The coagulant sometimes appears in dreams as cheese—mother nature turning into culture and differentiated sense—awareness through fermentation and putrefaction.

"Putrefaction extends and continues even unto whiteness," says Figulus;[86] yet "matter, when brought to whiteness, refuses to be corrupted and destroyed."[87] When does the putrefaction finally cease? Is the soul's resistance to destruction ever accomplished and when is its own capacity for corrupting and destroying overcome? Evidently, even after whiteness is there, the *putrefactio* extends and continues in some manner. One text speaks of "a white vapour, which is a soul that is whiteness itself, subtile, hot, and full of fire."[88] Other texts refer to a "white ferment," and we have already discussed the affinity of silver for sulfur as silver's inherent tendency to corruption (blackening, tarnishing, quick heating, etc.), its "phlegmatic leprosy."

We must therefore amend our notions of the white earth as a place of repose. Something else goes on in these anima states, despite the comforting whispers in the inner ear. Silver is copper within, says Rasis.[89] Copper was often used for the imitation of silver (*Leyden Papyrus* X),[90] and the majority of gold imitations, too, were alloys containing copper. So in which way does copper "falsify" the true silver? Of course, we turn to Venus, for copper was her metal: red in color, quick to heat, welcoming amalgamations, greening in time like her vegetative nature. Von Franz interprets copper as "man himself," the "microcosm," the term used in the texts she comments upon.[91] This "man himself," concealed in silver and able to falsify it, must refer to the human propensity toward all things Venusian—joy and beauty in the work, personalized feelings, the sensualism and passion as the transformations proceed, the heating up, the desire to connect out of the loneliness of whitened reflective isolation. Inside silver's cool lurks the all-too-human shadow of copper—which also serves to keep the work subjectively important, affecting "me."

86 *Figulus,* Canon 79.

87 *Figulus,* Canon 95.

88 J. Trinick, *The Fire-Tried Stone (Signum Atque Signatum): An Enquiry into the Development of a Symbol,* prefaced by letters from C.G. Jung and Aniela Jaffé (London: Stuart & Watkins, 1967), 81.

89 Rasis, *Book of Alums,* cited by Wyckoff in *Minerals,* 175 n 1; cf. Norton (*HM* 2: 59): "The redness is concealed in the whiteness."

90 V. Karpenko, "The Chemistry and Metallurgy of Transmutation," *Ambix* 39 (1992), 56–57.

91 M.-L. von Franz, *Muhammad ibn Umail's HALL AR-RUMUZ ("Clearing of Enigmas"): Historical Introduction and Psychological Comment* (Küsnacht: Verlag Stiftung für Jung'sche Psychologie, 1999), 63.

Otherwise, it would all be a matter of symbols and measurements, like chemistry, objective, going on only in glass vessels.

Within the whiteness lie the former stages. As whiteness emerges from blue, from black, and from great heat ("White medicine is brought to perfection in the third degree of fire"),[92] so these prior conditions are there within the *albedo* itself. It *must* tell us of itself as sweet, soft, and cool, just because it is always threatened by its own red copper, its propensity for sulfur, its hot and black inner nature. It is precisely this inherent putrefaction that distinguishes the *albedo* from the primary states of whiteness (innocence, purity, ignorance) and guarantees the soul against its own corrupting effects. Thus whitening gives the anima an awareness of its innate power, which comes from shadow that is not washed away and gone but built into the psyche's body and becomes transparent enough for anyone to see.

This brings us to four major *dangers* in the transition to white:

(1) *Transition as conversion.* The black all gone, born again, a new love, cure as loss of shadow. As clinicians know, the danger of impulsive suicide may be greater when coming out of depression into a manic phase or defense than when in the depths of melancholy itself. Thus every whitening needs clinical inspection.

Conversion, as regression to innocence, to the garden before the fall is the eternal seduction. There had to be killing at once on leaving Eden to make dead sure that all of them–Cain, Abel, Seth, Adam, Eve, and maybe the Biblical God too–wouldn't be tempted back. In the garden the serpent is the tempter, but once out in the vale of soul-making, it is the garden itself that seduces. Whenever whiteness–white lights, white ladies, white knights, white pages for a new leaf–draw us to them, keep the clinical eye. Remember your alchemy: the *albedo* must always be distinguished from the *materia prima*.

---

92 *Figulus*, Canon 106. Cf. *Bonus*, 342, referring to Arnold de Villanova's instructions on making white elixir: "Expose it to a good fire for twenty-four hours, to a still fiercer fire for another day and night, and to a very fierce fire proper for melting, in the third day and night."

Just here the difference is hard to discern. The urge to white is so close to the escape from black. Then the *ablutio* can become simply whitewashing, and *candida* can mean only a clean breast, a frank and open discussion, candid. "Albation," says the dictionary, still means dusting (off, away, over) with a fine white powder. Here the whitening converts back to primary innocence and the opus is back where it began.

Bonus of Ferrara offers a way through this danger. "When the Artist sees the white soul arise, he should join it to its body in the very same instant; for no soul can be retained without its body." "Now the body is nothing new or foreign; only that which was before hidden becomes manifest."[93] And what is this "body"? Bonus says: "Body is the form." Elsewhere: "The Ancients gave the name of body to whatsoever is fixed and resists the action of heat."[94]

I understand this body that resists heat and stays as it is (does not convert) to refer to those hidden forms within each of the manifest emotional changes that have led to the *albedo*. The occurrence of white can make us feel we are wholly in a new place because we are blanketed by the whitened condition. If, however ,the white is fixed in its *own* body of images, that is, its attention fixed upon the "hidden" forms that shape experiences (rather than the manifestations of those experiences), then we are less subject to conversion. For conversion here is nothing else than a consciousness submerged under its own white phenomena. Anima-enthused, anima-inflated, as the Jungians say. The soul has lost its body, the hidden form or image by which it can see itself.[95] The whitening can simply mean being unconscious in a new way, which is baptized (whitewashed) by the exalted name of "conversion experience."

We do not gain anima awareness (whitening) only by examining manifest experiences: remembering what happened and how it felt. Anima comes to its knowledge by an imaginative process: by the study of its own images. That's one reason why my version of psychoanalysis spends so much time on dreams (and less on reports of what happened)–to awaken the soul to imagination by the study of its images.

93 *Bonus*, 256–57.

94 Ibid., 261.

95 Ibid., 262: "The force of the body should prevail over the force of the soul, and instead of the body being carried upward with the soul, the soul remains with the body."

If the study of his images
Is the study of man, this image of Saturday,
This Italian symbol, this Southern landscape is like
A waking, as in images we awake,
Within the very object that we seek,
Participants of its being. It is, we are.[96]

Anima wakens in its images—of Saturday, Italy, landscape—becoming what it is by virtue of those forms, those bodies. Notice that the "body" of which Bonus speaks is *its* body—"nothing new or foreign." The whitening is present in any object that we seek once we seek it *as image.*

The body of the *albedo* is already there, the earth whitened, as the formal pattern that shows itself to the imagining anima as images. The lines of Wallace Stevens add to Bonus the further idea that these image-forms are participants in each being, including that being we consider to be ourselves.

(2) *Transition as "premature cooling."* The term is von Franz's interpretation of a passage referring to fearing "the cold of the snow."[97] Von Franz sees this as an inflation in which "feeling, relatedness to one's fellow men, perishes and is replaced by an intellectual form of relationship."[98] We have discussed above the potential silver that lies in coldness, and the innate coldness of the soul itself at some length elsewhere,[99] showing that the very word *psyche* is cognate with many words signifying cool and cold. Furthermore, coldness works in different ways at different times. For instance, "Digestion is sometimes quickened by outward cold... For cold drives heat inward and increases its action," says Norton in his "Ordinal" (*HM* 2: 43).

Since coldness is familiar to the soul and intrinsic to the whitening (as in Kundalini yoga), why *just now* the fear of snow? I think the danger to the work has less to do with feeling relationships than with a benign neglect of the alchemical fire which can occur at this moment.

Because the *albedo* brings relief from the tortures that instigated the process in the first place, we forget that the soul, whose body (its images now fixed) is better than ever able to bear heat, now requires a higher intensity than before. Bonus of Ferrara writes: "When the Alchemist... has

96 "Study of Images I," in *The Collected Poems of Wallace Stevens*, 233.

97 Von Franz, *Aurora Consurgens*, 233.

98 Ibid., 234.

99 Hillman, *The Dream and the Underworld*, 168–71.

reached the end of the first part of our Magistry in which is seen the simple white colour...then he must straightway set about the second part of the work, and this is the ferment and the fermentation of the substance."[100] By ferment, Bonus refers to "seething or bubbling," which makes the soul substance "swell and rise, exalting it into a nobler condition."[101] Premature cooling stops before the ferment. As things improve—and after all, the *albedo* is a betterment according to every text—there is less urgency. The whole work may go into the freezer, the baby abandoned in the snow. We forget that the long point of the opus is not resolving the *nigredo* nitty-gritty of our personal neuroses, but an exaltation, a multiplication of the soul's vermilion nobility to its full-blooded and manifold realization. Thus at this moment the analysis itself, as instrument of the fire, may have to turn up the heat deliberately in order to prevent cooling, which separates body and soul. "So long as the substance is volatile and flees from the fire, it is called soul; when it becomes able to resist the action of the fire, it is called body."[102] In order to keep the body, we must keep the heat.[103] We may have to invite new aggressions and passions; summon up the furies; force confrontations with essential questions that the white lady might prefer to cool. Active imagination, for instance, may now begin grappling with the angels of one's destiny, angels who are cores of fire. Now, "therapeutic support" means feeding the fire. The fire is the guardian angel and guards the angel from cooling. Analysis: place of fire. "The Spirit is Heat," says Canon 94 of Figulus.

(3) *Transition as premature calcining.* This is the caution against "burning the flowers." "Premature drying only destroys the germ of life, strikes the active principle on the head as with a hammer, and renders it passive" (*HM* 2: 188). Yes, the opus needs intense heat to dry up the personalized moistures: sobbing collapses, longings that flow out, sweet dopey confusions. These are dried in the soul-making process. But these conditions cannot just be hit over the head, taken to the (dry) cleaners,

---

100 *Bonus*, 264.

101 Ibid., 255–56.

102 Ibid., 262.

103 I suggest that analysis is instigator of "the ferment" because Bonus says, "The ferment of which we speak is invisible to the eye, but capable of being apprehended by the mind" (256). Thus what turns up the heat and generates ferment is an intensification of the mental work, i.e., deeper demands of analytical understanding.

caustically scorched. For in them there is a germ trying to flower. The flowers are burnt when anima seizures are blasted with scorn, with desiccating criticisms or abstract analysis. One of Figulus's canons states: "Those who... use sublimate, or calcined powder, or precipitate, are deceived, and err greatly" (134). So do those who "resolve Mercury into clear water" (135). What is wanted, as the pressure rises and the heat intensifies and anima infuses herself into everything, are not clear and distinct reasons. No dry powders. These kill the germ of life.

This is a curious warning. Though calcination (drying in heat) is essential for whitening, this same process can lead to an analytical burnout. When the therapeutic base in moisture, in permanent underlying humor, gentleness, and mercurial slipperiness (*aqua permanens*) is forgotten; then calcination blackens with mutual accusations, disappointments, exhaustion from too intense a heat at the wrong time. A new *nigredo*, cynical, bitter, burnt. Analysis failed.

Instead, like cures like—even while calcining is the main operation, responses to anima effusions can be in kind, i.e., feeling-toned images and reflective speculations, but only if held in the right mirror. Mirrors catch images because they are "moist," like the anima effusions themselves. But the mirroring moisture is cool and *limited*, contained by the act of mirroring. A modicum of moisture, humorful mirroring helps then, and personal effusions that start off by flowing out everywhere hysterically will, surprisingly, achieve a more objective telos: the white earth flowering, a sense of Flora in matter, the whole earth alive with her, amused by her.

(4) *Vitrification.* This is the sudden solidifying of the soul work into glass. Bonus says, "If by calcination a metallic spirit becomes vitrified, it is not capable of any further change." Unlike cold metals, he goes on, "on which one can either engrave or stamp any image... and it will retain that image; but glass will do nothing of the kind."[104] Vitrified materials have lost their "metallic humour" and can no longer amalgamate with the perspectives of other metals.

We find several specific dangers. The vitrified soul can no longer receive an image. It cannot imagine and so it cannot move. What isolates,

---

104 The reference in Bonus has escaped my pursuit. "An Open Entrance" (*HM* 2: 194) states: that the vitrified substance becomes "unsusceptible to any further change."

then, is the lack of imaginative receptivity. (Conjunctions take place when subtle bodies join, that is, when fantasies open to one another, take each other in.)[105] Here, the isolation results specifically from the soul's loss of insight into itself as an image in a "metallic" process. The "metallic humour" in alchemical psychology may refer to the realization that all personal events are objectively produced by the basic metals. What goes on in the soul is not of your or my doing, but refers back to the germination in us of the gods in the earth, the seven metals of the objective psyche or world soul. Vitrification closes us to this awareness; we become glassed into our personal individuality.

Vitrification "may happen at any time from the middle of the Reign of the Moon (into) the Reign of Venus" (*HM* 2: 194). It is a danger in the anima process. As the sweetness of the albedo passes into a Venusian love of life, a copper-greening of the material (ibid.), the heat can rise beyond the capacity of the material. It glazes, fixes, and petrifies. The intensity of the psychic process, fused by desire, creates an *idée fixe,* a globular obsession or glassified idol. "Be on your guard against the danger of vitrification; too fierce a fire would render your substance insoluble and prevent granulation" (*HM* 2: 195–96). No longer can one release the psyche from the form in which its passion is cast; no longer can one deal with it in particulars, piecemeal.

Silvering as granulation needs special comment. During the Reign of the Moon while the substance coagulates into the many shapes of silver, dissolving and coagulating "a hundred times a day," then "you see it all divided into beautiful but very minute grains of silver like the rays of the Sun ... This is the White Tincture" (*HM* 2: 193). Vitrification prevents the particularization of awareness, the tininess of insight, analytical precision that separates reflection within itself. Not the large mirror reflecting broad vistas and whole perspectives all at once, but rather a granulated, gritty, grainy consciousness that picks up "very minute grains," each spark, the little intensities, "a hundred times a day."

The passage from "An Open Entrance" (*HM* 2: 194) continues: "Do not irritate the spirit too much – it is more corporeal than before, and if you sublime it to the *top* of the vessel it will hardly return ... The law

---

105 Cf. R. López-Pedraza, *Hermes and His Children* (Einsiedeln: Daimon Verlag, 2003), chap. 4, for an understanding of erotic unions based on the attraction between and commingling of fantasies.

is one of mildness, and not of violence, lest everything should rise to the top of the vessel, and be consumed or vitrified to the ruin of the whole work."

We tend to forget that work on the psyche (soul-making) does indeed make the spirit more embodied. We forget that what goes on in the mind is gaining more and more substantial reality. If these newly-made psychic realities rise to the top, they tend to take on a life of their own, up and out, in behaviors "glazed and unsusceptible to any further change." Evidently, the body that is gained through the work is to be substantiated lower down in the vessel, as the body of the images themselves rather than as sublimed into hard truths, real values, factual persons and hot projects. Ideational inflations, highs, "that's the tops" can be vitrifications that, at this moment of anima substantiation, spell "the ruin of the whole work."

Glass is an ideal analogy for psychic reality: it mirrors, warms, and cools with its content, becomes transparent, appears like its contents though is unaffected by them, and it forms them according to its shape. It is the material par excellence for the opus. It both contains and allows seeing-through. Or seeing-through events is a way of containing them, as containing events is a way of seeing them as psychic images and processes. But glass is *not* itself the substance of the opus, and when it becomes so, vitrification has occurred. When the vessel becomes the focus of the work, when we take psyche itself substantially, when we literalize containment or seeing-through, then we are vitrifying. Psychology as a subject of its own, rather than a mode of seeing through, reflecting, shaping and containing other substances, is simply a vitrification, a glazed and fixed consciousness without humour, without imagination, without insight. Psyche has become Psychology. The paradox here is that seeing-through, as an act that makes any substance transparent, puts it into glass, and so can tend to vitrify the act of seeing-through. When an insight coagulates into a truth (because of too much heat, because it is compelled by Venus, because it rises to the top), this is vitrification.

Let us now turn to three alchemical versions of the whitening in order to grasp better what goes on in this process. The first is a statement from Maria the Jewess:

> If the two do not become one, i.e., if the volatile does not combine with the fixed, nothing will take place which is expected. If one does not whiten and the two become three, with white sulfur which whitens (nothing expected will take place)...[106]

We are told that nothing happens to the soul unless its gaseous state becomes solid, and its solidities mobile. All the scattered flying about and lofty arrogances of the spirit need fixation. At the same time, those certainties that we feel unquestioningly shall find wings and take off. To volatilize the fixed is to realize that things as they are are not as they are. Nothing takes place until we can see through the fixed as fantasy, and coagulate fantasy into forms and limits. The precondition for whitening is simply this embodiment of spirit and inspiriting of body. Until this simultaneous action occurs, we do not feel psychic reality, we perpetuate the "realm of the two" (body vs. spirit, inner vs. outer) and are vexed into every sort of "difficult decision."

When we recognize that all these hard matters are in the mind, then a whitening is happening. We are now in a new, third place where both being scatty and being stuck, being in the world yet not of the world, being volatile and being fixed, are reflected as *psychic* realities necessary to each other, setting each other up within the retort of an alchemical attitude. The two have become one, as Maria the Jewess says they must. But not by joining them, not by living them as oscillating alternatives, not by compensating one with the other.

They have become one because they have lost their literal pulls. And they have lost their oppositional tension, because our attention is on their relations (rather than on their substantiality), the movement between them, how they resound or require each other, and how we have required them. Realizations dawn; insights, illuminations; the sulfur active and whitened. The whitened sulfur here is not so much a purified

106 A.J. Hopkins, *Alchemy: Child of Greek Philosophy* (New York: Columbia University Press, 1934), 99. More on Maria the Jewess (Maria Hebræa) and the use of so-called called witches' multiplication tables in kabbalistic writings on alchemy, see G. Scholem, *Alchemy & Kabbalah*, trans. K. Ottmann (Putnam, Conn.: Spring Publications, 2008).

will power that can hold the opposites and hold from acting them out (cutting off the green lion's paw). Rather, this white sulfur refers to the coagulation of psychic reality as a third place that holds, a sticky stuff, a gum or mucilage,[107] that keeps the doer in the soul, making a third place between "the two," *esse in anima.*[108]

One finds oneself standing on a new ground, the white earth. But the earth does not necessarily come before the standing; the standing may make the ground. To stand one's ground, in the soul and for the soul, helps make the very ground one stands on.

Here is another discussion. It is a tale told by John Trinick, whom Jung called "one of the rare alchemists of our time."[109] (I remember meeting him while he was working on his version of Eirenaeus Philalethes's text, *Introitus Apertus or An Open Gate,* a text Jung examines in the *Mysterium Coniunctionis.*)

Trinick describes the white earth much like a pale young English lady, a virginal spirit, who is in love with a slim, aristocratic, but distant and winged youth. Trinick's vision shows two white "spirits" attempting to join: the dried white earth waiting to be released from salty encrustations and the refined white sulfur wanting to fecundate. But–the white lady is also being pursued by another sulfur, "the red thief," vile, coarse, active, and smelly, and so she cannot escape her imprisoning room.

We must note in passing that *salty* whitening is not sufficient. "Luna is never fixed... having only been washed, and fixed (as they call it) with Salt... O foolishness! O blindness of mind! Can common Salt be the

107 "Gum" is a frequent reference to the "holding stuff between," that which joins but is different from what it joins. Cf. *CW* 12: 336, 484; *Bonus,* 279; Trinick, *The Fire-Tried Stone,* 79.

108 Cf. *CW* 6: 66–67, 71, and 77. These passages present the alchemical gum in the intellectual language of philosophy. *Esse in anima* remains a third conceptual position, a mere rational argument. unless anima has become utterly real, so sticky that one can't shake it off, staining and smearing whatever one touches. Abelard, who promulgated the philosophical position *esse in anima* (though it is already present in the Platonic metaxy) was one for whom anima was a desperately convincing experience in the person of Héloïse.

109 Letter dated 12 June 1961, in Trinick, *The Fire-Tried Stone,* 12.

Soap of the Philosopher?"[110] The lady's tearful pining, the soul locked into its private introspective room, is not enough to fix the white earth. The ablution is not performed by tears alone; nor by memories, repentance or remorse. Not salt but sulfur.

But which sulfur? Who will break through the door and open the space, white puer or red thief?

In Trinick's account[111] it is the lady herself, in a moment of negligence, who unbolts the door. At the same instant the white sulfur, forgetting his anxiousness and resorting to his own style, enters on a rush of wings, and the sulfuric thief is left on the other side of the threshold to vanish gradually away. Notice that the two come together in a double unconsciousness: neither reason nor will bring this pair together. The scene, says Trinick, is tumultuous and dark, which describes the state of consciousness as one tosses tensely looking for what is wrong, yet that very upset signals the opening door, the sulfuric wings. The alchemical process of whitening happens *to* sulfuric consciousness, but not necessarily *in* consciousness.

To go on: The two white lovers within—the virginal anima whose imagination is caked in fearfulness and the crusted images of childlike knowings, and the white puer spirit of sulfur—have no vital instinct. They do not know what to do, how to conjoin. Slowly, the white lady, delivered from her fear of the red thief, its fat, its smell, its violation of her timing, comes to life through melting: "The pores of the Earth will be loosened"; "The youth enters easily through the pores."[112] What was passivity and immobility of the salted condition becomes a receptivity, a capacity for fusion. This conjunction is not a sexual penetration—a juxtaposition of dissimilars—but a fusion of likes, a gentle exchange through the pores as windows in and out of the body, the interchange of subtleties: the conjunction here a flowing conversation of images.

The substance in question (the "medium" of the conjunction), Trinick writes,[113] is a vapor, "unctuous, yet highly subtilized—a smoke, or

110 Hitchcock, *Remarks upon Alchemy and Alchemists,* 174.

111 Trinick, *The Fire-Tried Stone,* 38.

112 From Trinick's translation of "An Open Entrance" in *The Fire-Tried Stone* (cf. *CW* 14: 189–213). On the pores and puer, see J. Hillman, "Notes on Opportunism," in *Senex & Puer, UE* 3: 96.

113 Trinick, *The Fire-Tried Stone,* 80.

fume; that is, an exhaled matter... It is exuded—as milk from a nipple; or exhaled—since it is usually described as a 'thick white vapour.'"[114] The crucial white "medium" occurs concomitantly with the "dissolution of the two bodies." Another text says: "At last you must see that nothing remains undissolved. For unless the Moon or Earth is properly prepared and entirely emptied of its soul,"[115] it will not be fit for the conjunction. Now what is going on here?

The Moon or Earth becomes whitened when its own identity as Moon or Earth is emptied out, dissolved, losing its old ground in order to enter the new middle ground. Anima is now no longer defined by its own feminine principle. With the dissolution of the two bodies goes also *the dissolution of gender.*

This conjunction, unlike many others in alchemy, is not described in sexual terms where gender represents extreme opposites whose opposition is solved by the apposition of these (sexual) extremes. This conjunction teaches us something about gender thinking: it derives from the opposites, maintains them, and prevents the formation of the middle ground. Both radical feminism and male chauvinism are inherently unpsychological; the imagination remains trapped in the oppositions of gender. The dissolution of the two "bodies" (substantiations) does not occur and the white earth of psyche cannot seem to dawn out of the *nigredo* of physical naturalism.

Now we can understand why in this paradigm the "red thief" is the wrong lover. His vision is bodily; he emphasizes the opposition in natures of male and female, red and white. The white sulfur, however, joins the anima at that place where they are most similar: the mutual experiencing of fantasy and feeling. An imaginative conjunction is a conjunction in imagination.

But what happened to the red sulfur? Is it enough to say with Trinick that "the young lover... recognizes... that his own evil shadow is departing from him, never to return"?[116] Here we must recall

114 "For this water is a white vapour, and therefore the body is whitened with it. It behooves you therefore to whiten the body and open its infoldings," from Artephius, cited in Trinick, *The Fire-Tried Stone,* 81.

115 E. Kelly, "The Theatre of Terrestrial Astronomy," in *Alchemy: Pre-Egyptian Legacy, Millennial Promise,* ed. R. Grossinger (Richmond, Calif.: North Atlantic Books, 1979), 62.

116 Ibid., 39.

the "wateriness"[117] of the sulfur within silver, its latent copper, the potency of the white ferment, how suddenly silver heats—themes discussed above.

As an Artephius text says, "A white vapour, which is a soul which is whiteness itself, subtile, hot, and full of fire." "It is whiteness itself which quickeneth..."[118] The red sulfur is no longer thief when he is already "within," as that liveliness that sulfur brings to soul. His activity gives images their sense, their palpability and musk, their sexual attraction as well as our delight in being seized by them. He remains a thief only when the psyche remains like a lady in a small space, door closed against the visitations of clamoring images. These she then must see as dirty (fat and smelly), as a moral problem which divides the sulfur into good and bad kinds, and as literal demands on her for carnal actions. Fantasy then seems like an assault, a red thief, demonic and compulsive.

We learn from this text that imagination does not come into life directly. The anima of fantasy does not find its way to the world, unless mated with sulfur, and yet the red phallus is not the answer to the maiden's prayer—though the puer's wings are. She meets the spirit side of sulfur first from which the body later comes. The maiden here of course is not a woman, but a soul, i.e., that condition of psychic inability: of waiting in boredom and fret for something just beyond the threshold to come in, when tears are no use, nor is hope, only a sense of being threatened by life and knowing it would be too direct and too concrete to bear.

That it is *white* sulfur, which does the job of releasing the soul points to the operations upon desire itself: it must become white to be effective. This sulfur is like the image of Pan, white as snow, mentioned in Vergil (*Georgics*, 3: 391), a sense that the sulfuric fulminate generating within all nature is the imaginal force of the world soul. Sulfur, too, is soul, as Figulus says. And sulfur whitens when it is seen not as will or compulsion or desire only, but as soul; or, when we recognize soul in compulsion, will, and desire. This recognition releases the imprisoned soul from feeling itself cut off from life since life too has now become whitened as a sulfuric aspect of soul, i.e., life fused with *psychic* reality through and through.

117 *Minerals*, 3: 1.5.

118 Trinick, *The Fire-Tried Stone*, 81.

Trinick' s account has come from a young man's text: Philalethes is said to have written it at twenty-three. The problem and resolution are mainly sulfuric. But this is not the only method of whitening. For example, the text of Artephius is by an old man over eighty. It insists that "without antimonial vinegar no metal can be whitened." This antimony "is a mineral participating of Saturnine parts." It is "a certain middle substance, clear as fine silver," which receives tinctures so that they be "congealed and changed into a white and living earth."[119] Evidently the effective "middle substance" can be many things: the souring of depression as well as puerile sulfur (and of course it can be Mercury, which we are not discussing here), as long as the experiential mode produces a vivid sense of psychic reality, Whether vinegar, sulfur, or the processes of calcining or fusion, the experiential mode is extremely *active*. Anima refinement may lead through blue moods to cool silver, but the way to that refinement seems no less rending and intense than the torments of the *nigredo*.

My third alchemical example of whitening refers to the Doves of Diana, also mentioned by Philalethes, but here as they were worked by Isaac Newton in his *Clavis* ("The Key").[120] For Newton, the Doves of Diana meant both the mediation between mercury and antimony (puer and senex?), and especially, it seems, an amalgam of silver with the metallic center body (or *star regulus* as it was called) in the ore of antimony.[121] Newton suggests an anima possibility in this antimony, this saturnine substance of Artephius (who spoke of its vinegar). In Newton's

119 Hitchcock, *Remarks upon Alchemy and Alchemists*, 80–81.

120 B.J.T. Dobbs, *The Foundations of Newton's Alchemy or, "The Hunting of the Greene Lyon"* (Cambridge: Cambridge University Press, 1983), Appendix C (text of "The Key" from which come these passages): "Thus join the mercury, the doves of Diana mediating, with its brother, philosophical gold... Another secret is that you need the mediation of the virgin Diana (quintessence, most pure silver); otherwise the mercury and the regulus are not united."

121 Dobbs, *The Foundations of Newton's Alchemy*, 177; cf. also 183 and 207. For an entire text on antimony, with many references to its poisonous nature and the curative powers of its vinegar, see B. Valentinus, *The Triumphal Chariot of Antimony*, trans A.E. Waite (London: Stuart & Watkins, 1962).

alchemical psychology this substance amalgamates with silver. There is more to an old man's vinegar than your common sourness.

Sometimes this *star regulus* was called *corleoni* or lion's heart,[122] so that Diana's Doves also means a silver that has joined with the heart of the lion, a silver that has become amalgamated with the heat and light and desire of the animal king, his sulfur, his drive. A lion-hearted dove; a white-winged lion.

Philalethes's text, *Secrets Reveal'd,* which was the basis of Newton's, says: "Learn what the Doves of Diana are which do vanquish the lion by aswaging him."[123] He continues that it is especially the green lion (Ruland says a ferocious dragon) "killing all things with his Poyson" who is pacified in the embrace of the doves. In "An Open Entrance" (*HM* 2: 170), the bestial enemy is a rabid dog. Jung, commenting on this passage (*CW* 14: 185), prefers (for the word *mulcere*) "caress" for the action of the doves. Similar to Trinick's dry earth that loves the white sulfur, Newton's Doves of Diana contain a kind of love. There is a sensuous heart in the mineral body. The doves make possible "melioration," "sociability," and "mediation" of substances.[124] We should expect this Venusian aspect since the dove traditionally belongs to Aphrodite (cf. *CW* 14, p. 157n). The dove tames the dragon because "like cures like."[125] These doves have the heart of a lion. One animal spirit cures another.[126]

Newton compares work with silver with the mediating action of "Animal Spirits," a long-lasting psychophysical idea[127] that includes our concepts of emotion, instinct, libido, and imagination. The animal spirits, or spirits of the soul to translate the term rightly, were what we might today refer to as psychosomatic functions, emotions, vegetative nervous system, or unconscious fantasy—all of which work "between"' the conscious will and the physical body.

---

122 Dobbs, *The Foundations of Newton's Alchemy,* 148.

123 Ibid., 68.

124 Ibid., 207.

125 Ibid., 209.

126 On the motif of one animal spirit curing another, see my *Animal Presences.*

127 Dobbs, *The Foundations of Newton's Alchemy,* 207; cf. also J. Hillman, *Emotion: A Comprehensive Phenomenology of Theories and Their Meanings for Therapy* (London: Routledge & Kegan Paul, 1960), 75–76, on animal spirits.

Newton's analogy between the alchemical doves and the animal spirits does lead us to "learn what the Doves of Diana are." They are the mediating activity of the anima that can present as images of fantasy what goes on in the green lion of our nature. They can tame the green lion's passion because they are also passion—though of an other kind. This is a silvered passion that descends through the air, in whiteness. They are the *capacity to imagine passion* (rather than to rage it only). They are other than lions, dragons, rabid dogs, that is, images of emotions; the doves are the *emotions of images,* the animal in the air, in the mind, the mind as winged animal; and they are the excitation and tenderness released by imagining. These doves of alchemical fantasy present the mediating power of fantasy itself. They express, as they do in the traditional symbolism of the Third or Holy Ghost, Jung's transcendent function of active imagination (*CW* 8: 67).

The transition from passive fantasy, as Jung calls it (*CW* 6: 712) to active imagination is announced by the doves—and these doves belong to Diana. As Diana (Artemis) is a goddess of nature and the moon, the whitening here suggests a transition from reflective consciousness that is only natural and only moony—the garden of plants and animals, all things passing in somnambulist vegetative grace—to the active perception of the lunar forms—the images within nature, the presence of Artemis as an elusive White Goddess within all natural things.[128] As I see it, these Doves of Diana refer to a fundamental *reunion of nature and imagination,* where nature is seen as a vast coming-to-be and perishing of images, and imagination is experienced as a natural and necessary process, not merely human, not a faculty of the psyche, not psychic at all in the usual sense of subjective, but as given and autonomous as nature. Nature becomes the display of images, and images become the forms of nature. I would even hazard that this vision of imagination in the heart of nature, the imaginal white earth as nature's ground, corresponds with Isaac Newton's vision of

128 We see Artemis-Diana only if we are already in her train, that is, already hunting in the vegetable matter of our symptoms and slow growth and tangly underbrush of feelings for the elusive "animal spirits." Diana's sign is not only the animal and the forest; it is also the bow and arrow. Active imagination inspired by Diana will therefore be intentional. It will aim to seize fleeing images, and it will draw our puer intensity for quest into their pursuit, even at the one-sided risk of abandoning the pleasures of the flesh for the joys of the chase.

alchemy as an essay in the middle ground or Mediation,[129] for which, as he says, silver, the middle term,[130] is the secret.

The cliche that Newton's alchemical-religious-philosophical writings were the old-age crankiness, even tragedy, of a puer who had finished his genius at age twenty-four[131] is being dispelled as more of his manuscripts have been opened and published. Rather, it seems, he was engaged in mediating a Neoplatonic vision[132] of the universe and its world soul (*anima mundi*), a universe that proceeds from above downward and whose pull is an *epistrophé* upward—much like the pull of Corbin's white earth—with the gravitational forces of a mechanical world and its corresponding interpretation from below. His was a lifelong attempt from two sides, physics and alchemy, at a "wedding of the Hermetic tradition with the mechanical philosophy which produced modern science as an offspring."[133]

129 On Newton and "middle natures": Dobbs, *The Foundations of Newton's Alchemy,* 204–10 and 228–30. We recapitulate in Newton the theme we developed in Stevens and Cézanne (above, chap. 5, "Alchemical Blue and the *Unio Mentalis*"): the reunion of imagination and nature, which is also the reunion of imagination and reason, since for Newton, nature is rational. This reunion requires an alchemical work, the work of an art. The great landscape painter John Constable stated it thus: "The whole object and difficulty of the art (indeed of all the fine arts) is to unite *imagination with nature,*" Cited in E.H. Gombrich, *Art and Illusion: A Study in the Psychology of Pictorial Representation* (Princeton, N.J.: Princeton University Press, 1961), 386.

130 Dobbs, *The Foundations of Newton's Alchemy,* 183.

131 Cf. S. Sambursky, "Von Kepler bis Einstein: Das Genie in der Naturwissenschaft," *Eranos Yearbook* 40 (1971). Dobbs, *The Foundations of Newton's Alchemy,* chap. 1.

132 Dobbs, *The Foundations of Newton's Alchemy,* 19, 36ff. Cf. F.A. Yates, *The Rosicrucian Enlightenment* (London: Routledge & Kegan Paul, 1972), chap. 14.

133 Cited by Dobbs in *The Foundations of Newton's Alchemy,* 211, from R.S. Westfall, "Newton and the Hermetic Tradition," in *Science, Medicine and Society in the Renaissance: Essays to Honor Walter Pagel,* ed. A.G. Debus, 2 vols. (New York: Neale Watson Academic Publications, 1972). In his early work on light Newton had captured Iris, the mediating rainbow (and anima mediatrix), in a prism of glass and dissected her into seven colors. Iris, the Rainbow Girl, and colors themselves lost their mediating role (which Goethe tried to restore) between the phenomenal and the invisible. Colors were once the visibilities of the planetary principles; or, colors are planetary "messages" carried from above downward by Iris—hence they must be understood by *epistrophé,* or interpretation upward. When color becomes merely subjective (not really given with and in things), things do indeed become soulless, mechanical, and dead. Even in his mature work Newton was still trying to connect changes in color to changes in particle size (Dobbs, *The Foundations of Newton's Alchemy,* 221–24), a quantitative, mechanistic reduction, searching for the source of color in the colorless, soul in reason. Newton's optics deprived

My own view is that Newton was wrestling as must we all with the anima, "the secret... of the virgin Diana," in his own arcane, experimental, and seventeenth-century style—and this imaginal meditation helped keep him going into very old age. The key to "Newton's Key" is the enigmatic figure called "Philalethes" (or two figures Eirenaeus and Eugenius) who was "one of Newton's favorite alchemical writers."[134] This "Philalethes" was perhaps the last of the great alchemical philosophers[135] of the late Renaissance whom, some have said, was none other than Thomas Vaughan,[136] the Hermetist twin brother of Henry Vaughan, the English mystic, Platonist, and poet.

But what are these doves in *our* whitening? How are they *our* silver? Jung remarks in passing that "the tender pair of doves" "would be capable of an interpretation downward." (*CW* 14: 205) Here he has been brushed by their wings.[137] Interpretation from above downward follows their descending motion that announces a new vision of things. This is the moment, in Corbin's language, of *ta'wil,* that shift in mind enabling us

---

the world of its multicolored soul so that the restitution of anima ("mediation" in Newton's terms) by alchemical means became his ever-growing concern. Further on theory of color and the Rainbow Girls in James Joyce, see B. DiBernard, *Alchemy and Finnegans Wake* (Albany: State Univ. of New York Press, 1980), 87–91.

134 Dobbs, *The Foundations of Newton's Alchemy,* 67.

135 Ibid., 179.

136 The controversy concerning the true identity of "Philalethes" is discussed by Jung in *CW* 14, p. 33 n 183, and more recently by Dobbs in *The Foundations of Newton's Alchemy,* 53 n 25 (referring to investigations by R. S. Wilkinson).

137 Jung goes on, unfortunately, to moralize the doves, placing them into a pair of opposites with the evil rabid dog, Two does not always have to mean opposition. Twos are also cooperative as pairs, partner, mutuals, lovers—especially the last, when the two comes in the soft flutter and bicker of two turtledoves. Two feet, two eyes, two lungs, two shoulders—must they always be seen as opposites? *In alchemical psychology we must never abstract a number from its image.* Is the image two entangled serpents, two beasts, two fish swimming away from each other? My "two"'may be opposing currents in the stream passing by and bypassing each other, whereas your "two" may be a raging conflict of fighting beasts, or a mating *folie à deux* that cannot do without each other. The alchemical images of Lambspring (*HM* 1: 271 ff.) depict many kinds of animal pairs. The image always takes precedence over the abstraction, shapes it, and adjectivizes it. This is the perspective of psyche over and against the abstract numbers and laws (of opposites) of spirit.

to experience the sensate world of perception by means of the imaginal world. And it is this move that tames the lion, depriving him of his usual power as king of the physical world. We can now see all things, not spiritually through a glass darkly or naturally through a green lens, but first through a silvered imagining, an exegesis of events that leads them out of their physical encasement.

"Interpretation from above downward" is another way of describing the gift of tongues brought by the dove. This is not some peculiar pentecostal babbling, but rather a recognition that the dove is forever possible within our spontaneous speech, that speech is a gift and that the love of speech, its *peitho* or persuasiveness, is a tongue of fire as strong as love's desire which can at any moment ignite any thing with the whiteness of a silvered image simply by use of an inspired word. We wrote above of a psychology based in the *viśhuddha* chakra of the throat, psychology as an act of speech, a work of sound and listening, and we are trying to continue in that style of psychology here. Yes, Freud was right: therapy is a talking cure, and the doves cure the tongue of its *nigredo* talk: opaque concepts, deadening ideas in dull language, densities of plodding protocols, prose–interpretations from below. The doves teach trust in the sudden word, that miraculous appearance of the silver, which interpretations from below have called complex indicators, slips of the tongue, poetic license, puns, and lunacy.

Interpretations from below are necessary when reduction in Berry's sense is necessary.[138] Then we need *nigredo* talk, the hermeneutic of shadow: mortifying, depressive and nasty. But to carry on reduction when the dove is dawning from the lead occludes the whitening and frustrates imaginal realization. The shadow is not a panacea.

The hermeneutic of shadow is misplaced especially when literalized as the *nigredo*, shadow as only black. For this misses the shadows in whiteness, protecting the *albedo* from primal innocence.

Shadow conceived only as darkness forces the *albedo* to defend itself by intensifying its whiteness, thereby returning the albedo to the very condition for which it is under attack: innocence, ignorance, smoothness, purity. Then, whiteness is driven to anima extremes, becoming lofty, cold, and hard. Cure of white is not by opposites, but by sames, or

138 "On Reduction," in Berry, *Echo's Subtle Body*, 151–70.

at least similars—the blues, gray areas, foggy densities, mooniness, and other cloudings of consciousness that are the true shadows of white.

The actual shadow lies concealed in the nature of whiteness itself. For as the writers on color say, and the alchemists including Jung (*CW* 14: 389) concur, all colors unite and disappear into the white. So now the sense of discrimination is absolutely crucial, else one can lose the plurality of soul in a naive and simplistic *unio mentalis*. The doves do not herald unity. As von Franz observes, "The dove was generally interpreted as the 'multitude of the righteous'... as an image of plurality."[139] *The idea of unity is the primary shadow of the whitening*, an indication of delusional lunacy. It makes us forget that the alchemical psyche intends toward *multiplicatio* and *rotatio* through all degrees of the compass, i.e., an orientation by means of multiplicity and the precision of its tiny differences in direction. *Multiplicatio* already begins with the dove, as a sense of psychic plurality, those multiple perspectives emerging from the soul's myriad fantasies.

Unless the multiplicities of white are kept as its shadows—as blues, as creams, as the wan and pale feelings of grey—the whitening becomes sheer blankness. Here is a reflective consciousness that perceives without reaction, a kind of frank stare, chilled and numbed, lunar, curiously deadened within its own anima state that should have brought it life.

To keep whiteness from blinding itself with simplicities (instead of multiplicities), a reduction needs to be performed on the *albedo*, but in its own style, which means turning up the heat in an anima fashion. New lunatic intensities, demanding active imaginations and fermentations that lead to ever finer discriminations (white against white),[140] adding weight to light and rubbing the silver to more clarified reflections. This means friction, more accurate tuning of responses, and keeping to the lunatic fringe—noticing the oddity of behavior and feeling when images

---

139 Von Franz, *Aurora Consurgens*. She understands the plurality here differently: for her it is tied with a problem of evil so that "pluralization" becomes "regression."

140 The artist Robert Ryman, in response to a question regarding his supposed all-white canvases, said: "I'm not really interested in white as a color, although I have at times used different whites for different purposes. White is used instrumentally and for itself; but 'whiteness' as such is not the work's subject or essence. When it snows, you see things clearly that you didn't see before. So the white can eliminate certain visual clutter so that you can see nuances and certain things that you wouldn't be aware of ordinarily," http://www.praemiumimperiale.org/eg/laureates/rymanhtmlpages/rymansummarycontent.html (accessed 10 March 2009).

are first reality. We whiten the earth by earthing our whiteness. So, put the heat on anima attractions, soulful philosophizings, delicate aestheticisms, petty perceptions, global moods, lovey-dovey coziness, and the nymphic gossamer illusions that promise lions. Don't literalize the relief of the *albedo* into relaxation: pull the plug on Mary's bath. Silver is hard and it likes heat and truth; its eventual telos is yellow and red: vivification. Get at essentials. Stick to the image. Greet the angel.

This white earth of the imaginal is also a territory of essences, principles, *archai* (as we saw above from Corbin). The aim of reduction is not to stay stuck to the *nigredo* nose in the dirt but, as Berry writes, to come to "the essential oil, the quintessence of one's nature."[141] To achieve this intensity of soul, whether in an hour of analysis, in a close relationship, in language, study or art, takes as much sweat as shoveling through the stable with Hercules. These essences stand out the further we can move into each image, each fantasy, each event, working at distinctions within them rather than comparisons between them. For in the *albedo* the very method of psychoanalysis changes from an Aristotelian observation of similarities (and its ultimate reduction downward to common denominators) to the study of singularity, each phenomenon a thing in itself, allowing and forcing the necessary angel to appear as the body in the image making its behavioral demands on the soul.

A double dove, both male and female, appears in one of Jung's own dreams, and from that dream and Robert Grinnell's analysis of it,[142] we can take a final cue as to the doves' significance, or how the silvered psyche works in our consciousness. I shan't recapitulate the dream. It is in Jung's biography.[143] But the result of the dove's appearance, its transformation into a little girl—and do not such girls "belong" to Diana?[144]—its speech to him and its vanishing into *blue* air, adds something more to the gift of speech and the gift of interpretation from above downward. The result of the dove was, as Grinnell brings out, the gift of faith in images, a

---

141 "On Reduction," in Berry, *Echo's Subtle Body*, 169.

142 "Reflections on the Archetype of Consciousness: Personality and Psychological Faith," *Spring: An Annual of Archetypal Psychology and Jungian Thought* (1970), 15–39. See also J. Hillman, *Re-Visioning Psychology* (New York: HarperPerennial, 1992), 42–44, 50–51, on "Anima" and "Psychological Faith."

143 *MDR*, 166.

144 Cf. K. Kérenyi, "A Mythological Image of Girlhood: Artemis," in *Facing the Gods*, 39–45.

psychological faith, which permits belief and enjoins conviction, a fervid animal faith in the depths, a dove in the belly that gives one the sense that the psyche is the first reality and that we are always soul.

We have returned to that place of soul described above: What is reflection then when there is no subject reflected, neither emotion nor external object? No fact at all? The very idea of reflection transmutes from witness of a phenomenon, a mirroring of something else, to a resonance of the phenomenon itself, a metaphor without a referent, or better said, an image.

Mental events as images do not require and cannot acquire further validation by reference to external events. The soul's life is not upheld as correct by virtue of exteriority. But neither are mental events validated by virtue of my "having" a dream, "thinking" an idea or "feeling" an experience. We are beyond soul as a conglomerate of subjective functions, with imagination merely one function among others, a bureau in the department of mind. (Imagination imagines itself in this bureaucratic fashion only when it must give report of itself in the language of historical psychology that denied imagination any valid place to begin with.) Psychic events do not require my reports in the language of functions and experiences in order to be. They do not require my reports at all. Soul need no longer be captured by subjectivity, a mind owning its events and distinct from them. Neither wax tablet, cage of birds, ghost in the machine, iceberg or saddleback—functional models all, attempting to account for, give support to, a subjective base for psychic events. Let it go.

We can dispel subjectivity and yet still have soul. No subject needed, neither conscious nor unconscious, neither empirical nor transcendental, neither personal ego nor impersonal self. Personal pronouns can lose their hold: whose is that cat, this music, the idea which 'I' am writing now? The event is there, shining. Have we thought it, or has it appeared, ephiphanic amid that birthing turmoil which we call work. And who are "we" to say? Let events belong to themselves, or to the Others. "All things are full of gods," said Thales; it is *their* personal belongings that furnish our world. The event is there—though not in a mirror, for if the mirror vanish the event will still be there. Or better: the event is the mirror self-sustaining its own reflection. Have faith in the everlasting indestructible ground of images. They do not need us.

Do you recall the passage in Jung, who on the great Athi Plains watches the animal herds like slow rivers across the primeval scene of Africa: "Man, I, an invisible act of creation put the stamp of perfection on the world by giving it objective existence."[145] The objective world requires a human subject! *Horribile dictu:* "I" crown the creation, those herds, by my consciousness! But what if both, all, are images? Consciousness may be necessary to the *anima mundi* in specific ways she devises, but consciousness is not confined to my mind and is not only consciousness as "I" have defined it. The plains are, and their grazing gazelle, and these images move in the soul of the world unwitting of "Man, I" or any personal observation. Psychological faith affirms those gazelles, those images, whose appearance does not require my consent. Take joy in witness, but do not believe the world is held together thereby.

"Earth and moon coincide in the albedo" (*CW* 14: 154). All earthly things become whitened into lunacy; they are now apparitions, having dreamed themselves to death. All lunatic things become dense, real and slow, forms filled with earth. Lunar phantasms become ground on which to stand, because they themselves stand, faithfully. Images as things; as things in themselves; each phenomenon noumenal, yet utterly here. Perhaps things appear and have *durée* simply because they enjoy their images, themselves as they are in the display of their forms. They come into the world in such good faith, exuding such confidence that we test our reality, our theories and diagnoses by means of them. Their faith gives us our certainties.

Strange to find imagination as the ground of certainty, that nothing is more certain than fantasy—it is as it is. It can be subjected to the noetic procedures of cognition but these cannot negate it. It still stands, and more firmly than the doubts with which it is assailed by noetic inquiry. When the mind rests on imaginal firmament, then thinking and imagining no longer divide against each other as they must when the mind is conceived in the categories of *nous*.

Now *nous* can as well be *psyche*; the noetic, the psychological. Knowledge comes from and feeds the soul, the *epistrophé* of "data" to its first meaning "gifts." Knowledge is received by the soul as understanding, in exchange for which the soul gives to knowledge value and faith.

145 *MDR*, 240.

Knowledge can again believe in itself as a virtue. Here is knowledge not opposed to soul, different from feeling or life, academic, scholarly, sheerly intellectual or merely explanatory (*ein Erklärendes*), but knowledge as a necessity demanded by the silvered mind by means of which the soul can understand itself.

In this white country where the barriers between soul and intellect do not try to keep each other out, psyche is itself a kind of knowing, a keen accounting, a wit of what is there; and *nous* is psychological, engaged in intelligent interlocutions among its images. The entire dialectic of philosophy becomes whitened to talk among imaginal figures. We take part in a symposium going on forever; mental life, an extraordinary banquet. Through this inquiring conversation and this display of the image by means of its rhetoric, psyche becomes knowledgeable, noetically aware of itself, though not as defined by *nous* (which limits psychological knowledge to the cognition of experience, introspection of the interiority of time, structures of transcendental subjectivity and the operations of its logic). Instead of these philosophical constrictions on psychological knowledge, psyche becomes aware by means of an imaginal method: the ostentation of images, a parade of fantasies as imagination bodies forth its subtleties. *Nous* observer of *psyche,* seeing in her mirror how his mind actually proceeds. *Nous* at last psychological: all its cognitive instrumentarium become lunatic, the logic of images; psyche with logos. Here, in the white earth, psychology begins.[146]

Lunacy

We began by proposing, from Hegel, that soul purposely goes through a stage of insanity: lunacy belongs to soul-making. And we suggested that this necessary stage might be what alchemical psychology speaks of as silver and the whitening of the earth. All along, however, we have been begging a question: we have used terms like

146 The reader with interests in philosophy may notice that these last paragraphs play off from and comment upon the following obvious references: Henri Bergson's *durée,* Immanuel Kant's *noumenon*, Socratic dialectic (albeit altogether other than the *Symposium*), Wilhelm Dilthey's knowledge versus understanding, Edmund Husserl's transcendental subjectivity, as well as all philosophies that place imagination in the mind (rather than the mind in imagination) and consider it a function of a subjective knower.

"lunacy," "psychopathology," "madness," seeming never to have heard the arguments by Thomas Szasz against this medical language. But I think these maddening terms belong first to the moon,[147] and only incidentally to medicine. They are true coinages presenting true values, minted by the lunatic mind attempting to formulate a specific lunar state of its imagining that is underworld or otherworld, shocking and abnormal, and that therefore these terms themselves become vehicles of an *epistrophé*, a mode of carrying us to the archetypal principle to which they refer. On the one hand, I am agreeing with Hegel and with alchemy: lunacy is a necessity, as silver is a precondition of the conjunction. On the other hand, I agree with Szasz that lunacy becomes insanity when diagnosed as such by the medical model. Lunacy is a moon moment, and we must be aware of what happens to the moon when assaulted by Apollonic medicine. Lunacy calls for lunar understanding.

Let us look now at two forms of lunacy in the light of the alchemical moon. The first is *delusional literalism*, the core problem in what medical psychology calls paranoid behavior, and the second is *depersonalization*. A paranoid delusion is a factified imagination, a fantasy believed literally. The belief in this literal event, plot, or scheme cannot be shaken by appeal to feelings, by evidence of the senses, or by argument of reason. One who is held by this so-called "false belief" conforms precisely to what religions might call a "true believer," so that the border between fundamentalism in religion and delusional literalism is subtle indeed.[148]

What happens to an image that it becomes immutable and true? What congeals it into a delusion? Memories, dreams, reflections are usually so shadowed with uncertainty: they flicker and resonate in so many different ways. Besides, the anxious intuitions of the lunar night dispel quickly in the morning light. So what indeed happens that lunar

147 Pliny speaks of silver as "a madness of mankind" (*Naturalis Historia*, 33: 31.95). The relations between the moon and "madness" are legion; a footnote in *CW* 14, p. 156 (a page that discusses lunar madness) illuminates this relation: "Not only does Luna cause moon-sickness, she herself is sick or ailing." Lunacy is inherent in the archetypal principle, an infirmity of the archetype itself, and therefore lunacy must be understood on an archetypal (alchemical) level. For a discussion of "archetypal infirmity," see J. Hillman, "Athene, Ananke, and Abnormal Psychology," in *Mythic Figures*, *UE* 6: 31–73.

148 Cf. J. Hillman, *Eranos Lecture 8 – On Paranoia* (Dallas: Spring Publications, 1988), on "Revelation and Delusion."

imagination takes on solar certainty? Let us approach this psychiatric question by means of alchemical language.

Alchemy warns that only separated things can join.[149] Before any two things such as moon and sun can be conjunct or experienced as conjunct, they must be distinguished or else, says alchemy, a *monstrum* is born of a premature conjunction. Any union that does not differentiate its unity into distinct feeling realities is actually a monster. To go through the world seeing its pre-established harmony in synchronistic revelations—that inner and outer are one; that mother is daughter, and daughter, mother; puer is senex, and senex, puer; that nature and spirit, body and mind, are two aspects of the same invisible energy— fuzzes over the acute distinctions joined by these conjunctions. This wisdom, no matter how wondrous, is therefore both premature and monstrous. And by monstrous, alchemy means fruitless, barren, without issue.[150] Whenever we see sameness in two events without at the same instant recognizing their incommensurability, a sterile fusion has occurred, which means that paradox, absurdity, and overt enormity are more characteristic of a true union, than are androgynous wholeness and the harmony of the *unus mundus.*

The alchemical conjunction hears various disparate voices at once. The alchemical conjunction, in short, is metaphorical consciousness; or, it is metaphorical consciousness in short, more like an absurd pun than a bliss of opposites transcended. *Ananda* (bliss) in the joy of a joke: the alchemy books illustrated by grotesque cartoons, ridiculous terms, doing it in the bathtub, exact formulas laced through with metaphors—who said they did not know what they were doing. These monstrosities provide antidotes to the *monstrum,* the principal among which is the delusional unity of the Great Opposites, silver and gold. "The colour of the Sun does not enter into the Moon, nor that of the Moon into the Sun," says Arnold de Villanova.[151] "What is occult in gold is manifest in silver, and what

149 "The ancient philosophers have enumerated several kinds of conjunction, but to avoid a vain prolixity I will affirm, upon the testimony of Marsilius Ficinus, that conjunction is a union of separate qualities." Kelly, "The Theatre of Terrestrial Astronomy," 63.

150 *Lexicon,* 234: "The fruit of an unlawful and accursed copulation. They generate nothing in their turn ... not produced by any honourable means but by the guile of men ... These monstrosities are impotent and useless for breeding purposes ..."

151 *Bonus,* 332.

is manifest in gold is occult in silver," says Rasis.[152] Their union requires that each must be *stubbornly* different. Silver can only rightly join gold when it hides its gold, when it is not colored by the Sun, remaining manifestly silver, loyally itself, an unalloyed seed of its own planet.

We have to look carefully at our notions of conjunction. The conjunction is not a balanced mixture, a composite adding this to that; it is not a blending of substantial differences into a compromise, an arrangement; it is not a symbolic putting together of two halves or two things into a third. As a psychological event it takes place in soul, as a recognition, an insight, an astonishment. It is not the reconciliation of two differences, but the realization that *differences are each images* that do not deny each other, oppose each other, or even require each other. In fact, as differences, they have gone away. The notion of difference itself dissolves into shadings, tonalities, possibilities, implications—the multiple relations that are in the nature of any image. Once the logical category of "difference" gives way to the imaginal "image," then gold and silver can be perceived in the same way, having *the same imaginal nature:* "From these considerations we see clearly how silver and gold are of the same nature," writes Bonus.[153]

A conjunction occurs when the problem of conjunction is no longer our focus. The problem dissolves into metaphor, which is to say that the kind of consciousness that imagines in problems, the tension of opposites, the law of contradiction and paradoxes has itself dissolved into a metaphorical mode of hearing so that there is doublespeak, polysemy, going on everywhere. Each thing is a conjunction when consciousness is metaphorical, and there are no halves or realms to be joined. There are also no overvalued meanings that have to be held and unified by a symbol; metaphorical consciousness does not have to refer an event to a larger realm of meanings for its significance but rather enjoys the allusions that spring from the event. Nor is there anything to be unified since what is there, as an image, is already that which it is.

Here is an example of the difference between symbolic and metaphorical perception: if I say "cross" in an association experiment, your *symbolic* reply might be: suffering, Easter, to bear, mandala, Greek, Lorraine, martyrs, cosmic compass, sun wheel, protection—or any of the

152 Cited by Wyckoff in *Minerals,* 175n.

153 *Bonus,* 260.

meanings of the cross as worldwide symbol. The word "cross" would be deepened by reference to these larger meanings. Your *metaphoric* response might not neglect these, but it would also include: crosspatch, crossed, your fingers, my heart, the street, transgression, court, stitch, tic-tac-toe, and other spontaneous associations arising from the word as sound and image beyond its symbolic meaning. For the symbolic reply, Jung might be your guide; for the metaphoric, Joyce—and these two guides were often at cross purposes.

It is in this metaphorical way that we must read alchemy's hundreds of terms for its major symbols—Mercury, or *materia prima,* or whitening. That is, it is precisely with a whitened mind of metaphorical understanding that alchemy proceeds, dissolving even its own favorite symbols into images—and images that shatter meaning, that are so freakish, so absurd and funny, so vexing that they refuse to stand up as symbols with universal significance. The symbolic reading of alchemy would reverse alchemy's own metaphorical method. It tries to establish definite symbolic meanings, so that in all alchemical psychology, including what I am writing here, we may lose the alchemy in the psychology. Hence the importance of the white earth, which provides an imaginal ground for hermeneutics rather than a symbolic one.

We have had to expose the usual symbolic understanding of the conjunction because it bears on the lunacies we are examining. Lunacy as paranoid behavior begins already when we think symbolically: when the test of the conjunction is the synchronous appearance of an event in two realms of meaning, gold and silver worlds conjoined. Then, I feel a *conjunctio* has been confirmed, meanings appear in multiplication, and I believe myself to be in symbolic reality. But, these very terms—"symbol," "meaning," "two," "synchronous," "unified"—are part of the delusional construct itself. What actually has happened is the concretization of metaphor. We have gone tone deaf in the amplified system of symbolic meaning; we have exchanged metaphorical illusiveness for symbolic delusion. The notion of the symbol indicates, even produces, the *monstrum.* Instead of saying: the *monstrum* is an alchemical symbol, let us now say the symbol is an alchemical *monstrum*.

A proper alloy does not "stutter"—this we saw above. It takes the blows of the hammer because it is relatively malleable (*malleus* = hammer). An alchemical conjunction that is not a *monstrum* holds the distinct images in a loosely federated manner, precise in lines though not fixed in meaning, a malleable sort of consciousness, bending, supple, like the Chinese Tao or a Rabbinical or Sufi story–it could mean this, it could mean that–but always the image remains right under your nose, and its meaning does not congeal into allegory, parable, or symbol.

The test of the amalgamation of silver with gold is not witness of itself in the day world, imagination witnessed in literality, fantasies "coming true." The test is rather standing to the blows of the hammer as silver: that mental and imaginational realities are ungraspable elusives, quick and silver, and yet remain self-same, as they are, permanent as the white firmament in which they are lodged. They can take every sort of pounding (query, analysis, concentration, reproduction, emotional challenge) without coming apart into two interpretive halves, a physical side and a psychic side, a good side and a bad, a female side and a male–or the image and its meaning. "A poem should not mean/but be."[154]

So pound these delusions, therapists! Hammer away at those meaningful coincidences that seem to confirm psychic reality with physical evidence. Make them stutter. Ask what stance of mind requires this sort of literal witness. Don't let the work fall back into cloudy whiteness, taking sweet comfort as "meaning" dawns. Hit meanings with a stick until the images stand clear, by themselves, silver.

Why this urge to meaning just now in the work? Why the need to prove the psychic silver process by means of solid gold? What is this move defending against? "Terror in poems," says Bachelard in *Air and Dreams*. As the volatile becomes fixed and the fixed more volatile (Maria the Jewess), imagination usurps the field–and this lunacy, this *poiesis* is terrifying. The psyche moves from prose to poetry. Bachelard calls it

> a *kind of Copernican revolution of the imagination* ... In fact, images can no longer be understood by their objective *traits*, but by their *subjective* meaning. This revolution amounts to placing:
>
> dream before reality,
> nightmare before event,
> horror before the monster,
> nausea before the fall;
>
> in short, the subject's imagination is vigorous enough to impose

154 The famous last stanza of Archibald MacLeish's "Ars Poetica."

> its visions, its terrors, its unhappiness...it is a reminiscence about a state that comes before life, the state of a life that is *dead*...We could go one step further and put the image not only before thought, before the account of it, but also before all *emotion.* A kind of *nobility of soul* is associated with terror in poems...[that] guarantees the primacy of the imagination forever. It is the imagination that thinks and the imagination that suffers...The dynamic image is a primary reality.[155]

In this revolution we reach back for old structures, attempting to meet the lunacy, the poetic fright of the whitening, by "subjective meanings" in prosaic accounts of thought, narrative and emotion, all the fictions of our case history, desperately in search of a meaning to which we can fix the image, somewhere, anywhere outside the imagination itself. The mere being of the image, the image as a being, without recourse to meaning, psychic reality as such, is too much unless the soul be whitened. Or, shall we say, this poetic fright is one way the necessary blanching can occur. Lunacy, a necessary initiation to *poiesis.*

This brings us again to our first form of lunacy, delusional literalism. When silver conjoins with gold before psychic reality is hardened and cooled, then it easily yields to gold in such a way that the sun dominates and covers over the moon. "The man will dissolve over the woman," as Philalethes says it (*HM* 2:265). Lunar imagining becomes "solified": images reveal themselves as blazing truths, the night-world vision and its fright converted into day-world certainties: "It all makes sense. I see meanings everywhere." Moreover, a surging rectitude seizes the lunar world, attempting to establish its reign by means of solar energy. Fantasy speech becomes delusional declaration; lunacy becomes insanity, paranoia. The psyche can no longer hear its speaking as its own voice. Its silver resonance gilded, it hears only the overt content of its voice as literal statement, the stuttering disguised in positive and clear assertion. We can no longer see through: "Sometimes, too, the glass looks as though it were entirely covered with gold...it is a certain indication that the seed of the man is operating upon the seed of the woman, is ruling it and fixing it," says Paracelsus.[156]

---

155 G. Bachelard, *Air and Dreams: An Essay on the Imagination of Movement,* trans. E.R. and C.F. Farrell (Dallas: The Dallas Institute Publicatins, 2002), 101–2.

156 *Paracelsus,* 1:83.

Psychology may also become one of these stuttering alloys, a gilding of silver that covers over the woman, ruling it and fixing it. Whenever we define soul, declare it to be death or image, experience, reflection, or anima, perspective or metaphor, we are deluded with gold, making declarative statements, blinded by our logos brilliance, covering over psyche with an "ology." Psychology can take the blows of the hammer only if its glass remains backed with silver so that we can reflect as metaphor each of the psyche's "ologies."

"Sow gold in the white foliate earth,"[157] say the instructions. Not over the earth, covering it; but inside the silvered mind; let the sun shine in. Or, let it out: "Gold is hidden in silver and extracted from its womb," says Bonus of Ferrara.[158] The gold reaches the silver from within itself, life emerging from within psychic realities, charging the images with heat and beauty from within themselves. Glow, not gild.

The second lunatic condition psychiatry calls "depersonalization."[159] It can occur in organic psychoses, toxic states and anxiety states, in hysteria and in schizophrenic psychoses, in neurotic phobias, compulsions, and depressions, and also in normals. This symptom cannot be tied specifically to any syndrome; it can come and go or last, and it can happen at any time from puberty to old age. As one of the more universal psychic vicissitudes, it must be recognized as archetypal, therefore having a background in the poetic basis of mind and its fantasy processes to which alchemical psychology directly speaks.

During depersonalization, it is as if myself and world have become irreal and de-souled. Despite a fretful sort of introspection, there is no animation. Everything is as it is, but there is no dimension, no importance. All my functions are intact–sensing, remembering, orienting, thinking–but something primary has gone dead. Apathy, monotony, flatland, the world and my experience of it behind glass, in a vacuum or on another planet. Mechanical. Personal common life, the warmth

157 Cf. von Franz, *Aurora Consurgens*, 384.

158 *Bonus*, 260.

159 Cf. on anima and depersonalization, Hillman, *Re-Visioning Psychology*, 44–46, and *Anima: An Anatomy of a Personified Notion*.

of the sun-baked world and my responses to it, suddenly useless, frozen, formally automatic. A mirror image of the daily; underworld *eidola*; moonlit shadows of substance. Philalethes says (*HM* 2: 265): "The woman has become coagulated over the man."

Let's turn to poetry rather than to medicine for understanding this condition. Wallace Stevens, in "The Man with the Blue Guitar,"[160] describes depersonalization in the language of sun and moon:

> It is the sun that shares our works.
> The moon shares nothing. It is a sea.
>
> When shall I come to say of the sun,
> It is a sea; it shares nothing;
>
> The sun no longer shares our works
> And the earth is alive with creeping men,
>
> Mechanical beetles never quite warm?
> And shall I then stand in the sun, as now
>
> I stand in the moon, and call it good,
> The immaculate, the merciful good,
>
> Detached from us, from things as they are?

Depersonalization reverses the condition of paranoid delusion. There, everything fits together into a deluded sense of meaningful coincidences and subjective importance: everything means me, quite literally. The silver of the soul has been coated over with gold into absolute importance and highest value. All things resonate (silver) with truth (gold); psychic images receive indestructible, ultimate, ontological status. Omnipotence. Here, however, the warm world turns into the great cold sea, sharing nothing. The earth and its works and human bodies become merciless mechanical beetles, never quite warm. Impotence. Everything is as it is, things as they are, coagulated and present, but detached like shades departed from the sunlit world, because, as Stevens says, "I stand in the moon."

In this *monstrum* of gold and silver, the silver dominates the gold, coagulating the day world so that it is sicklied over with a pale cast of mooning, of introspective reflection; stale, flat and unprofitable become the uses of this world. When Luna usurps the Sol's place, the

160 *The Collected Poems of Wallace Stevens*, 168.

solar world remains, but transfigured, as if transported to the moon, the heat gone out of it, gone the *calor inclusus,* which distinguishes the living from the dead. Then we find no values such as mercy and compassion, no caring or wanting (only creeping), no good of any kind because the solar world has been silvered and resonance now means only hollowness. The very danger alchemy warned of, vitrification, has taken place. Glassiness of animation, the world a glass menagerie.

Back to Hegel, back to alchemy. Even should we envision these two basic conditions of lunacy in terms of gold and silver and their relation, must the soul go through these stages? Are overgilding the imagination and overwhitening the warm workaday world not mistakes? Is lunacy necessary; could it not be otherwise? Can't insanity be prevented?

Here, I am wholly with Thomas Szasz: *insanity* can indeed be prevented by one major simple measure—call off the medics who turn lunacy into insanity by the medical model of literalizing: accounting for what happens in the soul in positivistic clinical terms. But—the pathologizing, the lunacy and its "mistakes," cannot be prevented because it is necessary, according to both Hegel and alchemy. The only prevention I can imagine would be an education of the psyche along the lines of an alchemical training, so as to keep the lunacy, but not its clinical literalism. We would learn the metals, the seeds of the gods in our depths, and enter a long apprenticeship to the purpose of their workings. The meaning of the word *prevention,* "to come before" would be our guide: that is, we could prevent the "mistakes" of lunacy by turning to the primordial factors that come before all else and by relating what happens in lunacy to what comes before—not causally in a medical case history, but archetypally to the primordial seeds. Yet even then there is no guarantee; one may succumb to their purposes.

What then are the purposes of the metals, and what is accomplished in the soul by these "mistakes" of silver, such as depersonalization? Perhaps *depersonalization is an activation of the seed of silver,* asserting the impersonal over the personal, detachment over warmth, by whitening and deadening the sun of the shared world. It shows us that we are shades who can stand on the moon at any time and that what is truly real, according to the silver, is not the object and the world or even the gold as such, but the psychic imagining that the silver brings to the gold, that anima resonating factor on which the solar world actually depends for experience of its reality. We are told by this "mistake" that we do not and cannot properly inhabit the common earth until we have sojourned alone on the moon.

Or, take the first condition, the paranoid delusion which we have placed against the background of the "solification" of fantasy. This, too, can be accepted as a purposive, necessary moment. These literalistic delusions are attempts by the sun to seduce lunar fantasy into the world of persons and things. The intention in the seed of gold is to turn the psychological faith of the silvered dove into living conviction, giving width and connectedness to the moony reflections that by themselves remain unshared and private.

A paranoid delusion—a plot against me or a cosmic revelation or a jealousy obsession—each involves, as Freud first pointed out, an erotic component, indeed, a homoerotic component, a moment of libidinal connectedness with sames. Here is the gold attempting its conjunction with silver, *as if it were gold,* the sun mounting upon and covering the body of the moon as if silver were the same as gold. An archetypal or alchemical therapy will approach paranoid delusion as a *gold*-silver *monstrum,* seeing there the sun's desire to unite with the moon's fantasy and bring it into the common world. And this therapy will approach depersonalization as a *silver*-gold *monstrum,* seeing there the moon insinuating its importance by whitening and deadening the sun.

Our approach attempts to prevent insanity by recourse to lunacy, where lunacy is understood as the first appearance of the white earth in the solar world, the first recognition of psychic, imaginal reality, yet still couched in that notion of reality given by solar definitions. Solar consciousness responds to the white earth in a solar style: the response of Apollonic medicine, so that in its clear eyes lunacy must be insanity. The medical response serves only to fix the white earth into a solar literalism, furthering the wrong conjunction and creating that monstrum called the psychiatric case.

Our task lies neither in curing what is called lunacy nor even in using the term in the old and common sense of moon-mad, passing strange, out of one's mind, deluded. Rather our task—and by *our* I mean everyone engaged in soul, not merely professional specialists—is the recognition of moon moments, of silver states, so that they can be understood as phenomena of the white earth and reverted (*epistrophé*) to it. Then we can see these conditions as inherent to, purposeful and intentional, and necessarily appropriate in the work of the soul's silvering.

The medical model is a theology, according to Szasz. It is indeed a model that represses the gods as images and serves them as diseases. Lunacy becomes insanity, a secular diagnosis that no longer echoes Luna. The myths have been driven out only to return as the myth of mental illness. Szasz is right to insist that the problem of mental illness and mental health, and therapy, too, is myth. We need a polytheistic theology, old in the manner of Vico or new in the manner of David L. Miller,[161] new *logoi* to hold the *theoi* and give them articulation, each in his and her own form.

This long essay has been working at one example, a principal one, reverting lunacy to its metallic seed and planetary principle so that we can understand lunatic processes as whitening of the psychic body and silvering of soul. This example implies that there might be other planetary modes of pathologizing, such as leadenness, mercurialness, martial ironing, manic sulfurism (that we today call "ego") and so on. A psychopathology might better be derived from the principals of the heavens and their seeds in the earth, from the elements and the myths, a psychopathology which starts in the white earth of the imagination where the mind itself begins, than deriving psychopathology from secular behavioral categories. This archetypal psychopathology returns the conditions we suffer to their authentic home in cosmic and divine events. For if we are created in divine images, so, too, are our afflictions. Archetypal psychopathology gives credit to these events, where credit means faith in them as bearing transpersonal seeds that will out through our individual lives. What's more—and last—this mode of psychopathology, which considers silver the prime ingredient and necessary origin of psychological thinking, turns to those smiths of silver—the poets—as physicians and musicians of the soul.

161 D.L. Miller, *The New Polytheism: Rebirth of the Gods and Goddesses* (Dallas: Spring Publications, 1981).

Postscript

This essay was originally drafted to be delivered at a conference in Niagara Falls, N.Y., in January 1979, held by the Analytical Psychology Club of Eastern New York and chaired by Paul Kugler. The conference brought together Charles Boer, Robert Creeley, Rafael López-Pedraza, David Miller, and Thomas Szasz. Its theme was "The Lunatic, the Lover, and the Poet." The conference allowed the speakers to play upon these three parts and to show their commonality. It offered me the occasion to elaborate the poetic basis of mind (a major theme since the 1972 Terry Lectures)[162] and to expose my lunatic penchant toward re-forming clinical language so that it speaks to clinical conditions in their own tongue. Our tongues must become silvered; to reach souls on the dark side of the moon, we must talk from the *viśuddha*. A poetic basis of mind implies that a psychology truly representing mind will have to find its way into poetic speech—a task that may not be left only to poets anymore than the tasks of lunacy be left only to the insane.

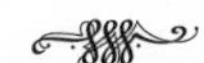

162 Hillman, *Re-Visioning Psychology*, xvii.

7

The Yellowing of the Work

A statement of Jung's in *Psychology and Alchemy* launches this chapter on its course. Jung wrote:

> Four stages [of the alchemical opus] are distinguished, characterized by the original colors mentioned in Heraclitus: *melanosis* (blackening), *leukosis* (whitening), *xanthosis* (yellowing), and *iosis* (reddening... Later, about the fifteenth or sixteenth century, the colors were reduced to three, and the *xanthosis,* otherwise called the *citrinitas,* gradually fell into disuse or was but seldom mentioned... There were only three colors: black, white, and red.
>
> The first main goal of the process... highly prized by many alchemists... is the silver or moon condition, which has still to be raised to the sun condition. The *albedo* [whitening] is, so to speak, the daybreak, but not till the *rubedo* is it sunrise. The transition to the *rubedo* is formed by the *citrinitas* [yellowing], though this, as we have said, was omitted later.[1]

Some questions arise from Jung's statements: What is the nature of the omitted yellow? What are the specific qualitative consequences of this omission beyond the ominous reversion from a fourfold symbolic system to a trinitarian one? Since the color yellow continues to appear in the material of contemporary alchemy—analytical work, as an opus of imaginative sophistication—can this work shed light on the nature of yellow? Can a more precise understanding of the alchemical yellowing shed light on our analytical practices?

Because the alchemical craft supposedly developed from hand workers' arts of metallurgy, embalming, jewelry, shamanistic medicine, cosmetics, and cloth-dying, the alchemical mind perceived changes in color

---

1 *CW* 12: 333–34.

in the material at hand to be changes of essential nature. A bit of iron changes color when fired and when cooling. Red iron is malleable; black iron, rigid. A cotton cloth dipped in a blue tint irreversibly alters its plain white state. Dyeing, as bathing or dipping—the Greek word is *baptizein*—affects essence. The unbleached muslin now colored blue has been baptized; its soul has been changed. A gilded statuette was considered more precious than one of solid gold because the gilded piece signified the transmutation of a baser metal to a golden state. Gilding indicates an *opus contra naturam,* while the sheerly gold is merely nature.

Our usual view of colors is derived from Western philosophy. For example, Newton, Locke, Berkeley and Kant considered colors to be not inherent in things but secondary qualities effected by light upon our subjective eyesight. Conflicting with this view is the earlier and alchemical proposition that change of color reveals change of essence. This earlier proposition corresponds with the way we actually live in the world. Colors of the sky, sea, sunset portend the coming storm. As a fruit sweetens on the stem, its color changes. As a patient sickens, we see pallor, jaundiced skin, cyanotic lips, brown urine, empurpled nose, raspberry tongue, red rashes, white exudates, black stools. The human eye's ability to distinguish 20,000 varieties of hue helps us read the inherent intelligibility of the world.

Yellow signifies a particular kind of change—usually for the worse: withering leaves, aging pages, and long-stored linen, old teeth and toenails, liver spots, peeling skin, indelible stains of food and semen. The process of time shows as a yellowing. The alchemists spoke of it as "putrefaction" and "corruption."

English and American common speech continues to use yellow in a manner that is, as the *Oxford English Dictionary* says, "often disparaging." Cowardice is yellow; so is jealousy. A yellow dog is craven, and a canary informs on friends. The yellow press and a yellow-back novel are cheap and lurid. The yellow star pinned on Jews reflects the jaundiced eye of prejudice.[2] The "yellow peril" raised, in Americans, engulfing fears of Asians. The yellow flag of quarantine is the international sign for dangerously contagious disease. The Spanish *amarillo* relates to the bitterness of bile and the Hebrew *yerek* derives from *yarak,* to spit.

---

2 The omitted fourth (yellow) in the Nazi trinity of red, black, and white becomes the rejected Other (Jews).

Yet yellow has a host of cheerfully sunny implications, from the etymological link of "yellow" with "yolk" to the metaphorical association with ripening grains, spring flowers, honey, sunlight, and the apotropaic use of lemons to ward off death. The German *gelb* and the Latin *galbus* and *galbinus* derive from roots meaning radiant and shining, like gold; so the Homeric Achilles and Apollo are yellow-haired, blond, fair, and sunlit. In addition, the most luminous of all hues (least saturated) is yellow and the yellow spot in the middle of the retina is where vision is most acute.

Thus, it would be easy to neglect Freud's insight into the contrary meanings inherent in the basic terms of language, and instead to look at yellow via Jung's lens of opposites. Then we would oppose yellow with purple as in our kindergarten color wheels, or with blue as did Goethe, or with green as did Jung himself in opposing yellow, for intuition, with green for sensation.[3] But definition by opposition restricts the meaning of a phenomenon to that face to which it is opposed. If purple is mysterious, then yellow must be crass and blatant. If green is growth and concrete nature, then yellow must be mental and loftily abstract. If blue is cold, withdrawn, deep, and sober, then yellow must be hot, active, shallow, and crazy.

The opinion that yellow is crazy floats through the arts. It was Edgar Allan Poe's favorite color, as well as Van Gogh's—leading Ellis[4] and Birren[5] to state that yellow frequently appeals to troubled minds. Kandinsky wrote that yellow "may be paralleled in human nature, with madness,... with violent, raving lunacy."[6]

The lens of opposites tends to ignore the context in which a yellow appears, its precise hue, and the words that describe it (butter, lemon, primrose, sulfur, gold, chrome, cadmium, mustard, amber, straw, etc.), its relation with other hues in the same image, and the personal myths perceived in the experience. For Van Gogh, for instance, yellow was the color of love, as it was in Gauguin's painting *The Yellow Christ* (1889). For Kandinsky, yellow was aggressive, trumpet-like, acidic, eccentric. I draw

3 *CW*9.1:582 and 588n.

4 H. Ellis, "The Colour Sense in Literature," *Contemporary Review* LXIX (1896).

5 F. Birren, *Color in Your World* (New York: Collier Books, 1962).

6 W. Kandinsky, *Concerning the Spiritual in Art*, trans. M.T.H. Sadler (New York: Dover, 1977), 38.

your attention also to the fearless, brilliant, triumphantly luxurious joy of the yellows in the old-age paintings by the French painters Rouault and Bonnard. Thus it is not easy to become clear regarding even this, the clearest of all colors. The most we gain by imagining in terms of opposites is seeing clearly a divine, goldlike, incorruptible yellow on the one hand and on the other, corruption and decay.

Here I need to intersperse some supposed facts from anthropological research. By compiling lists of the words for different colors from languages the world over, Berlin and Kay[7] state the following conclusions: all languages have terms for bright and dark, that is, white and black; if a language has a third color term, it is always red; if a fourth term, yellow or green; and if a fifth, either green or yellow. If we imagine colors along a scale from simple to sophisticated, then yellow-green—the hue the Greeks called *chloris*—becomes the essential bridge between black-white-red and the color terms that follow: blue, brown, purple, pink, orange, and gray; in that order, more or less universally.

Newton's chromatic prism, curiously, locates green-yellow in the center of its spectrum and da Vinci's six primary colors (black, white, red, yellow, green, blue) also give yellow a median position. Today the green-yellow of *chloris*, which for the Greeks described the earth goddess Demeter, reappears in English electrical wiring where a spiraling green and yellow insulation signifies the grounding or earth line, neither positive nor negative.

It is well to bear in mind this median position, allowing yellow to remain indicative of both Apollo's sunny brightness and the green of Demeter, *chloris* never definitely restricted to singleness. *Citrinatis* and *xanthos* in alchemy's texts and commentators tend to present yellow's more favorably "sunny" side as the nominative noun "yellow," and the other side as the gerund (*-ing*) or verbal noun referring to staining and decay.

To draw a first conclusion: neither by translating yellow into a symbolic meaning nor by dividing it into positive and negative poles can we uncover its significance for an alchemical psychology. Rather, we must

7 B. Berlin and P. Kay, *Color Terms: Their Universality and Evolution* (Berkeley: University of California Press, 1969).

find answers to our questions within the context of alchemical relations in which yellow appears as a specific transitional quality in a temporal process. (See below, "Postscript: The Missing Yellow.")

An Excursion on Sulfur

In the often-quoted passage from Maria the Jewess (Maria Hebræa) to whom is attributed one of the earliest alchemical formulations of the transitions in the process, we find this sentence: "When one yellows, three becomes four, for one yellows with yellow sulfur."[8] Albertus Magnus says, "The yellow color in metals is caused by sulfur, which colors them."[9]

Another name for sulfur is *hudor theion,* Holy Water, because of its vivifying power in bringing about substantive change. These changes are intensely sensate, as when raw sulfur heated with lime results in calcium sulfide, which, when added to water, results in the gas hydrogen sulfide. Hydrogen sulfide–spirit of sulfur–stinks. By introducing this gas into solutions of a variety of metals, various colors appear also on the surface of metals. The alchemical mind regards these changes perceived by the nose and eye as evidence of the dictum "By means of rot essential change takes place." The organic process of putrefaction is fortified by sulfur. Sulfur hastens nature toward its decay and thus toward its next season. Thus, when things stink, when they yellow with decay, something important is going on, and what is going on is sulfuric.

Since the texts so often warn that the sulfur of which they speak is a "sophic" material and not your common or vulgar sulfur (despite the fact that the texts also specifically refer to a yellow material mined and

8 A.J. Hopkins, *Alchemy: Child of Greek Philosophy* (New York: Columbia University Press, 1934), 99. Zosimos (ca. 300 CE), "the first Greek alchemical writer whose actual writings have survived" (R. Patai, *The Jewish Alchemists* [Princeton, N.J.: Princeton University Press, 1994, 60), entitled one of his treatises "The Standard of Yellow Dyeing." The role of yellow can be attested to even further back, for Zosimos refers to the Maza of Moses," a metallurgical work purportedly coming from Maria the Jewess and a possible school of Jewish alchemists prior to Zosimos (J.G. Gager, Moses in Greco-Roman Paganism [Nashville: Abingdon Press, 1972], 154–55). On Maria Hebræa, and the color yellow in Jewish mysticism in general, see also G. Scholem, *Alchemy and Kabbalah,* trans. K. Ottmann (Putnam, Conn.: Spring Publications, 2008).

9 *Minerals,* 193.

refined in definite geographical locations), we need to translate the term "sophic" into "metaphoric" or "psychic." We are speaking, therefore, of psychic change, which appears as "something going wrong," and going wrong in two particular ways. First, when things corrupt, rot, decay; second, when they become physically hyperactive because sulfur is defined as the principle of "combustibility"—flaring up, "easily kindled to violence or passion" (*Oxford English Dictionary*), "tumult" (*Random House Dictionary*). "It hinders perfection in all its works"[10] because sulfur hinders sublimation. Sublimation, as Ruland's 1612 alchemical dictionary says, "is effected by means of Distance."[11] Yellowing caused by sulfur therefore impedes detachment and distancing.

"Sophic" best translates as "not natural"—sulfur mediated by *sophia*, sulfur sophisticated by an imagination and craft of *anima*, sulfur as having an esthetic and reflective interiority beyond its crude compulsion. Sendivogius (1566–1636) gives a hint of this hidden potential within sulfur in his parable of wounded sulfur bleeding as "pure milk-white water."[12] Within my choleric greed for the fatness of life, my desirous reach into the world—what analysis long condemns as manic defense, projective identification, and acting-out—there lies an *anima*, a soul significance. Sensationalism, consumerism, and compulsions have other than common or vulgar significance. They have a *suksma* aspect, a sophic interiority beyond sheerly appetitive goals. This interior intention disguises itself in the vivid object of desire, but sulfur's desire is its own true intention, that leonine heat, that "earthy feculence"[13] without which the opus has no life and the *lapis* cannot redden. In each hunger there lies the whiteness of anima, which is revealed in the wounds suffered by sulfur.

Similarly, when things go wrong as rot—my job stinks, my marriage stinks, this analysis stinks, I stink—this stench signifies sulfur making changes. These changes, however, do not have to appear as the result of a process, as a clearer reflective consciousness *after* the putrefaction. The feeling of putrefaction is itself an awareness; feeling bad and wrong is already sulfur experiencing its own wound.

10 *CW* 14:138.

11 *Lexicon*, s.v. "Sublimation."

12 M. Sendivogius, "The New Chemical Light Drawn from the Fountain of Nature and of Manual Experience to which is added a Treatise Concerning Sulfur," *HM* 2.

13 *CW* 14:138.

To say it again: combustion and decay are the two ways sulfur sophisticates. Sulfur becomes aware of itself cholerically, violently. Hence, some alchemists said sulfur could not be worked with until it had first been calcined, that is, had been dried of its moisture or abstracted from its propensity for emotional attachment.[14] They were afraid of its eruptive inflammability. We, too, are afraid, most of us still enchanted by Anna Freud's dictum that the patient who acts out cannot be analyzed; most us are afraid of an analysis going wrong, beginning to stink. Jung devoted a chapter to sulfur in *Mysterium Coniunctionis:* not many pages, but wondrously condensed information and interpretation. He considered sulfur to be the active principle in the opus and thus of human life. He equated sulfur with what psychology calls the motive factor: on the one hand, the conscious will; on the other, unconscious compulsion.

The extreme language to which alchemy resorts to describe sulfur indicates to Jung that sulfur has affinities with the Devil—as corrupter and compeller—and with Christ, giver of warmth and life. In either direction, Devil or Christ, sulfur is usually imagined as male, hot, of an obdurate earthly body, fat and oily, desirous as a dragon or lion. Though it is the urgent agent of change, sulfur at the same time resists not only sublimation, but is that very component of the psyche, as Jung said, "responsible for our resistance to psychology in general."[15]

The innate *extraversum*[16] or turning outward of sulfur (despite its milk-white interior) corresponds with the place of yellow in Japanese medical color symbolism, where yellow and red are outside; black and white, inside. According to this four-color set, black is inside and cold; white, inside and chill or tepid; yellow is outside and warm; red, outside and hot. The transition then, from white to yellow would show both as an increase in warmth and a conversion from inside to outside.

Warm and outside: like the games we played as children, where clues to the hidden are given by temperature. The closer you get, the warmer

14 A man in analysis dreams that someone like his analyst is playfully handing out yellow paper napkins, trying to get him and his group to buy them as memorial tokens of their years in the group. Possibly, the drying is also accomplished by a more pleasurable, less *nigredo*-like attitude to remembrances, perhaps by using paper for absorbing experiences.

15 *CW* 14:152.

16 Ibid., 134.

you are, as if drawn outward and toward the object by its *calor inclusus*, its innate sulfur, that hidden warmth concealed in the world.

"Outside"—that is our clue for the relation between the yellowing and sulfur. "In what substance is this Sulfur to be found?" asks Sendivogius's Alchemist. "In all substances," is the reply. "All things in the world—metals, herbs, trees, animals, stones, are its ore."[17] Outside: wherever interest is kindled, wherever the active attention (or what Freud named "object libido") turns away from itself to things, things lighting up to be consumed. The "I" is called forth by its counterpart, the sulfuric element in the world, which calls the soul from the chill lunar reflection of the *albedo* into a combustible fusion with the warm-bodied objects of desire. As things light up and catch fire, we get burned by the sulfur lurking in each tree, lurking from behind every stone, like the Devil tempting us into the body of the world.

Between White and Red

So far we have been explicating yellow *per se*. Our main concern, however, is with yellow*ing* as transitional process in which something is yellowed. The "something" yellowed is the *albedo*, that lunar style of consciousness, when the *anima* or soul infuses the work with its whiteness.

This *albedo* whiteness, achieved after the soul's long exile in *nigredo*, must be distinguished from the primary white of the *materia prima*, the *candida* of unmarked and unremarking innocence. In alchemy, *albedo* refers to both a complete separation and a complete conjunction: the separation between sulfur (concrete urgency) and mercury (psychic fusibility and intellectual volatility). Life of mind and life of the body can be kept distinct, even go their separate ways. The conjunction occurs in mind, in the *unio mentalis* of soul and spirit (as elaborated below, in Chapter 10, "Alchemical Blue and the *Unio Mentalis*"). In both conditions—separation of sulfur and mercury, and conjunction of soul and spirit—the absent component is the solar power of sophic sulfur, which gives body to the clarified mind and is necessary for the *rubedo*.

In analysis, this whiteness refers to feelings of positive syntonic transference, of things going easily and smoothly, a gentle, sweet safety in

17 Sendivogius, "The New Chemical Light Drawn."

the vessel, insights rising, synchronistic connections, resonances and echoes, the dead alive on the moon as ancestors who speak with internal voices of the activated imagination—all leading to the invulnerable conviction of the primacy of psychic reality as another world apart from this world, life lived in psychological faith. In this tepid and shadowless lunar light, everything seems to fit. As Jung said,[18] this is the first main goal of the process and some alchemists were satisfied to stop here, bringing the opus to rest in silvery peace.

This condition does not want more light, more heat. Like the lyric cry of the lunatic, the lover, or the poet, it asks for asylum, poetic reveries, and love. "One night of love"—a forever lunar night that would be spoiled by dawn. Petrarch provides a classical example of the anima's song:

> *Con lei foss'io da che si parte il sole*
> *et non ci vedess' altri che le stelle,*
> *sol una notte et mai non fosse l'alba*
>
> Might I be with her from when the sun departs
> and no other see us but the stars,
> just one night, and let the dawn never come![19]

Having absorbed and unified all hues into the one white, the mirror of silvered subjectivity expands to reflect all things at the expense of differentiation of itself. It takes something outside subjectivity to see into oneself. Hence Jung's insistence on "the other" for individuation. This other, however, does not have to be confined to the other person in the analytic situation. Rather, "the other" refers to anywhere that the different appears, anything outside subjective reflection, any moment that intrudes upon white consciousness's love of its own lunar illumination, which is precisely where its blindness lies.

As Figulus says, "Matter, when brought to whiteness, refuses to be corrupted."[20] The white refuses to be yellowed. It seems a spoiling. Yellowing rots the perfection. White is cool, self-content; yellow is hot, smelly, earthy, male, active. To use an alchemical simile, the yellowing

---

18 *CW* 14: 388.

19 Poem 22, in *Petrarch's Lyric Poems: The* Rime sparse *and Other Lyrics,* trans. R.M. Durling (Cambridge, Mass.: Harvard University Press, 1976), 58–59.

20 *Figulus*, 287.

of the white is like milk becoming cheese. The white coagulates, takes on body, flavor, fatness. White resists this physical substantiation, for it feels like a regression to the vulgar drivenness of earlier moments in the work—*materia prima* and *nigredo*—which the arduous hours of analytic reflection have finally sophisticated and pacified.

Yet Figulus also says that whiteness remains imperfect unless it be brought by heat to highest redness and, in fact, remains "dead" until that occurs.[21] Other authors agree that the yellowing brings life, calling the yellowing a "resurrection." "*Citrinatio est resuscitatio*" (Johnson's *Dictionary*). To achieve this resuscitation, as another treatise says, the artifex "goes on increasing his fire till it assumes a yellow, then an orange or a citron colour."[22] The increasing yellow is imagined as growing within the belly of the white, its lunar mother and, as Hopkins says, "It was not only silvery on the outside, but was yellow on the inside ... 'At the same time you whiten on the outside, you yellow on the inside.'"[23]

Clearly then, the yellowing is more than a spoiling of the white. It is also its brighter, more vivifying illumination, a richer, more expansive clarity. This clarification is particularly intellectual. The sixteenth-century alchemical writer Gerhard Dorn, on whom Jung relied for many insights, made this explicit: "The form, which is the intellect, is the beginning, middle and end of the procedure; and this form is made clear by the saffron color."[24] This should come as no surprise. Since the yellowing operates upon the *unio mentalis*, it would have to be a transmutation of the mind, a change in intellect. "Birds play a prominent part in the *citrinitas*."[25] A mental analysis of *citrinato* will be looking through a white glass only. It will see coloring or discoloring of the albedo harmony, but not fattening, not warming, as if these qualifications of mind do not belong to the province of thinking. In other words, the yellowed mind cannot be captured by whitened reflection.

21 Ibid., 264.

22 *Collectanea Chemica: Being Certain Select Treatises on Alchemy and Hermetic Medicine*, ed. A.E. Waite (London: J. Elliot and Co., 1893), 116. See also *Figulus*, 143.

23 Hopkins, *Alchemy*, 96.

24 *CW* 12: 366.

25 J. Fabricius, *Alchemy: The Medieval Alchemists and their Royal Art* (Copenhagen: Rosenkilde & Bagger, 1976), 146.

"The growing light of solar illumination helps [one] discern more clearly the imperfections of the lunar sphere."[26] Therefore, one may expect a growing, though hidden, critical discernment of analyzing itself; for "yellow observes whiteness."[27] The yellow flowers of celandine (*chelidonium maius*) mentioned by Dorn at this juncture of the transition become a "precious ingredient" because celandine "cures eye disease and is particularly good for night blindness."[28] Paracelsus gives similar prominence to the *cheyri* or four-petaled yellow wallflower, both an abortive (out of the belly) and a restorative (*resuscitatio*).[29] "When the *citrinitas* (*xanthosis*, "yellowing") appears, there is formed the collyrium (eyewash) of the philosophers."[30] Many eyes appear in the *cauda pavonis*, and these peacocks' tails are yellow, heralding a new yellow ground of seeing. Where white unifies all colors[31] into a monotheism of subjective reflection, the yellow clarification is also a dawning of multiple vision, seeing each thing as it is, beyond subjectivity, and thus bridging to the *rubedo*'s sanguine tincturing of the world out there.

The intellect, too, goes through changes; not only the heart, the body and the imagination. "Thinking and being are the same" according to Parmenides (fr. B3, 17–18), a position shared by Gnostics and Zen teachers as well as alchemists. Alchemy (and analysis) clarifies the mind and sophisticates its thought since thought derives from psyche. During early phases of the work alchemy speaks of clouds, haze and fog, of the *massa confusa*, of white smoke, metaphors equally viable for the mind at beginning moments in analysis–and beginning moments occur not only at the literal beginning. They recur all through the work.

The mind in *nigredo* shows characteristics of downward and backward thinking, an intellect caught in reductive and depressive reasonings and figurings out: past history, materialized fantasies, and concretistic explanations, coupled with a bitterly stubborn protest against its condition. The *nigredo* psyche knows itself as victimized, traumatized, dependent, and limited by circumstantiality and substantiality. The

26 Ibid., 143.

27 S. Klossowski de Rola, *The Golden Game: Alchemical Engravings of the Seventh Century* (New York: George Braziller, 1988), 51.

28 *CW* 14:687.

29 *CW* 13:171.

30 *CW* 9.2:195.

31 *CW* 14:388.

nigredo psyche is *eo ipso* substance-abused. The mind in *albedo* more likely dreams. Receptive, impressionable, imagistic, self-reflective and perhaps comfortably magical. "But in this state of 'whiteness' one does not *live*...it is a sort of abstract, ideal state," as Jung states. No problems, except the vast generalized abstractions of spirit—for spirit and soul are indistinctly unified.

Dorn's intellectual account of the yellowing as an aurora of the moon becoming sun does not describe adequately the nature of the yellowed intellect. It is not the continued expansion of white consciousness, an increase of reflective capacity. It is more than aware, more than enlightened. It must be hot and male, beginning with the light yellow or dirty yellow-brown of Mars[32] and even putrid, if it is to spring the mirrored prison of reflection. Since sulfur with all its corruption, intensity, and feculence has been instrumental in its change, this mind "burns" with its own bitter bile, yellow *choler.*[33] In sum: during *nigredo* there is pain and ignorance; we suffer without the help of knowledge. During *albedo* the pain lifts, having been blessed by reflection and understanding. The yellow brings the pain of knowledge itself. The soul suffers its own understanding.

"The yellowing phase in Senior is expressed by an arch of armed eagles...[which] adds yet another image to the cutting swords, splitting arrows, cleaving serpents, and piercing rays of the *citrinitas.*"[34] Brighter, more coagulated and more combustible, the yellowed intellect is complicated with emotions, as one is indeed acutely aware and alive when in the grips of jealousy, cowardice, fear, prejudice, aging, or decay. It is like an instinctual smoky light shining through reflections from within, thought jaundiced with prejudice, fear, envy, the mind like a smoldering yellow effusion staining with intellect whatever it meets. "The yellowness of the sulfur has brought out all the hidden yellow of the metal and changed it into a kind of gold in which yellow was abundant and overflowing."[35]

---

32 Fabricius, *Alchemy,* 147.

33 *Saturn and Melancholy: Studies in the History of Natural Philosophy, Religion and Art,* ed. R. Klibansky, E. Panofsky, and F. Saxl (London: Thomas Nelson & Sons, 1964), 53.

34 Fabricius, *Alchemy,* 147.

35 Hopkins, *Alchemy,* 97.

This is not the usual intellect, dried with concepts, abstracted, pulled away; this is the fat intellect, physical, concrete, emotional, fermenting with instinctual interiority, an unctuous passion. Having first been whitened, its desire is not simple and driven, but desire aware of itself through intellectual fervor—an *intellectus agens*—dawnings of the winged mind, sure as gold. No longer that separation between mercury and sulfur, between fantasy flights and dense emotional body. In the carcass of the lion[36] a new sweetness, thick and yellow and sticking to all things, like honey, like oil, flowing like wax and gilding as it touches. One's nature goes through a temperamental turn, a change in humors from choleric to sanguine, which the dictionary defines as confident, optimistic, cheerful. So does *citrinitas* become the reddening.

Here, the yellowness of sulfur brings the riches of jovial, solar blessings. Ficino, describing the traditions of amulets and graven or painted images depicting states of the soul, writes:

> For longevity and a happy life, they made an image of Jove on a clear or white stone. It was a man sitting above an eagle or a snake, crowned, in the hour of Jove, when he is in exaltation happily ascending, wearing yellow clothes ... For curing diseases they crafted an image of the Sun in gold ... an image of the king on his throne, with yellow clothes ... For happiness and strength of body, the image of Venus as a little girl ... wearing yellow and white.[37]

About the red only this: Whatever its many names and equations, it indicates the inseparability of visible and invisible, psyche and cosmos, a *unus mundus*. It requires the most intense heat: "The spirit is heat."[38] The operations coincident to the reddening are exaltation, multiplication, and projection, according to the fifteenth-century English alchemist George Ripley. These expansions together perform the tincturing, staining all things as the sun shines everywhere. The image of the King

---

36 The reference is to the story of Samson (Judges 14:5–9) who killed a lion and recovered from its carcass a hive brimming with honey—a story traditionally used to tell of the hidden potential within sulfur. The exultation of the alchemical lion appears in Libavius's image (*CW* 5:287), and the lion appears in Jung's detailed case, in the same volume (276), following images of yellow balls and yellow light (266, 270).

37 M. Ficino, *The Book of Life*, trans. C. Boer (Putnam, Conn.: Spring Publications, 1994), 146–47.

38 *Figulus*, 287.

dominates. The King as a political figure redresses the balance of the introverted process that has led to his crowning, now toward the *polis*, the city on earth.

The *rubedo* as a purple-red is also called in Greek terms the *iosis*, which means poisoning. It would seem that the *rubedo* deconstructs the very matter from which the King arises. "All corruption of matter is marked by deadly poison."[39] The Ouroboros, which can also indicate the *rubedo*, at this red juncture signifies a final dissolution of sunlit consciousness and all distinctions—all the stages, phases, operations, and colors. It is a moment of the *rotatio*, a turning and turning like the cosmos itself, requiring endless numbers of eyes to see with, like the King seeing and being seen by each one in the realm. The work is over; we no longer work at consciousness, develop ourselves, or possess a distinct grid by means of which we recognize where we are, how we are, maybe even who we are. "The dissolution of Sol should be effected by Nature, not by handiwork," concludes Figulus.[40] Psyche is life; life, psyche.

Psyche is also death, an equation investigated in my writings on the Underworld. The "death" in this moment of the alchemical work is the "dissolution of Sol," which occurs "by Nature," as if a homeostatic self-correction of solar optimism. This process is similar to the insidious dark strength of Yin afflicting bright Yang from within. The sure optimism of solar clarity is the blind spot itself. Sol dissolves in the darkness of its own light. Or, to put it another way: yellow at this moment is nothing other than the visible presence of the black in its depth.[41]

Albrecht Dürer as witness to the black-in-yellow. In keeping with his unsurpassed commitment to melancholia (the nigredo affliction of black bile), Dürer drew himself naked to the pelvis, extended index finger pointing to a yellow spot just below the rib cage as focus of his pain. Above the self-portrait is the handwritten phrase: "Do wo der gelb fleck ist und mit dem finger drauff deut, do ist mir we."[42] (There, where the yellow spot is, to where I point with my finger, there it hurts.)

39 Ibid.

40 Ibid., 296.

41 Cf. G. Bachelard, *Earth and Reveries of Will: An Essay on the Imagination of Matter*, trans. K. Haltman (Dallas Institute Publications, 2002), 308.

42 The pen and watercolor, half-length self-portrait is in the collection of the Kunsthalle Bremen, Germany. It is reproduced, with commentary, in *Saturn and Melancholy*, fig. 145.

Another witness: Proust's character, the art critic Bergotte, in ill health and ordered to rest, nonetheless is compelled to seek out a painting by Vermeer with its remarkable "little patch of wall so beautifully painted in yellow." Overcome by dizziness while climbing the first steps towards the gallery, Bergotte quickly submerges the weakness by the thought of "sunshine." As he falters, he repeats to himself as if an incantation "Little patch of yellow wall, with a sloping roof, little patch of yellow wall." "Meanwhile he sank down on a circular settee... and reverting to his natural optimism, told himself: 'It's nothing, merely a touch of indigestion from those potatoes, which were undercooked." A fresh attack struck him down; he rolled from the settee to the floor... He was dead."[43]

A Case

Turning now to a case for further amplification and using alchemy as grid for conceiving the psychology of analysis, I confess myself a Jungian rather than of another school that relies on other basic metaphors such as infancy, typology, chronological development, mythical gods, diagnoses, transference. I take Jung seriously, even literalistically, when he claims that alchemical metaphors best provide understanding for what the psyche goes through in deep, long-term analysis. I also confess myself a Jungian by introducing a case as further amplification of the metaphors and figures: "Instead of deriving these figures from our psychic conditions, [we] must derive our psychic conditions from these figures."[44]

The analysand: a woman in her forties, professional, married though not closely, childless, intensely introverted, yet adapted. After a second bout of analysis lasting two years, she was required to return to her home country on a fixed date. Although she often had dreamt of colors, at this juncture with the departure date firm in our calendars, her dreams began to yellow, as follows and in brief:

January 18: A cat dozing on and off; yellow and white stripes.
January 20: Yellow cloth with letters on it.

---

43 M. Proust, "The Captive," in *Remembrance of Things Past,* vol. 3, trans. C.K.S. Moncrieff, T. Kilmartin, and A. Mayor (New York: Vintage Books, 1982), 185–86.
44 *CW*13:299.

January 24: White lustrous letters.
January 24: Yellow legal-size note-pads.
January 27: "I remember I had a baby; baby is wrapped in a yellow robe."
January 27: A yellow book opened to where it says, "end Chapter One; beginning Chapter Two."
January 28: Big eye on the wall. Eye looking through a hole in a curtain. "I said the word 'origin' in English."[45]
February 1: Big rooster, Black, "but some part had a different color."
February 2: "It became daylight."
Later in February: Bright light even with eyeshades (dark glasses).

Themes in this material correspond with the *citrinitas:* alternating yellow and white in the striped cat's dozing on and off; the logos clarifications in letters, words and books; eyesight; awakening; daylight; new life. The yellowing of her dreams also corresponds with the phases of the analysis itself: ending to return to her obligations in the world.

Hers had been a very white analysis: two or three times a week; many dreams each session which she worked on assiduously; hours of solitude; reading, reflection, reverie, imagination, memory, nature; few relationships; eating alone; isolation owing to language difficulties; feelings and fantasies focused on the analysis and on me, the analyst. Now she was planning her work for the next months at home: arranging schedules, letters and phone calls, parting ceremonies, shopping, and imagining further activities such as dancing, cooking, friends, and translating.

She suggested translating one of my books into her language. Then, we found a white interpretation for this suggestion. We understood translation as a way of remaining in the work by maintaining the relationship, abstract and distanced as exigencies had decreed.

Since then, I see that this turn to words in her dreams and plans accords with the yellowing, not only as solar clarification described in the "Ninth Key" of *The Golden Tripod,*[46] where "Grammar, bearing a yellow banner" precedes the Sun in the parade of planets and the virtues and arts associated with them. Dorn's emphasis on the activation of intellect during the *citrinitas* seems borne out in this case. Now I have a more

45 "Origin" comes from *orire* = to arise, from which orient, east, sunrise.
46 In *HM* 1.

yellowed and sulfuric interpretation for her suggestion to translate. It did not merely represent a backward move to retain the transference; it was also a move outward into publication, a *multiplicatio* and *proiectio*, her embodied mind entering the world. Besides, isn't translation a copulation, a meeting of tongues in linguistic intercourse?

Perhaps I have not made clear that her yellowing differs from another sort I have seen. Just as all whites are not the *albedo*, since the primary material can be *candida* rather than *albus*, white as innocence rather than white as reflection—so there is sometimes a primitive yellow-orange of raw and burning activity, a pleasure principle of *id* fire, the uncooked sulfur of manic brightness. This figures in dreams as a boy with orange hair or a yellow shirt, a bright yellow car going like mad, a construction worker with yellow hard-hat on a high-voltage line, a lion escaped or a yellow dog, a yellow propeller plane crashing into mud. These examples of sulfuric intensity do not result from white as interior to it, like butter from milk, but require whitening the yellow as an anterior *materia prima*. Again: colors have no single meaning; they must be placed with image, mood, time, context.

Despite the preparations for departure, the yellowing was mainly internal, where Fabricius's "yellow death"[47] was taking place, as symbolic with aging and ending of life. "Fall'n into the sere, the yellow leaf," as Macbeth says,[48] herself no longer the girl, her safety in whiteness no longer assured. How would her husband react? There occurred fear of losing what had happened; jealousy over others who did not have to leave, smoldering anger over what was not accomplished, not fulfilled concretely in the martial urge toward me. Remember: "Yellow is a true sign of Copulation of our Man and Woman together."[49] Sometimes, a bitter look, a curled lip, a lapse into suppressive silence. A killing was also going on.

Looking back, I ask where was the smelly, oily, fat sulfur that brings richness, lightness, and waxy receptivity to the *lapis* as *rubedo*, the ease and joy and capacity to float along? I remember feeling that an underlying depression had not all lifted and an acidic bitterness had not all sweetened; I was myself then disconsolate by what I felt had cut short

47 Fabricius, *Alchemy*, 140.
48 W. Shakespeare, *Macbeth*, Act 5, Sc. 3.
49 Philalethes, in Klossowski de Rola, *The Golden Game*, 27.

the work. Our rapport had become complicated—she seemed suddenly so dense—by the increasing presence of indelible emotions that seemed bent on destroying the harmony and illuminating insights that nevertheless still kept coming. Then, I rationalized these perceptions by attending mainly to what we were achieving. Today, looking back through my yellow-tinted lens, I believe that what was also being achieved—besides the evident yellow illumination—was actually a thorough spoiling of the white harmony which her emotions and my perceptions were clearly indicating, a spoiling which my own analytic whiteness resisted and tried to smooth over.

The Analyst, Too, Is Yellowed

Jung said alchemy has two aims, "the rescue of the human soul and the salvation of the cosmos."[50] Yellowing rescues the soul from the whiteness of psychological reflection and insight: "In this state of 'whiteness' one does not *live*... In order to make it come alive it must have 'blood.'"[51]

I understand this rescue operation to apply to psychology itself. Let me explain: as the alchemical opus rescues the soul of the individual, so this opus can rescue the psyche of psychology conceived only in terms of the individual human. From the alchemical perspective the human individual may be a necessary focus but cannot be a sufficient one; the rescue of the cosmos is equally important. Neither can take place without the other. Soul and world are inseparable: *anima mundi*. It is precisely this fact that the yellowing makes apparent and restores, a fact which the white state of mind cannot recognize because that mind has unified into itself the world, all things psychologized.

If psychological practice neglects its yellowing, it can never leave off psychologizing, never redden into the world out there, never be alive to the cosmos—from which today come our actual psychological disorders. Remember: sulfur is found in all things and out there; the yellow turns *outward*. The inwardness habit of psychologizing follows

50 *C.G. Jung Speaking: Interviews and Encounters*, ed. W. McGuire and R.F.C. Hull (Princeton, N.J.: Princeton University Press, 1977), 228.

51 Ibid.

consequently from the *albedo* condition that, as an "undivided purity,"[52] loses distinctions among the opposites it has united. Therefore, the *albedo* seeks mental integrations of the disturbing yellowing emotions of transference by means of psychological grids. Yet each new grid, each new analytic refinement–object relations theory, Kohut, Laings, Winnicott–continue to polish further the *albedo* mirror so that we may see more clearly, but what we see is still the human face and what we hear is still human language. Getting "out there" requires the yellow death, that poisoning prepared by a putrefaction of the *unio mentalis* that is analytic consciousness.

This poisoning awakens. The *pharmakon* kills as it cures. Our eyes open to the narcissistic corruption inherent to our theory, our diagnoses, treatment and training. We begin to see the addictive codependency of analyst and analysand disguised and glorified by theories of transference/countertransference, which intensify the mirror's gleam to the world's neglect.[53]

As analyst I, too, am yellowed; I cannot escape the *opus* since the *artifex* is myself, the material worked on. I therefore feel a fermenting discomfort of interior doubt, that yellowing inside the white which treacherously observes it from within. We feel ourselves betraying what we were, the realizations we believed, our very psychological faith and its achievements, even our former pain and the scars of identity it gave. For pain, too, changes color. As the *nigredo* has its inconsolable wounds that lift into the whitened suffering of aesthetic sensitivity, so the yellow brings the pain of further knowledge derived from piercing insights, critical, cruel, the eagles and arrows of seeing sharp and true, insights that arrive suddenly together with the fire and fear regarding the cowardice, jealousy, choler, and decay that taints both *opus* and *artifex*.

To evade the death by yellowing, that is, going straight from white to red, soul to world, is not what alchemy recommends. The texts warn against the reddening coming too fast, warn against direct flame, warn that if a red oil floats on the surface the work has been spoiled. Without the yellow, the whitened mind converts directly to red, enantiodromia,

52 T. Burckhardt, *Alchemy: Science of the Cosmos, Science of the Soul,* trans. W. Stoddart (London: Stuart & Watkins, 1967), 188.

53 See J. Hillman, "From Mirror to Window: Curing Psychoanalysis of its Narcissism," in *City & Soul, UE* 2: 66–79.

moving straight forward by converting psychic insights into literal programs, red bricks without straw. We reflect the world in the mirror of psychology, reducing its political conflicts to shadow projections, its exploitation of the earth to body problems, the destruction of nature to repression of our interior unconscious wilderness. We prescribe more of "the feminine," more anima, more lunar consciousness (though the yellowing is a time of Mars where the "male is on top of the female."[54]) We believe magically that self-transformation trickles down (multiplies and projects) into the world. As our learned colleague Edward Edinger, who does not mention yellow in his major work on alchemical symbolism in psychotherapy, wrote: "*Multiplicatio* gives us a hint as to how psychotherapy may work... the consciousness of an individual who is related to the Self seems to be contagious and tends to multiply itself in others."[55] No matter how the Self "multiplies itself in others," these others, too, are psychological entities (selves), and the opus remains one which psychologizes the world instead of mundifying the psyche.

Yet alchemy itself tempts away from the yellow which gives an inherent reason for its eventual neglect and our urge to jump over it. Because the last operations are so extraverted, the heat of the spirit so high, the King constellated in the *rubedo*, there is an exalted mission to multiply psychic projects in the world. Go forth and multiply. Mercurius as *multi flores* (many flowers) "tempts us out into the world of sense," says Jung, and his habitation is "in the vein swollen with blood."[56] This blood, identified in the secular unconscious with the redemptive and missionary blood of Christ,[57] urges ever forward to spread by conversion of the heathen (those "in need of psychology"). Large-scale film showings of Jung, his summer institutes including tours of his tower, his grave, teaching missions, and their appropriations for extending the study of Jung to "underdeveloped" start-up societies, even Jungian training programs may be driven by the sudden reddening, which prompts a countermovement to slow the training process by increased numbers of analytical hours.

---

54 Burckhardt, *Alchemy*, 90–91.

55 E. Edinger, *Anatomy of the Psyche: Alchemical Symbolism in Psychotherapy* (La Salle, Ill.: Open Court, 1985), 228.

56 *CW* 13:299.

57 Cf. ibid., 383–91.

We began by recalling that the yellowing phase faded from the alchemical schema after the sixteenth century, which is precisely when alchemy itself began to fade partly into the Rosicrucian movement, or to coagulate into either mountebank gold-making for temporal princes, or into spiritual directions for esoteric Christian redemption, or into experimental physical sciences.[58]

Against this scientific coagulation of subtle alchemical spirit, the alchemists themselves were ever on guard. "Beware of the physical in the material" was a basic caution. "Those who, in place of liquid Mercury, use sublimate, or calcined powder, or precipitate, are deceived, and err greatly."[59] There is an ever-present danger in regarding psychic materials by means of dry (calcined) metaphysical abstractions or from the naturalistic perspective of physical literalism (right-brain/left-brain, concrete holistic medicine, genetics, information theory, etc.). "The highest mystery of the whole Work is the Physical Dissolution into Mercury."[60] Keep the metaphors fluid.

Can we not draw a lesson from history? If the practice of Jungian psychology continues the alchemical tradition, then we too—unless we are fully yellow—simply repeat its fate, falling prey to either physical scientism, spiritual esotericism, or the business of professionalism as princes of this world—or all three mixed. For our work to approach its cosmic purpose, for it to reach the world, it must spoil itself. "The withering away of the state" (Marx). "Displacing the subject" by deconstructing its own consciousness (Derrida). Self-destruction as damage control. Kill the Buddha. Apocalyptic *via negativa.* Catastrophe theory. *Shevirath Ha-Kelim* (the Breaking of the Vessels).

If we washed our vision in the yellow collyrium we would be able to observe the whiteness of psychology with a fully jaundiced eye. We might then recognize that the issues plaguing professional psychologists—sexual misbehavior, ethical rules, lawsuits, insurance payments, licensing laws, warring societies, training regulations, regional and international organizations—expose the fermenting corruption breaking the white psyche out of its self-enclosure, which it defends by intensely, narcissistically, focusing on countertransference, training supervision,

58 See below, chap. 9: "The Imagination of Air and the Collapse of Alchemy."
59 *Figulus*, 293.
60 Ibid., 295.

childhood, and the Self. The fermenting corruptions, which seem diversions from the main job of therapy, may actually be how the psyche is yellowing into the cosmos. If so, there will be more psychology actually going on, more soul actually to be made, in the ferment of these corruptions than in the enlightened discussions of cases and theories. The esoteric is always in the outcast area; today, the stone the builders reject is the building itself.

Furthermore, those analysands who turn on us, turn on analysis, who condemn, sue, expose, violate the trust, may actually be angels of the yellow road to the emerald city, angels in the salvation of the cosmos from the psyche closed long enough into individualism, sulfuric angels pointing the way at the end of this analytic century to an end of analysis that omits the world. What I hoped to do in this text I feel is done: to disclose the yellow light within a process we ourselves are in and to leave on it an indelible yellow stain.

Finally this, inasmuch as every objective exposition is also a subjective confession and inasmuch as I have said that thought derives from psyche, what one thinks reflects where one is, the coloring of the *intellectus agens* as it filters through imagination. Let me bear empirical witness to these assumptions and to the *citrinitas* in my own case. I have, in part, been yellowed. Like Albrecht Dürer's self-portrait, I point to my own yellow spot.

Nine months ago I ceased practicing private analysis. I continue to practice psychology with large groups, in public speaking and teaching, publishing and writing. These activities are permeated with the same sulfuric fumes that have characterized this paper and others corrosive to the white psychology which other parts of me have long championed. In the white mirror I see myself as having simply walked out and closed the door on the consulting room of transference entanglements, too yellow-bellied and too withering in age to refine my skills further, and so, instead, I am acting out my countertransference on analysis itself, globally, with the destructive vision of prophetic inflation, convinced that what takes place in the depths of one's soul is taking place as well in other souls, in the cosmic soul of the world. I attribute this conviction to a predominance of sulfur in conjunction with mercury. What else to say save that for me the white moon is down even if the red is not risen, and my choler not sanguine.

Postscript: The Missing Yellow

When we read alchemical hues as distinct phases, the colors become bound to temporal process. Yellow as a state becomes yellow*ing* as a phase between an earlier condition and a later one, e.g., white to red. The narrative of transformation subjects each color to a stage in the narrative. Because of its median position in the various scales mentioned above (Newton's spectrum, Leonardo da Vinci, Berlin and Kay), yellow implies transition, even invites the fantasy of progression. The very title of this chapter, "yellowing," casts our comments in accord with this model. We find ourselves in a developmental fantasy.

Yet yellow itself, apart from relations with other hues, presents a state of soul with conventional significations, some of which Jung mentions in his 1929 *Dream Seminar:*[61] cowardice, jealousy, unfaithfulness, infectious contagion, prostitution, warning of danger, as well as the bright and joyful ones drawn from nature—ripe grain, sunrise, egg yolk, spring flowers. I have tried to show that the illumining and decaying or threatening significations are coterminous and that there is no either/or dividing yellow into sharply opposed halves.[62]

Can we do the same for a deeper division constellated by yellow: between yellow, the nominative noun, and yellowing as a gerund or verbal noun signifying motion, process, even intending toward a goal? In the contrast between yellow and yellowing are we confronted in the depths of yellow with the classic philosophical conundrum of Being and Becoming?

In these depths lies the defeat of the gerund form itself. The *Tabula Smaragdina,* perhaps the root text of the entire alchemical enterprise, states: "The combination of white and black, if the black predominates,

61 C.G. Jung, *Dream Analysis: Notes on the Seminar Given in 1928–1930,* ed. W. McGuire (Princeton, N.J.: Princeton University Press, 1984), 268.

62 The yellow traffic light means neither "go" nor "stop" but a transitional median between them.

produces a saffron color...[W]hite is motion, black is identical with rest...the essence of night is rest and blackness...all blackness is death."[63] At least since Aristotle, blackness has continually signified stasis, like the stuckness we feel enduring the *nigredo* and its immovable depression. Freud was absorbed by this same archetypal analogy between stasis and the death drive as he called it.

May we imagine that within yellow lies the blackness whose intention is stopping, bringing to the dead stop of stasis all forward motion whatsoever? Remember Dürer's morbid yellow spot, Bergotte's tiny yellow patch in contemplation of which he falls dead. Thus the yellowing of the work feels to be a regression, decomposing and putrefying what has been achieved. But "regression" is a term also belonging within a developmental fantasy. In fact, there is just plain cessation, stasis.

Yellow as a reversal of progress appears in a woman's dream: "A man is painting the walls of a church yellow. Half the church is already painted yellow. I am amazed, since the church had only recently been freshly renovated." A man dreams: "Cleaning up stuff; packing. I use yellow tooth paste before leaving to brush my teeth." Yellowing the white interior, the white teeth, reverses and vitiates progress, perhaps the belief in process itself, that the soul's life moves in time. At least and for sure, yellow here suggests a breakdown of the phallic thrust forward.

A woman dreams: "I'm pissing in the stall at the conference center. After the day's vitamins, the piss is extremely yellow. I'm standing up like a man to piss—no penis. Just able to do this. My Timex watch plops down into the piss. I am laughing as this happens, feeling clarity about how I don't care." No penis, and no penis-envy, since the mechanical forward march of time, its fallen idol, plops into the vitality-colored *citrinitas.*

A dreamer in Jung's *Dream Seminar*[64] reports that "parts of a machine are out of order and these parts are marked with little yellow labels..." Then, "the machine that is "injured" "disappears," and the dreamer sees his "little daughter." In the discussion which follows, Jung speaks of the patient as being shocked out of his righteousness (may we call this "the phallic patriarchal," "the masculine protest," or "progress fantasy"),

63 J. Ruska, *Tabula Smaragdina: Ein Beitrag zur Geschichte der Hermetischen Literatur* (Heidelberg: C. Winter, 1926), 156–57; cited in P. Dronke, "Tradition and Innovation in Medieval Western Colour-Imagery," *Eranos Yearbook* 41 (1972), 76.

64 Jung, *Dream Analysis,* 259.

so that Jung concludes the yellow labels were "the anima flag," that is, the dawning of soul which simultaneously illuminates and corrupts a mechanistic attitude. The black stasis within yellow seems to bring to a complete stop the belief in development through time, that Timex *watch*fulness, which runs Western consciousness.

If yellow brings process to a halt, then yellowing is stopped from within by yellow per se. We do not need to know about the white which it has stained and left behind or the red which it is heralding.

The famous maxim[65] declares: "the three becomes four" and the third of the four traditional colors is yellow. As we have seen, the third is not simply to be considered a stage on the way to four, yellow progressing into red. Rather, the fourth is red that is also a tincturing gold, both yellow and red, three and four at once, so that the *citrinatio*, is fully implicated *a priori* in the *rubedo*. The secret of the fourth—that ultimate mystery of an alchemical psychology—is concealed in the gerundive "ing" of yellow, an ever-active, ever-becoming, and clarifying *sol* of the *rubedo*.

Now we can better grasp the Ouroboros as basic to alchemical psychology. The Ouroboros is both active and static because its activity is within itself and not aimed beyond itself. As stasis-in-motion, the Ouroboros is like a living-dying, analogous with entropy, an ongoing movement intending to stand still, intending its own cessation by swallowing itself.

The *rotatio* also characterizes the end of the *opus*. It, too, is a movement that arrives nowhere, a becoming that stays in being, self-same. Being is a Becoming because, by continually rotating, it never stands

65 Maria Hebræa (aka Maria the Jewess): "One becomes two, two becomes three, and out of the third comes the one as the fourth." C.G. Jung, "Psychology and Alchemy," *CW*12: 26. Source: M. Berthelot, *Collection des anciens alchimistes grecs* (Paris: Georges Steinheil, 1888). An opportunity for reinstating the missing yellow occurs in Jung's essay "The Visions of Zosimos" (*CW*13: 123). Jung is discussing the idea of personification (of alchemical substances), and the Zosimos text introduces the figure of a "Yellow Man" who is "not pretty to look upon but you should not fear him." Although the text explicitly invites the Yellow Man to speak and give counsel, Jung's comments (124) skip to personifications of red and white. The problem of the three and four is constellated by the colors. Jung next quotes (125) the vigorous alchemical claim that "Four are the natures which compose the philosophical man." "The elements of the stone are four..." Yet the third, yellow, has been neglected, which, in fact, leaves only three.

still, neither advances nor regresses despite always moving. No point on the rotating circumference can be a "stage" of time's progress. There are no phases, no advances, no regressions, since a wheel's rotation always returns it to the same point.

The *rubedo* is imagined as a final moment of the *opus*—not because a result is finally achieved (the King, the gold, the elixir), but because Becoming is overcome and Being is released from static immobility.

Hence the alchemists can speak of eternity, less as an extension of time, or beyond time and altogether independent of any considerations of temporal process: utterly timeless, pure stasis, yet fully lively. The *opus*, that *via longissima*, ends here because alchemy as a psychological process with all its procedures has brought time to a stop.

We may now hazard a supposition regarding the issue that opened this chapter: the omission of yellow and the reduction of the color scheme to only three.

For Jung, fourness or the quaternity was like an article of faith condensed into a numerical or geometric symbol. The quaternity presents psychic wholeness, his highest valued concept and named the Self. Jung elaborated fourness in a variety of works apart from alchemy—typology, dream interpretations, mandala symbolism, in distinction from Trinitarian thinking (*CW* 11), in connection with Mercurius (*CW* 13), and into his late work, *Aion* (*CW* 9.2), and his account of synchronicity as a fourth, acausal principle at work in the cosmos (*CW* 8).

Regarding the colors of alchemy, however, Jung lets the tradition of threeness prevail. Yet colors, no less than numbers, must be considered archetypal powers. "They provide a kind of primordial classification of reality." They are like "forces" "biologically, psychologically, and logically prior," says Victor Turner.[66]

Consequently, I am led to propose that the omission of yellow as the neglected fourth color eliminates the earthly stasis and inherently dark (even "devilish") (*CW* 11: 243–95) materiality of the quaternity. This neglect or denial influences even Jung's own psychology of alchemy and those in his footsteps (von Franz, Edinger). Alchemical hermeneutics remains confined by the Trinitarian milieu in which so many of its texts were composed, offering ascensionist, progressivist, and redemptive

66 V. Turner, *The Forest of Symbols: Aspects of Ndembu Ritual* (Ithaca: Cornell University Press, 1967), 90.

fantasies that all too easily can be absorbed into the Jungian schema called "the process of individuation."

Hence this account of mine, which, by restoring the crucial significance of yellow, returns to the fourfold model, sticking with the phenomena of images and their inhibiting stasis on progress for analogies with the soul's conditions and motions, neither upward, backward nor forward.

James Hillman
October 2009

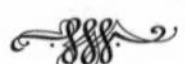

8

Concerning the Stone: Alchemical Images of the Goal

PROLOGUE

We begin by offering tribute to the ancestors, by acknowledging the almost sixty years of devotion to an idea in which still lies a large measure of hope—that word is rare in my vocabulary—that the intellect of the human animal bears witness to the cosmos, and that the good of society requires both the courage of disciplined imagination and the courage of the imaginative disruption of discipline.

By ancestors I mean the dead whose spirits continue to protect our work and urge it onward. What we say is for them and to them, in hope that they be not displeased and that they return our gesture by blessing the spirit of the living, you, here, who have made your way to take part in this *Tagung,* offering the generosity of audience.

When the Eranos rituals of mind began in the thirties, the historical world was at the threshold of peril. Today the ecological world is in equal peril. However, neither the historical nor the ecological stand on their own; their perils and all the others we live amidst daily reflect the culmination in this century of the perils of the soul owing to the pathologies of the spirit, its bulimia called economic consumerism, its manic inflation called technological progress, its schizoid *Wortsalat* called information, its paranoia called interpretative meaning. The contrast between the dedication of the ancestors of Eranos to the passionate intellect and courageous imagination, my way of describing "spirit"—and the apathy of spirit among official bureaucracies of church, government, arts, and academia could hardly be more extreme. Spirit has become marginal, and only in the marginal, liminal, occasional moments such as

Eranos can spirit return from its exile. I have come, as I have said at other Eranos meetings, for the sake of the Eranos vision, and to renew my tie to the ancestors and to the vocation that I feel their presence will claim from us.

I. GOALS

Our theme—the ideas and images of the alchemical goal—cannot be better introduced than by this statement from C.G. Jung:

> The goal is important only as an idea; the essential thing is the opus which leads to the goal: that is the goal of a lifetime.[1]

"The goal is important only as an idea" de-literalizes goals right at the beginning. We may not take alchemy's images of the hermaphrodite, the gold, or the red stone as actualized events. Nor may we even consider these images, and the many others, to be symbolic representations of psychological accomplishments. Not the goal; the *idea* of goal; goal as *idea*.

We are thus obliged to inquire into the goal idea before we look at goal images, asking why the psyche invents these goals. What is the function of goal-thinking, goal-fantasying? What do goals do for the soul? Why does the psyche need them? Or does it? Are goals merely delusions, projections, overvalued ideas, or neurotic fictions as Alfred Adler said? Before we turn to some of the main images for the alchemical goal, we best make sure we have placed them in the acid bath so that not a trace of their actuality remains, that they are wholly recognized as fantasies, projects of the psyche, serving some pragmatic purpose. I read Jung to be saying the purpose of the goal-idea is to impel the psyche into the *opus*. We shall have extraordinary and marvelous goals, like gold and pearls, elixirs and healing stones of wisdom, because then we shall be motivated to stay the course, that *via longissima* called a lifetime. Were the goal not imagined as gold, the highest value possible, were the goal not healing, were redemption and immortality not promised

1 *CW*16:400.

in the image at the outset, who would risk the leaden despair, tortured mortifications, ageing putrefactions, the sludge, and the corrosive fires? *An inflated vision of supreme beauty is a necessary fiction for the soul-making opus we call our lifetime.*

Moreover, the goal (*telos*) is one of the four Aristotelian causes,[2] entering into the consistency of each event. *Telos* is the long-range aim, the ultimate final purpose or "that for the sake of which" any thing or act exists. These goals, as inherent to the work, need to be kept interior to it, as the toward pull, the urging impetus, without ever being exteriorised into an objective literal aim. *The purpose of the work is purposiveness itself,* not this or that formulated purpose, which quickly degenerates into an ideology and just as quickly loses effectiveness as motive power. Not the attainable but the idea of the unattainable stirs the course of action—in fact, the task set by the theme, resurrection, is not to be attained. Rather, it is the beauty of the idealized goal that has brought us here. One such idea of the goal is the Pearl of Great Price, the name of an early printed text of alchemy by Petrus Bonus of Ferrara (flor. ca. 1323–1330).

The pearl as goal expresses the idea that the *materia prima,* the worthless gritty bit we call a symptom or problem, when worked on constantly, slowly becomes coated. An organic process turns the bit of grit into a coagulated jewel. The work goes on in the depths of the sea, where light does not reach, inside the hermetically closed oyster. Then it must be fished up and pried loose, extracted. It is not enough to have a pearl in the depth of the sea, not enough to be gifted with riches and blessed with talents. For they may remain there, still sealed away in the oyster when we are sealed away in the coffin. It is a "goal hard to attain"—it must be worked at as does the oyster, and it must be dived for, deep into the dissolving waters.

Moreover, pearls must be worn. Pearls kept in a jewelry box lose their luster; they need skin. Skin is the best polishing agent for pearls. They must be exposed, taken out, into life, carried about, shown, their beauty delighted in. Alchemy spoke of the congelation, or exposing a substance to cooling in the air, which is more than "reality testing." Bringing forth to shine refers as well to the revelation of beauty, no hiding of the Venusian, the sensate skin as the place of the pearl, the final

2 Aristotle, *Physics,* II.7.

goal of the *magnum opus*, the sensitive incarnate nudity of our aesthetic reality—exposure. Bonus writes:

> "Freely ye have received, freely give." What is the use of concealed diamonds, or a hidden treasure, to the world? What is the use of a lighted candle if it be placed under a bushel? It is the innate selfishness of the human heart which makes these persons seek a pious pretext for keeping this knowledge from mankind.[3]

Bonus's language seems to say that the esoteric is not the goal. Despite the endless warnings in alchemy against the vulgar, and alchemy's deliberately arcane mystifications, the goal, evidently, is display, and this gives another sense to the psychology of alchemy. Rather than emphasis upon the closed vessel as the modus for self-knowledge, we are to "freely give." Revelation.

If the goal is an idea that motivates the *opus* all along the way, then ideas of display and exposure must lead the mind.

Extraverted display not as the last stage of a long process of introverted secrecy; instead, disclosure. Man revealed is man known; as if self-knowledge were only truly that in the act of revealing that self; oneself and the glass vessel, the *vas hermeticum*, one. The conjunction between container and contained. Then containment becomes the transparency of each act. *As if transparency was containment.* My substance is my appearance. My inner is my outer. No hidden inner truth behind outer pretense. Remember Adolf Portmann and the idea of *Selbstdarstellung* (self-display) as the presentation of each animal's *Innerlichkeit* (inwardness). Jung, using the language of alchemy, writes of an innate *extraversion* in the sulfur of the *opus:* it will out. And, Bonus gives the reason with his phrase: "What is the use of concealed diamonds... to the world?" To the world," that little phrase, suggests a wholly social, political, ecological, communal aspect to the entire *opus*, an unnamed goal named" world." We shall come back to this.

Bonus mentions the diamond. Diamonds are not usual alchemical symbols, but as the most perfect and most precious stone, they deserve our notice. The root of the word, *dama*, expresses power. It is related to "dominate," "tame"; "adamant" means an impregnable hardness, and hard as steel. In Western natural history, which has become for us mere

3 *Bonus*, 16.

folklore and symbolism, the diamond had the properties of the *lapis* in that it was both a poison and a cure. Pliny, for instance, claimed the diamond "overcomes and neutralizes poisons, dispels delirium and banishes groundless perturbations of the mind."[4] Like Vajra, Indra's thunderbolt, or the Buddha's diamond ecstasy or diamond throne, or that diamond throne on which the Angel of God sits in Dante's *Purgatorio* (Canto IX: 104–5), the diamond mind can overpower and subject disorder to spiritual crystallization and perfected clarity. Not just the mind: the Japanese Shin sect speaks of a heart strong as diamond, which I read to correspond with Henry Corbin's *himma* of the heart, the power which perceives imaginal realities as hard and luminous and fixed as a diamond.

These precious stones are gathered in the Valley of Diamonds. Alchemical texts often describe the geographies for locating the metals and minerals and discriminating one kind of sulfur or salt from another according to geography. The geographical descriptions symbolize with psychological states. For instance, the inaccessible diamond valley is a place of intense heat, where the diamonds are in the power of serpents or adhere to sheep's flesh. Great birds of prey, vultures and eagles, eat the flesh and carry the diamonds up to their nests. They are even called "eagle-stones."

I have written about eagle images in dreams, and how this great bird of the spirit can visit a human life not only with transcendent revelation but also with intimations of paranoia.[5] Precisely here the toxic and the curative become indistinguishable. What is impregnable is also self-satisfied and self-enclosed, as the lore says of the eagle; it dies because its powerful beak never stops growing so that the beak's slowly increasing curvature eventually prevents the bird from taking in food, until finally it punctures its own throat.

Fierce, impregnable, unbreakable, steel-willed. In the Moslem world, and in China as well, there are close and interchangeable expressions for diamonds and swords. The Arabic word for diamond is *almas*, and in Khirgiz, *almas* also means steel. For the warrior, the children of eagles, to

4 *The Natural History of Pliny*, trans. J. Bostock and H.T. Riley (London: George Bell and Sons, 1898), Vol. 6, Book XXXVII, chap. 15.

5 J. Hillman, *Animal Presences*, *UE* 9, chap. 1: "The Animal Kingdom in Human Dreams," 24–28.

live and die by the sword is also to live and die by the diamond-body, to be fully self-realised.

In order that the diamond satisfy the alchemical requirements for the goal, adamantine hardness is not enough. Not enough to shine in the dark, as the lore says; not enough that it be the most luminous and powerful presentation of self-sure enlightenment; not enough that it dominate confusions. *It must as well be vulnerable.* Else this adamantine quality of soul be poisonous as described by the Pseudo-Aristotle, by medieval Muslim writers, and also by Hindu texts.[6]

What then prevails against the diamond? Pliny (and Augustine, in *The City of God,* XXI: 4) say that it can be softened by goat's blood and ram's blood though it is unassailable by iron, fire, and smoke. Sacrificial blood–for ram and goat are sacrificial animals–has more effect than the furious intensities of the iron will. Dioscorides, in the first century CE, claims that lead can pulverize a diamond; later Syriac and Arabic writers state that lead "makes the diamonds suffer"; and a Persian text by Muhammed Ibn Mansūr of the thirteenth century states that lead breaks the diamond.[7]

Of course, lead, the softest of the alchemical metals would make no mark on an actual diamond, let alone break it; but in alchemical psychology, sorrow, solitude and misery can break even the most indomitable spirit; and the indomitable spirit in its inaccessible valley or in its eagle eyre, with its all-clear paranoid certitude will indeed be subject to just these attacks of leaden despair.

The alchemical idea of gold is difficult to recapture today except through fantastical language, since gold has been debased to mean vulgar gold, gold of so many francs a kilo, dollars an ounce. As Bonus says: "The gold of Alchemy is not true but fantastical gold."[8] Only language retains the golden touch, the heart of gold, the winner's gold, the golden lads and lassies, golden hair and crown of gold, golden apples of the sun, golden age, golden key...

Once it was imagined that the corporeal substance of the gods was gold. Pythagoras, the story goes, had a golden thigh, which he exhibited in the theater showing that his origins were suprahuman, immortal.

6 B. Laufer, *The Diamond: A Study in Chinese and Hellenistic Folk-Lore* (Chicago: Field Museum of Natural History, 1915).

7 Ibid., 26.

8 *Bonus,* 67.

For gold is the incorruptible not because like a diamond it is hard but because it is the very body of the divine. Homer uses "golden" as an epithet for the divine, and not only Apollo and Aphrodite are golden; Dionysus has golden hair (Hesiod), as does Zephyrus (Alceus) and Eros (Anacreon). Truly, when we travel in the realms of gold, we are leaving the mortal condition, and so gold-making as a *telos* of alchemy clearly touches upon the theme of resurrection.

The two ancient methods of gilding (until the high Middle Ages) involved the two components we notice again and again: on the one hand, intense heat, fire-gilding; on the other hand, suffering, or gilding by means of lead. In the first, an amalgam of gold and mercury covers the material. Fire drives out the mercury by vaporizing it, leaving the substance coated with gold. The second method dips the substance in a molten lead bath, a corrosive acid removes the lead, again leaving the substance gilded. Both methods run the risk of poisoning, either by mercury or by lead. The *iosis,* the process of reddening or purpling corresponding with the gold-work, means also poison.

A gilded object, say a statuette of a divinity, had a higher value than one of pure gold, because the gilded object had been transmuted. It was an *achieved* gold, having moved from the mundane to the extramundane, from the *thnetos* condition of mortality or naturalness to the gilded condition of eternal godlikeness. Pure gold as given by nature in fragments and nuggets had not been worked, merely given, the *opus contra naturam* not accomplished.

Other modes of refining, reported by Forbes[9] as having been invented after 1100 CE are equally metaphorical. We can hear through the metallurgical descriptions to the psychological resonances. Gold ore was melted, fragments of sulfur laid on the molten gold, stirred by a black stick of charcoal (which itself does not contain moisture), and then poured into a rigid iron mould, its form fixed by iron. When cooled and solidified, the piece was beaten on an anvil to get all the black out of it. The black was the sulfur that had drawn the silver from the ore, leaving the gold pure. These methods used salt, nitric acid, alum, sal ammoniac, that is, bitter, pungent, and corrosive agents in order to raise gold to its finest condition.

9 R. J. Forbes, *Metallurgy in Antiquity: A Notebook for Archaeologists and Technologists* (Leiden: Brill, 1950).

Did the alchemists make gold? How often that question returns and how the mind clots trying to give reply. Clearly, the question sets up a literalist answer: either yes or no. All of our Cartesian and positivist history is packed into the question. The literalist answer emphasizes the gold as the end of the work and the making as a means to it. A psychological answer collapses the goal into the way, the substance into the process, the fact into its fantasy, the gold into the making (*poesis*). Then the end (gold) serves the means (making), the idea of gold motivates the making, justifies the struggles, and gives them the highest value.

Once we release gold from its financial materialization, we can imagine the desire for gold as feelings already familiar: to be good as gold, ourselves and our golden hair at last one, to be permanently glowing and untarnished, to have a consciousness ever-shining like dawn, like the sun, without fits of darkening, moods and meltings, to have the lucky golden touch, warm, radiant, cheerful, spreading light, and a value beyond corruption and beyond price. Gold is the lion and the crown and the king, the key to the kingdom, one's own kingdom come, to come into one's own. Able to be beaten and beaten, yet never crack under the hammer, to be bent, thin as a leaf and so cover mundane things with the shine of glory.

By imagining the goal as *feelings already familiar*, we are reiterating my goal of this talk about goals, that is, we are deliteralising the goal by removing it from a temporal presence and activating it as an idea already present in the human condition and intermittently available to our feelings, spurring the desire for supreme values.

It takes a supreme fiction to present the supreme value. The spirit approach takes these fictions of value as metaphysical realities, and measures progress toward them in literal stages. The soul approach maintains the images as supreme values but takes them always as fictions, thereby protecting the values from the inflating eagle's talons. The precious goals of alchemy are neither physical achievements (they did not make concrete gold) nor metaphysical truths (they did not redeem themselves). We are not in the realm of metaphysics or physics. The *opus* is neither physical nor metaphysical– as alchemy itself declares in one of its sagest warnings: "Beware of the physical in the material."

It does not say beware of the material, for the material is the concrete, the laboratory, the fire and stove, the charcoal and the acid, the lead and mercury, the tough struggle with the actual mess of life. "Beware of the physical in the material" warns about the *physis*, whether physical or metaphysical, the literalizing, substantiating mind which forgets the primacy of *imaginatio*.

When alchemists insist that everything at the beginning is not the ordinary, the vulgar, the common, they are saying we are not dealing with the natural but with the sophisticated. The literal *physis*, the substance as such, is washed so that its interiority, its imaginative principle stands forth. We must start, as Benedictus Figulus says, in the *caelum*, the sky-blue firmament over our heads, the mind already in the blue of heaven, imagination opened. The blue *caelum* of imagination[10] gives to the *opus* a rock-hard standpoint from above downward, just as firm and solid as literal physical reality. A sapphire stone already at the beginning. The sophic activity of the mind—and *sophia* also is clothed in blue—when dealing with concrete matters must be anchored in the imagination else it be lured into identifying the material with the physical. Since *imaginatio* is both goal and a starting point, the goal as idea serves to remove the mind at the very beginning to a *u*topic, non-*physis* condition, comparable with Henry Corbin's many descriptions of the imaginal. The risk all through alchemy, and which this warning about physical points to, is the loss of imagination to the physical spirit, the risk of poisoning by literalisms of the spirit as we work with the material.

The Christian spiritual allegorization of the alchemical *opus*, emphasized by Jung, is nowhere more evident than in these images of the goal achieved after torturous sufferings. But my intention is somewhat different. For if we regard alchemy through the Christian lens, that is, mainly as a *spiritual* discipline, then it becomes merely another—even if highly differentiated and materialized—allegory for the Christian opus. Then, why alchemy, why bother with it, learn it; why can we claim, as did Jung, its essentiality for psychological work? If it is merely another version of the Christian *opus*, then the Christian *opus* is the essential and alchemy a mere variation, an accresence, not fundamental. The basic story of the synoptic gospels suffices.

Instead, I prefer to read alchemy, and its goals, as *images of psychic conditions always available.* Then the pathologized aspects of the grit and

10 On the *caelum*, see below, chap. 10: "The Azure Vault."

the pearl, the lead and the diamond, the hammer and the gold are inseparable. The pain is not prior to the goal, like crucifixion before resurrection, but pain and gold are coterminous, codependent, corelative. The pearl is also always grit, an irritation as well as a luster, the gilding also a poisoning.

This accords with life, for we are strangely disconsolate even in a moment of radiance; we suffer an inmost irritation simultaneous with exhibition, for display harbours as well the feelings of shame and awkwardness. The superiority of clear-sighted surety—when we truly see and know, brilliant as a diamond, as an eagle—always carries with it, unredeemed, the loneliness of distance and the insensitivity of certitude. So, too, gold, again and again will press for testing in the fire, ever new blackness appearing, dark crows with the yellow sun, calling for ever more corrosions and salts, alums, and hammerings.

Each moment of shining forth invites the hammer. Gold's perfection is always at risk, the risk in fact determines gold's value, else how prove its incorruptibility? Yet, the perfected condition with its internal glow is also a poisonous state of splendid solar isolation that drives out the black and separates itself from the lunar silver. Ever thinner, ever more spread, touching into all things in this world, its beauty lies precisely in this friable, delicate, stretched-out state that allows it to gild the world, giving a glow of the incorruptible to the decay inherent in all matters.

II. OPERATIONS

The images of the goal—pearl of great price, jade body, diamond, gold, elixir, *lapis philosophorum*—correlate with particular operations. For instance, when one employs the *askesis* of torturing, this *mortificatio* brings about the complete blackening called *nigredo*. The life of the material must be wholly and fully mortified, that is, killed dead. All usual responses no longer effective, not even as possibilities. Then the *nigredo*, blacker than black, like the crow's head, has been achieved.

The state of blackness corresponds with the reductive work of psychological examination, mainly memorial: searching out old roots, pounding the past for its shames and traumas, grinding the smallest seeds so that they not spring up with fresh illusions and fresh despairs. The *mortificatio* means going back and down into the dark pathologized deeps of the soul. The *nigredo* mind's activity is characterized by explanations, especially those that search out origins and causal explanations which are concrete, material, historical, and fateful. The *nigredo* and its mortification occur not just once. The mind's explanatory attacks on the soul occur each time an accomplishment falls apart—and another *descensus ad inferos* begins. Once again, remorse, repentance, self-punishment, and a turn to fate. The fateful turn reveals the hidden purpose of the *mortificatio* and the *nigredo:* the objectification of psychic events beyond personal worth and intention. Something is being done to me beyond my doing. What is happening is a divine or natural process; I am its victim; *fiat mihi.* Not I occasioned this despair by my faults; fate has, and so eventually I come to the dawning recognition that something beyond my soul has intentions with my soul that the blackened mind cannot envision. A basic level of psychological understanding is characterized by *nigredo:* causal, reductive, depressing, or incomprehensibly dark.

Other operations correlate with other states of soul. For instance, the *separatio* distinguishes the elemental seeds within the *massa confusa,* that primary condition in which sulfuric desires, mercurial intuitions, and salt-bitter pains are all mixed together. Separation disconnects, allowing ideas, insights, and intuitions to appear as such, free of the sting of recriminations and remorse, and freed as well of the sulfuric compulsion to rush insights into action. Mercury loses its sulfuric smoky urgency, sulfur its mercurial sporadic fragmentation, and salt both the fantasies of attachment that feed its self-abused feeling and the willfulness that urges revenge. In other words, the substances become themselves by separating them one from another.

And so with the operation of putrefaction, which works particularly on and with sulfur. Putrefaction refers to the inner heat that brings about decay. It is an organic fantasy of disintegration, as if ripening and rotting can hardly be distinguished. Those encrustations that psychology calls fixations, resistances, and compulsions, give up their habitual routines. The psyche surrenders its unity and identity, falling into a messy yet fecund disarray, like a compost pile. Putrefaction is particularly suited to the inner change of any well-established form. It is especially necessary when life loses its organic imagination and instead has become mechanical, literal, and spiritual.

Remember: it is the nature of each bit of psyche to want to persist as it is. What succeeds wants to continue as it is. The drive to persist and resist alteration is the very nature of substance, according to Spinoza. Thus there will always be a profound and natural resistance to the psyche's own innate movement. That alchemy imagines movement in soul by means of the repulsive rot of putrefactions and the killing torture of mortification shows how obdurate and compacted, shall we say stone-like, is the stuff of the psyche and how hard indeed it is to bring about change.

I have mentioned only a few of the operations: separation, mortification, putrefaction. Some texts have as many as forty-eight, all lined up in an order, from first to last. From an alchemical dictionary you could collect many more. The differentiation of techniques and tools, methods and processes, and giving each particular bit of hand-work its instrument, its intensity, and its own name belongs essentially to the craft of any work. When the plumber arrives or the car breaks down, a florid new vocabulary blooms from the disaster.

Of all the terms, I must mention especially one pair of operations that have come to stand for the work of alchemy in general: *solve et coagula.* Dissolve and coagulate. Whatever is permanent and habitual must be dissolved by heat or water, and whatever is wishy-washy, floating, uncertain, and vaporous must be thickened, hardened, fixed and reduced.

These forty-eight operations conceived as one process through rime reflect another of the fundamental fantasies which permeate alchemical thinking: alchemy as an art of time. What makes the work actually work is knowledge of the secret of time. Just how long does each operation take? How much time is required for the gold-making work to be completed? Bonus of Ferrara, in a chapter on the "Chief Difficulties of Alchemy," writes:

> The time required for the whole work is stated by Rasis to be one year; Rosinus fixes it at nine months; others at seven; others at forty, and yet others at eighty days.[11]

11 *Bonus,* 115–16.

Part of knowing the secret of the time is knowing which steps precede and which follow others. Time shall be ordered. Stages. Success in the work depends upon succession; procedures proceed through processes; the *opus* is made of operations. Albertus Magnus insists that specific steps follow upon others:

> Above all I exhort you to be careful not to make any mistake, first in the pounding, then in sublimation, then in the fixation, then in the calcination, then in the dissolution, then in the distillation, then in the coagulation. Perform all operations properly, in their correct order, and you will not go wrong. If you reverse, or interfere with the order in any way, you are sure to get into difficulty.[12]

Here we see the obsessive literalism of laboratory magic. Albertus seems to present an infallible method utterly independent of the condition of the material, the quality of heat, the nature of the vessel. His orders sound like an instruction book. "Perform all operations properly, in their correct order, and you will not go wrong."

However, starting points differ since the *materia prima* differs from case to case. For instance, if the primary material (or presenting complaint as psychology now names the originating condition) that starts the alchemical *opus* is listless abulia, neurasthenic lassitude and somnolence, then one can hardly begin by pounding. Pounding is effective as a first step only if the material is hard-shelled and thick-skinned. Pounding the dissolved watery flux of a childlike psyche will not produce anything. If the condition shows a preponderance of sulfur, hot-tempered and willful, then sublimation, or "rising to the upper part of the vessel" (as sublimation is alchemically defined), may have to occur again and again in between and along with other procedures and not merely once as one step in an order of steps.

Of course, in the alchemical laboratory, like in any kitchen of the house or of the soul, certain operations come before others. You don't boil before you chop; you don't wield the cutting sword of acid criticism until you have first consolidated some matter in a vessel; you can't evaporate until you have first turned up the heat, just as you cannot coagulate into a relationship until you have first dissolved in passionate fusion.

---

12 "Extracts of Lacinius from Albertus Magnus, S. Thomas, and Other Great Sages," in ibid., 415.

Nonetheless, "first things first" means priorities (*a prioris*) as well as sequences (in time). What comes first and what comes after depends not merely on the rules of *techne* and *praxis*. Priority refers as well to value. To what we give first place therefore returns us to our starting point, those ideal goals of highest value that all operations serve. And since these goals—diamond and pearl, rubedo and lapis, elixir of immortality—are imaginal and mythical, they are beyond time, dissolving the literalism of the laboratory and its measures of time into images, rather than temporal steps, images of drying and moistening, distilling and condensing, therewith moving the method of alchemy itself into myth.

Then we recognize that we are in one or another of these mythical places, enduring the torture of being flayed alive, or volatilizing into empty-headed thin air, or fixating upon a despairing memory. Not sequence of steps but the idea of sequence serves to remind the practitioner, first, that there are other places to be and, second, that each and every single place connects with the overriding goal of the opus. This mode of viewing the phases of the work could be called mercurial (and Mercurius was one name for the goal), because it values each moment for its multiple possibilities, its potential for transformation in any direction without prescribed course.

Even if the illustrated texts sometimes show the twelve, sixteen or forty-eight technical operations as actual steps like a ladder of ascent, each stage the ground of the one above it, nonetheless *each step is a separable moment.* Terms for the processes are therefore descriptions of actions as images. Each provides recognition of what one is doing and where one is standing rather than only prescriptions of what should follow upon what. The operations appeal to imagination, to reflection, and to mythical amplifications of the craft of action rather than to the moral will of instruction.

I regard each rung for itself and apart from the ladder, each step a necessary standing place offering understanding for where one is and what one is undergoing. And, therefore, I understand the operations of alchemy as *topoi* rather than as pieces of a system for achieving the utopic. The best support for this disjunctive, asystematic, and imagistic reading of the texts are the texts themselves which can never solve the question of time, neither in regard to the length of the *opus,* nor through agreement as to which operations precede and succeed others.

If we literalize the ordering of time through phases towards a goal, we remain entrapped in what I cautioned against earlier: the notion of goal as a state achieved over time rather than as a mythical idea: goal as an end state rather than a *telos* or impelling image. The literalism of goal and the literalism of spiritual progress through steps and stages is the bane of alchemical language, capturing the imagination of alchemical thinking, and the depth psychology that has followed from it. Steps and stages in alchemy represent the historical, developmental thinking that permeates the Judeo-Christian tradition. The imprisonment of thinking historically, chronologically, developmentally necessitates that other aspect of the same tradition: freedom from history—eschatology, apocalypse, and resurrection as a condition beyond time. Were we to abandon historical thinking, we might also no longer be so engaged in freedom from it. We can break out of history, out of time and process and development, the moment we think in images, engaged in each thing as it presents itself, each step for itself, rather than linked by a process of individuation.

III. THE STONE

Why stone? What is stoneness; stonitude? What in particular does this image of the goal say to the soul and what does it have to do with resurrection?[13] Are we to come back as stones? Are the stones lying about our feet, paving our streets and stuck into our walls reincarnated ancestors? Is that where the dead now live: in the pebbles and cobbles we pass by with little care? Are the cemetery's gravestones placed there to secure the dead from rising, to separate two worlds, or are the dead already risen into the perduring condition of granite and marble? If we lived in the dreamtime of Australia and each held a Tjurunga in the hand, perhaps we would feel that resurrected life indeed lives in stones.

To begin with, the stone brings facticity, objectivity. It stands there emblematic of the final freedom from subjectivity. To be stone-like is to

13 See *CW* 13:126–33, on the stone, immortality, Christ, and redemption.

be in the world like everything else, among everything else, hard, simple, one, compact, defined, unambiguous, occupying definite space and of indisputable *durée*. Yet, each stone different from every other stone, fully individualized, like a self-enclosed monad, a solid presentation of this place and no other.

That stones give rise to philosophical metaphors—the eachness of William James; Johnson's famous refutation of Berkeley; the *durée* of Bergson; the monad of Leibniz—also states something about their importance for intellectual fantasy. There is something intellectual about the stone. It offers itself as exemplar of philosophical permanence—a dream as old as Parmenides, as old as the pyramids—for stasis and basis. To have thoughts as indestructible as a stone, to have arguments like builder's blocks, indisputable and infrangible, to buttress with rock-solid foundations—this is what the mind in its countless attempts to fiction the cosmos so diligently desires. The power of the stone impregnates fantasy to find meanings for the *petra genetrix*. The mind turns back on itself by this stubborn unthinking thing to search out the reason in the stone for the fantasies it fosters. This search for meaning and its frustration was brilliantly, overwhelmingly presented at Eranos in 1988 by David Miller,[14] surely one of the most extraordinary pieces of intellectual amplification ever to have graced the Eranos conferences.

Of all that one learns from Miller's essay, one thought stands very clear: the stone does not allow itself to be held in meaning. It does not yield to understanding. Its capacity to resist mental penetration is the primary wound to human hybris. Like Sisyphus and his stone, like Prometheus and his rock, *it defeats all human effort,* and therefore no word better symbolizes with stone than God.

The stone wounds, even the smallest, like gravel in the shoe or in the kidney. Ignored and common, nonetheless to be a stone requires that you be taken into account. Even a river must take account of the stones in its bed. The flowing water alters its course simply because you, the stone, are there. You lie still, no action, yet the river diverts accordingly. If you are a stone in the ground, the roots of the hugest tree must find a way around you. Growth, organic movement, the process of life must adapt to your being even if you are utterly passive. *Beharrlichkeit ist alles; stur, stumm, still,* even stupid: such stony silence.

---

14 D.L. Miller, "Prometheus, St. Peter and the Rock: Identity and Difference in Modern Literature," *Eranos Yearbook* 57 (1988).

The alchemical *lapis* was considered a ripened metal, a seed that had been brought to maturity by the opus; it was the made soul. But, before it could be ripened, it had already been in nature for a long, long time, the Stone Age (not the Golden Age of Hesiod). The stone has time in it, filled with time, a long life, the time of the world itself. Having been present through all time, it must of course be a *lapis philosophorum*, a philosophical stone, stone as philosopher, stone of wisdom. Because its body condenses in one solid object the history of time, it can overcome the conditions of history and serve as elixir to give longevity.

All the basic operations, whether 48, 24, 16, or 12, and all the basic substances—salt, sulfur, lead, mercury, the *tetrasoma*—are embodied in the stone. The *opus* stops here. As the operations on the substances conclude here, so the substances reach their goal and, by looking back on them from their achieved *telos* in the *lapis*, we can see more clearly why each was so essential. It must be composed of lead so that the alchemical stone will have weight, gravity, density, ponderousness; that is, the ability to ponder and outstay whatever events befall it, and the depth that only saturnine tragedy, isolation and melancholy can reach. So, too, it is made of salt, for it remembers and has the interiority of blood, sweat, urine, and tears, a sensibility that keeps pain acute and the volatile imagination from dissipating.

The stone is made of sulfur else it would not be rich and fat, vital and combustible, and so would not be able to tincture and multiply. Without sulfur it could bear no progeny, be but plain matter, colorless, odorless, a sanctified concept of pure spirit only. As well, the stone is the perfection of mercury, a *compositum oppositorum*, unable to be captured by definition, though nothing in nature be more sharply defined. Light and heavy, poisonous and healing, huge in effect and miniscule in size, bearing innumerable messages and lying about in multiples of millions, though differently unique in each instance, the *lapis* is able, because of mercurial fusibility, to participate, conjoin, dissolve, mean anything without loss of essence.

The two major operations that mark the beginning of the work, the *calcinatio* and the *solutio*, are also incorporated in the stone, giving it further specifications. The drying performed by calcination leaves the stone *secco, sec, trocken, torr,* cleared of moistures—marvelous sensate words that have been conceptualized into the term "objective." The stone's dryness bespeaks the psyche's move from subject to object, the subjective person no longer stuck to identifications, the gluey, gooey moisture dried to ashen powder, desert sand. Personal life reflects the objective psyche, thatness rather than me-ness, or better said, a me-ness that is simply thatness. Spiritual disciplines might call this compassion "that thou art," a kind of unity of feeling with any thing. Yet I believe the stone's feeling is yet more strange. It feels, let us imagine: "there is just that," "even I am just that." All that other people are and the world is, from rivers and elephants to teacups and toasters is essentially what I call "me" as part of an ensouled *anima mundi* and yet utterly depersonalized as molecules dancing in dry air.

The *solutio,* that other major initial operation mentioned in every text I have encountered, affects stone by reducing all its parts into consistent and equalized homogeneity. You will recall that the solution is defined as the dissolution of a prime matter in water, according to the familiar maxim: "Perform no operation until all has become water." That is, until all has been permeated with emotion, until mood permeates all parts, until whatever is the matter that was solidly fixed into definite diagnosis loses its sure definition and melts into indiscriminate fluidity. Instead of sloshing about in waves, the flux of emotions stabilize and the stone is self-same all through, no compartments, no divisions, no internal oppositions.

A new scale of values occurs because of the *solutio.* That most precious faculty, discrimination, the very faculty by which we define consciousness, dissolves. The stone is without distinctions and degrees of valuations. Sameness supersedes differences, and so the stone's self-sameness, its lack of inherent differentiations makes it seem utterly dull, boring.

In our usual lives, especially our usual psychologically introspective and therapeutic lives that so characterize the last decades of this century, we track every trace of emotion, wringing experience for every drop of moisture in great fear of desiccation and petrification. We work earnestly at differentiating the components of the psyche. We do not live as these stones are described. We are not on earth simply as a fact but imagine ourselves as subjective primal movers. We are Sisyphus pushing, not his stone. We imagine possibilities of further differentiation, "growth" as it is popularly called, tapping the flow of subjective events to provide the *succus vitae* for our romantic fantasy of organic expansion. Yet the stone indicates a crystallization, even a petrification of subjectivity;

all that passes through the heart and mind condensed into thingness. The psyche not fluid, not cloudy, not winged, but hard and real and dumb as any stone: the subject, you and me, studies in mineralogy.

I have already mentioned the metallic origin of the stone flowing from the idea that metals are seeds of the planets scattered deep in the earth. These seeds, or metals, ripen through time, all metals seeking to become gold. Their ripening can be hastened by the concentrated heat of the alchemist's art. Though the stone may be dry and dumb, it is nonetheless not quiescent. Its motion is of another sort than one appropriate to trees and flowers. The organic fantasy no longer dominates psychic life and so the soul's stony motion must be imagined in accord with its metallic nature.

"Metal" etymologically means "mine," the verb "to mine," from the Greek *mettallao,* means to search, inquire. The stone's movement is not growth, development, or metamorphosis but rather intellectual curiosity. Pray and study, work and read, oratory and laboratory, one book opens another, explain the unknown by the more unknown—these were the maxims for the stone, or *of* the stone, the stone's own teachings. Not grow, become healthier in mind and body, develop and transform but the seeking and searching of the awakened mind, the light of the *intellectus agens,* like a burning jewel in the stone. Learning is the key. Study. Experiment. Travel. Read. These are the processes that work the stone and follow from the idea of its metallic seeds. Dig. Mine. Quarry.

However, and I believe this caution to be important, the philosophy taught by the stone's intellectual challenge seems to be saying: beware of confusing significance with size. Not the hewn megalithic pyramid, Moses's Mountain, Peter's Rock, the Kaaba, Uluru (Ayres Rock), the Dome on the Rock—the pilgrim's distant goal that lifts the mind off the earth. Not the pragmatic saws and general truths we have come to believe are wisdom following from our addiction to handed-down written abstractions. The stone does not ask about life, or answer. It advises no way forward, pointing not to what's next, but what's nearest, what's right at hand, time become a specific place. Its philosophy seems altogether accidental, casual, taking daily pleasure in reactions to occurrences, as if lying in wait for kicks and hooves, plough blade and spade, roots and water, a kind of obstacular wisdom to life's events as they touch the stone and are taught a lesson by it.

The obstacular wisdom of the stone confronts and demands response. It acts like a learned teacher disguised in ordinary dress. Alchemy speaks of the stone as the *lapis philosophorum*. What is the philosophy? What is its wisdom? It is the wisdom of the "ultimate actuality" of the "singularity of individuals,"[15] first put forth by that subtle thinker of the medieval Church, John Duns Scotus (c. 1266–1310), and called by him *haecceitas*, haecceity or "thisness." It is the wisdom that logically establishes each thing as itself, individualized. In fact, "haecceity for Scotus is the principle of individualism."[16]

For Charles Sanders Peirce (1839–1914), *haecceitas*, which he calls "secondness," is the "shock" of experiencing the "brutal fact" of the Other: "We are constantly bumping up against hard fact."[17] The stubborn, indubitable presence of "thisness" provides a founding rock for William James's philosophical favoring of eachness over Idealism's allness, oneness, and wholeness.

David Ignatow put the haecceity of the stone into a short poem:

> Each stone its shape
> each shape its weight
> each weight its value
> in my garden as I dig them up
> for Spring planting,
> and I say, lifting one at a time,
> There is joy here
> in being able to handle
> so many meaningful
> differences.[18]

The factual, confrontational eachness of the stone teaches the mind to study and appreciate each contrary event more closely beyond comparison, concept, or category and, as well, to become wily and mercurial in searching for ways through and around each obstacle.

---

15 E. Gilson, *History of Christian Philosophy in the Middle Ages* (New York: Random House, 1955), 462.

16 "John Duns Scotus," *Encyclopedia of Philosophy*, ed. P. Edwards (New York: Macmillan, 1967), 2: 431*b*.

17 *Collected Papers of Charles Sanders Peirce*, ed. C. Hartshorne and P. Weiss (Cambridge, Mass.: The Belknap Press of Harvard University Press, 1960), 1: 324.

18 "Each Stone," in D. Ignatow, *Whisper to the Earth: New Poems* (Boston and Toronto: Little Brown & Co., 1981), 17.

There is a third kind of movement, besides the organic and the intellectual. The quality of this motion we might call the sensitivity of the stone. Sir George Ripley, the Yorkshire alchemist, writing in the second half of the fifteenth century tells how to keep a Philosopher's Stone once you've got one:

> These stones must be kept by themselves, in several glasses, or fair boxes, in a warm place, or dry at the least, as you would keep sugar, because they are of so tender and oily substance, as they are apt to dissolve in every moist place, which therefore preserve as is here showed.[19]

Let's review Ripley's advice, for it reveals more about the stone than we have so far discovered. First, it is well to keep it *warm,* a certain gentle attentiveness, an affection, like the care one gives a small child, or a pet animal. Second, it is sensitive and so best kept in a *glass* vessel, present, yet once removed; apart as a precious object, yet in full view. Third, since it is apt to dissolve in every moist place, it must be kept *dry.* Here we are given the advice dear to philosophers as far back as Heraclitus who claimed that, though souls love moisture, the dry soul is the best.

Evidently the stone is of such an oily and tender nature that it can melt on any occasion. It is easily affected. Imagine: after all the labor, the goal is not strength, power, and certitude but a stone tender, oily, easily dissolved. What sort of stone is this?

Ripley explains how the stone becomes oily:

> By pouring on it, as it were, drop by drop until the stone be oilish; then congeal it, and again imbibe it, and in this manner iterate this work, until this stone will flow in fire like wax, when it is put upon a plate of copper fiery hot, and not evaporate, and congeal it up until it be hard, white, and transparent clear as crystal.[20]

Ripley is here describing the *ceratio* (ceration), a process that makes a substance softer while giving it a waxy appearance and invented, according to Albertus Magnus, "to mollify a body with a view to permit penetration of other substances."[21]

---

19 "The Bosom Book of Sir George Ripley," *Collectanea,* 141.

20 Ibid., 138.

21 *Libellus de alchimia (Ascribed to Albertus Magnus),* trans. V. Heines (Berkeley and Los Angeles: University of California Press, 1958), 47.

Now we have an idea of the goal that is tender, soft, like sugar, malleable as wax. This stone melts easily; it receives impressions like a *tabula rasa* and then just as easily lets them go again. It asks to be affected, penetrated and, because transparent, seen through. As its borders are not fixed, its defense is yielding and its answers always indefinite. It allows itself to be pushed around without altering its substance. Like wax, its condition reacts to the climate of its surroundings. With the warmth of the human touch, it takes the shape of the hands that hold it, remaining, nonetheless, self-consistent despite the repeated meltings and congealings that wipe away all the struck and engraved typological characteristics. Any moment offers the fresh start, the innocence of a slate wiped clean: *solve et coagula*.

I used the term "typological characteristics" because both words, "type" and "character," refer at their Greek root to defined engraved markings. Ceration, making wax-like, seems intentionally designed to obliterate a psychological episteme of types, traits, characteristics—anything that would rigidify the idea of the goal into categories of knowledge.

An oily stone is lighter than water and can float upon it. Christos, Messias, the anointed one who is of oil, walks on water. The oil that walks on water, the stone that floats, gives a wholly surprising idea of the goal should we expect the heavy-weight rock of ages emblematic of senex seriousness. It would seem, therefore, that the stone as goal invites the archetypal program of the senex; and so the deliberate emphasis upon soft, oily, tender, and waxy subverts the rigidities of the senex, which always threaten alchemy with petrifications: such as dogma, as images of wise old men and magicians, of scholars of Greek and Arabic; as geometric diagrams and mathematical formulae; as moral remonstrances, pious cautions and instructive warnings; as long-winded histories and maxims like the *via longissima,* which champions old age; as metaphysical and theological appeals in secret isolate language; as the reference to the dead, to history, to authoritative masters; as cryptic rebus codes, wisdom initiations, madness and melancholy—that elaborate paraphernalia of senex consciousness.[22]

Alchemy's true wisdom, it seems to me, is that it is wise to itself, imagining operations of the goal, like *ceratio, rotatio,* and *rubedo,* which soften, sweeten, excite, loosen, and make impossible any fixed position,

22 See also J. Hillman, *Senex & Puer, UE* 3, chap. 1, 9, and 10.

thereby countering the senex propensity to crystallize the goal in doctrinal truths. Let us say, the *ceratio* saves the stone from stoniness, that literalization of its compact density to mean "simplicity," "strength," "solidity," "unity," as the symbol dictionaries declare. The stone's oiliness lets it slip that grip of *Begriffe,* which would capture it. Its waxiness lets it receive endless literalizations without being permanently impressed. Subject to change without notice.

It is the senex stoniness—and again I refer to David Miller's exposition: hard of heart and hard of hearing, ungiving and unyielding, stones instead of bread—that seems the major disease of the *opus major.* If this diagnostic conjecture is right, then we must note carefully maxims and operations that preclude the rigidities, which indicate usurpation of the idea of the goal by the archetypal senex.

One mollifying example is this dictum: as the work goes on toward the *lapis,* "its love will increase." Is this love for the work? Does this increase refer to the progress of love from the vilification and orphanhood of the primary matter, through the abject despair and self-hatred of the *nigredo* to the smooth comfort of the lunar *albedo*? Or does this increase of love symbolise with the higher heat required for the goal: as the work intensifies, the degrees of fire become doubled and redoubled. Perhaps these are parallels to love's "increase," yet the source of this love seems to be the increasing reality of the stone, as if a love rising from the stone.

A stone-like love, a love utterly dehumanized, as if there is something about me that loves something about you, like the love of two stones. Cool, distant, apathetic? As if our planetary bodies were asteroids sharing a mythical affinity? Rather, I feel this notion of love is not so much cold as simply unconcerned with love, stone-focused rather than love-focused. It is indeed a fevered concupiscence, engaged in a coupling conjunction soul to soul as the alchemical images show—naked, sexual, crazy—yet having nothing to do with anybody anywhere. Let us imagine it as a love of two stones. Externally solitary, yet interiorly they are not distant from one another because they are not different. They are akin in their impersonal stony essence, descendents of a common body, Gaia, brothers and sisters, their love the incestuous passion of kinship libido, that calor inclusus which urges all things, including humans, to participate in the cosmos. We love the world unspeakably because of what burns within our silent, lapidary essence.

Gabriel Marcel writes of fidelity as a permanent faith in loving. Alchemy speaks of an *aqua permanens,* the steady emotional state brought about by the *solutio.* This love lives and flows regardless of vagrant desires. It is without *pothos,* or that yearning for elsewhere beyond the given. It is without the *anteros* of love returned, a love that lasts like a stone and is constant in soul, whether alive or dead, as the gemstones in our finger rings of loving unions. This is not all of love, of course, nor is this "increase of love" the transmutation of passion into *agape* and the person into perfection. No, the lion's paw and the bear's clutch, the eagle's eye and the strutting peacock's pageant are ever active alchemical figures in the heart's imagination. They do not go away. But as the stone ripens, so does the idea of love increase, says the text, referring, I suppose, to the love for the work and work's love for the worker, the *artifex.*

For after all, what can possibly sustain the *via longissima,* the absurdities and loneliness of the opus major of the soul-making unless it be the love it gives us.

Not only do *I* love this work, not only does *my* love increase for it and increase the stone but the stone's increase loves my work. Something firm and forever keeps faith with me. Something in my nature is ever in love with the materials of the world, a libidinal attachment, a desire that alchemical texts call Sulfur, ever ready to ignite, a bit of it lurking in every object out there, luring my love to the world of sense and matter, a love that Freud called the "object libido." So, too, there is something in the world of sense, in the matter with which the *artifex* works that increases its love for the *artifex,* drawing him and her passionately into the *opus* by its increasing love. Curious to find that I am more and more "in" love as I imagine myself more and more stony, mineralized.

IV. *RUBEDO* AS RESURRECTION

Let us go back to the early operation called calcination and the dry objectivity to which it leads, and let us remember that dryness means neither *siccitas,* nor *acedia:* not an aridity of spirit, exhaustion of imagination, a deserted soul. It is not burn-out, and it is not cold irony or remote detachment.

Rather, calcination left an alum or salt as a dry white powder. These residual powders are the objectified substances that have been calcinated. They could be reactivated by the adjunction of moisture. One smile, one touch, a drop of humor, an instant of rending pain refreshes the essence of an objectified experience and makes it an *aqua vitae,* flowing with the water of life. A memory lies utterly quiescent, merely a distant cameo of history until moistened by some sudden motion of the soul, stirred by a similarity or a poignant nostalgia. The residual powders of objectified emotions remain available as everyday potentials, but all the subjectivity, the me-ness has been cooked out of them.

The objectification of the subject seems to be a major intention of all alchemy, as well as of spiritual disciplines and psychotherapy. Soul-making takes place where me-ness once was, in inverse proportion, so goes the basic theory of depth psychology whether in Freud's lifting of repressions or Jung's relativizing of the ego.

In brief: the psychotherapeutic cure of "me"—the desire for improvement; to become better, grow whole—would thus seem to be a subjectivized and secularized version of the archetypal urge toward salvation or resurrection, a completed condition where there is no further development. Thus we may claim that the end of improvement, its subversion, that condition imagined as "resurrection," must be the main *telos* of the *opus major*. The images we reviewed earlier—gold, pearl, diamond—each envision a superior condition that cannot be improved upon. No further addition, only multiplication; rotation, circulation, iteration, again and again.

Once we can recognize that the subjective urge to develop is an idea of a goal and not a goal as such, then process thinking itself comes to a halt and another motion takes over. Plotinus contrasts the linear motions of what I have been calling the one-ness of developmental psychology with the circular motion of the soul (*Ennead,* II.2.2). The goal images correlate precisely with this motion of circularity, since the *iteratio* (repetition, or as the maxim goes, "one operation does not make an artist"), *circulatio,* and *rotatio* are often considered among the last operations of the *opus*.

The *rotatio,* like a turning wheel, announces that no position can remain fixed, no statement finally true, no end place achieved. Development makes little sense when no place is better or worse, higher or lower.

As the wheel rotates what was up is now down, what was inferior, now superior and will become again inferior. What rises, falls, repeatedly: "Only the fool, fixed in his folly, may think he can turn the wheel on which he turns."[23] Linear motion as a line of development from any point of the rotation only goes off at a tangent. Developmental process actually moves away from the soul's goal which is turning in circles. As Figulus says: "What we seek is here or nowhere."[24]

The *rotatio* also returns *telos* itself to its root meaning. *Telos* does not simply mean end, goal, purpose, finis. "Instead," says Onians, "I would suggest that with this root notion of 'turning around' τέλος meant 'circling' or 'circle.'"[25] The goal itself circles, because it is a psychic goal; or, the goal is psyche itself obeying the laws of its own motion, a motion that is not going somewhere else; no journey, no process, no improvement. And so the images of the goal put to final rest the subjective urge that has impelled the entire work from the start. We awaken to the fact that the goal of the work is nothing else than *the objectification of the very urge that propels it.*

Let me say it again: the result is not merely the objectification of subjective "me-ness," but the objectification of its material basis. This has been dissolved, calcined, tortured, putrefied, and distilled to a clarity that can be completely seen through, as if it were not there at all, not a speck of literalism remains, not even spiritual literalism. The libidinal compulsion, the organic towardness of hope and desire that would always go further for a faraway grail, turns around on itself and dissolves itself. The snake eats its own tail—another goal image of deconstructive subversion. The snake of healing, transformation, and rebirth, the goals most dearly desired, and the *artifex*'s obedient service, all dry to dust, mineralized. The uroboric motion poisons (*iosis*)[26] the very idea of cure. Or, poison is the cure.

---

23 T.S. Eliot, "Murder in the Cathedral," in *The Complete Poems and Plays, 1909–1950* (New York: Harcourt Brace & Company, 1952), 184.

24 *Figulus*, 273.

25 R.B. Onians, *The Origins of European Thought: About the Body, the Mind, the Soul, the World, Time, and Fate* (Cambridge: Cambridge University Press, 1951), 443.

26 The Latin equivalent for *iosis* is *rubedo*, and Jung (*CW* 12: 333) equates *iosis* with the reddening. H.G. Lidell and R. Scott, *A Greek-English Lexicon* (Oxford: Clarendon Press, 1890), define the Greek word ἰός to mean both rust and venom. But it is also purple or violet, the hue deriving, according to Hopkins (98–102), from the

What is actually accomplished by the alchemical work? According to my psychological fantasies, it is the objectification of the libido—our lives are not *our* lives. The alchemical goal is the realization in its complete sense of Freud's "object libido."[27] The libido as a cosmic erotic dynamic that permeates the world because it loves the world of matter, even though it has been caught in the personal delusions of subjectivity, so that we believe we love the world, or can be improved or instructed to love the world. Whereas it is the object libido that loves the world through us, despite us. The anima in chains in the matter of "me," and we place it there each time as we ask psychologically, what is the matter with me? Alchemy answers, saying: you, I, everyone, the world is matter, elemental material, and we indulge in the materials, as the *artifex* in the laboratory, all along believing that you are working on you, your life, your relations, your processes until the day dawns, aurora. You awaken *within the idea of the goal,* the goal not somewhere else out there calling for attainment, but you are within the idea. But because the mind is still trapped in me-ness, we shamelessly assert that the idea is in me when your mind is in the idea. You awaken to the recognition that you are already in that stone, mineralized, stoned out of *your* mind.

If my reading is on track and the *telos* or "that for the sake of which" is the de-subjectification of the object libido, then we are obliged to imagine resurrection from this vantage point, which hardly conforms with a Christian reading of either alchemy or resurrection. For now resurrection would indicate not the confirmation throughout eternity of the personal subject and its body saved from the world and the devil

---

metallurgy of bronzing, a process that gives rise to an ephemeral iridescent violet. *Iosis* appears in the final phase of the famous formula of Maria the Jewess: "At the end...all things combine into Violet." A.J. Hopkins, *Alchemy: Child of Greek Philosophy* (New York: Columbia University Press, 1934), 99. Since both rust and poison describe the final goal, the aim of the work is its destruction. Or, the destruction (metamorphosis) of physical alchemy into a sensate display of imagination, happening not only to the mind of the alchemist but in the imaginal ground (*anima mundi*) of the material world. Here we must ask: Did Jung's long familiarity with the color language of alchemy influence the formulation of his comprehensive theory of archetype, first laid out in 1946 at Eranos ("On the Nature of the Psyche," *CW* 8), in terms of the color spectrum's extreme poles of ultraviolet and infrared (image and instinct)? There he writes of the violet pole as if describing the alchemical *iosis:* "a spiritual goal toward which the whole nature of man strives" (415).

27 S. Freud, "On Narcissism," *CP* 4:31 and 33.

of its flesh but rather the resurrection of the body of the world with an idea to its eternity. Not the lifting, the *Aufhebung,* of material worldliness but the full realization of desire for a world that pulsates in the materials of the elemental psyche, those substances that compose the stone and give it its enduring life, a realization that the world itself speaks through the desire in the materials; that desire is the language of the world, that the libido of each individual human is indeed a cosmic force, an eros or object libido which yearns toward and enjoys this world. And we who labor in the garden as if it were a stony ground would find our individual resurrection in attachment to our materials, which are the world's body, this body becoming a *jardin des délices,* the objectification of pleasure.

Object libido finds its pleasure in the other, the object, the world as a body. This dry term "object libido" calls for a moistened language. Terms such as cosmogonic eros, desire, *jouissance,* or *unus mundus* cannot do justice to what is implied. Libido brings with it the aura of pleasure and the Aphroditic world of the senses. Did not Plotinus attribute to Plato the idea that the soul is always an Aphrodite, which suggests that we cannot adequately speak of the libidinal soul without shifting immediately to an Aphroditic language?[28] Then we would imagine that this libidinal drive throughout the whole opus of soul-making and its increasing love has as its goal a resurrection in beauty and pleasure, and we would realize that even such terms as *opus* and *operatio* are work-words which distort the libido's nature. The Christianization of alchemy nonetheless retains the Aphroditic vision in the images it presents. She is the Golden One, the pearl is her jewel; the rose, her flower; the bath and the copulations in the bath of the *Rosarium,* her liquid territory. The translation of sensate images into spiritual value, as if a lifting improvement to the higher realm of Aphrodite Urania, succeeds only in losing the very sensate attraction of the goal as a pleasurable pull toward beauty. Hence Ficino, Valla, and other Renaissance Platonists insisted that Voluptas is nearer to the life of the spirit than the middle region or mediocrity of ataraxic rationality. Voluptas, according to

28 Aesthetic sensuality and judgments, even if disguised in the language of physics (Newton's color spectrum) and chemistry, infiltrate the work all through, enlivening the moralisms and obscure formulas with color and figure. "The free-ranging psyche of the adept uses of chemical substances and processes as a painter uses colours to shape out the images of his fancy." (*CW* 14: 687).

Apuleius, lies curled in the womb of Psyche and comes to birth only after all psychological effort is passed.

I beg you for a moment to convert your mind from Jung to Freud, and a conversion or reversion from a Christian to a more Pagan vision of our theme. For we may not speak of libido as energy only, as an abstraction equivalent to the energy concept of physics. "Beware of the physical in the material." Jung missed something essential, something essentially non-Christian, when he removed Freud's principle of pleasure, the eros, from the libido, leaving it as a bare concept without sensuous content.[29] Libido comes from *lips*; it means the drippings of pleasure, like honeysuckle from the vine, like the fat grape, like the excitation of lust. Libido belongs in a word cluster—and I take this from Onians[30]—that includes libation as pouring of liquid, *deliquare* (to make liquid, melt); *laetus* (moist, fat, fruitful, glad); and the German *lieben*, to love; as well as *liber* (free), the god Liber, the procreative fertility figure.

These meanings in the word "libido" amplify from another perspective the oily stone and even the oiled one, the Messias or Christ.[31] The liquid of life and strength, the seed, was conceived as "oil" and a new "spirit," even the "spirit" of Yahweh, was believed to be transmitted to the head by anointing it with holy oil, and this "oil" = seed was naturally derived also from the thighs, also from fat. The fat of the lower body of the sacrificial animal was appropriate to the god, for that is where the life force resided: "Thou shalt take of the ram, the fat and the fat tail and the fat that covereth the inwards..." (Exodus 29:22).

The oiled one is the libidinized one. In fact, there is a belief "that it is the tail-end of the spine, which grows into a new body in the Resurrection."[32] This tail end of the spine in Muslim tradition is the *'ajb* and in Rabbinic tradition it is the *Luz*. In ours, it is the *os sacrum*. This is the animal tail that I have amplified elsewhere[33] at length in regard to the monkey in the center of the mandala of that dream of which Jung spoke in his first lecture on alchemy at Eranos in 1935. In that dream the key phrase was "a gibbon is to be reconstructed." I am now making

29 *CW* 8:33.

30 Onians, *The Origins of European Thought*, 473.

31 Ibid., 189n2.

32 Ibid., 484.

33 J. Hillman, *Senex & Puer*, *UE* 3, chap. 13, "Of Milk... and Monkeys."

a correlation between the reconstruction of the ape and the resurrection of the libido as a material, generative, erotic power, which reddens into life. This imaginative step was once literalized by Freud in his attempts to rejuvenate, i.e. resurrect himself, by means of the Steinach (of monkey gland fame) operation on his testes.[34] In the testes, says the *Zohar*, "are gathered all the oil, the dignity and the strength of the male."[35] In common speech the testes are called "stones" and "rocks."

Because we have been held in a spiritualized and Christianized alchemy, the *rubedo* has remained enigmatic, usually explained in terms of Christ. The reddening has been conceptualized in higher abstractions like the conjunction of opposites and the *unus mundus*. The brilliant blood-red vitality of the solidification has been imprisoned in a lunar *albedo* vision. By that I mean the *unus mundus* has been apprehended within the *unio mentalis*.[36]

Therefore the yellowing, so crucial for the transition from white to red, silver to gold. The yellowing undoes the white, spoils it, decomposes it out of itself so that the psychologized mind cannot serve as vehicle for entry to the world. The *rubedo* can no longer be conceived to be a psychological activity only because it is as well a libidinal one, a movement in what Jung called the infrared end of the archetypal spectrum where he said "instinct" prevails.[37] "Instinct": another name for the first Adam who, legend says, had a tail. The *unus mundus* is therefore head-cum-tail as the Ouroboros depicts, mind as nature, image as instinct. The goal of the *unus mundus* occurs not necessarily at the end of the *opus* but whenever a mental image compels with the force of a natural phenomenon and whenever nature appears wholly as imagination. The end of the goal is thus a spontaneous creative event occurring whenever the adept's fantasy (violet) is empowered by (red) certitude, even if inherently subject to rusting and bearing poison within it.

The *unus mundus* as goal makes sense only if it is sensuous, is felt as a libidinal reality, an Aphroditic reality. Her pleasure in the world objectified as its beauty, the radiance in earthly things as Hilary Armstrong's

34 See D. Hamilton, *The Monkey Gland Affair* (London: Chatto and Windus, 1986).

35 Onians, *The Origins of European Thought*, 188.

36 See above, chap. 5, "Alchemical Blue and the *Unio Mentalis*."

37 *CW* 8:414.

Neoplatonic vision beautifully elaborates.[38] Pleasure objectified as beauty, pleasure perceived as the attractive enjoyable qualities of things–this is the definition of beauty, according to George Santayana and it suggests that without pleasure, no beauty.[39]

A final operation, a last effect of the stone, is called the tincturing.[40] The stone stains all that it touches, suffuses brightness and color, increasing value to that of gold. Things show themselves in a new light, an alchemical light, enlightened by the beauty of imagination, as if the touch of Venus is the final effect and ultimate aim of the entire opus.

Thus, at the end of the *Rosarium philosophorum*, the text that Jung examines in great detail in his penetrating and fascinating work, *The Psychology of the Transference* (*CW* 16), one image in the series of engravings is entitled "Revivification." It is figure 18 of a total of 22. Since Jung's famous commentary concludes with the tenth figure, we are now dealing with images not examined by Jung. This figure of Revivification shows the female soul with streaming long hair diving down from the upper right. The accompanying text says: "The soul descends here from heaven, beautiful and glad."[41] "Beautiful and glad" is the soul's descent into the world's material body.

Without beauty and pleasure of the world, why save it? Neither shaming for past exploitations, nor moralizing about future generations, nor theologizings about the great good mother Gaia, nor sophisticated scientific and economic ecologies, nor romantic sentimentalisms and politically opportune greenings so moves the individual soul to re-unite with the world soul as does the Aphroditic power of pleasure. Only the object libido can fully reconnect us. Not duty but beauty, and the pleasuring in things.[42]

---

38 A.H. Armstrong, "The Divine Enhancement of Earthly Beauties: The Hellenic and Platonic Tradition," *Eranos Yearbook* 53 (1984).

39 "Thus beauty is constituted by the objectification of pleasure. It is pleasure objectified." G. Santayana, *The Sense of Beauty* (New York: Charles Scribner's Sons, 1896), 52.

40 *Tinctur* is the name of the top step of the ascending operations depicted in the Mountain of Adepts (S. Michelspacher, *Cabala, Speculum Artis et Naturae,* in *Alchymia* [Augsburg 1654]), reproduced in E.J. Holmyard, *Alchemy* (Harmondsworth: Penguin Books, 1957), pl. 16.

41 *Le Rosaire des philosophes*, trans. E. Pérrot (Paris: Librairie de Medicis, 1973).

42 On the essential role of libidinal Venus (*voluptas mundi*) for the *rubedo,* see *CW* 14: 415–21.

Hence the stone is red; *krasny*, as the Russians say, beautiful and red in one word. Red as nature in tooth and claw, the color of Adam's first earth, the cinnabar rock that compounds sulfur and mercury, the red flush of shame, the red rose of erotic desire, the red coals of wrath, of devils, of Seth, and the furious gods of war, the red of revolution, challenge, danger, the holy heart of *himma*'s enthusiastic imagination, and the royal robe of kings, lords of this world. Let us be quite clear: red is of this world. Yet it correlates with an operation called exaltation. Exaltation of what? The *Rosarium*'s penultimate image showing Maria crowned states the "perfection of the stone as the crowning matter." *Matter* is exalted.

Ruland's alchemical dictionary defines exaltation as an "Operation by which a Matter is Altered in its inclinations, and is elevated to a higher dignity of substance and virtue."[43] This suggests that the reddening of the material is not its transformation. It does not become something else, transcended, spiritualized, but that rather a nobler notion of matter prevails. It is crowned; and thereby its virtues are revealed and its inclinations alter from being the lodestone of dumb concrete daily obstruction to the ruby rocks that provide our life with daily pleasure.

In a curious way, you and I crown matter, have been crowning matter, many times, perhaps since childhood. Recall the stones that we have brought back from our travels, from a desert, a river-bed or seashore, a temple precinct, the little pebbles smoothened, the striped or stippled granite, the flintstone, mica, plain grey rock, that we as pagan primitives set on our desks and tables and shelves, the unobstrusive occasional altars that have formed in our rooms, remembering beauty, love, the dead, mystery, sadness, hope, attaching the soul with the weight of stone to some specific sensate geography. In this compelling yet offhand urge to pick up and carry home, primordial Adam connects again with the material world's ordinary beauty. He reconnects, is this not *re*-ligion? Lifted from the ground, transported inside, singled out and raised in inclination, is this not that exaltation of the material body of the world, which religion calls Resurrection?

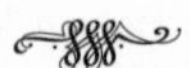

43 *Lexicon*, s.v. "Exaltation."

9

The Imagination of Air and the Collapse of Alchemy

Air is the element," says Plato, "which raises (*airei*) things from the earth or as ever-flowing (*aei rei*)."[1] Since the Stoics, as Samuel Sambursky has so well explained, this ever-flowing, continuing air has been imagined as an elastic continuum, the *pneuma*.[2] Pneuma pervades all things; it inheres, coheres, gives structural tension (*hexis, tonos*), as if to say that things are as they are because they are filled with an invisible breath. Pneuma or air is the body of the stars, the froth of animal sperm, the seed of the metals.[3] All things breathe. The entire cosmos manifests the imagination of air. Even Tartarus is a blasty place, tossing the images of souls hither and yon in ceaseless animation, sending us their dreams.[4] Geist, Logos, Pneuma, Spiritus, Prana, Ruach, Psyche, Anima/Animus—words of air, forms of its imagination. Air makes possible this perceptible world, transmitting the colors, sounds and smells that qualify and inform our animal immersion. As we breathe air and

---

1 *Cratylus* 410*b*.

2 Cf. S. Sambursky, *Physics of the Stoics* (New York: Macmillan, 1959), 1–16, 41–48, from which the substance of my paragraph is derived; also J. M. Rist, *Stoic Philosophy* (Cambridge: Cambridge University Press, 1969), 86–88; M. Putscher, *Pneuma, Spiritus, Geist: Vorstellungen vom Lebensantrieb in ihren geschichtlichen Wandlungen* (Wiesbaden: F. Steiner, 1973).

3 The *locus classicus* for the connection between pneuma, vital heat (*thermos*), and the stars is Aristotle, *De generatione animalium*, II: 3.736*b*30–737*a*. Cf. F. Solmsen, "The Vital Heat, the Inborn Pneuma and the Aether," *Journal of Hellenic Studies* 77 (1957), 119–23.

4 Agrippa von Nettesheim, *Natural Magic* (London: Aquarian Press, 1971), 48: "Whence it is that many philosophers were of the opinion that Air is the cause of dreams, and of many other impressions of the mind, through the prolonging of Images, or similitudes, or species (which are fallen from things and speeches, multiplied in the very Air) until they come to the senses, and then to the phantasy, and soul of him who receives them."

speak air, so are we bathed in its elemental imagination, necessarily illumined, resounding, ascending. Human life cannot keep from flying; "all God's chillun got wings." Aspiration, inspiration, genius is structurally inherent, a pneumatic tension within each soul. The song-bird and the choked voice, the hyperbole of the whirlwind, spiritual restlessness, and the dread of asphyxiation are given with imagination itself. Imagination is air: the Celestials (the *daimones*), says Plotinus, "are composed of air" (*Ennead*, VI: 7.11). These imaginative persons populate the middle realm of the imaginal, which consists of airy stuff and, in Plutarch's phrase, upholds the "consociation of the universe."[5] These bodies of air would be what we now call psychic images. The alchemist Michael Sendivogius (*CW* 12: 397–98) says that air is "uncommonly light and invisible, but inside heavy, visible, and solid." The invisible *anima corporalis* is visible and "real" (heavy and solid) as image to the *imaginatio*. Jung comments (ibid.), "as 'the images of all creatures' are contained in the creative spirit, so all things are imagined or 'pictured' in air..." Air is the confluent element of spiritus and anima,[6] appearing as imagination. Therefore the exercise that our subject, air, demands of us in this chapter is that of picturing in the air, imagining the sensate world of empirical chemistry as filled with airy bodies, psychic images. We shall be working with and by means of the *anima corporalis*, or soul embodied in imagination.

L'Air et les songes[7] was the great exploratory work in this medium and it is to Gaston Bachelard that we owe a first debt, although our texts shall not be those he would have chosen. Instead, we shall come in from his side, the side of the history of science. His study of the flame of a candle, for instance, does not occupy itself with the works on this very subject by Carl Wilhelm Scheele, Michael Faraday, or Antoine Lavoisier even though, or because, Bachelard begins as a natural scientist. He approaches the elemental air through the poetic imagination; we shall approach this same air through the chemical imagination.

---

5 Plutarch, *De defectu oraculorum*, 13: "Now if the air that is between the earth and the moon were to be removed and withdrawn, the unity and consociation of the universe would be destroyed, since there would be an empty and unconnected space in the middle..." (*Moralia* 416e, trans. F.C. Babbitt). Plutarch goes on to make the analogy between the middle realm of air and the middle realm of *daimones*.

6 Cf. Putscher, *Pneuma*, 38–77, on the close connections of spiritus and anima in Medieval and Renaissance thought.

7 G. Bachelard, *Air and Dreams: An Essay on the Imagination of Movement*, trans. E.R. Farrell and C.F. Farrell (Dallas: The Dallas Institute Publications, 2002).

This chemistry takes us to the Enlightenment. When this period (say from Cromwell's death to Napoleon's) does appear here, it is usually to contrast it pejoratively with the Renaissance before and the Romantics after, or to point to alternative currents simultaneous with the Enlightenment: Emanuel Swedenborg, Johann Kaspar Lavater, the Rosicrucians, Franz Xaver von Baader, Franz Anton Mesmer, Jacob Frank, William Blake ... (The eighteenth century anyway did not belong only to the Encyclopedists and Dr. Johnson. Alchemical publications thrived: fifty eighteenth-century editions of Paracelsus; Jean Jacques Manget's two-volume *Bibliotheca Chemico-Curiosa* (1702); Friederich Roth-Scholtzen's *Deutsches Theatrum Chemicum* (1728–32) in three massive volumes; Jean Maugin de Richebourg's four-volume *Bibliothèque des philosophes chimiques* (1740–54); five editions of Basilius Valentinus's fifteenth-century *Chymische Schriften*, one as late as 1775. And I have not listed the Rosicrucians.)

But instead of looking into the occult tradition, let us look into the enlightened ratio of our Western mind, right into its blinding self-centered light as it appeared most assuredly in the scientific Enlightenment, and there discover, as Gilbert Durand says, its occulted possibility within itself—not as an offshoot or outcast of the official position (Vico against Descartes; the alchemical Newton against the mechanical Newton; the mystic Pascal against the mathematician Pascal)—but rather to see within the enlightened mind the occulted configurations of imagination at work and expressing themselves by the very means of the age's own rationalist actions.

If we could "save the phenomenon," i.e., the air of the Enlightenment, we would be moving to save the phenomena that the Enlightenment bequeathed: rational science and technology, no less; no less than the present world as left to us by the Enlightenment. In attempting this unabashedly heroic move, I shall be extending an idea of Jung's from personal psychology to cultural psychology. Jung's idea says that the thing we believe we know most about, ego-consciousness, is a dark body full of obscurities. In the midst of the Enlightenment there are thus less visible images. How does the ego look from the soul, the Enlightenment from the anima? Not the whole Enlightenment, of course; merely essential bits of it as it appeared in its imagination of air.

Ballooning, Street Lighting, Soda Water

Let us now take to the air, in a balloon, constructed by the Montgolfier brothers, June 5, 1783, the first *aerial ascent.*[8] The Montgolfiers, Charles and Robert, repeated the demonstration by means of a hot-air balloon before the public of Paris on the Champ du Mars in August. Immediately a commission was appointed to "study" the phenomenon–a commission is itself a phenomenon of the Enlightenment. "Frappé par l'expérience," as they say in their report, the commission, which included Lavoisier and the Marquis de Condorcet, submitted already in December its *Rapport fait à l'Académie des Sciences sur la machine aérostatique inventée par MM. de Montgolfier.* The aerial imagination had entered the public, scientific, official domain.

Within a few weeks (January 16, 1784), Benjamin Franklin, then 78 years old, penned a letter to a scientist physician at the Imperial Court in Vienna, attesting to the event and advising that if the good doctor wants to make a similar balloon, send someone who is "ingenious" so as not to fail from "want of Attention to some particular circumstance."[9] Note Franklin's use of ingenious. Already the spirit of "genius," in the ancient sense of a fiery-airy nimbus around the head, was becoming clever dexterity, ingenuity, technological. Franklin goes on significantly:

> It appears, as you observe, to be a Discovery of great Importance, and what may profitably give a new Turn to human Affairs. Convincing Sovereigns of the Folly of Wars, may perhaps be an Effect of it...Five Thousand Balloons capable of lifting two Men each would not cost more than Five Ships of the Line.

Franklin imagines "Ten Thousand Men descending from the Clouds" making it quite impossible for Sovereigns to control the borders of their nations. Franklin's letter seizes upon the hope for peace within a fantasy of war that arises with this new move into air. Already by 1794 the

8 The way had been prepared in 1755 in a small treatise by M. Gallien, *L'art de naviguer dans les airs, amusement physique et geometrique.* Joseph Black, one of the first to examine air in the laboratory, had shown his friends in 1767 a balloon filled with hydrogen that rose to the ceiling. Black said they would never be useful for aerial voyages.

9 B. Franklin, *On Balloons: A Letter Written from Passy, France, January 16, 1784,* privately printed for his friends by W. K. Bixby (Saint Louis: Merrymount Press, 1922).

French had set up a military school for balloonists. Curious that the first public ascent was from the Champs du Mars. Curious that the Montgolfiers' balloon carried a cock, a dog, and a duck—prelude to Sputnik and the space shots, as if the *opus contra naturam* has to prove harmless to the bestial soul,[10] or as if the bestial soul, too, had to be uplifted by enlightened science.

Even more curious that these machines of air—the Montgolfiers' hot-air balloon, the Roberts' hydrogen (1783), and then the Wrights' airplane—were invented by pairs of brothers. Mythology has such brother-pairs: the Açvins, the Dioscuri, Gemini (first ascent in June), who sometimes bear the same name and come as healers and saviors through the air, bringing hope. They are sons of the sky and ride the wind on horses. They prove themselves especially by flight over water (crossing the Channel, the Atlantic).

The hope for peace, the horse of war—that ambivalence is archetypally present in the sky-born Twins.[11] In some cultures the birth of twins is regarded with terror and marvel, with foreboding over their freakish unnaturalism and joy over the prospect of salvation, a new day.[12] Within the same image is salvation upward and the prospect of danger from which to be saved.

By the end of the century, balloons were all over the place. Lavoisier himself made several ascents to study the atmosphere as did Joseph Louis Gay-Lussac in 1804. Besides balloons, there was the new, "scientific," ascent of mountains. Horace-Bénédict de Saussure climbed Mont Blanc in 1788, noting the effects on respiration of rarified air.

Next the literal enlightenment: *lighting by gas*. Despite the fascination with sight—philosophical works on optics, improvements in telescopes,

---

10 A cat, dog, cock, sheep, etc. were sent on another balloon flight from Ecouen to Paris; they survived the flight "with no damage to their reproductive powers."

11 J. Rendel Harris, *The Cult of the Heavenly Twins* (Cambridge: At the University Press, 1906).

12 During this period (1797), the MS. of Leonardo depicting flying was discovered. Erasmus Darwin in his *The Botanic Garden* (1789) wrote these lines: "Soon shall thy arm, unconquer'd steam! afar/Drag the slow barge, or drive the rapid car;/Or on wide-waving wings expanded bear/The flying chariot through the field of air."

lens grinding and microscopes, works on light and color, the prevalance of lions and suns and kings—the eighteenth century in physical fact was a dim age. Every room, workshop and palace was illumined by candles or oil. Not until coal gas was first described by John Clayton in England in 1739 could the physical enlightenment begin.[13]

Robert Boyle had already worked with coal gas and Lavoisier's first written chemical study at the age of twenty was on street-lighting, which led him further into the chemistry of combustion.[14]

But illumination by gas required more than chemistry; it took technology too: valves, filters, wicks, fittings; extracting, measuring, separating, transporting and cleaning the gas. By 1792 these problems had been solved, and in 1798—the year of Kant's *Anthropologie in pragmatischer Hinsicht,* and Wordsworth's and Coleridge's *Lyrical Ballads,* or more appropriate to our theme and more ominous, the year of Thomas Robert Malthus's *Essay on Population,* the birth of Auguste Comte, Alessandro Volta's electric pile, and the French conquest of Rome—gas lights were installed in a Birmingham foundry. In the next decades the cities were bathed in a new light: London's Pall Mall and Lyceum Theatre; Philadelphia; Baltimore, where the first public company distributed gas to private customers. By 1819 there were over fifty-thousand gas lights in London and hundreds of miles of gas lines.

The documents of the time advancing the new invention show a language of democratic positivism—gas lighting is labor-saving, clean, safe, and cheap, bringing benefits to all. One of the principals of the new engineering, Friedrich Christian Accum (1769–1838) writes: "No dread is felt of the darkness of night. It might be a curious speculation to enquire how far, and in what respect, the morals of men would become degraded by the want of the contrivance." For "gaslights really dispel the dominion of night" whereas oil lamps but "serve the purpose of making the darkness visible."[15]

---

13 Cf. J. le Clezio, *L'Industrie du Gaz* (Paris: PUF, 1947); W. V. Farrar, et al., "William Henry, Hydrocarbons and the Gas Industry," *Ambix* 22/3 (1975), 186–96.

14 A. N. Meldrum, "Lavoisier's Early Work in Science," *Isis* 19 (1933), 337. The Academy of Sciences offered prizes for a study on lighting a city at night. Lavoisier won a gold medal, and his study took up such questions as materials, wicks, costs, optics, reflectors, lantern design, treating the oils, etc. This, in the 1760s: how close to today and how far from the alchemy of the same period.

15 F. C. Accum, *Description of the Process of Manufacturing Coal Gas* (London: Thomas Boys, 1820).

The enlightenment literalized and moralized: deprivation of gas-lighting becomes a *privatio boni.* To light the night, and actually dispel darkness, its dreadful dominion, implies the upgrading of mankind.

The spirit in the bottle: The great investigative chemists–Scheele in Sweden; Lavoisier in France; Boyle, Henry Cavendish, and Joseph Priestley in England–were eager to understand the nature of the bubbly waters springing from the earth, such as at Bad Pyrmont in Germany.[16] Here was an air apparently trapped in water. What sort of air is this and how does the water hold the air? Lavoisier and Scheele isolated the gas in the water, *gaz acide carbonique,* and Priestley in 1772 published his *Directions for Impregnating Water with Fixed Air.*

While the Fathers of the American Revolution–Thomas Jefferson, James Madison, Benjamin Rush–studied mineral waters, two enterprising Englishmen produced a technical device for making effervescent waters and for manufacturing it on a commercial scale. Between 1789 and 1821 bottling plants were opened in Dublin, Geneva, Paris, London and Dresden, and the first artificial mineral-water business of Schweppe, Paul and Gosse began in Switzerland. "Soda Water" entered the language in 1798–that remarkable year. Experimental chemistry, ingenuity, and pop culture went hand in hand: Benjamin Silliman, a pioneer chemist of the new United States (who learned in Accum's manufacturing plant in England and in whose honor one of Yale's twelve colleges is named), among other contributions to science, produced and bottled soda water on a commercial basis and opened a public place for dispensing it, a soda fountain. This democratic artificial spa, a refreshing pause on main street, was now established in Western social life: the soft drink of aerated water for anyone, the spirit in the bottle in a six-pack, and now in the United States consumed more than milk, coffee or beer: 422 twelve-ounce containers per capita in 1980 (and by 1990, 10 gallons more per capita than consumption of water).

16 On the history of soda water and its early chemistry, see J.J. Riley, *A History of the American Soft Drink Industry: Bottled Carbonated Beverages, 1807-1957* (Washington, D.C.: American Bottlers Carbonated Beverages, 1958; C.A. Mitchell, *Mineral and Aerated Waters* (London: Constable), 1913.

New soda powders were dispensed to make water fizz. Scientific papers stated the benefits of aerated water. Physicians used "fixed air" (air of the laboratory) in treating putrid kinds of diseases such as small pox, driving out the *putrefactio* by means of enemas of fixed air and carbonated waters.[17] Soda water, like gas lighting by Accum and ballooning by Franklin, was presented as a public boon, hopes for peace and health, darkness dispelled. It is as if the chemical revolution brought forth advertising as part of its effervescence, bubbling up and spewing forth new words for new products and procedures. To pamphlet, pamphleteer, and pamphleting as active verbs entered the language in the 1700s. Gas, steam, hot air, windy, blowhard—we still use these epithets to mock the words of advertising, recognizing unconsciously that the ascensionism of air is what gives the original impetus to advertising's uplifting, improving hyperbole, its educative mission to inform the public. A huge multiplication of words accompanied the new chemistry in order to illumine the citizens and help them sail with the *Zeitgeist.*[18]

Yet it was in focusing upon the questions of bubbly water that John Dalton (1766–1844), in his 1803 treatise *On the Absorption of Gases by Water,* was able to distinguish clearly between chemistry and mechanics, between combining things and mixing them: "All gases that enter into water by means... of pressure, and are wholly disengaged again by the removal of that pressure, are mechanically mixed with the liquid, and not chemically combined with it."[19] Since water does not admit all gases equally, different gases have different ultimate particle weights, which led Dalton to publish in that same volume his first list of atomic weights.

---

17 Some curious pneumatic treatments are described by W.V. Farrar, et al., "The Henry's of Manchester: Part I," *Ambix* 20/3 (1973), 200–205. Humphry Davy (see below), while a very young man, was Superintendent at the "Pneumatic Medical Institution" near Bristol from where, probably, he acquired the nitrous oxide. An aim of the work at the Institution was to improve the health of factory workers with oxygen.

18 Advertising and pamphleteering were radically advanced by the invention of the paper machine in France in1798. Hitherto, all paper had been handmade.

19 Published in *Memoirs of the Literary and Philosophical Society of Manchester,* Second Series, vol. 1 (Manchester: S. Russell for R. Bickerstaff, 1805).

Intermezzo: The Psychology of Extraversion

I could go on and on with the aerial fascination of the Enlightenment: James Watt and the steam engine, steam boat, steam heat; blast furnace improvements under George III; the investigations of respiration that were then compelling physiology;[20] study and mathematics of wind force in sails, wind gauges,[21] and the measuring of storms by Admiral Beaufort's wind scale (1805). But what has all this to do with psychology for that matter? Has my removal from Europe to the United States blown me off course, a de-rangement toward American fascination with gadgetry? Or is it rather that the path of psychology has been single and narrowed to subjective experience? Investigations of the deepest collective unconscious have more or less stuck to introverted texts of theologians, mystics, shamans, alchemists, poets, dreamers. Even Jung's definition of the image, that starting point for archetypal psychology, states the introverted perspective: "I do not mean the psychic reflection of an external object, but a...*fantasy image,* which is related only indirectly to the perception of an external object" (*CW*6: 743).

What about the depth psychology of extraversion, the images within the soul of the world? Does not the *anima mundi* move its imagination also in the world of exterior manifestions? The psychology of extraversion has been upheld at Eranos by two men, Adolf Portmann and Samuel Sambursky. For years here they examined the external world and ideas about it so that this chapter is also in homage to them. More specifically my aim is psychology, the rectification of its focus from an imagination held narrowly to subjectivity and the therapy of the private individual, to the imagination of extraversion and the therapy of the public world, where an imminent radical breakdown threatens all our subjective lives, a world that has been deprived of its depth and subjectivity by the prejudices of our psychology. Archetypal, collective,

20 For two excellent examinations of respiration theories, see L.G. Wilson, "The Transformation of the Concepts of Respiration in the Seventeenth Century," *Isis* 51 (1960), 161–72; C.A. Culotta, "Respiration and the Lavoisier Tradition: Theory and Modification, 1777–1850," *Transactions of the American Philosophical Society, New Series,* vol. 62, no. 3 (1972), 3–41.

21 Cf. Col. Beaufoy, F.R.S., "Experiments on the Resistance of Air and on Air as a moving Power," *Annals of Philosophy,* vol. 8, ed. T. Thomson (London: Baldwin, Cradock, and Joy, 1816), 94–108.

unconscious—these adjectives apply as much to phenomena out there as in here, providing we release our minds from depth psychology's introverted bias.

Please: by a psychology of introversion I do not mean an extraverted psychology, using behavioristic, historical or sociological perspectives to study phenomenon, whether in the world or in the person. I do mean giving due recognition to the "ascendency of the object over the course of psychic events" (*CW*6: 569) where "interest and attention are directed to objective happenings ... Not only people but things seize and rivet ... attention" (*CW*6: 563). We can extend depth psychology from persons to things, places and ideas as manifestations of imagination. The same imagination, the same soul, that presented itself in fifteenth- and sixteenth-century alchemy showed itself in the extraverted psychology of the explorers seeking gold, the journey across the perilous seas, the seven cities, the impossible passage, the fountain of youth, the black man and lost Atlantis—the world as metaphor. Thus in chemistry, there is an imagination in every experiment and invention. The cosmos of things, their arrangement, displays archetypal patterns; the world's soul is subject to depth psychological analysis because imagination takes places in the construction of things as much as it takes places in the order of words. The spirit, that perennial concern of Eranos, cannot be limited to a literalization in events called spiritual; spirit blows through the world as it did on the first day of creation, and in ever-continuing creation.

Humphry Davy

So back to the world, and to *sniffing*. This was the first means of differentiating the airs, a diakrisis of the spirits: marsh-gas, coal gas, air after thunderstorms. Imagine the dangers: ammonia, chlorine, hydrogen sulphide—and no warnings on the bottles. The dare-devil assistant of Lavoisier, Pilatre de Rozier, the first human ever to ascend in a balloon also invented the gas mask with which he descended into beer vats and the Paris sewers (only to be killed soon after in an attempt to cross the Channel by balloon).[22] The chemists were in wine cellars, cesspools, swamps, breweries, prisons, collecting various airs.

22 Cf. C.N.A. Duval, "Pilatre de Rozier (1754–1785), chemist and first aeronaut," trans. R.E. Oesper, *Chymia* 12 (1967), 99–117.

Volta (1745–1827, born and died in Como) worked with a new gadget, the eudiometer, discovering methane in the bubbles of Lago Maggiore in November 1776.

But I want to tell you specifically about nitrous oxide, the laughing gas that Joseph Priestley had "discovered" in 1772 but was considered a noxious substance until a lad of twenty, Humphry Davy (1778–1829) tried it on himself in his attic bedroom near Bristol in 1798. After ten months of experimentation and three more of writing, Davy published his *Researches, Chemical and Philosophical; Chiefly Concerning Nitrous Oxide*.[23]

Davy writes that his early experiments were "attended by a highly pleasurable thrilling, particularly in the chest and the extremities."[24] Davy induced at least eighteen others to try the gas and they contributed descriptions of their sensations to his research. One said "I felt like the sound of a harp."[25] Davy took moonlight walks, composing verse under influence of the gas; Coleridge, a close friend of Davy's, enjoyed "a highly pleasurable sensation of warmth over my whole frame."[26] And the poet Robert Southey, then twenty-five, wrote his brother:

> Oh, Tom! Such gas has Davy discovered, the gaseous oxide! Oh, Tom! I have had some; it made me laugh and tingle in every toe and finger tip. Davy has actually invented a new pleasure for which language has no name. Oh, Tom! I am going for more this evening.[27]

Humphry Davy bears attention because he provides an illustrative example of the imagination of air in its turn to the world. In Davy two character streaks appear together, senex and puer. First, the puer

---

23 H. Davy, *Researches, Chemical and Philosophical; Chiefly Concerning Nirtous Oxide, or Dephlogisticated Nitrous and its Respiration* (London: J. Johnson, 1800).

24 Ibid., 458.

25 Ibid., 496. The harp simile has the profound cosmological implications of the *anima mundi* as air, as this well-known passage from Coleridge's "The Eolian Harp" (1795) shows (*Selected Poetry* [Oxford: Oxford University Press, 1997], 28):

> And what if all of animated nature
> Be but organic harps, diversely framed,
> That tremble into thought, as o'er them sweeps
> Plastic and vast, one intellectual breeze,
> At once the Soul of each, and God of All?

26 E.B. Smith, "A Note on Humphry Davy's Experiments on the Respiration of Nitrous Oxide," in S. Forgan, *Science and the Sons of Genius: Studies on Humphry Davy* (London: Science Reviews Ltd., 1980), 233.

27 Ibid.

experimenter with laughing gas, and poetic hero of whom Coleridge wrote, "the Father and Founder of philosophic Alchemy, the Man who *born* a Poet first converted Poetry into Science and *realized* what few men possessed Genius enough to *fancy*."[28] For Coleridge, Davy (after Wordsworth) was the greatest man of the age because his chemistry was poetry accomplished in nature, materialized: science was a poetic undertaking, a *songe* of the air. With Davy we move from the Enlightenment to the Shelleyian vision and Byronic stance: at age seventeen, Davy had written his *The Sons of Genius*, a puer testament in which science carries one on wings above terrestrial cares:

> To scan the laws of Nature, to explore
> The tranquil reign of mild Philosophy;
> Or on Newtonian wings sublime to soar
> Through the bright regions of the starry sky.[29]

In his early twenties we see the two streaks in his daily schedule: he worked on his epic *Lover of Nature* before breakfast and *The Feelings of Eldon* just after, followed by five hours straight of experimentation—Science and Poetry together. He could play with nitrous oxide *and* laboriously write the details and see it into print.

It was, however, his other character streak, a hesitant and practical attention to "the minute alterations in the external world,"[30] that made him famous in his time and renowned in the history of science. He invented the safety lamp for coal mines. He had immense influence on farming.[31] By 1813, Davy had identified forty-seven of the new chemical elements, having himself isolated by electrical experimentation, sodium,

---

28 *Collected Letters of Samuel Taylor Coleridge,* 6 vols., ed. E.L. Griggs (Oxford: Clarendon Press, 2000–2002), 5: 809.

29 T.H. Levere, "Humphry Davy, 'The Sons of Genius,' and the Idea of Glory," in Forgan, *Science and the Sons of Genius,* 35.

30 *The Collected Works of Sir Humphry Davy,* 9 vols., ed. J. Davy (London: Smith, Elder and Co., 1839–40), 2: 311.

31 W.D. Miles, "Sir Humphrey Davie, the Prince of Agricultural Chemists," *Chymia* 7 (1961), 134: "Davy was a prophet who showed farmers what might be gained from science ... Few chemistry books have had as much influence on the layman as [his] *Elements of Agricultural Chemistry.*"

potassium, calcium, strontium, barium, magnesium,[32] and pointed further to beryllium and aluminium.

What precisely tames the puer spirit of laughing gas and epic verse, placing it in the service of the public good? The question is both psychological and historical, since it refers also to the spirit of an age that moved its early pneumatic adventures in the gaseous realm into applied technology of democratic positivism. In Davy's case, some have answered "ambition," reputation, or *fama,* as it was called in the Renaissance. Idealism is inherent to the imagination of air. It soars with lofty *superbia*. Ambition is applied idealism; it harnesses the spiritual ideals to practical works that gain public recognition–recognition from the human world. Puer ambition must be more than mere vanity and opportunism.[33] It serves to bring puer ascensionism into the social nexus. Davy wrote:

> The voice of fame is murmuring in my ear–My mind has been excited by the unexpected plaudits of the multitude–I dream of greatness and utility–I dream of science restoring to Nature what Luxury, what civilization have stolen from her – pure hearts, the forme of angels, bosoms beautiful; and panting with joy and hope...[34]

When addressing the question of the public aim of science, Davy, in his last written work, used the image of the alchemist. The difference between alchemical charlatans and "true alchemical philosophers" is that the latter were concerned "to ameliorate the condition of humanity and to support the interests of religio...[so that] their discoveries [were]

32 C. Singer, *A Short History of Scientific Ideas to 1900* (Oxford: At the Clarendon Press, 1959), 346.

33 Davy was criticized for typically *puer* traits. We find these words in his biographers and in comments by his adversaries and critics: "mercurial," "fragmentary," "tentative suggestions rather than comprehensive theories," "reformer," "lifelong anti-materialism," "opportunist," "love of social glamour," "popular idol," "rebel," "romantic," "exuberance," "brilliant but unfocussed life." His last years showed a typical *senex* conversion: he worked on corrosion of ships' bottoms, chemical archeology at Herculaneum, geology, and suffered a stroke in Geneva leaving him crippled at the end. See further, J.Z. Fullmer, "Humphry Davy's Adversaries," *Chymia* 8 (1962), 147–65. On the psychological characteristics of puer and senex, see J. Hillman, *Senex & Puer, UE* 3.

34 Levere, "Humphry Davy," 43.

eminently useful."[35] The amelioration of human conditions coincided with the aims of an extraverted religion of good works; science could fulfill God's purpose, less by defining the mind of God and his universal laws of Nature in theoretical physics and more by furthering God's redemptive intentions through applied chemistry. Chemistry materialized the aim to restore to Nature her angelic anima.

This view must have led Davy further from his earlier, "starry sky" poetry about which he later wrote: "These were the visions of my youth/Which fled before the voice of Truth."[36] Truth as he grew older seemed now to lie wholly with Locke, for he asserted that all knowledge was acquired by means of the senses and declared (in 1812) that "Nature has no archetype in the human imagination,"[37] implying that nature can be known by direct experimentation only. Coleridge was appalled, complaining that Davy "was determined to mould himself upon the age in order to make the age mould itself upon him."[38] Coleridge saw only popularity, vanity, and a fall away from the *Naturphilosophie* of Schelling and the new Romanticism. For Davy, however, there was no such polarity–a favorite term of Coleridge, and not of Davy himself who actually worked with electricity and electromagnetism from which the term arose–between poetic and scientific genius or between ideal and practical action.

Davy gives us, further, a clue to the spirit of empiricism that informs the period from Jan Baptist van Helmont and Robert Boyle through Davy. These men played even as they measured:[39] Benjamin Franklin with his kite; Robert Hooke with his gadgets; Stephen Hales examining his animals and plants; Joseph Louis Gay-Lussac ascending to 7,000 meters in a balloon; Humphry Davy and his crowd sniffing. It was not merely that magical tricks and alchemical transformations still pervaded the new chemistry, but that the occupation with air constellated its elemental force: risk, flight, fancy. The spirit of experimentation–the puer

35 Levere, "Humphry Davy," 37.

36 *Fragmentary Remains, Literary and Scientific, of Sir Humphry Davy,* ed. J. Davy (London: John Churchill, 1858), 13.

37 Levere, "Humphry Davy," 40.

38 *The Notebooks of Samuel Taylor Coleridge,* Volume 2: 1804–1808, ed. K. Coburn (Princeton, N.J.: Princeton University Press,1961), 1855.

39 Cf. L. Thorndike, *A History of Magic and Experimental Science,* 8 vols. (New York: Columbia University Press, 1947–1953), 8:601n56.

impulse had not yet succumbed to the pre-arranged intentions of what experiments came to be in later science.

A lab experiment now is a senex ritual repeating what is already known. Less an investigative act of curiosity, it is more an initiation into the scientific paradigm by an imitative performance of what the figures of science, now senex patriarchs of scientific laws, did centuries ago. Even a research experiment is to test a law or gain evidence for (or against) it. Puer experimentation—let's try and see what happens; Davy in his attic chamber; the game and fun of it—this is now all but missing. Again, think of the puer risk of handling gases: methane, ethylene, chlorine, hydrogen cyanide, carbon monoxide, nitrogen—the noxious fumes, explosions, asphyxiations, collapse of balloons. The very dangers taught care; scientific method is not a pure senex invention. It arises as a protective necessity within the puer drive and it begins in the loyalty one gives to one's poetic excitement. Empirics is not only a senex preserve; it can lift a wing as well.

Balloons, soda bubbles, laughing gas—they demonstrate the new, extraordinary, and mundane imagination of air of the time. These examples also serve to demonstrate my method here. Psychological method requires that one go to the phenomenon itself, judgment suspended. We enter the material with the patient, as the chemist in the beer vat, the cesspool. Our discipline requires that we go where the air itself went, wherever it went. Just here, the spiritual attitude contrasts with the psychological. Where spirit can regard mundane phenomena against a background of eternal verities, reminding the mundane of its origin in the transmundane, calling the fallen phenomena, in outrage, compassion, or nostalgia, to rise up to redemption, the psychological method follows the phenomena downward into their pathologized condition, as did Freud and Jung with their cases, attempting redemption of the mundane and the material from within itself. From the psychological viewpoint, precisely there where the symptom is most crass, most manifest and embarrassing, is where the soul clamors for understanding.

Phlogiston or Oxygen

So what was in the wind? How did the elemental air inspire these inventions and transform itself into these useful tools: guns and pumps, lamps and drills, balloons and bubbly water?

The answer is well-known. Probably no scientific revolution has been so thoroughly documented as the foundations of modern chemistry[40] by Joseph Black, James Watt, Cavendish, Priestley, Scheele, and Lavoisier who himself used the term "chemical revolution."[41] Sometimes the revolution is called the overthrow of the phlogiston theory, or the death knell of alchemy. It occurred concurrently with the American and French revolutions. Both Priestley and Lavoisier were political "revolutionaries": Priestley, a highly active dissident theologian, finally driven to take refuge in Pennsylvania in old age; Lavoisier, though originally part of the republican administration, executed during the Terror.

Lavoisier's work ran parallel with and culminated the differentiation of air that, let us say, began with Robert Boyle's *New Experiments, Physico-mechanicall, touching the Spring of the Air and its Effects* (1660) and his tract on the *Relation betwixt Flame and Aire* (1672), John Mayow's *On Respiration* (1668), and John Evelyn's *Fumifugium* (1661) on the pollution of the air of London. With the eighteenth century came "A Specimen of an attempt to analyze the Air by a great variety of chymio-statistical Experiments," a long chapter in Hales's *Vegetable Staticks* (1727); Black's "Experiments upon Magnesia Alba, Quick-lime, and some other Alcaline Substances" (1756, his study of effervescence or "fixed air" (carbon dioxide); Daniel Rutherford's dissertation (1772), which described nitrogen; Torbern Bergman's *Om Luftsyra* (1773); Cavendish's "Three Papers Containing Experiments on Factitious Air" (1766) and his "Experiments on Air" (1784); Marsilio Landriani's *Ricerche fisiche intorno alla salubrità dell'aria* (1775); Watt's "Thoughts on the constituent parts of water and of

40 J.B. Conant, *Overthrow of the Phlogiston Theory: The Chemical Revolution of 1775–1789* (Cambridge, Mass.: Harvard University Press, 1950); see also T.S. Kuhn, *The Structure of Scientific Revolutions* (Chicago: University of Chicago Press, 1970), 53–56.

41 "All young chemists adopt the theory and from that I conclude that the revolution in chemistry has come to pass" (1791), quoted in the Introduction to the Dover Edition of Lavoisier's 1790 *Elements of Chemistry in a New Systematic Order containing all the Modern Discoveries* (Mineola, N.Y.: Dover Publications, 1965), xxix.

dephlogisticated air" (1784); Scheele's description of his experiments in Sweden, "Chemical Treatise on Air and Fire" (1777); and Priestley's three-volume *Experiments and Observations on different kinds of Air* (1774–77).

Priestley's chapters dealt with vitriolic air, vegetable acid air, marine acid air, mephitic air, red nitrous vapor, putrid air, and on and on. It is hard for us to realize what assiduous devotion it needs to examine and distinguish the components of the common air we breath. By means of their techniques and apparatus the ancient element of air was being rapidly dismembered into components and individual gases identified.[42]

Much as the subterranean earth and its minerals had fascinated the alchemical writers earlier and the celestial bodies, ether, light, and optics had fascinated the mathematical and physical philosophers (Spinoza, Galilei, Descartes, Newton), air was the focus of the chemical imagination. It was subject to the human hand: the invisible elastic fluid, the soul breath, could be pumped, expanded, exploded, evacuated, condensed, poisoned, separated and weighed. Air had become one of the new *tria prima* of matter: solid, liquid, gas. Chemistry arises as the materialization of air.

Let me demonstrate the paradigm shift, the death knell of alchemy, before your imagining eyes. If a strip or bar of metal is calcined, that is, dry roasted in the intense heat of a burning glass–the old alchemical operation of *calcinatio*[43]–the calx or powdery residue of the metal weighs more than the original metal. Does this heavy calx remaining

42 A century earlier, Boyle had already regarded it as a composite, a "confused aggregate;" "there is scarce a more heterogeneous body in the world" (*Suspicions about Some Hidden Qualities of the Air,* 1674). Hales continues the same idea:

"It is well known that air is a fine elastic fluid, with particles of very different natures floating in it..." (*Vegetable Staticks,* 1727). Once the idea that air was a compositum took hold of consciousness, it became fascinated with the differentiation and naming of its "particles."

43 The crucial operation of the transition to chemistry was calcination; the crucial material, mercury. Cf. C.E. Perrin, "Prelude to Lavoisier's Theory of Calcination: Some Observations on *Mercurius Calcinatus, per se,*" *Ambix* 16 (1969), 140–51. From the psychological viewpoint, the *calcinatio* is the *operatio* that dries out the emotional humors and moistures, rendering the material *sec* (dry) and objective, i.e., scientific; thereby, Mercurius, the fugitive spirit of alchemy and God of its imagistic transformations, received a new fixation in the objectivity of the chemical method.

mean that something volatile in the metal has been burned away, subtracted, leaving a heavy deposit? If this is your account, then you belong to the school of Stahl and would call the "something volatile" that has burned away *phlogiston*.

If, however, you consider the heavier residue to indicate that calcining has added something to the metal that is present in the calx and was not present in the metal (at all or to the same degree), then you belong to the school of Lavoisier and the "something added" is *oxygen*. Although Scheele and Priestley had earlier isolated "dephlogisticated air," Lavoisier recognized its significance, naming it "oxygen" in 1779. Burning is oxidation, the residues of metals are oxides, combustion is a combinatory process, hence the body left after the conflagration is heavier. Phlogiston became superfluous to chemical explanation.

Phlogiston had been imagined to have a negative weight or at least to be exempt from the laws of gravity.[44] As such it was akin to the Stoic's pneuma, Aristotle's absolute lightness, and to the vitalistic anima in Georg Ernst Stahl's (1660–1734) chemical medicine. Alchemy finally collapsed when this last breath of the religious-alchemical imagination expired. Its aerial fantasies burned out. It stopped imagining itself further and the new images appeared in chemistry.

Priestley clung to a notion of phlogiston to the end, perhaps because of its roots in an ancient religious sense of the material world. Moreover, the idea of phlogiston spoke to common sense, like the idea of the sun rising and setting as it revolved around the earth. Girolamo Cardano (*De subtilitate*, 1547) and Leonardo da Vinci, for instance, had believed that burning adds weight to things because in the process they lose their celestial lightness, their innate breath of the world soul; hence for Leonardo a corpse is heavier than a living body. (Today's materialism reads death otherwise: recent experiments attempt to compute weight *loss* at the moment of death as evidence for the departure of a material soul.[45])

44 Cf. J.R. Partington, *A History of Chemistry*, 4 vols. (London: Macmillan, 1961–70), 3: 614. Jeremias Benjamin Richter (1762–1807), who considered chemistry applied mathematics and was so important to the shift of chemistry toward physical-mathematical models, applied his mathematics and determined the "weight" of phlogiston.

45 See Ian Sample, "Is there lightness after death?" http://www.guardian.co.uk/film/2004/feb/19/science.science (accessed 14 July 2010).

Besides this archetypal trace of the celestial pneuma still to be found in phlogiston, it more directly derives from the sulfur of the Paracelsian *tria prima (sulfur phlogistos)*, and Johann Joachim Becher (1635–1682),[46] from whom Stahl took the idea, was an alchemist. Stahl says that phlogiston "is chiefly found in fatty materials." Its name, meaning *brennlich*[47] (combustible), he says, derives from its action within compounds, since it does not appear by itself. Phlogiston is that invisible, ubiquitous, inflammable richness in all things, its burning compulsion to life, using air as its medium, and like sulfur acts as the joyful, fat, and oily vivifier.[48]

Oxygen has a different ancestry. The word comes from the Greek prefix *oxy-*, from *oxys*, acute, sharp, hasty, pungent, shrill, bright, sour. It is an epithet of Ares (*Iliad* 2:440). Lavoisier asserted that oxygen is the necessary component in all acidity. (Hence, *Sauerstoff* in German for oxygen.) Lavoisier was wrong in his wide claim, and Davy, Richard Kirwan, Louis-Bernard Guyton de Morveau, and especially Priestley, did not go along with the elevation of oxygen into a single explanatory principle for acidity, a universal elemental essence much like the phlogiston it was replacing.[49] When Lavoisier designed the shorthand symbol for his *principe*

46 On Becher as alchemist, see Thorndike, *A History of Magic and Experimental Science*, 7:578ff.

47 Stahl's relevant passages on phlogiston are given in English in *A Source Book in Chemistry, 1400–1900*, ed. H.M. Leicester and H.S. Krickstein (Cambridge, Mass.: Harvard University Press, 1968), 59–62.

48 "Sulfur is a formative, partly gaseous, partly fiery, partaking of an ethereal nature; it is that whence strength proceeds, and life inheres in things." *Lexicon* s.v. "Sulfur." Cf. Jung's compact chapter on Sulfur in *CW* 14:42, and his remarks on Sendivogius's *De Sulfure* (*CW* 12:396–98) concerning imagination, which we referred to at the beginning of this chapter, and my passages on sulfur elsewhere in this volume. Further on the close relation of sulfur and phlogiston, see H.M. Leicester, "Lomonosov's Views on Combustion and Phlogiston," *Ambix* 22 (1975), 1–9.

49 "Several of [Lavoisier's] contemporaries...shared the view that the oxygen theory of acidity was in the tradition of explanation-by-principle dating back to Stahl and probably to Paracelsus..." H.E. LeGrand, "A Note on Fixed Air: The Universal Acid," *Ambix* 20 (1973), 94. "We may accuse Lavoisier of having made a whole philosophy out of oxygen," M.P. Crosland, "Lavoisier's Theory of Acidity," *Isis* 64 (1973), 325. "Lavoisier's oxygen theory was from the beginning as much a theory of acidity as a theory of combustion" (Ibid., 306), since the term he coined for air (oxygen) means "principle of acidity rather than principle of combustibility [phlogiston]" (Ibid., 307), implying that sour air is indeed the root metaphor of the chemical revolution. The metaphor was "right" even if the material was "wrong,"

oxygine, he drew it with sharp points[50] because acids were imagined in the eighteenth century to be composed of atoms with spikes, hence their biting, corrosive effect.

Phlogiston, through its sulfuric ancestry, was warm, oily, and generous; oxygen, through its acidic ancestry, was corrosive and aggressive. The chemical revolution brightened, and soured, the air. The exchange of alchemy for chemistry was, in short, an exchange of phlogiston for oxygen. What went was vitalism and the final cause; what came was atomism and the material cause. What went was Stahl's *anima;* what came was Lavoisier's *methode.* What went was the meaning in chemical transformations; what came was their explanation.

The soured air occurs together with the triumph of a nominalist theory of matter.[51] For the Stahlians, the stuff of the world, however particularized it may be on analysis, yet depends upon fundamental essences that should not be confused with the particulars themselves as they are in atomic theory. And the resistance of some chemistry of the time (Davy, for instance) to the table of atomic weights was the multiplication of elements seeming to indicate a multiplication of essences. The sharp, acidic eye was analyzing into ever more, ever smaller and more abstract particulars; in explanation, dissolution took precedence, and "element" lost its elemental, essential sense. The acid pollution of the world, its dissolution into particulates, and the loss of the essential

which raises questions about the place of mistakes—as they are called—in changes of *Weltbild:* "who" makes them; why do they "catch on"; and why are they necessary? In defense of Lavoisier, see H. Guerlac, *Lavoisier—The Crucial Year: The Background and Origin of His First Experiments on Combustion in 1772* (Ithaca, N.Y.: Cornell University Press, 1961).

50 Cf. M.P. Crosland, *Historical Studies in the Language of Chemistry* (Cambridge, Mass.: Harvard University Press, 1962).

51 Crosland, *Historical Studies in the Language of Chemistry,* 170–71. This nominalism went together with the mathematization of chemistry pursued so successfully by the French, Jeremias Benjamin Richter, and John Dalton to whom Coleridge passionately objected, struggling to keep his vision of chemistry as "poetry... substantiated and realized in nature: yea, nature itself disclosed to us... as at once the poet and the poem!" *The Friend: A Series of Essays,* vol. 3 (1818), in *The Collected Works of Samuel Taylor Coleridge* (Princeton, N.J.: Princeton University Press, 1969), 4:471. Against Dalton, Coleridge wrote: "an attempt to destroy chemistry itself." "Thus the theorist who reduces the chemical process to the positions of atoms, would doubtless thereby render chemistry calculable... by destroying the chemical process itself, and substitute[s] for it a *mote dance* of abstractions..." *Lay Sermons, Collected Works of Coleridge,* 6:173–74n.

sense of soul in the material world are all prefigured in the imagination of air as oxygen.

A shift in the significance of air is a shift in the *anima mundi*, a change of cosmos. The seventeenth century, largely owing to Helmont and Boyle, had dismissed air as a true element. Alchemy was mainly occupied with the discrimination of earths (metals), alterations of waters (distilling, condensing, dissolving, tincturing) and the art of fire. In eighteenth-century chemical thought, wherever the four elements did appear, earth, water, and fire remain while air is conspicuously missing. It was merely a facilitator, a pressure to keep a flame steady, a medium for refraction, a vehicle for phlogiston. The *souffleur* did not feed the fire with his bellows, for air itself did not enter into combustion. The invisible imagination, air, had been excluded from participating in the Cartesian-Newtonian world. Hence Enlightenment rationalism, mechanism, and turgid sentimentalism: it had no air in it.

Then came the chemical revolution. Air became the prime element in combustion and combustion the essence of chemistry. Where Helmont had eliminated air in favour of water, Cavendish could now show that water dissolved into gas. For Lavoisier, water was simply an oxide of hydrogen. The archetypal fantasy of the processional transformation of elements, familiar since the Presocratics, ever-continues as the air, and so does the archetypal argument concerning priority among them.

As technology could now be applied to air, it became materialized and took on weight. The powers dormant within it—demons, images, pneumatic tensions, underworld subtleties—also materialized. They did not materialize literally as in medieval visions but kept their invisibility as the pneumatic impetus within the *Zeitgeist*. The demons and angels of the aerial imagination took wing and filled the air with new notions, inventions, positive expansionism, a heavenward hope as explosive as aerial nitre[52]—our common air is mainly nitrogen. Upward, onward—the roots of revolution and romanticism lie in the air. Imagination itself became positivist, progressivist, material, active.

52 "Aerial nitre" or the explosive "air" in gunpowder played a devastating role in the persecution of both Priestley and Lavoisier. Priestley had used a gunpowder metaphor in one of his dissident, pro-revolution writings leading some to take him literally, and the charges against Lavoisier laid blame on him for mismanaging the powder magazine at the time of the Bastille riot. The chemical and political revolutions were fatefully entwined. Ironically, one of the major accusations brought by

Weighing the Air

With this we come to Henry Cavendish (1731–1810), the crucial figure in the mathematization of air. His first published works were his "Three Papers, Containing Experiments on Factitious Air,"[53] i.e., air produced through laboratory arts. He isolated hydrogen (inflammable air) and accurately set forth its weight in comparison with the density of common air. He synthesized water, thereby showing that it is not an element, but arises from two distinct airs. He theorized that cold is generated from substances transmuting into air. And among other extraordinary accomplishments he performed the task of "weighing the world," as he called it, calculating the density of this planet and arriving at a number remarkably close to the present estimate. This, called the *Cavendish experiment,* was also published in that year 1798. As well, he collaborated with John Michell's attempt to determine the weight of the stars.[54] Cavendish has been considered the most brilliant and accurate experimenter in physics, electricity, thermodynamics, and chemistry of the eighteenth century, but I want to spend a few moments on his character.

When Henry Cavendish was two, his mother died; he resided with his father, also a scientist. The father lived until Henry was fifty-two, immediately after which he opened his only longer term correspondence, with Michell and with Priestley, and engaged his scientific assistant, Charles Blagden.[55] Science was the content and spirit of these relationships. For as a recent biographer writes: "All who knew him were agreed about his striking deficiencies as a human being . . . 'he did not love; he did not hate; he did not hope; he did not fear.'"[56] The lack of affection appears especially in his morbid shyness regarding women.

Cavendish "ordered his dinner daily by note, which he left at a certain hour on the hall table" and "would never see a female servant."[57]

---

brought by Marat against Lavoisier was that the construction of the city walls around Paris, which Lavoisier authorized, polluted the air.

53 Published in *Philosophical Transactions* 56 (1766).

54 R. McCormmach, "John Michell and Henry Cavendish: Weighing the Stars," *British Journal for the History of Science* 4 (1968), 126–55.

55 Ibid., 129n11.

56 A. J. Berry, *Henry Cavendish: His Life and Scientific Work,* London: Huchinson, 1960, 22.

57 G. Wilson, *The Life of the Hon. Henry Cavendish* (London: Cavendish Society, 1851), 169.

Once he was so disconcerted by bumping into a maid on the stairs that he immediately had constructed a second staircase so as never to be faced with this phenomenon again. At the Club one evening, the gentlemen were assembled before an undraped window, peering out. Cavendish joined the group assuming they were studying the moon; but when Cavendish discovered it was a "very pretty girl" he "turned away with intense disgust."[58] His biographer writes in 1851:

> To the other objects of common regard which excite and gratify the fancy, the imagination, the emotions, and the higher affections, he was equally indifferent. The Beautiful, the Sublime, and the Spiritual seem to have lain altogether beyond his horizon. The culture of the external senses, which the prosecution of researches in the physical sciences, secures ... did nothing in Cavendish's case, to quicken the perception of beauty, whether of form or sound or colour. Many of our natural philosophers have had a strong and cultivated aesthetical sense; and have taken great delight in ... the fine arts. For none of these does Cavendish seem to have cared.[59]

Even his interest in his experimental instruments remained functional, a concern for accuracy only. Unlike Black or Accum, he took no care about elegance of form or value of material.[60] On his geological researches in open country, we find no response to the natural scenery or observations about the inhabitants or historical associations with the different localities. Cavendish had his eye only on his instruments, crossing the country, says his biographer "like a railway surveyor."

When he found himself dying in 1810, nearly eighty, an observer writes:

> He gave directions to his servant to leave him alone, and not to return till a certain time ... by which he expected to be no longer alive. His servant ... was anxious about him, opened the door of the room before the time specified ... Mr. Cavendish ... was offended at the intrusion, and ordered him out of the room ... commanding him not by any means to return till the time specified. When he did come back at that time, he found his master dead.[61]

58 Ibid., 170.
59 Ibid., 178.
60 Ibid., 178n.
61 Ibid., 182.

When Cavendish's trunks and cupboards were inspected for report to the next of kin, "they found parts of embroidered dresses, and much valuable jewellery, including a lady's stomacher, richly decorated with diamonds."[62]

Let us say that the "striking deficiencies" mentioned by Cavendish's biographers would today be referred to as an "anima problem." Some criteria of anima are:

–a sense of beauty: of which Cavendish was devoid;
–sensuousness: Cavendish ate mutton most nights of his life;
–vanity: Cavendish refused to sit for a portrait, and so we have no sure depiction of his face; he wore the same unchanging outmoded fashion his life long;
– fantasy: impelled by the flow of life, Cavendish was always concise and precise, living by the clock;
–delight in women, indolence, gossip: biographers and acquaintances report a void;
–affection for nature: Cavendish weighed it and surveyed it;
–fascination with death: he died on schedule, fulfilling a matter-of-fact prediction, his face to the wall.

My purpose here is neither to ridicule Cavendish nor to diagnose him.[63] Nor is it to judge. Judge not lest ye be judged by your very judgment. I have told this story to suggest that the Cavendish phenomenon—obsession with density, weight, number, and measure—was necessary to materialize the air, which in turn was necessary to differentiate it into a complexity of constituents, leading to Priestley's classic work on the *Different Kinds of Air.*[64]

Certainly, the act of weighing is a reductive move. Macrobius says: "Nature always draws weights towards the bottom; obviously this was

62 Berry, *Henry Cavendish*, 24; cf. Wilson, *The Life of the Hon. Henry Cavendish*, 184 n.

63 For an attempt at revising the eccentric view of Cavendish as an "incessant measurer," so as to perceive the originality and logic of his thought and a "whole life dedicated to science without precedent," see R. McCormmach, "Henry Cavendish: A Study of Rational Empiricism in Eighteenth-Century Natural Philosophy," *Isis* 60 (1969), 293–306.

64 J. Priestley, *Experiments and Observations on Different Kinds of Air*, 3 vols. (London: J. Johnson, 1775).

done that there be an earth in the universe."[65] By weighing the air, Cavendish took the ascensionism out of it. His move is prototypical for what today is called reductionism or "bottom-line" thinking—valuing invisible things, spiritual things, in terms of their weight in a material scale. The movement is toward the bottom and the effect on the ascensionism of spirit is depressing, and of course the justification for the "bottom-line" reduction is in the rhetoric of earth—common sense, solid facts, hard reality.

May we not link the rise of nineteenth-century economics and the domination of economics over the Western mind today with the procedures of weight, measure, and number introduced to perfection by Cavendish and the chemical revolution. (I must set aside the relations between the new technology and its immense demands for capital, and also set aside Cavendish's relation to his personal wealth—supposedly the wealthiest scientist who ever lived.) The barometric language used by economics for its basic directions—inflation and depression—seems to belong to what I am calling the Cavendish phenomenon, that is, reduction to a mode of thinking that is both abstract *and* material, presenting what seems concrete and tangible—material or economic "realities"—altogether abstracted by mathematization. As such, the Cavendish phenomenon is a symptom formation, a compromise with the material element of earth, using its rhetoric to measure all things, yet never touched by it by virtue of the measuring act itself.

Nonetheless—even as air is reduced by the Cavendish phenomenon it is also differentiated. This suggests that *the recognition of the complexity of an invisible seems to require materialization.* The reduction to matter is not necessarily a fall, a defeat of the wing; materialization is a means by which spirit becomes differentiated, makes itself knowable. The mind's invisible complexity, the air of its logos, its *Geist,* recognizes itself in the precision of the senses; and, action in the material world, rather than a mere acting-out, an escape, presents the sense-display of the spirit. In Adolf Portmann's language: the material world is where *Selbstdarstellung,* self-representation, takes place. As such, all action is aesthetic, and materialization is, as the Scholastics insisted, necessary to individuation.

65 Macrobius, *Commentary on the Dream of Scipio,* trans. W.H. Stahl (New York: Columbia University Press, 1990), 182.

Cavendish performed the materialization of air by means of counting, but the accounting or re-counting of a story, a *recit* in Corbin's sense, also brings invisibles down into the world of sense and differentiates them. Cavendish's mode was numerical counting by which air became precisely accountable for its various behaviors. In other words, counting is more than mere, sheer quantification: it is one mode of making differentiation visible, of precise description, of giving an account, a tale of things.

Even the angels dancing on a pinhead seemed subject to counting if the very air was susceptible to measure. Stephen Hales earlier in the century had introduced the book containing his work on air, *Vegetable Staticks*, with that verse from Isaiah 4:12 about God measuring the waters, the earth, and weighing the mountains (which Cavendish performed in a divine feat of mathematical literalism by means of a mountain in Perthshire). Hales said:

> Since we are assured that the all-wise Creator has observed the most exact proportions, of number, weight, and measure, in the make of all things; the most likely way therefore, to get any insight into the nature of those parts of the creation ... must in all reason be to number, weigh and measure.[66]

Cavendish's motto was precisely this: "To weigh, number, and measure"[67] (as later, J.B. Richter [1762–1807] was to use the motto on the title page of his major work). Counting had now become an imaginal carrier with as much force as a demonic possession.

With the materialization of air, fantasies became inventions. Elixirs and tinctures available at the soda fountain; the alchemical *exaltatio*, laughing gas; and the spirit's *acclivitas* rose up in balloon ascents, while the air's light-transmitting mission became gas-lit avenues in Baltimore. With the collapse of the ascensional principle, the pneumatic impetus spread horizontally–the *anemoi* of ideologies (congregationalism, republicanism, utilitarianism), which are vertical ideas in horizontal clothings. The alchemical *multiplicatio*, as a lofty, idealized end-stage of the work, became literalized in the method of counting, and moved as an axiomatic principle to touch all things: counting heads, counting

---

66 S. Hales, *Vegetable Staticks* (London: W. & J. Innys, 1727), "Introduction."

67 Wilson, *The Life of the Hon. Henry Cavendish*, 186.

votes, counting money; Bentham and Mill. The *rubedo* finally, utterly, exteriorized in the red *bonnet phrygien* of revolution.

Is the lady's stomacher studded with jewels left behind in Cavendish's cupboard a clue to the way the Cavendish phenomenon still works in science, and in us each when we enter this mode of thought? Does anima become both densely concrete and rationally abstract when driven out from nature, beauty, sensuousness, history, and personal affairs—the middle realm between concrete and abstract?

The soul returns through the same door of its exile. If exiled by means of abstractions and materializations, then it returns in the very modes of its repression, insinuating into numbers and weights the fascination that maintains the repression. The examination of the return of the repressed—a main task of depth psychology is not only an examination of the repressed *content*, but of the *style* of the repression. The style reveals the content; it is the content as its form. This is what Freud meant when he spoke of symptoms as compromises. This is what Jung meant when he said the unconscious shows the face you show it. If the new chemistry materializes the airy soul, then that soul will return in a materialized manner. We must look into the very style of repression: the method and apparatus itself, by means of which the materializing operations were performed to find where the fantasies of the airy soul now were lodged. For the soul is never lost nor the air forever dissipated. Air is "ever-continuing," says Plato. It merely becomes engrossed in matter in another style. The alchemical attempt to disengage and combine spirit and matter *(solve et coagula)* is ever-continuing even if the locus of the attempt changes. We can imagine that the soul might come and go through a door marked, as it was at Liebig's famous laboratory in Giessen: "Thou hast ordered all things in measure and number and weight." *(Book of Wisdom,* 11:20). Over the door into Jung's house, his "laboratory,'" is another motto: "Invoked or not, the god will be present" (*vocatus atque non vocatus deus aderit*). Then why not present as well in measure and number and weight?

God can thus be present in the method and not only in the material as alchemy thought. This is the watershed between alchemy and chemistry: where alchemy sought the secret in matter, chemistry imagined the secret in the modes of examining the matter—measure, weight, and number. Hence the importance of technical apparatus, mathematical models, laboratory experiment—these were divine instruments. To call this merely quantification or technology or applied science is to lose the inspiration, aspiration, effervescence, illumination, and ascension—the gas—that suffuses the discoveries and the heights of vision to which the methods led.

The collapse of phlogiston freed the spirit. It had been held in an alchemical vestige, for phlogiston was, as Stahl insisted, a kind of matter, yet one which no method could analyze. Lavoisier's accurate method overcame that subtle matter, releasing spirit from that style of alchemical materialization. Now the place of spirit was in the method of "free" scientific inquiry, which together with the social, religious and technical revolutions that inseparably accompanied the new method, breathed the aerial soul, and its inflations, into the free-thinking spirit of the times whose watchwords were both measure, weight, number and *liberté, egalité, fraternité.*

Before we go on, we need to go back before Cavendish and Davy to the 1600s, when a cluster of events began the movement from air to gas. The air pump by Guericke of Magdeburg (1656), and improved by Hooke and Boyle in Oxford in 1658, produced powerful vacuums from which the air gun was developed. The universal elastic fluid of air could be driven out, voided—space without air. Moreover, air could be used as a weapon. Robert Boyle's *The Spring of the Air* (1660) laid the groundwork for his famous law, which states that the volume of air varies inversely as the pressure upon it. The more the pressure, the smaller the volume. This too-simple rule established the mathematics for condensing air. Boyle's law placed the air in servitude, reduced in size, and then released at one's pleasure. Air's elasticity was wholly passive, suffering compression; he does not speak of it as exerting pressure itself. These were early steps in imagining air as a passive material. It was also through Boyle that air lost its elemental nature,[68] not even entering into the composition of fire but merely providing the containing environment for it.

68 "But *The Spring of the Air* was more than a new departure in scientific writing and the fore-runner of the accepted form of modern technical papers... by his 43 experiments [he] conclusively demolished the traditional view that air was an essential element, a mysterious all-pervading and almost mystical entity... the very

The control of air was demonstrated before the courts of the continent and fashionable folk: extinguishing the life of birds and mice under bell jars, explosions when a vacuum was pierced, raising water with suction pumps, making little wooden figures dance and spin inside glass tubes. Hooke opened a dog's thorax, applied a bellows to show the mechanics of respiration; Hales cut apart horses to study air.[69] The manipulation of air was like the capture and release of Ariel by Prospero in Shakespeare's *The Tempest* (1610–11), a play whose name itself derives from the imagination of air and in which the words *spirit* and *air-airy* occur more often than in any other of Shakespeare's plays.

Also in the seventeenth century (1686), Edward Halley published his first map of the winds of the globe, accounting for the winds and monsoons in terms of the laws of heat distribution over the earth's surface. The old maps showed great heads in the four corners with winds whose names like gentle Zephyr of the West, like blowy Boreus, the Northwind, appear as far back as Plato's *Phaedrus*. Now maps could have directional arrows instead; the air had lost the faces of its gods.

I might also mention the publication in 1678 of Alessandro Capra's *La Nuova architettura famigliare,* which sets forth devices for freshening rooms with cool air by fans and drafts drawn over water. Here begins the early domestication of air by air-conditioning which can so tame and denaturalize the elemental force that we may draw our daily breath wholly independent of the weather.

---

stuff of Nature herself." Roger Pilkington, *Robert Boyle: Father of Chemistry* (London: John Murray, 1959), 145. Boyle gave the first modern definition to element: "I now mean by elements ... certain primitive and simple, or perfectly unmingled bodies; ... of which all those called perfectly mixt bodies are immediately compounded, and into which they can be ultimately resolved." *The Skeptical Chymist* (1661), in *The Works of Robert Boyle* (Hildesheim: Olms, 1966), 1: 562. This definition of element led to its substantiation and identification with atom, thus moving the idea from *elemental* to elementary (primitive and simple). Air, of course, failed the definition.

69 Alexander Pope complained of Vicar Hales: "He commits most of these barbarities with the thought of being of use to man; but how do we know that we have the right to kill creatures that we are so little above as dogs, for our curiosity, or even for some use to us," in *The Works of Alexander Pope,* 8 vols. (London: Longman, Brown, and Co., 1847), 1: 447. Pope is picking on Hales less for vivisection than for curiosity, a primary Catholic sin (Fénelon) and a primary impulse in the experimental method. A century later, another poet-philosopher, Coleridge, used a similar metaphor regarding Davy's galvanic experiments: "To bind down material nature under the inquisition of reason, and force from her, as by torture, unequivocal answers to *prepared* and *preconceived* questions." Coleridge, *The Friend,* 4: 531.

Van Helmont's Gas

Our focus now must be upon another extraordinary figure, the Flemish alchemist, chemist, and physician Johannes Baptista van Helmont (1579–1644), who coined the term "gas"–though it did not find its way into chemistry as the third state of matter until the later eighteenth century, mainly through Lavoisier.[70] What Van Helmont means by gas appears in this passage published posthumously, as were all his works, by his son Franciscus Mercurius (himself a kabbalist):

> ...the live coal, and generally whatsoever bodies do not immediately depart into water, nor yet are fixed [i.e., combustible materials] do necessarily belch forth a wild spirit or breath. Suppose thou, that of 62 pounds of Oaken coal, one pound of ashes is composed: Therefore the 61 remaining pounds are the *wild spirit*... I call this spirit, unknown hitherto, by the new name of *Gas*, which can neither be constrained by Vessels, nor reduced into a visible body... But bodies do contain this Spirit, and do sometimes wholly depart into such a Spirit.[71]

Some say by "gas" Van Helmont may have meant *Geist*; or he may have derived it from *gaesan*, a Paracelsian term like the German *gären*, for fermentation of food in the stomach. Charles Singer says "gas" was the Flemish pronunciation of the Greek word *chaos*.[72] The demonstration makes clear enough what Van Helmont intended by "gas." It was the uncontrollable 61 pounds that had escaped. Van Helmont himself says: "Gunpowder doth most nearly express the History of Gas,... for there is not a vessel in nature which being close shut up doth not burst by Reason of Gas."[73] This was a wild spirit, or *spiritus silvestris* in the original Latin.

Van Helmont's experiment with oaken charcoal shows his chemical reasoning, while the experiment in the closed vessel is alchemical. The figure as a whole is imaginational. You surely remember the Grimms' fairy tale of the spirit in the bottle with which Jung opens his essay on Mercurius spoken first at Eranos in 1942 (*CW* 13:239). A woodcutter's

---

70 Lavoisier, *Elements of Chemistry*: "Henceforwards I shall express these elastic äeriform fluids by the generic name *gas*..."

71 W. Pagel, "The 'Wild Spirit' (Gas) of John Baptist van Helmont (1579–1644) and Paracelsus," *Ambix* 10 (1962), 1–2.

72 Singer, *A Short History of Scientific Ideas*, 269.

73 From *A Source Book in Chemistry*, 26.

son comes to huge old oak where he hears a voice calling from the ground: "Let me out, let me out." The boy digs into the roots of the tree and finds a well-sealed glass bottle. He opens it. The spirit rushes out and grows immense and frightening. (Boyle's law: expansion of gas as pressure is lessened.) The tale goes on: boy and spirit each out-tricking the other. The spirit, like Ariel, seeking its release; the boy desiring to keep the spirit imprisoned. Finally he is rewarded with technological gains: a wound-healing cloth and the transformation of his iron axe into silver.

Psychotherapy has made this tale a root parable. We are told to bottle the spirits—anima or animus—in the vessel so that they remain as voices without visible bodies, seen into and seen through (kept in glass), and thus prevented from expanding into giant inflations in the world, running free and wild: chaos. Whereas *in* the vessel, their *gären* or digestive fermentation generates the new self (*homunculus*). We work with a paradigm of alchemist as imprisoner. Let us not forget that the spirit itself wants out.

The term *spiritus silvestris,* the wild spirit that now became gas, had already been used by Paracelsus. His Sylvani or Sylvestres are "Airy men or Airy Spirits."[74] The natural world abounds with these *Luftleute.* Each is endowed by God with a quality and a specific task. They have a "subtle flesh," give birth, eat, drink, talk and walk about, and die. Their realm is intermediate between the invisible immaterial world and the world of flesh and blood—like the daimonic metaxy of Platonism, or what we call today psychic reality. The spirits of Fire are salamanders, those of Water are nymphs, those of the Earth are like goblins, gnomes, and sylphs.

The spirits of the airy element are *sylvani.* Curious—since "sylvan" means most simply forested. So it is in the woods and wilds that the airy spirits abound. Since they are sylvan, of course they could be trapped and weighed in the oaken coals of Van Helmont's experiment. Van Helmont insisted that the gas "is the body itself" in its volatile form. Hence when the coals were burned to ash both their body and their gas were gone. From Van Helmont's notion that gas is a body to Cavendish's weighing this body is a logical step. Also, Van Helmont's notion that

74 Pagel, "The 'Wild Spirit' (Gas) of Van Helmont," 8. See also *Lexicon,* s.v. "Sylvestres or Sylvans": "Sylvestres are Men of the Air, Spirits of the Air, Aerial Spirits which inhabit the woods ..."

each of these wild spirits had its own quality and purpose was but one step away from the divisibility of the single elemental air into its component gases and Dalton's proportional table of atomic weights.

Instead of taking these historical steps forward, we could take a mythological step. We could understand this invisible body of wood that is a gaseous soul as the body of the nymph in the wood, what Greek myths called the hamadryad. Classical literature shows many occasions where the wood nymphs are one and the same as the tree they inhabit, living and dying with it. They too are not visible, only audible, as for instance the oracle of Dodona spoke through the Priestess from an oak tree.[75] (We cannot take the time to go into the special role of the oak–Van Helmont's choice of wood; Graves, Jung, Cook, and Frazer have exhaustively discussed it.) Important for us is the cosmological implication of Van Helmont's idea, for it is a vision of matter (*hyle*, which means originally in Greek, wood, copse, brushwood, forest) in whose body is a wild spirit, a gas. Van Helmont's vision says the material world is not merely wooden, but speaks; each coal, each thing is composed of a subtle flesh, is constituted of a sylvanic nymph, a hylic anima with a specific quality and task.

What moves each thing in its specific way, its *vis motus*, or motive power, is its *blas* (a term Van Helmont invented and defined in his *Ortus Medicinae*[76]). The *blas* originates in the stars. It is the dynamic impulse within natural phenomena such as air motions, weather, storms, and the subtle dynamics of human beings in their neurovegetative symptoms. Yes, we are affected by the weather (whose root means "blow"), since a *blas* moves in the spirits of the soul as in the atmosphere. Weather is simply the "middle realm" in our everyday lives, and the climate (*climax*) is like a diagonal ladder sloping between above and below, higher and lower, anagogical and concrete meanings. Weather talk cannot help but be metaphorical. John Dalton's last words as he died, "little rain this day," is a scientist's observation and also a report on the state of psychic affairs, the climate of his dying nature.

75 *Lexicon* s.v. "Nymphae"; H.W. Parke, *The Oracles of Zeus* (Oxford: Blackwell, 1967), chap. 3 and 4; *CW* 13: 418–20 on the feminine tree numen.

76 Originally published in Latin in 1648 and translated into English as *Oriatrike, Or, Physick Refined* in 1662.

The *blas* works within things as an Odor (also called by Van Helmont a Ferment and an Image).[77] It gives to the seed of each thing its "time" and its "notion of what has to be done." Or, let us say, the image of its purpose. The imagination of gas and *blas* shifts the object of perception from the visible to the invisible, and thus the organ of perception to ear and nose so that images can be imagined as airy events, climates, atmospheres, vibrations, timings, pressures, vapors, odors.[78] Not only mass, motion, gravity and direction of Newtonian physics determine the vectors of change in physical bodies and so in our lives, but odors. Chemistry as a science of airs, the determination of the *blas* in the world, a truly pneumatic study.

I must interpose something here about the forests, home of the hamadryads. Eighteenth-century science encouraged vast deforestation, especially in America.[79] Was this an attack on the hylic anima, the *spiritus silvestris*? Like the air, driven out by vacuum, made to dance and whistle, harnessed to pump, compressed, turned acid, so too the air associated with woodlands, especially in America, required enlightened intervention. It was considered cold, damp, and bilious, a source of diseases, and a place of gloom and daimonic temptation back to the amoral liberty of nature (a frequent trope in early American novels).[80] By clearing the forests, man could have a warmer, dryer and lighter earth, hence, a healthier climate. By affecting our relation to trees, the *siècle des lumières* also affected the *Luftleute* in the trees. Perhaps these hamadryads turned into sylvan demons are the sources of our images of savages living in primeval forests—from *sauvages, sylvani*. Forest animism[81] was now both brutalized and sentimentalized (Rousseau) at the same time. In the

77 "The 'Odour' is also called 'Ferment' or 'Image' of the thing which is to be formed or 'Notion of what has to be done.'" W. Pagel, "The Religious and Philosophical Aspects of Van Helmont's Science and Medicine," *Supplements to Bulletin of the History of Medicine* 2 (1944), 17.

78 Cf. the discussion of smell in my *The Dream and the Underworld* (New York: Harper & Row, 1979), 185–88 and notes.

79 This complicated subject is illumined in C. J. Glacken, *Traces on the Rhodian Shore: Nature and Culture in Western Thought from Ancient Times to the End of the Eighteenth Century* (Berkeley: University of California Press, 1976), esp. 318–45 and 659–81.

80 R. W. B. Lewis, *The American Adam: Innocence, Tragedy, and Tradition in the Nineteenth Century* (Chicago: University of Chicago Press, 1955).

81 Cf. Alexander Porteous, *Forest Folklore, Mythology, and Romance* (London: Allen & Unwin, 1928), chap. 4.

eighteenth century, the word savage began to be used more frequently as a verb: to savage something or someone. May I refer you here to Portmann's insightful piece on the *Urmenschenmythos*?[82]

Thus, Van Helmont's experiment with coals of oak out of which came the concept of gas has profound mythological underpinnings and implications. Gas arose from the funeral pyre of the wood nymph. There was a death of soul and its rebirth in a new form, from mythic body to chemical body. And it was, as I believe we are coming to understand, this gaseous vapor of the anima that was the fascinating and elusive object pursued in the chemical revolution.

Anima

I am suggesting that what escaped the vessel was the old phlogiston, that this mysterious combustible substance was the aerial soul or anima, and that this escape produced those escapades of mountain ascents, laboratory explosions, laughing gas—and the attempts to recapture this soul by weight, measure, and number. Besides the lightweight fascinations were the turbulent revolutions in science, politics and society. What goes on in the individual soul also takes place in the world soul, and vice versa. What goes on in the soul of chemistry goes on in the chemists' souls. A Platonic view does not divide psyche into subjective and objective, so that changes in the air of the times show also as anima phenomena in the principals involved. This means we must attend to the role of anima in the development of a science; paradigm shifts will manifest themselves as much in anima symptoma—her mystifications, obsessions and dramatizations—and may be their result, as in societal and theoretical phenomena. For science to consider itself also subject to anima means examining the roots of its disputes, inspirations and formulations with a more subjective, though not personalistic, eye; an eye which scientific method is designed to exclude.

A case to point is psychoanalysis. Think of the role in the development of its thought played by the behaviors of Charcot's and Bernheim's suggestible women.[83] Think of the remarkable women patients

---

82 A. Portmann, "Vom Urmenschenmythos zur Theorie der Menschwerdung," *Eranos Yearbook* 38 (1969).

83 Cf. J. Hillman, *The Myth of Analysis* (Evanston, Ill.: Northwestern University Press, 1972), part III.

by means of whom Freud's theories developed, and the figures in Jung's thought, Helly,[84] Sabina,[85] Babette,[86] and Miss Miller (*CW* 5). In fact, it was only at the culmination of this development of ideas, refined through confrontation with the dramatic expressions and mystifications of these women and their symptoms, that the idea of anima itself appeared and could be distinguished from actual women.

What we saw of Cavendish gave us a clue to the behavior of the aerial anima in experimental chemistry. His absolute disjunction from women and his senex peculiarities seem to epitomize what was happening in the soul of the chemical revolution as its air turned sour and grew heavy, becoming more physical, mathematical and industrial. Does the figure of Cavendish indicate that enlightened technical science requires dissociation from anima? Evidently the mind of experimental pneumatics is peculiarly detached from women.

Here Cavendish may be extreme but no exception. Louis Vauquelin, a major figure in the Lavoisier school, was cared for by two old ladies.[87] He never married. The great German mathematical chemist Jeremias Benjamin Richter never married. Joseph Black, who first named "fixed air" and whose experiments were "the first intensive study of a chemical reaction" never married. Alessandro Volta never married. Stephen Hales, whose capture of gases in his "pneumatic trough"[88] made possible their isolation and identification, lived all of eighty-four years; he was married for one of them. The Swedish chemist Jöns Jacob Berzelius, who determined the molecular weight of hundreds of substances, did marry at age fifty-six; Guyton-Morveau married at sixty-one. Both couples

84 Cf. J. Hillman, "Some Early Background to Jung's Ideas," *Spring: An Annual of Archetypal Psychology and Jungian Thought* (1976), 123–36.

85 Cf. Aldo Carotenuto, "Sabina Spielrein and C.G. Jung," *Spring: An Annual of Archetypal Psychology and Jungian Thought* (1980), 118–45.

86 Cf. *CW* 3: 198–316; *MDR*, 125–30.

87 About Vauquelin, Davy writes: "Nothing could be more singular than his manners, his life & his menage. Two old ladies, the Mademoiselles Fourcroy, sisters of the Professor [a major successor of Lavoisier]...kept his house...the first time I entered it, I was ushered into a sort of bed chamber which likewise served as a drawing room. One of the ladies was in bed but employed in preparations for the kitchen & was actually paring truffles." J.Z. Fuller, "Davy's Sketches of his Contemporaries," *Chymia* 12 (1967), 136.

88 See J. Parascandola and A.J. Ihde, "History of the Pneumatic Trough," *Isis* 60 (1969), 351–61, on this crucial apparatus invented by Hales by means of which gases are collected by displacement of water.

remained childless. Of Carl Wilhelm Scheele, the German-Swedish genius, whose name we associate with oxygen, chlorine, and innumerable compounds such as hydrogen sulfide, hydrogen flouride, glycerol, oxalic acid, etc., it is written: "He literally had no private life. In his entire correspondence there is ... hardly one note which is not devoted or does not refer to his work. There never was a woman in his life."[89] (He did marry on his death bed to assure his elderly housekeeper an income.) John Dalton never married. He wrote this of his temptation to it by a widow of great intellectual ability and personal charm: "During my captivity, which lasted about a week, I lost my appetite and had other symptoms of bondage about me, as incoherent discourse, etc., but have now happily regained my freedom."[90] Lavoisier, a biographer writes, had "for twenty-seven year ... verily shunned all womankind except his devoted Aunt Constance and his great aunts, who had given his undivided attention to scientific labors, and had passed by with case the love fancies of youth ..."[91] He married a girl of thirteen who was his translator and aide; they remained childless. After his beheading she was accused by some for not having made the right effort to save him. That she could be so blamed furthers my case that there is a disjunction, a soured air, between the new chemistry and the notion of anima as relationship to woman. Humphry Davy's marriage "deteriorated after about two years and some sort of separation was worked out between them." The satirical magazine *John Bull* gossiped: "They never interchange a word but ... are continually talking at one another ... He considers her as having grown too old, and therefore a bore; she evidently looks upon him as an ass."[92] It is said of both Priestley and Faraday that they enjoyed long, affectionate marriages. Yet Priestley wrote: "It has been a happy union to me ... so that I have been able to give all my time to my own pursuits. I always said I was only a lodger in her house."[93] And Sarah Faraday said, when

89 G. Urdang, *Carl Wilhlem Scheele: A Pictorial Biography* (Madison, Wis.: American Institute of the History of Pharmacy, 1958), 13.

90 Partington, *A History of Chemistry*, 3 :760; cf. 756: Dalton contributed an early piece on love to the periodical *Ladies' Diary*.

91 S.J. French, *Torch & Crucible: The Life and Death of Antoine Lavoisier* (Princeton, N.J.: Princeton University Press, 1941), 53.

92 Fullmer, "Davy's Adversaries," 155.

93 F. W. Gibbs, *Joseph Priestley: Revolutions of the Eighteenth Century* (New York: Doubleday, 1967), 231.

asked why she didn't study chemistry to be closer to her husband: "Already it is so absorbing and exciting to him that it often deprives him of his sleep and I am quite content to be the pillow of his mind."[94]

Of these examples Robert Boyle may yield the most insight since he at least wrote his theory of woman and love.[95] Boyle never married. He was an apprehensive hypochondriac, haunted by fear of early death though he lived to be sixty-four. "He ate and drank only enough to keep his body in health ... never from choice or indulgence." Even the air seemed an enemy: he was terrified of thunder and "kept a range of cloaks to wear according to varying temperature, selecting the appropriate one for the moment with the aid of a thermometer. "[96]

Boyle's experiments were serious and entertaining, a curious mixture of carelessness and exactitude (not that obsession with method as experimental science proceeds into senex professionalism). "Distinguished foreign visitors counted Mr. Boyle and his air-pump one of the sights of London."[97] *On the Spring and Weight of the Air* was not his first book: that was a religious romance, *The Martyrdom of Theodora,* a theological novel written when Boyle was twenty. In it, Boyle displays through the voice of a woman character his arguments against marriage and his mistrust of human love compared with the love of and for God. In another early work, *Seraphick Love,* Boyle shows the delight he found in service of God as amateur scientist, whereas love of woman is "devotion misaddressed... for when you give your mistress the style of a goddess, and talk of offering up of hearts, adoring, sacrifices, martyrdoms, does not all this imply that it is meant to a divinity?"[98]

94 L.P. Williams, *Michael Faraday: A Biography* (London: Chapman & Hall, 1965), 99.

95 Pilkington, *Robert Boyle,* 107–26.

96 Ibid., 107, 128. A visitor to Boyle reported how Boyle "had chemical cordials calculated to the nature of all vapours that the several winds bring; and used to observe his ceiling compass every morning that he might know how the wind was, and meet the malignity it brought by a proper antidotal cordial. So that if the wind shifted often he was in danger of being drunk." M. Boas, *Robert Boyle and Seventeenth-Century Chemistry* (Cambridge Univ. Press, 1958), 18–19. Another Irish pneumatic philosopher uncomfortable with the climate was Richard Kirwan (1733–1812) who wore his hat and overcoat always indoors. His marriage was brief; he lived forty-seven years as a widower.

97 Boas, *Robert Boyle,* 207; cf. Pilkington, *Robert Boyle,* 135.

98 Pilkington, *Robert Boyle,* 122.

The clue is clear: the divinity to whom went the "adoring, sacrifices, martyrdoms" was the invisible soul in the world of matter. The fascinating mistress was not woman, but the mystery within the natural world; the laboratory[99] was the thalamus, and the experiment, the rite.

When Boyle refuses to worship anima embodied in woman, it was not that he was utterly estranged–he wrote his thoughts to his elder sister throughout his life, living with her for thirty years and dying within a week of her death. Also, he records a moment of anima enchantment, watching a milkmaid drilling her pail in a green pasture singing to her cow "with the melody of larks in her voice."[100]

What did claim his eros was the invisible soul of the world and the "invisible College"[101] as he called his fellow thinkers and tinkerers at Oxford who, under Charter from Charles II became the Royal Society of which Boyle was several times President. (Charles "was reported to have laughed at his gentlemen of the Royal Society for spending their time only in weighing air."[102])

If air was the object of eros, then air was the locus of soul; or vice versa, since air was the locus of the hiding soul, then it was the object of seeking, curious eros. The new weightiness of air corresponded with a new substantiation of soul in the material world. Physical experiment made the invisible more visible. No longer the mottoes of alchemy: to explain the obscure by the more obscure; the secret art, blacker than black; the hidden treasure. The vessel was opened by Boyle, and by Helmont, through public demonstration, discussion among colleagues, and the airing of ideas in the language of the layman. The enemy was not merely the old paradigms of thought–Aristotle, Galen, Paracelsus, the Scholastics, the Vitalists. The enemy was thinking itself as deductive reasoning in difficult language closed into the head, without hands, without visibilities. Newton's writing was obscure; he lived in an academic atmosphere and wrote in Latin. Boyle's forty-two books went into two-hundred editions. He employed professional editors and proofreaders to keep pace; the opus now had democratic intention. Of Scheele, a

99 Cf. Boas, *Robert Boyle*, 21, where Boyle compares crossing the threshold into the laboratory with Lethe–forgetting the world and entering the realm of souls.

100 Pilkington, *Robert Boyle*, 100.

101 Ibid., 76–77.

102 Boas, *Robert Boyle*, 185.

century later, a biographer writes: "... esoteric discussion of the abstract was superseded by the democratic search for the concrete ... with no inclination to generalize, he occupied himself mainly with experiments."[103] This statement represents not merely the new Baconian method but the new Boylean love that supports the method.

In examining the case of the chemists' anima we could use the perspective of feminism. Then the exclusive maleness and singular traits of the puer-senex pattern does indeed stand out. The dandyness of Davy and his sudden aging; Lavoisier, Noble Martyr; Cavendish, obsessive misogynist, and Stahl, too, called a misogynist;[104] Kirwan with his pet eagle, odd clothes, and chemical study of manures; Faraday, withdrawing from social affairs, ending senile and amnesiac in a chair; Priestley, firebrand, then retreating to Pennsylvania, writing religious tracts and clinging still to the old theory of phlogiston; Black's "scrupulous frugality;" Hooke, unproductive after the age of forty-two, in the same room for forty years, a dedicated hypochondriac, "who never permitted himself the luxury of feeling well for the length of a full day."[105] Boyle was "often ill" and when not, believed himself so; Black was "feeble;" Kirwan for years ate only ham and milk as Cavendish mainly ate mutton; Scheele supposedly wasted away. This estrangement from the body. And their voices: Boyle's tammered seriously; Priestley had a speech impediment for which he took breathing lessons; Kirwan had a "weak throat;" Vauquelin, a "weak voice" that prevented his lecturing career; Dalton spoke with mumbling diction and an indistinct voice; the voice of Cavendish was squeaky, shrill, or wispy. Witnesses evidently were struck by these vocal distortions. Ficino says that the voice pertains directly to the soul, a primary attribute.[106] Could the air be taking its revenge?

---

103 Urdang, *Carl Wilhlem Scheele*, 7. Coleridge could not comprehend the new method, much as he was fascinated by chemistry, keeping up with it in some detail. Rather than Scheele's (and others') "democratic search for the concrete ... with no inclination to generalize," Coleridge considered the materials "of the *Laboratory* ... to be symbols of elementary powers, and the exponents of a law, which, as the root of all these powers, the chemical philosopher, ... is instinctively labouring to extract ... striving after unity of principle through all the diversity of forms." Coleridge, *The Friend*, 4: 470.

104 *Dictionary of Scientific Biography*, ed. C.C. Gillispie, 16 vols. (New York: Scribner's, 1970–80).

105 Ibid.

106 M. Ficino, *Commentary to Plato's Symposium*, V: 2. Perhaps the earliest connec-

The French *Encyclopédie* (Diderot & D'Alembert, 1753) says that the Chemists "are a distinct people, very few, with their language, their laws, their mysteries, and living almost isolated." Men, all men, says the feminist perspective, in the company mainly of men, generous to their friends, faithful to their clubs, exhibiting their apparatus to one another, little boy's games with valves and troughs and asphyxiations and explosions; experiments on animals, ascents in balloons, fascination with gunpowder. And the disputes, the vanity over priorities mixed with patriotism, the paradigm of which is the discovery of oxygen (Scheele or Watt or Priestley or Lavoisier); discovery of the gaseous composition of water;[107] of nitrogen (Rutherford or Cavendish or Scheele); the constancy of the co-efficient of the expansion of air (Boyle or Volta or Gay-Lussac); the steam-engine; the steam-boat; iodine and chlorine—who was first? Or the many new names, new systems of atomic relations, of classification of compounds. Whose was best? Who won?[108]

From the feminist perspective, the chemists' anima reveals the anima of chemistry, that chemistry is estranged from anima owing to the archetypal constellation of the puer-senex whose method of exploring air removed soul from it, leaving both it and them fanciful, eccentric, dry—and in the long run destructive.

Air plays a singular role in both senex and puer phenomenology: the puer's wings, inflations and collapses; Saturn, lord of foul air, chronic ailing of the spirit, concretization of the invisible mind.[109] Our discussion showed also that the puer revolts against sensuous nature and

tion of voice and psyche occurs in a fragment of Xenophanes (Burnet, 7): "Once they say that he [Pythagoras] was passing by when a dog was being beaten and spoke this word: 'Stop! don't beat it! For it is the soul [*psyche*] of a friend that I recognized when I heard its voice.'"

107 Cf. S.M. Edelstein, "Priestley settles the Water Controversy," *Chymia* 1 (1948), 123–37 on the "discovery" of the composition of water and the various priority claims among Waltire, Monge, Watt, Priestley, Cavendish, Macquer, and Volta.

108 Priority disputes need to be re-imagined. To consider them as vanity and opportunism is to read spirit phenomena (genius) in ego terms. (Opportunism belongs to the puer spirit, necessary to seeing and seizing insights; cf. J. Hillman, "A Note on Opportunism" in *Senex & Puer*, 96–112.) If the aerial spirit was now out in the world it demanded its recognition in outward ways. Public recognition of priority is simply the outer way of recognizing the originating power of spirit, where and when its primacy and generativity manifest in the world.

109 Cf. Hillman, *Senex & Puer.*

must overcome it, while Saturn, the senex, rules with scientific instruments and systematic classification, taking his delights in abstraction, laws, and the extreme reduction of body to its bones. Neither was ever "in favor with woman or wife" as the old lore said. Anima was the major problem and only solution of that puer-senex constellation.

As chemical science continues, we cannot expect otherwise than suffering in the soul of the world: puer explosions and senex poisons. The very definition of air implies that all things it touches oxidize; its constituents are violent, noxious and sharp. Stratospheric pollution, acid rain, exhaust fumes, pneumatic drills, commercial air waves, aerial heroics and gas warfare, soda-pop culture, forests become packaging and ephemeral words, freon climates and neon lights—and above all the sense that the world no longer breathes with soul, the air gone out of it; gas, chaos.

Such is the contemporary view—sometimes called feminist or ecological, a rhetoric of the element earth, expressing its soul. We are all pervaded with it. It moves us to sadness and outrage, a fear of technological doom, a feeling we must go back before the chemical revolution. This view appears in several guises; for instance, in phenomenological metabletics with its nostalgia for pre-reformational, pre-scientific consciousness—the restoration of innocence; man, nature, and God not fallen apart. It appears, too, in some Jungian psychology with its longing for a restoration of a *unus mundus*, contemptuous of extraverted modernity and distrustful of the spirit escaped from the bottle.

But we can take another tack, borrowing Stahl's own motto: "Where there is doubt, whatever the greatest mass of opinion maintains... is wrong."[110] Or, as a modern scientist, G.H. Hardy, says: "It is never worth a first class man's time to express a majority opinion."

Actually, there are two majority opinions: the nostalgic, feminist one we have just sketched, and the one we learned in school, the heroic, progressivist view taught by science about its history.

We can move from both these majority opinions, from opinion altogether, by returning to the images we have been examining. What happened to the imagination of air once alchemy collapsed? Once the bottle came unstoppered, where did the anima of the chemical

110 *Dictionary of Scientific Biography.*

enlightenment appear? This question belongs to the ordinary procedure of psychological inquiry. We do not tell a patient where the anima should be–in wife, or daughter or friend. It may be in his boat, his cabin in the woods. But we do assume that as archetypal *numen* anima does appear, somewhere. Clearly, in the chemical revolution, the anima did not appear in "the feminine," as it is usually conceived, not in marriage, woman, relationships, nor in the sensuous body. We saw the aerial soul go into the world–into fascination with air itself in soda fountains, steam engines, winds and gases. We may discover where the aerial anima actually was by searching the intention in the inventions of these men.

The last thirty years of Stephen Hales was devoted to alleviating human problems. Chemical and mechanical solutions for kidney and bladder stone; installation of his ventilators on merchant ships and slave ships, prisons and hospitals. He rebuilt the church in his parish, and engineered a new water supply for his village. His major work on the respiration and mechanics of plants would, he was confident, improve agriculture and gardening. Hales's writings on the effects of spirituous liquors led to the passage of the Gin Act in 1736.

Humphry Davy attempted to reform the Royal Society itself by expanding it to include women and to improve the relations between science and government. His work in tanning, on the corrosion of ship bottoms, the miner's safety lamp, and especially in agricultural chemistry, fulfilled his intention to make science immediately useful.

Usefulness was the result of even Hooke's mechanical eccentricity: he invented the cross-hair sight for the telescope, its screw adjustment and iris diaphragm; he perfected the air-pump, the weather clock, the wheel barometer and founded scientific meteorology. He coined the term "cell" for botany, advanced geology, set the freezing point at zero, and invented the universal joint. Robert Hooke added something to every important instrument developed in the seventeenth century, and like it is said of Bach, he left no form as he found it.

Lavoisier's "whole adult life had been given to public service."[111] He was engaged in press, prison and hospital reform, unemployment insurance; he was a founder of the society of scientific agriculture and farm credit, addressed problems in gas-lighting, plaster of Paris, porcelain,

111 A.J. Ihde, *The Development of Modern Chemistry* (New York: Harper & Row, 1964), 82.

soda water, ballooning, tobacco preservation. As prominent and active member of the Academy of Sciences he was instrumental in initiating the metric system. The standard metric bar of platinum and the definition of a kilogram were finally established, by the way, in that year 1798.

I could add further examples of usefulness. But we are better served by understanding the overriding intention in the inventions. Walter Pagel says this of Helmont: "His was the desire to help his fellow Creatures by detecting and opening up the divine resources in Nature." Pagel calls this "religious pragmatism."[112] These men were not mechanists, materialists, atheists. In them was no warfare between science and religion, no two worlds such as we find later in Shaw and Snow.

Helmont was a mystic: he had retreated from the world for seven years; read Epictetus, Johannes Tauler, Thomas à Kempis, "all Avicen." For him empirical research was a divine vocation. God himself is a chemist with nature as his laboratory. In 1633, at age forty-six, Helmont visualized his soul, which appeared as a light in human shape with its own radiance. He identified this epiphany with an apparition of "something indescribable" announcing his vocation to chemistry that had appeared in the wall of his room twenty-three years earlier.[113] Anima appeared to Boethius as Philosophy; to Helmont as Chemistry. Chemical pragmatism was a religious call of soul.

Boyle was an orthodox Anglican. His apologia for religious pragmatism is entitled: *The Christian Virtuoso: shewing that by being addicted to Experimental Philosophy a man is rather assisted than indisposed to be a good Christian.* Dalton was an earnest Quaker schoolteacher; Hales, a Vicar; Stahl, a devout Pietist; Priestley, a founder of and preacher in the new Unitarian Church; Kirwan had been a Jesuit; Volta wrote a defense of religion against science (1815); Faraday was an Elder of the Sandemanian Church and a devout practitioner of its beliefs his entire adult life. Most were deeply concerned with finding medical solutions for the miseries of human health. Unlike physics and mechanics, chemistry had from its inception in alchemy a close tie with medicine; it had a therapeutic concern.

112 Pagel, "The Religious and Philosophical Aspects of Van Helmont's Science and Medicine," 12 and 38.

113 Pagel, "The 'Wild Spirit' (Gas) of Van Helmont," 9–10, referring to Helmont's *Imago Mentis.*

Love for the World

Alfred Adler considered the aim of psychotherapy to be *Gemeinschaftsgefühl,* translated as "social interest," "the feeling of intimate belonging to the full spectrum of humanity." In Adler's view, "a man of genius is primarily a man of supreme usefulness." "Mankind only calls those individuals geniuses who have contributed much to the common welfare. Contribution is the true meaning of Life."[114] Humphry Davy believed that genius "consisted in the perpetuation of individual existence through ideas that in their application transformed society."[115]

In my essay on Adler I brought the case of a sophisticated psychotherapist who held dialogues in imagination. The alter-voice with whom he spoke was his breath-soul. It spoke from his chest and was called anima. When he asked this soul what it wanted, it replied, "I want out." It demanded release from his bottling like the *spiritus silvestris.* He was afraid of releasing it for the wildness, the chaos it had caused and might cause again. As the conversations progressed, he found himself surrounded by its presence, "an air that had density."[116] The psychological development in him compared with "the *coagulatio* of the soul in alchemy; its becoming thickened, sensed as a presence. This had evidently happened like a chemical process. After long cooking, stirring, and containing, suddenly ... a coagulation takes place."[117]

It is as if the process that went on in that individual case took place in the world soul during the chemical revolution. After a long period of concentrated attention—for what else is the weighing, measuring, experimenting—which cooked and stirred the aerial soul, the hamadryads returned to the physical phenomena, to *hyle,* the world of material things. We can read the collapse of alchemy and the transformation of chaos into the differentiation of gases as the aerial soul's own intention—to be out, public, free, and to invest itself in objects, giving them a new intention. Objects became instruments of its upward aspiration, ascensionism, now called—by the rationalist French minds of Turgot, Condorcet, and then Comte—"progress."

114 These quotations from Adler's psychology are documented in J. Hillman, *Healing Fiction* (Putnam, Conn.: Spring Publications, 2005), 107–8; 124–25.

115 Levere, "Humphry Davy," 49.

116 Hillman, "Psychotherapy's Inferiority Complex," 166.

117 Ibid.

Dreams of progress, liberalism, humanitarianism, religious pragmatism was where the old element of the air now lodges. New dreams. *L'air et les songes*. The atmospheric metaphors of Wordsworth, the revolutionary dreams of Shelley,[118] that master phenomenologist of the poetics of air; the progressivist dreams of Priestley who wrote in 1790:

> While so favourable a wind is abroad, let every young mind expand itself, catch the rising gale, and partake of the glorious enthusiasms; the great objects of which are the flourishing state of science, arts, manufactures, and commerce, the extinction of wars... the abolishing of all useless distinctions... so that the world would be "re-christianized."[119]

Even the conservative answer to Priestley employed the same metaphor. Edmund Burke, speaking of the revolution in France and against its supporters in England, said: "The wild *gas*, the fixed air is plainly broke loose."[120] Burke tried to put the spirit back in the bottle: "We are resolved to keep an established church, an established monarchy, an established aristocracy, and an established democracy, each in the degree it exists, and in no greater."[121]

The imprisonment of Van Helmont by the Inquisition, the reactionary orations of Burke, the persecutions of Priestley—the violent destruction of his house, church, books, and the laboratory—, and the beheading of Lavoisier could not put the new air back into old bottles. As Jung writes about the objective wilfulness of the Spirit: "The crucial point is that so long as the... spirit cannot be proved to be a subjective psychic experience, then even trees and other suitable objects would have, once again, to be seriously considered its lodging places." (*CW*13:249)

The air was out of the subjective mysticism of alchemy. It got out first through those transitional alchemists, Van Helmont and Boyle, and their skeptical attacks on the element itself. It got out in the puer play of experimenting: "I shall not scruple," says Boyle, "to confess to you that I disdain not... even of Ludicrous Experiments, and think that the 'Play of

---

118 For an extraordinary documentation of Shelley's imagination of air, see J. Perrin, *Les structures de l'imaginaire shelleyan* (Presses Universitaires de Grenoble, 1973).

119 Gibbs, *Joseph Priestley*, 195.

120 E. Burke, *Reflections on the Revolution in France and on the Proceedings in Certain Societies in London Relative to that Event* (London: J. Dodsley, 1790), 8.

121 Ibid., 135–36.

Boys' may sometimes deserve to be the Study of Philosophers."[122] The alchemical *ludus puerorum* (*CW* 12: 302 and fig. 95), the play of the puer spirit in public exhibition, was the image within Boyle's experimental method. The airy element was playing freely; even iron vessels, says Van Helmont, could not hold it. Now it lit the darkness, bubbled up at soda fountains, and whistled through the steamboat.

All these inventions facilitated the air's release, but where did they originate? The Grimms' story says they come from the air in the bottle: the invisible spirit itself gives the boy the wound-healing rag, the silvered axe. The imagination of air invents its own technology by means of which it can return to the material world. The technological achievements of Hales and Black, Scheele and Davy, on which the new chemical theories themselves depended, where after all did they come from? Genius?

It is easy enough to attribute inventions to genius, but genius is also an air, a nimbus around the head. Genius was the Roman word for *psyche* or *daimon*, for a vapor-like spirit that "blows."[123] It is not an ego, but breaks in upon it—*invenio*—a gift of the genie in the bottle who speaks to the "boy," a guiding presence telling the attentive worker how next to move his hand, waking him in the night with flashes of intuition as to how best respond to the demands of the invisible to become visible by means of invention. Of course, these men were often solitaries; they reserved their ears for the subtle "invenio" of the airy genius.[124]

---

122 Thorndike, *A History of Magic and Experimental Science*, 8:181.

123 R. B. Onians, *Origins of European Thought* (Cambridge: Cambridge University Press, 1954), 129–32.

124 Gerald J. Holton, "On Trying to Understand Scientific Genius," *American Scholar* 41, no. 1 (1971), 96, includes these traits among those essential to men of scientific genius: "a tactile coexistence with natural phenomena: sometimes the mind seems to move into a problem of nature as if it were a hand slipping into a glove ... intensity and wide scope of his alertness, for example, to small signals in the large 'noise' of any experimental situation ... extraordinary energy and persistent dedication—in manipulation of equipment, in the making of apparatus or tools, in computing or writing ... ability to ... give his whose life over ... to near exclusion of satisfactions of drives other men find irresistible." As paradigmatic figure, Holton depicts Einstein, a quote from whom is relevant to Holton's thesis and to one of mine here: "My passionate sense of social justice and social responsibility has always contrasted oddly with my pronounced lack of need for direct contact with other human beings and human communities" (ibid., 97). One more trait in Einstein needs mentioning, since we have seen it in the chemists: "The objects of imagination were to him evidently persuasively real, visual materials, which he

"I do not think I could work in company," Faraday said, "or think aloud, or explain my thoughts."[125] The genius of making, *poesis:* apparatus as poem. Their thought and enquiry were focused by technological images. Volta was "a genius for instrumentation and measurement."[126] James Watts (1736–1819) started as an instrument maker; his engineering inventions fed the imagination of others, just as the engraved drawings of apparatuses in the texts of the period, and the public demonstrations, visualized extraordinary new images. Lavoisier's *Elements of Chemistry* (1789) revolutionized the field largely because, it is said, he described in such excellent detail the technical instruments of chemistry and their uses. The aerial soul was registering itself in the patent office. "The poem," says Bachelard, "is essentially an *aspiration toward new images.*"[127] "The poet of fire, of water, or of earth does not convey the same inspiration as does the poet of air."[128]

We must therefore read the chemical revolution neither with progressivist heroics for what had been conquered nor with nostalgia for loss of feminine soul. The genius of air was still imagining by making new images, and these men were still serving soul as it seems to have asked to be served. Should Mrs. Faraday have become a chemist too, or Cavendish tried to get on better with servants, or Dalton caved in to the widow? Love was there in the work itself because psyche was there when, following Jung, we see that "suitable objects" can be "lodging places" of psychic events. The experiment, the laboratory, the apparatus,[129] and the paper (Black, Davy, Dalton, Faraday, Boyle each wrote hundreds of papers or delivered hundreds of popular and scientific lectures): here was eros, anima, joy; and an aesthetics of usefulness. When Davy first isolated potassium, he danced furiously through the laboratory. Boyle called his laboratory "a kind of *Elysium*" where he was

voluntarily and playfully could reproduce and combin... The key words are *Bild* [image] and *Spiel* [play]" (ibid., 103).

125 *Dictionary of Scientific Biography.*

126 Ibid.

127 Bachelard, *Air and Dreams,* 2.

128 Ibid., 4.

129 Even the exception that proves the rule turns out to be a false exception: Dalton is usually considered to have had the least, the cheapest Quaker-style equipment—chemistry in "penny ink-bottles." This was not at all the case; cf. K.R. Farrar, "Dalton's Scientific Apparatus" in *John Dalton and the Progress of Science,* ed. D.S.L. Cardwell (Manchester University Press, 1968), 159–86.

"transported and bewitched."[130] Read the experiments themselves as documents of loving-care, of patience, of appreciation of the qualities and respect for life in things; read of the relations of the men with their instrument makers.

Technology

We are led by these thoughts to technology. Technology is widely bemoaned as the logical and terrible consequence of empirical science. Robot, Golem, Frankenstein's monster—is this technology or a view of it? That we speak of technology with these fantasy images ought to tell us that it too is a psychic expression. Not the apparatus is a soulless machine, but the Cartesian-Newtonian world view that declares things so. As long as soul had been removed from the world of *res extensa,* anima could not appear in worldly things or, if it did, it was fallen, in projection, in need of redemption. Things *had* to be robots, monsters, the apprentice's demonic broom. That demonic broom at least reminded us that it was not dead, as Descartes had said.

Technology is cursed by our mechanical idea of it. It is the great repressed, the unconscious, the realm of the dead, forced to carry the egocentric unimaginative demands we put on it: labor-saving, cost-efficiency, productivity, uniformity, speed. It may not break down—only wear out and be thrown away. If the chemical revolution was, finally, the restoration of an imagination of air to material things by means of technical inventions, then technical things may still harbor that imagination. Technical things are neither silent, obedient slaves, nor mere manufactured products of other machines, the dead creating the dead, obsolescent litter in a throwaway culture. They are concrete images of animation, locations of the hylic anima with names and faces whose natures need to be perceived individually, subjectively. Each is a potential *objet parlant.*

It is not the dead who create the dead mechanical world but we, our subjectivism. Our private sense of soul deprives things of their images, leaving mere objects out there, without subjectivity, calcined, impersonal, dead. These things have taken their revenge. The repressed always does, by insinuating our notion of them into our notion of ourselves:

130 Boas, *Robert Boyle,* 21.

ourselves as mechanical functions, assemblies of parts, enduring stress and friction, attempting objectivity, until we, too, oxidize in "burn-out." Moreover, if the world is already dead, then our present cataclysmic fantasies are simply statements of the case—even if their pathologized imagery does announce a new concern of soul, a new return of love to the suffering things of the world.

The Newtonian *Weltbild* no longer rules; technology can be freed from its mechanism. The soul of the world returns to the world. A vast cosmological shuffle is taking place, new Aquarian dance steps in heaven called The Paradigm Shift. *Anima mundi* is moving from her clean celestial attic. *La folle du logis* is descending the staircase, nude, radiant, descending even into the streets. *Anima mundi* now means soul-in-the-world, which means also a new anima sense of technology. Only as we appreciate the beauty in the things of the world can our love return to the world.

Again, our minds must keep pace with what our hands construct. Boyle's invisible college of virtuosi that became the Royal Society presented a new mode of education *within the material world:* "To apply the eyes, and the hands of Children, to see, and to touch all the several kinds of *sensible things.*"[131] "It is *matter,* a visible and sensible *matter,* which is the object of their *labours,*"[132] wrote the historian of the Society. "Matter would make its own patterns of meaning [by] the hands and eyes of the virtuosi ... ,"[133] handling and watching the hylic anima.

The chemical enlightenment also proceeded from hand to mind. Experiment and invention, technical *poesis;* making taught thinking. Thus today: cheery, friendly R2D2 has replaced soulless Robot. The maintenance of your motorcycle, the Apple on your desk, and the calculator in your breast pocket imply that Dr. Frankenstein has died because, like Nietzsche's god, he has become superfluous. Though our minds are still ruled by the mechanical enlightenment, animation works in the laboratory hands, elaborating fantasy, inspiring things with new life, like the puer spirit now playing in computers. Alchemy, therefore, did not collapse—if we mean by alchemy a *poesis* of matter.

As we have distinguished genius from ego, so we can view the chemical enlightenment, not from the ego in enlightenment terms, but from

131 T. Sprat, *History of the Royal Society* (1667) (London: Routledge, 1959), 329.
132 Ibid., 339.
133 Ibid., xxx (introduction by J. Cope and H.W. Jackson).

the imagination of air. We learn, as children, from the enlightened hands,[134] from what they did rather than what they said they did. Their formulations can deceive us: Lavoisier prefaces his *Elements* with an epistemological account taken straight from Condillac's theory of language.

Because the chemical enlightenment required an imagination of air, the chemists were not merely weighing and naming the gases. They were as well inspiring the world with a new vision of things,that balloons and ventilators, wind charts and air pumps were carriers of highest aspirations, a pneumatic vision parallel with free-thinking, public knowledge, and the Bill of Rights.[135]

Their inventions were the new mode of access for the *genie,* the *invenio* of the daimon. The technical thing, moving with its own pneumatic power like the statues and icons of the gods, was now the *numen,* acting like a *spiritus rector,* the invention leading the inventor to think new thoughts, to imagine more deeply into the soul of the world.

We can turn to these men for guidance through the present technological crisis. Remember Helmont: each thing has its *blas,* its atmosphere that comes from the stars and must be studied as such, for in each thing there is an odor or a seed or an image by which its specific nature, timing, value, and purpose can be known. The turn to matter means concern with specifics; as the main Scholastic tradition insisted, matter is the individuating principle. Each thing differs from each other thing. Scheele, Davy, Boyle pressed toward specifics. "Per nudam observationem," said Helmont, "quaerere et pulsare."[136] "Matter [...] is not subordinated to soul but is the active vector of specificity."[137] The individuation of our soul requires recognition of the individuality of soul in things, that each thing has its own 'privacy,' distinct from the public and uniform laws of physics.[138] Because there is soul in things, even our

134 J. Brun, *La main et l'esprit* (Paris: Presses universitaires de France, 1963), whose profound and broad study restores the hand to its primary place in human comprehension.

135 Bentham's utilitarian, popularist phrase, "The greatest good for the greatest number" was admittedly derived from a similar phrase in Priestley's *An Essay on the first Principles of Government* (1768). See *A Scientific Autobiography of Joseph Priestley,* ed. R.E. Schofield (Cambridge, Mass.: MIT Press, 1966), 348.

136 Pagel, "The Religious and Philosophical Aspects of Van Helmont's Science and Medicine," 11.

137 Pagel, "The 'Wild Spirit' (Gas) of Van Helmont," 27.

138 Ibid., 6–8: "Helmont asks with Plotinus, how can variety in nature, how can

modern hi-tech things, they can be received into our souls, imagined as images, their "odors" perceived with aesthetic sensitivity, considered animistically. Such is the thought of the heart.[139]

At the close I should distinguish what I have been doing from what I have not been doing in this chapter. Although we have dug into a period of time, we have not been engaged in an archeology of Enlightenment chemistry à la Foucault; we have not been engaged in a phenomenological metabletics à la Van den Berg. Such would be to historicize, to consider the interrelations of political revolution, scientific method, technical invention, religious philosophy, and poetic expression as phenomena of a single *Zeitgeist*, one idea manifesting in many phenomena. This approach, which literalizes the historical period into the fundamental determinant, leads back to Hegel and the objectivation of air as *Geist* in its historical procession, and eventually to the literalisms of Marx.

For us, an archetypal idea such as air, and its phenomenology in a segment of time, does not require an approach through the spirit. The phenomena can as well be reflected by means of anima, by means of an airy imagination which is both the subject and object of the method, appearing in our own anima fantasies as we work as well as in the personal lives, chemical ideas, and actions in the world of those we work with. History is not the determining factor; psyche is—the timeless, the archetypal psyche is what manifests in the phenomenology of air, requiring the approach of an archetypal psychology. As such, the phenomena we have been witnessing—transposition of soul from self to public world; materialization, souring and collapse of air as a primordial element; its rebirth in method, apparatus and progressive aspirations—are psychological events taking place in soul, in individualized *anima corporalis* and collective *anima mundi*. Its movement "out" is the soul's own psychology of extraversion, an archetypal movement that is not the result of historical conditions as much as the condition of historical results. History is inside us, as Henry Corbin always insisted, not we inside history. History

specificity be ever explained by uniform motion and its laws. Motion ... must take place *in* something ... and it is this something which has to be investigated." Because "a modification of matter [is] different in each individual being ... Helmont reserved for things vital the 'private' right and privilege of specificity," leading to a cosmology of "vitalistic Pluralism."

139 J. Hillman, *The Thought of the Heart and the Soul of the World* (Putnam, Conn.: Spring Publications, 2014).

is a psychological material where the eternities of soul leave their traces in time. As the soul moves in circles, so does history display the soul's *ricorsi* as records. The enlightenment phenomena we have been witnessing continue to circle, to return, in our souls. We run the same risks of puer playful destruction and intoxication, of senex abstraction and abstractedness, of materialistic blindness and aggressive souring of atmospheres, wherever soul moves out from private concern to animation of matter. Soul can always be lost, for that is its nature;[140] lost even as it is found in the noblest intentions of *fraternité* or *Gemeinschaftsgefühl.* Soul is necessarily shadowed, its enlightenment never accomplished.

These historical, biographical reflections have not been merely historical and biographical, about those men in those two hundred years of the extended Enlightenment. They have been about our own enlightenment as a psychological phenomenon. The virtuosi I have evoked did not die with their period. They are eminences who haunt the soul as psychic attitudes in the imagination of air. History does not simply go on then; it is also psychology going on now. Otherwise why examine the facts? We study history to find a way out of it. Its paradigmatic figures of science present imaginative modes of working the elemental powers. Engagement with the elemental constellates elemental responses, heightening a biography to archetypal proportions. The figure of Coleridge, who has been shadowing our theme like an ancient mariner himself, is yet with us as an archetypal questioner. He is the Romantic voice who identifies the *poesis* of experimental science with its philosophical ideas rather than seeing through to the *poesis* of the laboratory hands, their methods and technical apparatus. Biographies of historical giants thus become mythical tales in which we trace archetypal patterns. These biographies show how air can blow within an individual life, take up its lodging and make its demands.

We have seen that the elemental force of air constellates puer and senex, requiring revolution in thought, experiment in action, precision of detail, differentiation by quality, and a solitary's devotion to an invisible fascination. And, a further trait of major importance: an *imagination of extraversion,* the perception of depth in the object, focus upon the public physical world, and the apparatus of realization—technology. Even Cavendish, most painfully introverted as a person, shows this imagination of

140 Hillman, *Healing Fiction,* 128–29.

extraversion, a life given to the soul in the physical world. His house "had a laboratory in the drawing room, a smith's forge in the adjoining room, the upper part being an observatory."[141] He lived in the crucible; designed, built and tested his instruments with his own hands, like an alchemist. Unlike an alchemist, the concern of his imagination was the world.

We have also seen in the accumulated denials of marriage that the anima of air requires impersonal attachment, a higher husbandry. The adored mistress (Boyle), the woman in the window (Cavendish) become distractions from Helmont's religious pragmatism, Boyle's seraphic love, Lavoisier's betterment of human conditions, Priestley's courageous idealism, Davy's usefulness. You remember our patient mentioned above: after his airy anima "got out," he entered public service; the end of personal analysis as *Gemeinschaftsgefühl.*[142] Similarly, in cultural psychology the end of chemical analysis was public concern.

Gemeinschaftsgefühl is even more impersonal than Adler foresaw. It expands beyond unselfish action intending the common good. The soul in the world of things calls our feelings to recognize *their* participation in that common good, things not just for our sake but also for theirs, thereby restoring a psychological appreciation to constructed things left too long for dead, returning soul to the world. Progress, that airy dream turned sour, now means *ricorsi*, return to the *anima mundi.*[143] Davy's statement that "the progress and improvement of civil society is founded in mathematical and chemical inventions"[144] takes us only half way. The other half is psychological, or cosmological: returning soul to those inventions. An invisible spring of air, a combustible phlogiston, a wild gas still imbues each thing, making possible the animation of the actual world of things among which, or whom, we live.

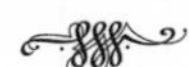

141 Partington, *A History of Chemistry,* 3: 303.

142 Hillman, *Healing Fiction,* 124.

143 For the restitution of Air to its primordial authority, see D. Abrams, *The Spell of the Sensous: Perception and Language in a More-Than-Human World* (New York: Vintage Books, 1997).

144 Levere, "Humphry Davy," 50. Cf. this statement of practical idealism with another from Davy during the nitrous oxide period (1799) as recorded by Southey: "A paradise wholly immaterial—trees of light growing in a soil of ether—palaces of water refracting all rich colours." *The Notebooks of Samuel Taylor Coleridge,* 2:191.

10

The Azure Vault: Caelum as Experience

We shall begin along two parallel paths, one aesthetic, one psychoanalytic; the first, a poem by Lisel Mueller called "Monet Refuses the Operation"—a cataract operation; the second, a moment in the analysis of Anna O. reported by Josef Breuer, Freud's friend, mentor, and co-author of *Studies in Hysteria*.

These paths intend toward the azure vault, particularly the experience of the alchemical *caelum*, a blue intimated earlier in Chapter 5 above, and here to be more brightly illumined and more clearly contrasted with the blues of that earlier chapter.

The Latin word means the blue sky; heaven; the abode of the gods and the gods collectively; the sky as the breath of life, the air; and also the upper firmament or covering dome, including the Zodiac. The alchemical *caelum* or *coelum* is expanded upon especially in Jung's last great work, *Mysterium Coniunctionis*, and, as he says, the *caelum* has "a thousand names." These few will also help us as we proceed: "a Heavenly Spirit that makes its way into the essential forms of things"[1]; the "anima mundi in matter," "the truth itself," "a universal medicine," "a window into eternity," radiating "a magic power," "the *unus mundus*" as a "*unio mystica* with the potential world, or *mundus archetypus*" and the final realization of the alchemical opus.[2] We are headed to the edge.

Now to the poem, and the first of many stories:

> Doctor, you say there are no haloes
> around the streetlights in Paris
> and what I see is an aberration
> caused by old age, an affliction,

1 *Lexicon*, 10.

2 *CW* 14:761–70.

I tell you it has taken me all my life
to arrive at the vision of gas lamps as angels,
to soften and blur and finally banish
the edges you regret I don't see,
to learn that the line I called the horizon
does not exist and sky and water,
so long apart, are the same state of being.
Fifty-four years before I could see
Rouen cathedral is built
of parallel shafts of sun,
and now you want to restore
my youthful errors: fixed
notions of top and bottom,
the illusion of three-dimensional space,
wisteria separate
from the bridge it covers.

[...]

I will not return to a universe
of objects that don't know each other,
as if islands were not the lost children
of one great continent. The world
is flux, and light becomes what it touches,
becomes water, lilies on water,
above and below water,
becomes lilac and mauve and yellow
and white and cerulean lamps,
small fists passing sunlight
so quickly to one another
that it would take long, streaming hair inside my brush to catch it.
To paint the speed of light!
Our weighted shapes, these verticals,
burn to mix with air
and change our bones, skin, clothes
to gasses. Doctor,
if only you could see
how heaven pulls earth into its arms
and how infinitely the heart expands
to claim this world, blue vapor without end.[3]

3 *Second Language: Poems by Lisel Mueller* (Baton Rouge, La.: Louisiana State University, 1986).

Now, Anna O. as told by Josef Breuer:

> She told me there was something the matter with her eyes; she was seeing colors wrong. She knew she was wearing a brown dress but she saw it as a blue one.[4]

Breuer tested her color vision; it was not impaired. Breuer interprets this curious "misperception" as an incursion of a secondary state of mental functioning into "her first, more normal one." Breuer writes: "She had been very busy with a dressing-gown for her father, which was made with the same material as her present dress, but was blue instead of brown." The visual mistake—or visionary experience?—is reduced by Breuer to the blue material of the father's dressing gown.

Could there be something more? Could the patient's own avowal that she saw blue despite knowing "she was seeing colors wrong" indicate a wish, not for the father only, and for dressing *his* body, but for clothing hers in blue? And, what might it imply for her, for that analysis, for the field of analysis itself—since Anna O. is a *fons et origo* of our psychoanalytic heritage—for the body of the patient, of every analytical patient, the *opus* itself to be clothed in blue? We shall return to both Monet and Anna O. But first a few more blue stories.

Again one from the beginnings of our field, the devastating crisis starting at age thirty-nine in the life and work of Gustav Theodor Fechner (1801–1887), to whom both Sigmund Freud and William James pay effusive tribute, claiming him to be the most valuable thinker in psychology of the nineteenth century. Fechner was a brilliant physical psychologist, observer, micro-measurer, laboratory experimenter.

Then his eyes gave out. He couldn't observe, he couldn't read. He was not blind, but he could no longer see. Nor could he eat or drink. His digestion gone, shriveled, despairing, sleepless and silent, he protected his eyes with lead cups and retreated into a blackened room, kept alive by his wife. After close to three years in this black hole, gradually recovering physically, he emerged, lifted the bandages and allowed light into his eyes:

> I stepped out for the first time from my darkened chamber and into the garden... It seemed to me like a glimpse beyond the boundary

4 J. Breuer, "Case Histories: Fräulein Anna O.," in S. Freud, *SE* 2:33.

> of human experience. Every flower beamed upon me with a peculiar clarity, as though into the outer light it was casting a light of its own. To me the whole garden seemed transfigured, as though it were not I but nature that had just arisen. And I thought: So nothing is needed but to open the eyes afresh.
>
> The picture of the garden accompanied me into the darkened chamber; but in the dusk it was all the brighter and clearer and more beautiful, and at once I thought I saw an inward light as the source of the outward clarity... and the shining of the plants' souls.[5]

Fechner felt giddy with joy of this moment of the *multi flores*. Fechner went on to live healthily to age eighty-six, immensely productive, exchanging his professorship from natural science to the philosophy of nature. The first lectures he delivered after his recovery were devoted to pleasure, formulating for psychology the pleasure principle later expanded upon by Freud.[6] The book on the soul that followed his return to life was subtitled "a walk through the visible world in order to find the invisible." Fechner now wore blue glasses. To protect his eyes? Or to protect his vision from the materialist perspective that preceded his blindness and which he now called the "night world", i.e., the *nigredo* from which he had emerged.

Two stories from childhood, one from an Irish poet, the other from an American musician. "Æ" (George William Russell), friend of Yeats and pivotal figure in the Irish literary revival, describes a moment when about four or five years old, he was lying flat on some grass recalling a story of "a magic sword with a hilt of silver and a blade of blue steel":

> The word "magic" stirred me, though I knew not what it meant... It lay in memory... until a dozen years later its transcendental significance emerged as a glittering dragon-fly might come out of a dull chrysalis. The harmony of blue and silver at once bewitched me. I murmured to myself "blue and silver! Blue and silver!" And then, the love of color awakened... one color after another entered the imagination... This love of color seemed instinctive in the outer nature.[7]

---

5 W. Lowrie, *Religion of a Scientist: Selections from Gustav Th. Fechner* (New York: Pantheon, 1946), 211.

6 H.F. Ellenberger, *The Discovery of the Unconscious: The History and Evolution of Dynamic Psychiatry* (New York: Basic Books, 1970), 217f.

7 *Song and its Fountains* (Burdett, N.Y.: Larsen Publications, 1991), 12–13.

Here, says Æ, is "the birth of the aesthetic sense," in harmony with the natural world and its colors that were, as he says, "of its nature and not of that unthinking child's."

"The very first thing I remember in my early childhood," says the incomparable Miles Davis,

> is a flame, a blue flame jumping off a gas stove…I remember being shocked…by the suddenness of it…that stove flame is as clear as music is in my mind. I was three years old.
>
> I saw that flame and felt that hotness of it close to my face. I felt fear, real fear…But I remember it also like some kind of adventure, some kind of weird joy, too. I guess that experience took me someplace in my head I hadn't been before. To some frontier, the edge, maybe, of everything possible…The fear I had was almost like an invitation, a challenge to go forward into something I knew nothing about…everything I believe in started with that moment. I have always believed and thought since then that my motion had to be forward, away from the heat of that flame.[8]

"Away from the heat of that flame" and into the "cool": his inventive use of the mute, his solos as "thinking" the music, the titles of his great pieces such as "Kind of Blue," "Blue in Green," his wearing "shades" already in the 1940s. I can imagine that both Goethe and Kandinsky would approve of Miles Davis's feeling for blue. "Blue," says Goethe, "gives us the impression of cold…and reminds us of shade. A Blue surface seems to recede from us…it draws us after it." Kandinsky adds, "[B]lue…retreat from the spectator…turning in upon its own center…active coolness." For Davis, a challenge to go to the edge; for Æ, the sympathy for revolt.

The call of Æ's aesthetic sense and the spirit of revolt marked the Romantic impulse of which Novalis's "blue flower" is the undying example—although he himself, as Friedrich von Hardenberg, died at twenty-nine. That famous blue flower appears in Novalis's novel of the poetic education in which the hero, Heinrich, dreams a vision. Climbing through a strange geography, the hero comes to a place filled with "a holy stillness," where "a basin of water emits a faint blue light."[9] Blue, veined cliff…The sky was blue, clear, and he was "drawn to a tall

---

8 *Miles: The Autobiography* (New York: Simon and Schuster, 1990), 11.

9 C. Bamford, *An Endless Trace: The Passionate Pursuit of Wisdom in the West* (New Paltz, N.Y.: Codhill Press, 2003), 228.

light-blue flower. The flower then leaned towards him and...upon a great blue corolla, hovered a delicate face."[10]

Novalis regarded the blue flower as "the visible spirit of song." Curious that Æ entitles the little book describing the evolution of his poetic calling *Song and its Fountain*. Novalis writes: "One thing recalls all..."[11] "No more the order of time and space...the great soul of the world moves everywhere, blooms ceaselessly...World becomes dream, dream becomes world."[12]

Another report from the history of our field. This time: Wilhelm Reich. Reich combined the libido of Breuer and Freud with the physical science of Fechner. Reich imagined that the libidinal charge flowing through the body is the orgone energy of the cosmos. Freud's later theory of Eros as a cosmic force Reich would capture in a box in which a patient could receive orgone radiation. The radiation, according to Reich, came in three variations of blue.[13] Whether Reich was a crackpot or a brilliant therapist does not concern us here: but his witness to blue as the color of libidinal Eros that embraces the phenomenal world adds another page to our collection of stories. Besides, why not imagine libidinal desire as blue? Weren't porn shows once called "blue movies" and the suppression of libido attributed to puritans named "blue stockings"?

Reich's blue orgone shifts the source of erotic arousal. Instead of blood and glands, arousal becomes an impulsion from the sky, a bolt from the blue imagination. Hence, perhaps, that sense of immutable destiny in sexual attractions, as if ordained by Heaven—and Hell.

Backing for Reich's blue Eros as the universal energy that joins phenomena together comes from Cézanne. I quote from one of his most astute and studious biographers: "Cézanne gave blue a new depth of meaning...by making it the foundation of the world of objects 'existing together.' Blue was now recognized as belonging to a deeper level of existence. It expressed the essence of things and their abiding, inherent permanence."[14]

---

10 Ibid., 229.

11 Ibid.

12 Ibid., 230.

13 M.V. Adams, *The Fantasy Principle: Psychoanalysis of the Imagination* (Hove and New York: Brunner-Routledge, 2004), 89.

14 K. Badt, *The Art of Cézanne,* trans. S.H. Ogilvie (New York: Hacker Art Books, 1985), 82.

Cézanne himself wrote: "Blue gives other colors their vibration, so one must bring a certain amount of blue into a painting."[15] Zola, referring indirectly to Cézanne, writes: "The flesh colors are blue, the trees are blue, surely he went over the whole picture with blue."[16] In his old age, Cézanne drew with a brush loaded with aquamarine. May we say Cézanne painted with the color of the *caelum* in order to present the *unus mundus*?

Again from the history of our field. Two stories from Jung's biography. In 1944 Jung suffered a heart attack:

> I experienced dreams and visions which must have begun when I hung on the edge of death... I had reached the outermost limit... It seemed to me that I was high up in space. Far below I saw the globe of the earth, bathed in a gloriously blue light. I saw the deep blue sea and the continents... its global shape shone with a silvery gleam through the wonderful blue light.[17]

Jung's vision goes on for pages. It made his return to the normal hospital situation disappointing and difficult. He writes: "Now I must return to the 'box system' again. For it seemed to me as if behind the horizon of the cosmos a three-dimensional world had been artificially built up."[18] Again that theme: cosmos without horizon, without partitions, as if a deeper layer of existence, which is "the foundation of the world of objects," and is initiated by the blue experience.

When Fechner subtitled his revisioning book "a walk through the visible world in order to find the invisible," did he know Hölderlin's poem "The Walk" (*Der Spaziergang*) and the phrase "Divinity escorts us kindly, at first with blue (*Die Gottheit freundlich geleitet / Uns erstlich mit Blau*)?[19]

A particular moment in the three-week course of Jung's vision needs remarking. He felt the presence of "inexpressible sanctity" that had a "magical atmosphere."[20] "I understood then why one speaks of the odor of sanctity, of the 'sweet smell' of the Holy Ghost."[21]

---

15 Ibid., 57.

16 Ibid., 56.

17 *MDR*, 273.

18 Ibid.

19 F. Hölderlin, *Sämtliche Werke, Briefe und Dokumente,* ed. D.E. Sattler (Munich: Luchterhand Literaturverlag, 2004), 12:44.

20 *MDR*, 275.

21 Ibid.

Here I want to use poetic license by inviting Heidegger to explicate Jung's moment of sanctity, the presence of holiness in the hospital room. Heidegger writes: "Blue is not an image to indicate the sense of the holy. Blueness itself is the holy, in virtue of its gathering depth which shines forth only as it veils itself."[22] Robert Avens explains Heidegger's holiness of blue: "Holiness is not a property of a God ... but a name for all entities insofar as they display a numinous aspect; it is an ingredient that awakens, ensouls, and vivifies everything. Specifically, the holy [in Heidegger] is identified with the blueness of the sky."[23]

The next tale of Jung's encounter with blue occurs in Ravenna on entering the Baptistry of the Orthodox. "Here, what struck me first was the mild blue light that filled the room ... I did not try to account for its source, and so the wonder of this light without any visible source did not trouble me." It was here that Jung and his companion envisioned "four great mosaic frescoes of incredible beauty ... and to this day I can see every detail before my eyes: the blue of the sea, individual chips of the mosaic ..."[24]

These mosaics on the walls of the Baptistry did not exist, simply not there—though they were seen and remembered in detail by both viewers. The light which introduced the vision was blue; the most vivid of the images: "the blue of the sea."

The last of these stories of the azure vault I take from Marcel Proust in *Time Regained*, the concluding part of his many-volumed masterpiece, the author as himself and as character reflecting on his lifelong literary effort recounts the rising of his psyche to joy from "gloomy thoughts" about the "life of the mind" which he calls "unfertile," "boring," "tedious," "useless," "sterile," and "melancholy."[25]

While crossing a courtyard he stumbles on an uneven paving-stone, and suddenly the oppressive blue mood becomes visual and visionary: "A profound azure intoxicated my eyes, impressions of coolness,

22 M. Heidegger, *On the Way to Language*, trans. P.D. Hertz (New York: Harper & Row, 1971), 166.

23 R. Avens, *The New Gnosis: Heidegger, Hillman, and Angels* (Putnam, Conn.: Spring Publications, 2003), 56.

24 *MDR*, 265–66.

25 M. Proust, "Time Regained," in *Remembrance of Things Past*, vol. 3, trans. C.K.S. Moncrieff, T. Kilmartin, and A. Mayor (New York: Vintage Books, 1982), 898.

of dazzling light, swirled around me."[26] Then, "a new vision of azure passed before my eyes, but an azure that this time was pure and saline and swelled into blue and bosomy undulations, and so strong was this impression that the moment to which I was transported seemed to be the present moment."[27] No sooner is Proust out of this sentence then the *cauda pavonis* appears: "The plumage of an ocean green and blue like the tail of a peacock. And what I found myself enjoying was not merely these colors but a whole instant of my life on whose summit they rested."[28]

Recording his reflections, he concludes with a cogitation about time past and present "and I was made to doubt whether I was in the one or the other."[29] Experiences that so moved him and had given him such felicity were those that joined past and present, "outside time."[30] The doubt about the life of the mind as writer and "anxiety on the subject of my death had ceased... since the being which at that moment I had been was an extra-temporal being."[31] "The being which had been reborn in me... with a sudden shudder of happiness... is nourished only by the essences of thing... A minute freed from the order of time has recreated in us, to feel it, the man freed from the order of time."[32] The azure vision had brought together the pleasures of the world and the life of the mind, placing time within the timeless, the timeless within time. And with joy he can now say, "My appetite for life was immense."[33] Proust presents this azure vision in temporal terms, where time's ineluctable continuity is intersected (as in a flash of lightning)[34] by the joyful certitude of his extra-temporal essence beyond the reach of death.

The harmony of world and mind, resolving doubt and death, brings us to Wolfgang Pauli's dream vision of the world clock, a centerpiece of Jung's 1935 Eranos Lecture published more fully in Jung's Terry Lectures at Yale (*Psychology and Religion*), and later in his *Psychology and*

26 Ibid., 899.
27 Ibid., 901.
28 Ibid.
29 Ibid., 904.
30 Ibid.
31 Ibid.
32 Ibid., 905–6.
33 Ibid., 905.
34 Ibid., 905.

Alchemy.[35] Allow me to recapitulate only that component of Pauli's vision bearing on our theme: the vertical blue disk that intersects the horizontal one, each disk having its own pulse or time rhythm. A letter from Pauli to Jung shows Pauli still working on the world-clock dream of several years before. On 15 October 1938 Pauli writes:

> I have come to accept the existence of deeper spiritual layers that cannot be adequately defined by the conventional concept of time. The logical consequence of this is that death of the single individual in these layers does not have its usual meaning, for they always go beyond personal life.[36]

Pauli emphasizes the "sense of harmony" bestowed by the word-clock vision, much as Proust wrote of joy and an appetite for life and Fechner of the beauty of the garden.

What intersects, breaks into the normal (to use the word from Breuer) world of time's minutes and three-dimensional existence, what moves one outside that "box" (to use Jung's language of his own vision after the heart attack) is blue's verticality. The break in Proust's step-by-step forward motion, his stumble, parallels Jung's late unusual definition of God:

> This is the name by which I designate all things which cross my willful path . . . all things which upset my subjective views, plans, intentions and change the course of my life for better or worse.[37]

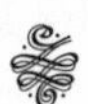

Proust's was the last of the stories I have collected so far. There are surely more waiting in the wings. Now the temptation arises to form the scattered occurrences into a metaphysical conclusion. It would be expected now to leave the earth for the blue yonder and a literalization of the spirit, outside of time, outside the body. Don't the stories support a hypothesis of earthly transcendence? Have we not been encountering the Celestial Kingdom, the "effulgent blue light of the Buddha body,"[38]

35 *CW*12.

36 *Atom and Archetype: The Pauli/Jung Letters, 1932–1958*, ed. C.A. Meier, trans. D. Roscoe, with a preface by B. Zabriskie (Princeton, N.J.: Princeton University Press, 2001).

37 *C.G. Jung Letters*, 5 December 1959.

38 *CW*11:852.

visitations of ethereal Sophia, of Mary in her blue dress, the ultimate transcendent anima?[39]

Not quite; not yet; not today. I shall go on insisting until I am blue in the face that Miles's music stayed dark, that blue is the color of the deeps, as Heidegger says, that the poetic fantast Æ was earth-born and earth-bound, invited by the United States Department of Agriculture to lecture on rural economy; that Cézanne stood day in and day out in the fields among rocks and mountains, painting peasants and apples of this earth; that Novalis, whose degree was in mining, felt called "to cultivate the earth,"[40] and that he took the pen name Novalis from the Latin for "newly ploughed field"[41]; and that Fechner acknowledged the earth's consciousness to be far superior to that of humans; and that Proust captured every fiber of the earthly emotions in touch and smell and taste; indeed embodied, and very much in the natural world of phenomena. Embodiment: is that not what is meant by macrocosm and microcosm together, a *unus mundus*? If embodiment is presaged already in the "blues" that sing of sadness and pull the soul down into the body's longings and mournings, then the *caelum* expands skyward (Jung's vision in the hospital, Pauli's cosmic clock), the senses awakened to the presence of the whole wide world, urged forward as Miles Davis felt, enlivened as Proust says, as Fechner perceiving the dazzling flowers. Blue initiates "the birth of the aesthetic sense."[42]

The aesthetic—*aisthesis*, Greek for sensation[43]—born from the *caelum*'s blue is marvelously elaborated by Maurice Merleau-Ponty who uses this one hue to lay out his theory of sensation. A body or attitude corresponding with, influenced by, under the aegis of blue is utterly different from one of red, for instance, for a person "adopts the bodily attitude corresponding to blue."

---

39 Cf. Jung's dream of Toni Wolff after her death: "On Easter Sunday he dreamed that Toni visited him, garbed in a dress of many brilliant hues whose primary color was royal blue. He remembered her carriage as regal and floating, majestic and like a bird, a kingfisher or a peacock." (D. Bair, *Jung: A Biography* [Boston: Little, Brown, 2003], 559.)

40 Bamford, *An Endless Trace,* 198.

41 Ibid.

42 Æ, *Song and its Fountains*.

43 F.E. Peters, *Greek Philosophical Terms: A Historical Lexicon* (New York: New York University Press, 1967), s.v. "*aisthesis.*"

> As I contemplate the blue of the sky I am not *set over against* it as an acosmic subject; I do not possess it in thought, or spread out toward it some idea of blue ... I abandon myself to it and plunge into this mystery, *it 'thinks itself within me,' I am the sky itself* [my italics]as it is drawn together and unified ... my consciousness is saturated with this limitless blue.[44]

"I am the sky itself ... drawn together and unified." How better express the *unus mundus* experience, which occurs, as he writes, when his "consciousness is saturated with this limitless blue." Merleau-Ponty's use of blue for the demonstration of his theory of sensation (or perception) expresses the blue thinking within him, the archetypal *caelum* embodied in his being.

If spiritual ascension is not my intention with these tales, what am I intending to convey? First of all I am elaborating a method for psychology of *storytelling*. Stories claim neither proof nor truth. Instead of argument, anecdote; individual cases circumambulating a theme. The theme? The *caelum* of alchemy in actual lives, particularly lives open to fresh perception. The method follows Jung's method of *amplification*: building the power of a theme by amplifying its volume with similarities, parallels, analogies. The method is also *empirical* in that it starts and stays mainly with actual experiences. Further, the method is *phenomenological*: let the event speak for itself, bracketing out concepts of spirit, of the numinous, the *coniunctio*, and the self.

Most valuable of all, I believe, is the aesthetic of the method which I am attempting. I am employing a rhetorical device, *peitho*, as the Greeks sometimes called Aphrodite, to invite, seduce, charm, enhance, and convince by rhetorical, even poetic, means. An aesthetic method relies on texture, images, language, emotion, and sudden mysterious arrivals. The method complies with and submits to the content. Logos in the embrace of psyche. Like blue itself, an aesthetic method conceals and reveals, withdraws from our prehension, tempts us to follow after it, and connects invisibly, analogously, all the stories and persons existing together in the same field. The method is relieved of interpretations and personalistic contexts. It aims to present things as they are and also as played upon the blue guitar—to use Wallace Stevens's famous phrase,[45]

44 *Phenomenology of Perception*, trans. C. Smith (London: Routledge, 1998), 214.
45 *The Collected Poems of Wallace Stevens* (New York: Alfred A. Knopf, 1978), 165.

following also his statement "I am thinking of aesthetics as the equivalent of *aperçus* which seems to have been the original meaning."[46] Sudden openings of the heart and mind and senses, especially of the eyes; insights, aha's, analogies, unique epiphanies that shake the soul, carry it to an edge, and free it from the box.

The box is also psychology: not psyche, but the "ology," the parasitical suffix that sucks the psyche dry. Long before there was a field called psychology, there were tales, old wives' tales, grandmothers' tales, oral accounts of origins and great deeds, theater of tragedy and comedy, the gossip of the day carried by messenger, lessons learned at the feet of a teacher, stories passed down rich in the ways of the world and the ways of the soul. Long before psychology there were the bedside observation of physicians and nurses, of captains on the field of battle, painters of portraits, breeders of animals, and of trappers, of midwives and judges and executioners. Psychology's case reports are too often botched attempts to continue the storytelling tradition. Too soon we draw theoretical conclusions obliged by "ology" to package psyche in a box. We would win from every story the trophy of meaning.

An aesthetic method, if I may call it that, ideally would let the beauty of an event, its sweet shock, instruct the soul, educate it by leading it to an edge, out of the box of the already conceived and into pondering and enjoying. The method suits the correspondences that compose the cosmos itself, each thing implicating other things by likeness rather than only by causality, in an implicit order of the world. Metaphors and analogies abounding. The display of images addresses the "poetic basis of mind,"[47] which is our most native mode of comprehension.

Display: The display of the cosmos beyond the box of mind, beyond even metaphor. This is the shift from the blues of the *unio mentalis* to the *caelum* of the *unus mundus*. If the first conjoins mind and imagination, the caelum displays a world wholly embraced in blue. "I am the sky itself." Mind/imagination/world conjoined without necessitating conceptual structures to hold them together—valid as these may be for a mind in search of comprehension (Pauli's clock).

---

46 *Letters of Wallace Stevens*, ed. H. Stevens (New York: Alfred A. Knopf, 1972), 469.

47 J. Hillman, *Re-Visioning Psychology* (New York: Harper & Row, 1975), xvii.

Display: "Things as they are" call to be noticed. Display speaks aesthetically, provoking and pleasuring the senses, and the aesthetic response becomes the favored method for working the *opus*. Hence Æ can write that the assault of blue gave birth to the aesthetic sense, and hence we have here turned particularly to great aesthetic practitioners—Proust and Davis, Novalis and Stevens, and, yes, Merleau-Ponty and Jung—for evidence of the azure experience.

Alchemy caught me and taught me with its aesthetics—its colors and minerals, its paraphernalia, freaks, and enigmatic imagistic instructions. It is like a vast collective artwork built through centuries. It offers an aesthetic psychology: a myriad of aperçus, images, sayings, stories, formulae; and all the while engaged with the matters of nature. It tells us to throw away the book of conceptual systems; no need for male and female, typology, stages, opposites, transference, self. Conceptual systems may be useful as a scaffolding for better access to the *massa confusa*, which alchemy presents to a logocentric mind. Too soon, however, the conceptual scaffold replaces alchemy itself, reducing it to merely providing examples to support the conceptual scaffold. *¡Que lastima!*

Allow me one more story, one more from Jung. This is the moment in the articulation of our field when Anna O.'s poetic blue is saved from Breuer's prosaic brown.

It is the moment of Jung's "steep descent," when he felt he was "in the land of the dead." "The atmosphere was that of the other world." First, he met Salome and Elijah which he interpreted as Logos and Eros, but then retreated from this intellectualization. Then, "another figure rose out of the unconscious ... I called him Philemon."[48] Jung had already met Philemon in a dream:

> There was a blue sky, like the sea, covered not by clouds but by flat brown clods of earth. It looked as if the clods were breaking apart and the blue water of the sea were [sic] becoming visible between them. But the water was the blue sky. Suddenly there appeared from the right a winged being sailing across the sky ... He had the wings of the kingfisher with its characteristic colors."[49]

48 *MDR*, 175.
49 *MDR*, 176.

These pages in *Memories, Dreams, Reflections* are legendary—more: they belong to the "creation myth" of Jungian psychology because it was Philemon who taught Jung "that there are things in the psyche ... which produce themselves and have their own life."[50] Here, too, I would claim, begins Jung's alchemical authority based not only on his scholarship, insight, and accumulated cases of evidence from his practice. Here begins his blue visionary mind, that opening to the vault that makes alchemy and his work mutually comprehensible.[51]

Jung later placed a kingfisher's wing in one of his paintings, a wing whose color has given its name to a particularly brilliant blue. That blue with its shimmer of coppery gold recalls Stevens's poetic way of stating psychic objectivity: "When the sky is so blue, things sing themselves."[52] The painted image of a blue wing sailing across the sky announces the arrival of Jung's new knowledge of the autonomy of the psyche.

The autonomy of the psyche is preserved by an aesthetic method. Jung's term "the objective psyche" refers to more than the spontaneous production of "internal" events. Psychic events are not atomistic particulars only; they bode forth analogous affinities such as Freud sought in free associations. Events "sing themselves" further, dream the myth onward, even "infinitely" as Mueller's poem says, and in this way they are objective, freed from the given—the feeling or fact or fantasy—by their analogous embodiments. Events dissolve their own edges and overreach themselves, creatively objectifying psyche in the production of complex forms that bring their own norms which seem to usual judgments as irrational, amoral or abnormal, and give rise to the prejudice that the aesthetic and the ethical are incommensurables.

To the great misfortune of our tradition, Josef Breuer could not hear the transposition to psychic objectivity, the singing of things themselves.

---

50 Ibid.

51 This encounter with teaching voices also brought his mind to aesthetics. He heard a female voice declare that his active imaginations were "art." As I have written elsewhere, "had Jung listened more receptively to that voice of the soul ... Jungian psychology might have taken a different tack: less division between aesthetics and science, aesthetics and nature, art and morality, less distrust of beauty and anima—and more sense for aesthetics." (*The Thought of the Heart and the Soul of the World* [Putnam, Conn.: Spring Publications, 2014], 44, where the "aesthetic" difficulty in Jung is discussed more fully.)

52 "Debris of Life and Mind," in *The Collected Poems of Wallace Stevens*, 338.

Despite his arduous devotion to his case, he did not recognize the poetic basis of mind. He called Anna O.'s seeing blue a "secondary state" invading the "more normal view." Her dress was simply brown—*basta la musica,* enough said. Yet Anna's fantasies were breaking into, and her out of, the historical, literal, and personal. Her symptoms were mainly bodily and the analysis was wrapping her body in blue material. Breuer describes Anna as "markedly intelligent with penetrating intuition [and] powerful intellect... She had great poetic and imaginative gifts."[53] The patient was being led by her very eyes and the call of her symptoms to follow the blue in keeping with her gifts. (The only recourse the psyche seems to have had for moving her analysis toward the promise of blue was to bring into play blue's erotic energy [Reich], constellating the sexualized transference from which Breuer fled.)

The blue incursion early in the case of Anna O., upon whose psyche our field is founded, requires us to make a small correction to the poem about Monet's cataracts with which I began. Lisa Mueller has Monet saying: "I tell you it has taken me all my life to arrive at the vision of gas lamps as angels. Fifty-four years before I could see Rouen cathedral is built of parallel shafts of sun..." Fifty-four years! Jung, too, places the *caelum* at the end of his *opus maior* and the end of his scholarly life. And an implication from Proust requires a correction. Is it only as death enters our thoughts and we are near the last page of that novel's *via longissima* that the azure vision, with peacock tail, flowers, and joy finds us?

Others tell a different story. Miles Davis as a tiny boy; Little Æ with the silver and blue of the magic sword; Anna O. barely out of her teens. Fechner in his early forties; Jung with Philemon also in midlife—not at the end of an *opus contra naturam*, a work that struggles to arrive. Rather, we learn that the "arrival," if it be that, is outside of time altogether and what is outside of time cannot be achieved through time. Either the achievement is never reached: analysis "interminable" to use Freud's term. Or, timelessness is eternally present from the beginning and potential in each moment of the work. Far out is where we start from! Hence, *caelum* is one of the names of the *materia prima,* the starting stuff and permanent basis of the work.[54] The striving toward healing on the *via longissima* is

53 Breuer, "Case Histories," 21.

54 C.G. Jung, "Lecture VIII, 20 June 1941," in *Alchemy: E.T.H. Lecture Notes,* ed. B. Hannah (mimeograph, Zurich, 1960).

present from day one in the very fantasy of wholeness as an impulsion of the *caelum* as *unus mundus*. The fantasy that things are "coming together," integrating, and Jung's synthetic or prospective method, too, are modes of stating in terms of time the *caelum* that is always there as the *mundus archetypus*, that potential to which all things desire to return.

Although the *caelum* as quintessence is often presented at a later stage, it is also said (Paracelsus, Figulus) to be the prerequisite for alchemical operations of any kind. The mind from the beginning must be based in the blue firmament, like the lapis lazuli and sapphire throne of mysticism, the azure heaven of Boehme, *philos-sophia*. The blue firmament is an image of cosmological reason; it is a mythical place that gives metaphorical support to metaphysical thinking. Metaphysics in image form. These upper vaults of stone confirm the solidity of invisible thought in a mythical manner; they reveal the mythical foundations of thought. They allow, even command, a philosophy that reaches to just such cosmological heights and depths, the full extension and glory of imagination as philosophy, philosophy as imagination in the *terra alba* of the imaginal as described by Henry Corbin.

A warning is here in order. Alchemical authors love to warn—about heat, about sudden change, about wrong colors at the wrong time such as red rising to the surface or the surface occluded by black. So I would add a warning about blue, although I have never come across one in a text. Psychological alchemy remains within the psyche. It is an alchemy of imagination and built of sensate metaphors and poetic concretisms. The psychologist may never forget that the blue firmament, azure stone and sapphire throne are mystical. Hard and solid these images may be: nonetheless they are not literal. Here we must keep in mind the basic alchemical caution: "Beware the physical in the material." The hardening of imaginal vision into program (the vitrification discussed above, in Chapter 6) coagulates the transparency of a process or phenomenon into a fixed idea, an immutable law, or a final state. Most simply defined, the *caelum* is the blue sky in which the world has its home; but the sky is not the world, not physically mundified. The durabilities of the *unus mundus* are supernal durabilities that infuse things as they are with imaginal vitality.

This warning is especially relevant for Yves Klein's remarkable experiments with blue pigments and his truly blue vision of *unus mundus*, announced in lectures and manifestos.[55] Though prompted by an alchemical impetus and himself a devotee of Bachelard's poetics of the material imagination, Klein's "Blue Revolution" aims to incorporate the metaphysical into the physical (and vice versa), a *unus mundus* for all nations and achieved in society. A- and H-bombs to be colored blue; oceans renamed their true color rather than seas marked on maps as Red, Yellow, and Black; human flesh put in service to the monochromatic cause (using the bodies of his models as "living brushes" saturated with blue paint, and his own body (the famous leaping vault into blue air): "We shall become aerial men. We shall know the forces that pull us upwards to the heavens..."[56] Compare Klein's "body" with Merleau-Ponty's, which remains noetic, body contained within consciousness "saturated with this limitless blue."[57] No physical leap required. But then, Klein's obsession with the physical body correlates with out-of-body metaphysics. Two literalisms inciting each other.

Clinicians might conceive Klein's extraordinary insights and breakouts to be signs of an archetypal possession by the *caelum* as one may be possessed by the *nigredo* or the *albedo*. I would rather argue that Klein did not pursue his alchemy diligently enough, remaining monochromatic, too truly blue, not incorporating the innumerable and interminable processes of *solve et coagula,* forgetting that alchemy is never monochromatic, never "mono" anything. In the blue, yellow is present; in the white, black; and in the red are the *multiflores* and eyes of the many-hued peacock's tail, rotating in multiplication.

If the *caelum* must be present to begin with, then to do alchemy one must be confirmed in imaginal durabilities. The metaphorical twist that the adjective blue gives in the immense variety of its uses in vernacular speech, removing ordinary things from their ordinary sense, is only the beginning of the epistrophic return of all things to their imaginal ground. The mind itself, embodied in shadows, must be drenched in blue, cosmological, transcending psychology.

Alchemy begins before we enter the mind, the forge, the laboratory. "For before the sapphire existed there was no arcanum," says

---

55 See *Overcoming the Problematics of Art: The Writings of Yves Klein,* trans. K. Ottmann (Putnam, Conn.: Spring Publications, 2008).

56 Ibid., 64.

57 Merleau-Ponty, *Phenomenology of Perception*, 214.

Paracelsus.[58] A precondition for the arcane practices of psychoanalysis is a mind established in the blue vault, in the deep seas; a mind thinking in both images and analogies, in words that turn things into flashing ideas and ideas into lively little things that crawl across the paper like inked letters and brush strokes, the blue streak of free association. Freud's "talking cure," which locates this verbal consciousness in the voicing throat of the *viśuddha chakra* whose dominant hue is a smoky bluish purple with a central blue area.[59]

The idea "blue" as formed into a color word "was probably borrowed by prose from poetry."[60] "Blue"—a poetic invention that trickled down from the azure vault, splitting itself into many descriptive shades and hues (indigo, ultramarine, cerulean, turquoise, cobalt, prussian...), but in origin vanishing to the grasp like the blue of bird feathers, the blue of the sky, the blue tremor on the surface of water. No blue stuff there at all; all in the mind.

The *caelum*, then, is an aesthetic condition of mind, on which the entire *opus* depends. Envision it as a night sky filled with airy bodies of the gods, those astrological images that are at once beasts and geometry[61] and participate in all things of the world as their imaginal ground. The *caelum* does not take place *in* your head, *in* your mind, but your mind moves in the *caelum*, touches the constellations. The thick and hairy skull opens to let in more light, their light, making possible a grand new idea of order, a cosmological imagination whose thought speaks for the cosmos in the aesthetic forms of images.

Because the sapphire belongs to Venus according to Paracelsus,[62] blue infuses the work with beauty, with love for the work and erotic delight in its pursuit. A blue mind may be a deep mind and a wide mind, but also it is a place of pleasure, the pleasure of thinking, the libidinal pleasures of secret study, of teasing meanings in the dark; revelations, uncoverings, fresh insights laid bare.

---

58 Cited by Jung in *CW* 14: 641.

59 M. Eliade, *Yoga: Immortality and Freedom*, trans. W.R. Trask (New York: Pantheon, 1958), 242.

60 C. Rowe, "Conceptions of Color and Color Symbolism in the Ancient World," *Eranos Yearbook* 41 (1972), 351.

61 Plato, *Timaeus* 55c.

62 *CW* 13: 234.

Practitioners of analysis who carry an alchemical imagination in their devotion will keep faith with the primordial firmness of their vision. Like Fechner they will wear blue glasses and like Cézanne they will hold a blue brush in their hands, hearing things as they are played upon Stevens's blue guitar. Practitioners will be remembering that practice itself is an aesthetic activity that awakens the soul from anesthesia by re-visioning from the first hour. And, like Miles Davis, they will feel the blue flame pushing forward to some frontier, the edge, and out of the box, loosed from the logic of opposites and the coercion of centering, without tops and bottoms and lines of horizons. Certitude and trepidation, both; and like Proust, with an immense appetite for life.

All along our blue theme has been haunted by nostalgia, *Heimweh*, a nest from which we have flown, the harbor where we have not arrived, a longing that imagines an elsewhere that is "not here." Not here: that is the essential plaint of the émigré, of the mercenary by the campfire in a foreign land, of the displaced, the exiled. A mood of wishing, "mixing memory and desire," and the disconsolate regret of heartbreak. Nostalgia gives a particular hollow ache to the "missing blue" mentioned by Jung in his *Psychology and Alchemy*.[63]

Though the *opus* is dominated by black, white, yellow, red, and blue is not missing, for it is present in the missing—the "not here," not yet, or long ago and faraway—those feelings of *pothos* or longing, which, too, was also a blue flower.[64]

The "soulful awareness that glows with a vision of blueness"[65] is the moistened, saddened eye. "Tears," writes Derrida, "are the essence of the eye—and not sight."[66] Or, rather, the eye sees by means of tears. The *caelum* vision reclaims the blues of melancholic nostalgia.

---

63 *CW* 12:287 and 320.

64 See J. Hillman, "Pothos: The Nostalgia of the Puer Eternus," in *Senex & Puer*, *UE* 3:182.

65 S. Marlan, "The Metaphor of Light and its Deconstruction in Jung's Alchemical Vision," in *Pathways into the Jungian World: Phenomenology and Analytical Psychology*, ed. R. Brooke (London and New York: Routledge, 2000), 185.

66 Ibid.

Blue withdraws from us, says Goethe; it is the absence shadowing the alchemical process, the essentially missing. Not-hereness profoundly motivates the work all along the way: not enough, not right, not fulfilling, something else, something more. Intensely present in its utter absence, reminding the soul of its exile. The inevitability of exile as the necessary ground for removal of all supportive identities: the very idea of identity, of self-identity, of self itself are the structural straws to which loneliness clutches. Exile reveals that we are each foundlings and that there is no other home but the cosmos itself from which no single particle can be severed, to which all aches belong, and homecoming takes place continually–Proust crossing the courtyard, Fechner entering his garden–occurring in our very breathing the globe's blue air. Cézanne drenched all things in blue, keeping them from separateness, making visible "how heaven pulls earth into its arms." The azure vault folds hard edges into its cosmic comprehension. No elsewhere, no exile, no nostalgia.

Precisely here we can make yet another a distinction, between, on the one hand, the blue of the *unio mentalis* that occurs, writes Jung, before the *unus mundus* and, on the other, the celestial blue of the *caelum*. That first blue is more mood than effulgence. Its blue roses are intertwined with lunar subjectivity, called "pleurosis" in the case of Laura in Tennessee Williams's *Glass Menagerie*. That first blue emerges as the *nigredo* clears into the *albedo* and the mute mind finds voice, lightens up, can sing the blues, and express melancholy. But now, as the famous song "Blue Skies" announces, "Blue days, all of them gone/Nothin' but blue skies from now on..." In painting, the two blues show in the contrast saturated blue like Matisse's late cut-out shapes of lively blues, dancing and swimming in white. This azure blue is the "visible spirit of Song," wrote Novalis,[67] the source of song itself (Æ), of vision beyond reflection. If the *unio mentalis* signifies the confluence of understanding and imagination, an understanding by means of images, the *caelum* is beyond understanding–though we may work at it as did Pauli. It feels unimaginable, incomprehensible–as to Jung after Ravenna. Magical. It simply happens, out of the blue, simple and evident and truthful as the sky happens, as death happens, unfathomable and undeniable both. A universal

67 Bamford, *An Endless Trace*, 229.

given, a gift. The eyes no longer able to grasp what they see; the eyes become the ungraspable air by which they see. It is vision.

Jung declared his blue visions of 1944 "the most enormous experiences" he ever had.[68] Yet another is described in a letter to Victor White following a heart embolism a month previous: "A marvelous dream: One bluish diamond, like a star high in heaven, reflected in a round quiet pool—heaven above, heaven below. The imago dei in the darkness of the earth, this is myself...The dream meant a great consolation. I am no more a black and endless sea of misery..."[69]

"No more... endless sea of misery" correlates with Proust's shift from self-centered despair to joy, perhaps Cézanne's move from furious frustrations to the blue of Mont Ventoux. What makes this transcending of misery possible is the vision of transcendence itself. The bluish diamond (Jung), the blue flower (Novalis), the azure and bosomy undulations (Proust) are each the ungraspable objectified. The *caelum* consoles the present not by taking experience away from what is, but by offering the box an image of transcendence, so that vision is delivered from its pain and circumstance, freed even from the very desire to transcend the misery simply by the *prospect* of transcendence, the inquiry it evokes, the light it sheds, and the balm delivered.

Science fosters separations into boxes. Science, its root *scire*, to know, has a further root in Greek, *schizo* (cleft, splinter, separation) and further, Sanscrit *chyati* (divides). Science splinters the *unus mundus*. Instead of "science," why not "séance" for these sessions that invoke our common ancestor? Séance is defined by the dictionary as a meeting of a learned society and also a meeting that attempts to connect with the dead. Jung's expansive vision in hospital took him to the edge of death. Return to life meant divisions, separations: "the grey world with its boxes."[70] But there are other ways out of the box, other ways for the grey world to discover a blue vision.

---

68 Bair, *Jung*, 500.

69 *C. G. Jung Letters*, 18 December 1946.

70 *MDR*, 275. Worth noting: Miles Davis's "Kind of Blue" couldn't quite be boxed. "The truth is that no two editions of 'Kind of Blue' have sounded exactly the same...undetected problems with the speed of one of the tape recorders resulted in a quarter-tone sharpness of pitch... the tonal ambiguity... created the seductive illusion of music that inhabited its own, dreamlike space." (F. Davis, "Blue Heaven," *The New Yorker* [December 4, 2000], 96.)

In this vision, the world appears as analogies. All things refer, imply, connote. Likenesses everywhere and so things cure one another by means of similarities. "Objects existing together" (Badt on Cézanne). Edges banished, says Monet in Mueller's poem: "I will not return to a universe of objects that don't know each other." "The human soul recognizes itself in the world, as the world."[71] Descartes's separations dissolve. Analogy, says William James,[72] is the mark of Fechner's method and genius, for it reaches in all directions and finds subtle strands of implications. "Attentiveness to subtle signs and traits," writes Novalis.[73] The method of discovering analogies carries further than symbols, further than images as such. It is a poetic connection. Reich might add, "an erotic connection." "Poetry," writes Wallace Stevens, "is almost incredibly the outcomes of figures of speech."[74] So incredibly is healing. Analogy disrespects definitions, leaps over defenses, listens through walls to overhear reverberations. The poetic mind resolves the need for meaning, Jung's underlying reason for psychotherapy. "The poet is the transcendental doctor," wrote Novalis.[75]

Is the transcendent move not precisely the poetic sleight-of-hand, the healing magic of art? Jung's term, "the objective psyche," refers to the psyche's unboxed spontaneity and autonomy. But more, the term indicates the power of the psyche to objectify itself, transcend the given by means of analogies (imagistic, linguistic, sensate) that are strange and alien, outlandish, as are those prescriptions and figures of alchemy that have supported the condemnation of alchemy as amoral and crazy. Alchemy is therefore singularly able to reveal the "transcendent function"[76] of the psyche, its native overreach and its delight in excursions out of every box, including the formulations of alchemy itself.

James goes on to describe Fechner's *unus mundus*: "All things on which we externally depend for life—air, water, plant and animal food, fellowmen, etc.—are included in her [the earth]... She is self-sufficing

71 Bamford, *An Endless Trace*, 230, on Novalis.

72 W. James, "Concerning Fechner," in *A Pluralistic Universe* (London: Longmans, Green, and Co., 1909),151.

73 Bamford, *An Endless Trace*, 224.

74 "Effects of Analogy," in W. Stevens, *The Necessary Angel: Essays on Reality and the Imagination* (New York: Alfred A. Knopf, 1951), 117.

75 Bamford, *An Endless Trace*, 220.

76 *CW* 8:131–93.

in a million respects in which we are not so."[77] Then, like an astronaut's vision of the globe, and like Jung's vision from his hospital bed, James captures Fechner's vision with this paragraph: "Think of her beauty—a shining ball, sky-blue, sunlit over one half, the other bathed in starry night... she would be a spectacle of rainbow glory... Every quality of landscape that has a name would be visible in her at once... a landscape that is her face." Novalis saw the face of the blue flower. "Yes," writes James, "the earth is our great common guardian angel who watches over all our interests combined."[78]

Fechner perceived this through his blue glasses, the *unus mundus*, the earth as angel. The deep ecology of the Gaia Hypothesis becomes truth because seen and felt, not because believed in or scientifically buttressed. "We are called to form the Earth," wrote Novalis.[79] "Doctor, if you could only see ..." This vision is the *caelum* experience, and "without vision," continues James famously at the end of his rapture recapitulating Fechner's, "the people perish."[80] And we perish, the patients perish, our psychology perishes without reminiscence of the vision that impelled us to Jung in the first place, a vision that is there from start to finish as *materia prima* and *unus mundus*, a recollection that gives reason for Jung's turn to alchemy for the amplification and substantiation of his life's extraordinary work, leaving us with the charge to recollect that our work, however boxed and clocked, however bandaged our eyes, is always under an azure vault.

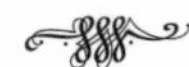

77 James, "Concerning Fechner," 157.
78 Ibid., 164.
79 Bamford, *An Endless Trace*, 220.
80 James, "Concerning Fechner," 65.

Source Notes

"Therapeutic Value of Alchemical Language" was delivered in 1977 at the 7th International Congress for Analytical Psychology in Rome and first published in *Methods of Treatment in Analytical Psychology*, ed. I.F. Baker, (Fellbach: Adolf Bonz Verlag, 1980), 118–26.

"Rudiments" is previously unpublished.

"The Suffering of Salt" originally appeared as "Salt: A Chapter in Alchemical Psychology" in the publication of papers of the *Dragonflies* conference in Dallas in February 1979, and subsequently published in *Images of the Untouched: Virginity in Psyche, Myth, and Community*, ed. Joanne Stroud and Gail Thomas (Dallas: Spring Publications, 1982), 111–37.

"The Seduction of Black" was originally prepared for and delivered at the Inaugural Evening of the "Colors of Life Conference and Festival," Turin, Italy, August 1995, and subsequently published in *Fire in the Stone: The Alchemy of Desire*, ed. S. Marlan (Wilmette, Ill.: Chiron Publications, 1997), 42–53.

"Alchemical Blue and the *Unio Mentalis*" was originally published in *Sulfur* 1 (1981), 33–50, and reprinted in *Spring: A Journal of Archetype and Culture* 54 (1993), 132–48.

"Silver and the White Earth" was originally given as a talk at a conference held by the Analytical Psychology Club of Western New York in January 1979 at Niagara Falls, N.Y., and subsequently published in two parts in *Spring: An Annual of Archetypal Psychology and Jungian Thought* (1980), 21–48, and *Spring: An Annual of Archetypal Psychology and Jungian Thought* (1981), 21–66.

"The Yellowing of the Work" was originally delivered at the 11th International Congress for Analytical Psychology, Paris, September 1989, and subsequently published in *Personal and Archetypal Dynamics in the Analytical Relationship*, ed. M.A. Mattoon (Einsiedeln: Daimon Verlag, 1991), 77–96.

"Concerning the Stone: Alchemical Images of the Goal" was originally delivered at the 1990 Eranos Conference "Resurrection and Immortality" in Ascona, Switzerland, and subsequently published in *Sphinx* 5 (The London Convivium of Archetypal Studies, 1994).

"The Imagination of Air and the Collapse of Alchemy" was originally published in *Eranos Yearbook* 50 (1981), 273–333.

"The Azure Vault: *Caelum* as Experience" originally appeared in *Edges of Experience: Memory and Emergence: Proceedings of the 16th International IAAP Comgress for Analytical Psychology* (Barcelona 2004), ed. L. Cowan (Einsiedeln: Daimon Verlag, 2006), 43–57.

JAMES HILLMAN (1926–2011) was the founder of Archetypal Psychology. His pioneering imaginative psychology spanned five decades. It has entered cultural history, affecting lives and minds in a wide range of fields. For the creativity of his thinking, the author of *The Myth of Analysis, Re-Visioning Psychology, The Soul's Code, The Force of Character, A Terrible Love of War,* and *Lament of the Dead: Psychology After Jung's Red Book* (with Sonu Shamdasani) received many honors, including the Medal of the Presidency of the Italian Republic. He held distinguished lectureships at the Universities of Yale, Princeton, Chicago, and Syracuse, and his books have been translated into some twenty languages.